BASIC PROGRAMMING FOR BUSINESS
■ a structured approach

BASIC PROGRAMMING FOR BUSINESS

■ a structured approach

Larry R. Fry

DELMAR PUBLISHERS INC.

TO

- Delmar Publishers Inc. for providing the opportunity to write this book.
- My wife, Jean, for her encouragement, support, and proofreading help.
- One Chocolate-point Siamese cat, known as Pudding, for the company during those many hours.

Cover photo: Image by Cliff Hollenbeck, Cliff Hollenbeck Photography

Production editor: Patricia O'Connor-Gillivan

For information address Delmar Publishers Inc.
2 Computer Drive West, Box 15–015,
Albany, New York 12212

Printed in the United States of America
Published simultaneously in Canada by Nelson Canada,
A Division of International Thomson Limited

10 9 8 7 6 5 4 3 2 1

Library of Congress Cataloging in Publication Data

Fry, Larry R.
   BASIC programming for business.

   Bibliography: p. 296
   Includes index.
   1. Basic (Computer program language)
2. Business—Data processing. I. Title. II. Title:
B.A.S.I.C. programming for business.
HF5548.5.B3F79 1984   OC1.64'25   84-14268
ISBN 0-8273-2245-3
ISBN 0-8273-2246-1 (instructor's guide)

BRIEF CONTENTS

CONTENTS

PREFACE

BASIC Programming for Business: A Structured Approach is a comprehensive business data processing textbook in which structured BASIC methodology is presented. The primary objective in the writing of this book was to satisfy the perceived need for a volume in the BASIC language that successfully presents structured business-oriented programming. This book is designed to clearly explain the standard business-related programming techniques.

If this or any textbook is to be successful in training people for business programming, it must cover several areas. The essential elements of structured BASIC programming must be developed, so that the student has a strong foundation of knowledge. Input/output procedures and calculation operations, which form the core of any programming language, must also be presented. Business applications, such as comparisons, subtotals and final totals, headings, tables, arrays, searches, and sorts, should be clearly presented. Accounting reports, including journals, ledgers, balance sheets, and income statements, should also be covered. Statistical techniques utilized in business and industry should be described. The widespread use of video display terminals necessitates an introduction to screen management. And, disk file handling of data in sequential and random storage is almost required in today's training.

This book is structured in chapters of related programming topics. Several learning objectives are provided in each chapter. The first chapter contains introductory material regarding business data processing, hardware, software, flowcharting, problem analysis, and program design. Designed as a review chapter, it does not provide comprehensive presentations of the material. A wide range of textbooks and reference materials that treat these areas individually and comprehensively are published. Instructors may use or omit the review chapter to suit their individual classes.

In Chapters Two through Four, the BASIC statements used to enter and print data are presented. They are designed to provide detailed treatment of these BASIC language operations for those users who find it necessary. Many students have previously taken courses in BASIC and may be able to proceed to Chapter Five. This determination is left to the instructor.

The chapters that follow describe comparisons, BASIC business applications, screen management, control breaks, one-dimensional tables, arrays, sequential disk data files, and random access disk data files. Self-tests, exercises, problems, and programming assignments are included to challenge the student.

A glossary and four appendixes are presented as resources for the student. In Appendix A, the ANSI BASIC key words are listed. Appendix B contains the non-ANSI key words and common BASIC language specifications supported by the various systems. A general introduction to time-sharing and microcomputer systems is provided in Appendix C. In Appendix D, the key words used by the most popular systems are compared. Space is provided in Appendix D for the student to note specific machine-dependent key words. This can also be used to note specific differences the user may require.

The introduction of the microcomputer and the small business computer caused an increase in the variety of hardware that supports the BASIC language. This increase in the variety and number of computers, and in the forms of BASIC available makes writing a textbook that is not dependent on a specific hardware or software design difficult. However, by utilizing ANSI Minimal BASIC as successful business-programming textbooks written for COBOL have utilized ANSI COBOL, this textbook is designed to be machine-independent. The essential core of the language is provided by ANSI Minimal BASIC. All program statements in the textbook are described in detail. Alternate program statements used by the most popular manufacturers of hardware and software are provided as is practical.

Exercises are presented throughout the text to help the student learn the technical and operational characteristics of the computer system being used. These exercises require the student to refer to the system manual to research the computer system and dialect of BASIC being used. Professional programmers refer to system manuals constantly; it is important that students learn how to use these manuals as reference tools early in their careers.

It should be recognized by students that the business data processing field involves much more than writing programs. A wide range of courses in the business area, such as accounting, management, marketing, and statistics, is necessary to develop an understanding of business. Practical work experience in the business world is certainly recommended. Since verbal and written communication with users of programs, management, and other programmers consumes much of the programmer's time, verbal and written communications development programs, such as public speaking, technical writing, and business communications, should be included in training. The student who recognizes the importance of business and communication courses and takes advantage of them will be well prepared for today's job market.

ACKNOWLEDGMENTS

Preliminary thoughts of writing a textbook began surfacing in the late 1970s when attempts to find a suitable BASIC language book for business usage proved fruitless. As a result of a survey conducted for DELMAR PUBLISHERS INC., I was contacted by them to consider writing such a book.

Mr. Mark Huth, Administrative Editor at DELMAR, provided the initial impetus for this project. He has had a positive and encouraging influence on this work from the first day.

Mr. Jonathan Plant, Project Editor for this book, offered guidance and suggestions. He was the "point man" handling my contact with project reviewers and the DELMAR staff. I am sure there were many days when deadlines were missed that he felt as if he were sitting on a "point."

The project reviewers sharpened my thought and helped me avoid the perils and pitfalls of publishing a flawed product. My humble and belated thank you to Arthur J. Phares, James W. Cox, and Mary Rigsby.

The text and program examples in this book were prepared using an International Business Machines Personal Computer. WORDSTAR, by Micropro International, was used to enter the text.

I accept full responsibility for any technical errors that may have been overlooked.

APPLE, APPLE COMPUTER, and APPLESOFT BASIC are registered trademarks of APPLE COMPUTER INC., Cupertino, CA.

IBM, INTERNATIONAL BUSINESS MACHINES, and INTERNATIONAL BUSINESS MACHINES PERSONAL COMPUTER are registered trademarks of INTERNATIONAL BUSINESS MACHINES CORPORATION, Armonk, NY.

MICROSOFT and MICROSOFT BASIC are registered trademarks of MICROSOFT CORPORATION, Bellevue, WA.

TRS-80, TRSDOS, TRS-80 BASIC, and RADIO SHACK are registered trademarks of TANDY CORPORATION, Fort Worth, TX.

WORDSTAR is a registered trademark of MICROPRO INTERNATIONAL CORPORATION, San Rafael, CA.

INTRODUCTION TO DATA PROCESSING AND BUSINESS ORIENTED BASIC

1

OBJECTIVES

At the end of this chapter you should be able to identify and describe the following items:

- The emergence of the electronic computer and business data processing.
- The common types of computers that utilize the BASIC language.
- The types and sources of data used in data processing.
- Proper program documentation procedures.
- Steps in the development of structured programs.
- Flowchart symbols, construction, and interpretation.
- BASIC language structured methodologies.
- The ANSI Minimal BASIC Language.
- The differences between interpreters and compilers.
- The required parts of BASIC program statements.
- The syntax rules for BASIC program statements.
- BASIC variable name rules and procedures.
- The procedures used for direct, or immediate, execution.
- The components of a BASIC program.
- The procedures for creating or changing a program in the current memory (work space).
- The procedures for creating, storing, and retrieving a program in auxiliary storage.
- The debugging procedures used to eliminate syntax/logic errors.

COMPUTER DEVELOPMENTS

The importance of computers in the business and scientific communities has only recently been realized. Thirty years have elapsed since the installation of the first commercial electronic digital computer, but only in the past few years has it been possible to place a computer at the work station of every employee within an organization. American dominance in the primary production industries is being replaced by an emphasis upon the high technology areas. A widely proclaimed fact is that over one-half of the work force in the United States is now involved in handling or processing data or information, rather than in producing products.

The computer era is only now reaching the growth stage and probably will not reach maturity in the current generation. Robotics and computer-aided manufacturing are barely underway. The shortage of people trained in the new high technology areas will continue. New people must be trained in these areas and those workers displaced by computers and robotics must be retrained to take their places in the computer-based information society.

The time line shown in figure 1–1 records the major events that have occurred since the development of the first computer. The first generation of computers with technology

```
                SOFTWARE                                    HARDWARE


                              1945 !
                                   !
           "Hard-Wired" Hardware   !     ENIAC - Vacuum Tubes-1st Gen.
                                   !
                                   !
                                   !     Transistor - Bell Lab
                                   !
                                   !     First business computer
                                   !              installed
                                   !
                                   !
                                   !
                                   !     IBM - RAMAC Disk Developed
         FORTRAN Released - IBM    !
                                   !     Transistor Computer-2nd Gen.
                              1960 !
                                   !
         CODASYL Released COBOL    !     Integrated   Circuit
         FORTRAN IV Released       !
                                   !
         ASCII Character Code      !
         BASIC Developed           !     IBM System 360 - 3rd Gen.
                                   !     Minicomputer Developed
         PL/1 Released             !
         ANSI FORTRAN              !
                                   !     Large Scale Integration
         ANSI COBOL-68 Released    !
         PASCAL Operational        !     IBM System 370 - 4th Gen.
                                   !     Microprocessor Chip
         ANSI COBOL-74 Released    !
                                   !
                              1975 !
                                   !
         CP/M Developed            !
                                   !     APPLE   II & TRS-80   Micro
                                   !
         ANSI Minimal BASIC        !
                                   !     TRS-80  -  Level II
                                   !     APPLE  III
                                   !
         ADA -  Chosen as standard !     IBM Personal Computer
            high-level language  by!     TRS-80  Model 16
            Department of Defense  !     DEC and WANG Professional
                                   !
                              1983 !     APPLE "LISA" Computer
         ANSI MINIMAL BASIC-Draft  !
            Revision               !     Coleco  "ADAM"
                                   !     IBM  PC JR
                                   !     APPLE "MACINTOSH"
```

FIGURE 1–1
Hardware and software
time line

based upon vacuum tubes is a distant memory. The implementation of new technologies over the years has involved the vacuum tube, the transistor, the integrated circuit, and currently the very large scale integrated (VLSI) circuit. The evolution of computer equipment, commonly referred to as hardware, has replaced old machines, which literally filled entire rooms, with small desk top and even handheld computers.

The personal and small business computers of today's world use a microprocessor, which is often called "the computer on a chip." One silicon chip contains all of the components necessary to perform the processing functions of a computer. The resulting personal, home, and small business computers have made computers accessible to most people. The downward slide in prices brought about by competition and technology will accelerate the information explosion and, thus, the need for trained people.

Hardware advances have been followed slowly by changes in computer programming languages, which are referred to as software. The gap that has existed between the technological advances in hardware and the progress in software development continues with only modest improvement. High-level computer languages, those which are "closest to

English," such as BASIC, COBOL, and PASCAL, minimize the programming burden of writing instructions in binary code or machine language. These advances, however, have not kept up with the frantic pace existent in the development of the machines.

COMPUTER ENVIRONMENT

The term computer has generally been associated with the large central processing units known as mainframes (see figure 1–2). These computers have large main memory capacity and extensive auxiliary storage in the form of disk drives or tape drives. In the past they were used in batch processing situations in which one program after another was put through the machine in batch sequence. Today they are found performing a variety of duties in an interactive mode where many terminals are connected to the computer.

The use of a central computer to support terminals is called *time-sharing*. The computer supports several programming languages at one time and controls, or drives, all of the terminals. This is called *multiprogramming*. These large computers are essential in a center that has a data base that supports the major programming tasks of an organization. The only practical way to maintain the large data files and the wide variety of programs necessary to support the management information objectives of an enterprise is to possess large mainframe computers. The procedures used to access time-sharing computers are summarized in Appendix C.

FIGURE 1–2
IBM 3084 mainframe computer. *Courtesy of International Business Machines Corporation*

Minicomputers were introduced in 1965. The term minicomputer resulted from comparing the size of this system with the mainframes of that day. Minicomputers (see figure 1–3) are capable of using a wide variety of programming languages, including BASIC, and are usually used in a time-sharing environment. These computers expanded the market because many businesses that could not afford mainframes could afford to purchase or lease minicomputers. The market for minicomputers remains strong today.

The microprocessor was developed in the early 1970s. This device placed all the logic, memory, and other circuits necessary to perform the tasks of a computer on one silicon chip. The first production microprocessor was the INTEL 4004 (see figure 1–4). The technology had moved significantly forward.

By 1977, a large variety of computers utilizing a microprocessor as the "brain" had been introduced. These included computers manufactured by APPLE, Radio Shack, and Commodore (see figure 1–5). The personal computer opened the market to private individuals and small businesses for whom the price of a computer had been prohibitive. Microcomputers soon included diskette drives, printers, telecommunications ability, and network options. By 1981, the home computer went into mass marketing. These computers, which now sell for under $500, are marketed by Sinclair, Coleco, Atari, Commodore, and others. The procedures used to access microcomputer systems are summarized in Appendix C.

Microcomputer main memory was initially limited because of the size of the microprocessor, but the introduction of 16-bit processing units by companies such as Interna-

FIGURE 1–3
Digital Equipment
Corporation PDP–11/24
minicomputer. *Courtesy
of Digital Equipment
Corporation*

FIGURE 1—4
Intel 4004
microprocessor.
*Courtesy of Intel
Corporation*

tional Business Machines, Digital Equipment Company, and Wang Laboratories (see figure 1–6) greatly expanded this ability. Microcomputers are now offered with a 32-bit microprocessor. The APPLE Macintosh is a 32-bit machine.

BASIC is the dominant "first language" supported by microcomputers. Other languages such as PASCAL, COBOL, and FORTRAN are also offered.

Probably in excess of one million microcomputers for personal or business use were sold in the United States by 1980. In 1982 alone it is estimated that over one million microcomputers for personal or business use were sold. The estimated potential market for personal-use and business-use microcomputers in the United States probably exceeds 50 million units.

TYPES AND SOURCES OF DATA

The proper identification and classification of data is an essential part of program construction. The programmer must determine the types of data to be used in the program before going on to other tasks. Since the program user is the source of these facts, communication between the programmer and the user is an important part of the programming process.

The procedure of identifying the facts necessary to solve the problem is called *capturing data*. Once the data has been captured it must be transferred to some form of input media such as magnetic tape or disk for storage and processing.

The program should be tested under operational conditions before it is added to the management information system. The internal historical records maintained by the or-

FIGURE 1–5
Apple II Plus
microcomputer with
monitor and diskette
drive. *Courtesy of Apple
Computer, Inc.*

ganization are an excellent source of test data. External data sources, such as government or trade organizations, may also be utilized.

A single fact is known as a data item or field. A *data field* is a single fact such as the employee identification number, employee name, hours worked, or rate of pay. A data item or field is called a *variable* in the BASIC language.

A *record* is a collection of related variables. Within each record of a single type the variables must be arranged in the same relative sequence. For example, a payroll record contains all of the relevant data pertaining to an individual employee—identification number, name, hours worked, and rate of pay. When the company's first payroll record was written, the variables were placed in the order just mentioned; therefore, the variables in all of the payroll records must be placed in that sequence.

A *file* is a collection of related records. The records can be grouped in any sequence within the file. For example, the records in the payroll file could be arranged in ascending order by employee number.

Variables, records, and files are interrelated. Files contain all related records. Records, in turn, are made up of related variables. Most importantly, the variables within the records must be arranged in relative order. Any changes in the relative sequence of variables within records will cause errors. GIGO (Garbage In—Garbage Out) will result if this rule is not strictly followed.

THE PAPER CHASE—PROGRAM DOCUMENTATION

Program documentation is absolutely necessary in the development of programs. Although it adds expense to the overall data processing operation, its benefits outweigh its cost. A "paper trail" supporting every program in the overall information resource management operation is essential.

FIGURE 1–6
IBM Personal Computer
with monitor, diskette
drives, and printer.
*Courtesy of
International Business
Machines Corporation*

Two areas in which the benefits of program documentation are evident are program maintenance and computer failure. Program maintenance, or updating programs to keep them current, is necessitated by changes in the environment. Changes in such areas as tax rates, pay scales, the general economy, governmental regulations, and negotiated agreements can make programs obsolete. In the course of updating programs proper documentation helps by supplying the user with a record of the logic and decision-making process used to write the program.

Computers have a tendency to suffer failures (referred to as going down or crashing) from time to time. One of the critical decisions at such a time is whether or not the program caused the failure. Program documentation helps unravel this mystery because a complete record of the program is readily available for review.

Program documentation should begin early in the developmental phase of each project. As each task is accomplished the documentation should be kept current. Proper documentation consists of a program package often referred to as a run book. The package should include the following:

1. User's request—The user's original request as well as records of any communication or conferences concerning the program.
2. Flowcharts—Both top-level and detailed logic flowcharts.
3. Coding forms—The language coding forms with amendments.
4. Program listing—A printout showing the operational version of the program.
5. Normal output—The printout that should result from normal execution of the pro-

gram. This shows the computer operator what normal execution should look like making it easier to detect abnormal execution.

6. Program trace—The independent verification of the program results. This procedure is known as a hand trace.

7. Program documentation within the program—Most computer languages allow documentation statements within the program. In BASIC, the REMARK (or REM) key word is used. REMARK lines should be coded in such a manner that they are distinguishable from regular program statements. This can be done by indenting REM key words or by varying spacing.

Program documentation packages should be updated to reflect program maintenance and they should be kept in an available but secure place.

PROGRAM DEVELOPMENT

Structured programming follows the top-down approach: a problem is divided into large segments called blocks or modules and as the problem solution is developed the segments are filled with details. Top-down programming is also known as stepwise refinement because each step in the developmental process provides more detail.

The following are the fundamental rules referenced in structured methodology.

1. Eliminate the use of GO TO. Although structured methodology calls for the elimination of GO TO, this is not possible in all forms of BASIC. Those dialects of BASIC that do not support the IF-THEN-ELSE statement or other features, such as ON-GOSUB and WHILE-WEND, may have to continue using GO TO.

2. Each program module shall have one entry point and one exit point. This rule is used to keep the program modules short and limited to one task.

3. BASIC program modules shall be limited to performing one task. Generally, a module should not exceed one page.

4. A *hierarchy* exists in structured programming. Top-level modules control detailed modules. Modules may be used for control only, processing only, or a mixture of control and processing.

Although the BASIC language was not originally designed for structured methodology, recent adaptations have given it added flexibility. Future language standardization releases concerned with BASIC should refer to structured programming.

FLOWCHART PROCEDURES

A *flowchart* is defined as a logical and graphic step-by-step solution to a given problem. Flowcharts are road maps that are used to get the programmer from point A to point Z.

This text uses two levels of flowcharts—top-level and detailed logic flowcharts. In structured methodology the *top-level flowchart* presents the problem as it has been divided into subroutines, or modules, and the *detailed logic flowchart* provides precise step-by-step directions for each of the modules. Program instructions written for each of the subroutines should correspond with the modules in the detailed logic flowchart. Seven standard flowchart symbols are used at the beginning level (see figure 1–7).

STRUCTURED METHODOLOGY

BASIC was designed as a general purpose language before structured programming methodology was implemented. Recent enhancements in the BASIC dialects used on most systems have given additional flexibility to the programmer.

The subroutine procedure is used in structured BASIC to execute program modules. This is done through the use of the GOSUB-RETURN statement. Execution of a subroutine means that program control is shifted to the procedure indicated in the statement. When a subroutine is completed, control shifts to the line following the statement that invoked it. RETURN is used in the program to identify the end of a subroutine.

BEGIN/END   The oval symbol is used to begin
             or end a flowchart. It is also
             used to identify, begin, and
             terminate subroutines.

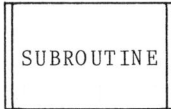

SUBROUTINE   This symbol identifies a
             predefined procedure or subroutine.

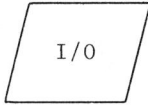

I/O   The parallelogram symbol is used
             for input/output operations.

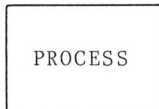

PROCESS   The rectangle is used for all
             process steps such as calculations.

DECISION   The diamond is used for a decision
             or branch.

1   The small circle is used   to
             connect points.

5   Off-page connector.

FIGURE 1–7
Flowchart symbols

There are three program control structures that can be implemented with most BASIC systems: the simple sequential, the program branch or decision, and the program loop. In the *simple sequential control structure,* the program or module is executed in a straight flow with no branches, or decision blocks.

When the program *branch,* or decision, control structure is used, there are changes in the flow of logic that depend on operator selection, variable values, and programmed decision, or branch, conditions. The simple branch is a commonly used procedure where changes in program control are accomplished through the use of the IF key word.

Another program branch control structure is sometimes described as the CASE OF procedure. In BASIC, two procedures are used for this purpose: the ON-GO TO and the ON-GOSUB. The CASE OF procedure is commonly used in menu operations where the user is asked to select certain program options.

The final type of control structure is the program *loop* in which certain program modules are repeated. When a loop is used, program control is shifted repeatedly to a specified point in the program. The number of times the loop is executed is a programmable option that is determined by operator selection, variable values, or programmed decision, or branch, conditions.

The two BASIC control structures for executing loops are the FOR/NEXT and the WHILE-WEND statements. The FOR/NEXT structure is used when the programmer wants the loop to be executed at least once. The WHILE-WEND structure is used to test for a condition before the loop is executed.

STRUCTURED FLOWCHARTING

The first type of BASIC program presented in the text is an input/output listing. Data is entered into the computer and a listing is printed. The top-level and detailed logic flowcharts for this type of program are shown in figure 1–8.

The top-level flowchart identifies the modules that are part of the program. Each of the blocks in the top-level flowchart are then charted step-by-step in the detailed logic flowchart.

The top-level flowchart in the listing program contains three blocks. The first block is the mainline module, which controls all processing functions. The next block is the read module, which is used to enter the data. The last block is the output module, which results in printing of the information.

The detailed logic flowchart provides the step-by-step program flow. The mainline

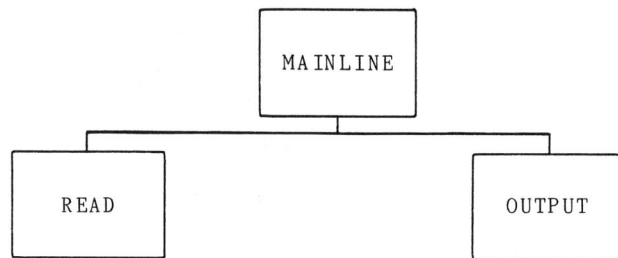

TOP–LEVEL FLOWCHART

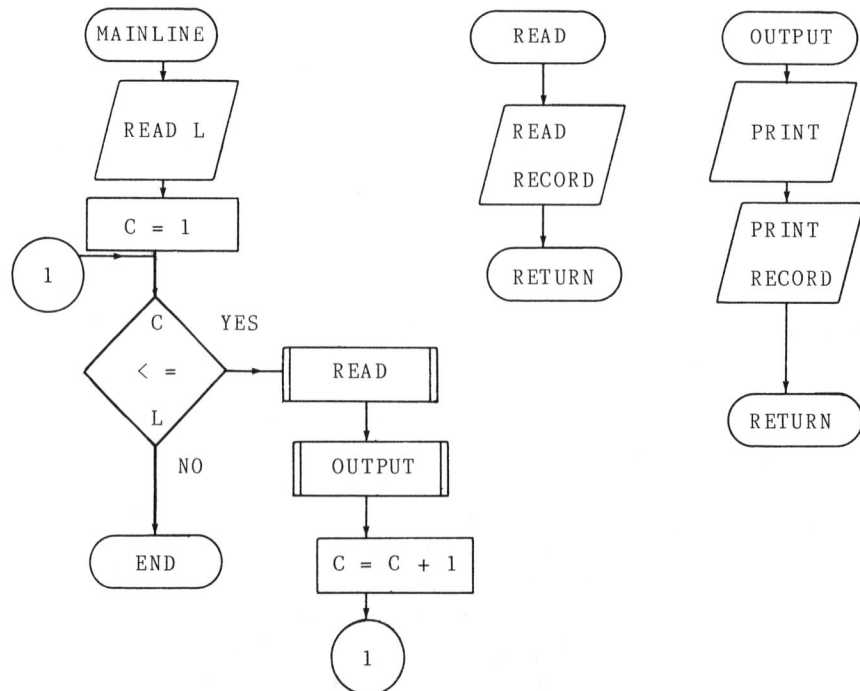

FIGURE 1–8
Top-level and detailed
logic flowcharts for
listing program

DETAILED LOGIC FLOWCHART

module contains the loop control structure, the FOR/NEXT loop, which is repeated as long as variable C is less than or equal to variable L. The loop is composed of the read and output subroutines. The read module causes the data record to be entered. Variable values are entered as the loop is executed. In the output module the actual data is printed. Output is controlled by the print statements. When variable C exceeds variable L, the program loop ends.

The complete listing program for this flowchart is discussed in Chapter 3.

THE BASIC COMPUTER PROGRAMMING LANGUAGE

The BASIC (Beginner's All-Purpose Symbolic Instruction Code) language was developed by Professors John Kameny and Thomas Kurtz at Dartmouth College in Hanover, New Hampshire in the early 1960s. It was developed in an interactive mode using a General Electric time-sharing computer and was used in educational environments with limited general purpose or business application until the late 1970s. As the microcomputer and small business computer markets exploded, BASIC became the standard small machine language. This development moved it into the forefront as a business problem-solving language.

The American National Standards Institute (ANSI) released its first standard dealing with the BASIC language in January 1978. The document, entitled *American National Standard for Minimal BASIC,** defines the minimum set of syntaxes and features that must be operational on computers supporting the Minimal BASIC Standard. It establishes 26 key words for standard usage (see Appendix A) and gives examples of applications for each of them. The ANSI standard also describes the BASIC character set, syntax, and usage. Future standards dealing with BASIC will be released as developed by ANSI.

The large number of hardware manufacturers and software companies, each with its own particular product, has resulted in a variety of forms of BASIC. Many additional key words/commands are offered by the manufacturers in addition to those defined in the ANSI standard (see Appendix B). The use of different dialects of BASIC by the various computer companies has undermined standardization efforts. It is uncertain whether or not this range of products and dialects can be brought under control. Among the problems created by the variety of dialects is the task of writing a BASIC textbook that is not limited to one computer system. Since each manufacturer has the option of going its own way, the student's system may differ from the system used in the text. To avoid confusion the textbook must include the options used by the most popular manufacturers and must also refer the student to the system manual for specific instructions.

BASIC LANGUAGE TRANSLATOR

Computers communicate internally using a binary-coded form called machine language. Since BASIC is a high-level language, one that "is close to English," the computer needs a translator to change the BASIC language instructions into machine language instructions. To accomplish this task, the computer uses an interpreter. An *interpreter* is a control program that translates and monitors execution of BASIC programs. When a high-level BASIC program is executed, the interpreter performs the following functions:

1. Converts the high-level BASIC program into binary form, known as machine language. Each BASIC statement may generate more than one machine language instruction.
2. Checks each BASIC statement line by line for errors.
3. If necessary, provides error messages, called diagnostics.

Interpreters are called low-level programs because they are written in assembly language, which is usually done in an intermediate numbering system, such as hexadecimal. They are prepared by computer scientists or system programmers.

---

*American National Standards Institute. *American National Standard for Minimal BASIC*. X3.60–1978. New York: ANSI, 1978.

Recently, compilers have been added to microcomputers. *Compilers* perform the same tasks as interpreters, except that compilers translate the BASIC program into machine language as a whole, rather than line by line. They also consider the entire program, rather than each separate line, when looking for errors. The result of compilation is referred to as an object program. Generally, compiled programs execute faster than interpreted programs.

A BASIC PRIMER—BASIC SYSTEM COMMANDS AND PROGRAM STATEMENTS

System commands are used in BASIC to cause the computer to execute certain operations. A BASIC command is distinguishable from a BASIC statement because it consists of only one word. Such BASIC system commands as CATALOG, CLEAR, DIRECTORY, END, FILES, HOME, LIST, LOAD, RUN, and STOP cause the computer to perform a specific operation each time they are entered. Some of these commands may be entered as part of a program with a statement number while others may not. This varies with the computer system.

BASIC *program statements* are the individual instructions written to cause the computer to execute in a certain way. These statements must be constructed following usage rules to result in proper syntax. Statements consist of three elements: the statement number, the BASIC key word, and the parameter, or imperative. BASIC program statements must be written in the following form.

100 KEY WORD ⟨ PARAMETER ⟩

The statement number must be listed first. It must be a positive integer between one and the ceiling indicated by the system. Conventional practice calls for statement numbers to begin at 10 or 100 and to be increased in increments of 10 or 100. This is done to allow the insertion of program statements between the original numbers at a later time. Listing the program statements in even increments also creates a tidy program.

Most systems provide automatic statement numbering through the use of the AUTO command. The RENUMBER command, or utility, is also provided on some systems to renumber program statements in a predetermined sequence.

Program statements can be entered into the system in any sequence. The computer automatically places the statements in line number sequence whenever the RUN or LIST commands are entered. If two statements with the same line number are entered, the last one to be keyed replaces the first one.

BASIC key words are the system reserved words that cause the computer to perform specific tasks. Key words such as DATA, GO TO, IF, INPUT, LET, PRINT, READ, and REM are reserved for specific usage. They must be spelled correctly and follow the statement number.

The *parameter* is the variable name or the operation being processed as part of the statement. Parameter format depends upon the purpose of the program statement. The parameter may consist of a list of variable names or multiple program instructions on the same line.

BASIC program statements must include the line number, the key word, and the parameter. Individual program statements are terminated by depressing the RETURN or ENTER key. The maximum length allowed for individual program statements varies with each computer system; however, most permit over 200 characters in one statement.

The spacing between statement elements is not critical in BASIC. Most systems permit the insertion of blank spaces between statement elements to improve readability.

BASIC program execution begins at the smallest statement number and proceeds through the program line by line. Program termination occurs when the END or STOP statement is executed.

The following are examples of valid BASIC statements.

```
100 PRINT A
200 LET A = B + C
300 READ A
400 REM A BASIC PROGRAM TO LIST EMPLOYEE NAMES
```

BASIC VARIABLE NAMES

Computer programs must include a method for storing data values that vary as the program is executed. The procedure used is to designate a memory location for a specific use. Because the contents of this memory location can change as the program is executed, this is known as a variable.

Variable names are used in BASIC programs to define and describe data fields, which are single units of data. Two types of variables, numeric and string, are recognized by most systems. *Numeric variables* consist of integer (whole number) or real (decimal fraction) data. Numeric data values may include only digits or decimal points; dollar signs, commas, percent symbols, and other marks of this type are not permitted.

String variables are alphabetic or alphanumeric fields. Alphanumeric data is formed by mixing alphabetic characters, digits, and other special characters. String data values are defined, or delimited, by quotation marks. Although spacing in BASIC program statements is not critical on most systems, it is important in string data values.

Variable name rules are as follows:

1. Numeric variables—The first character of the variable name must be an alphabetic character. This may be followed by one to twenty alphabetic characters or digits on some systems. Certain systems can accommodate thirty characters in a variable name, but they actually use only the first one or two. Other systems allow only one character in the name. Blank spaces are not recommended in variable names. Examples of valid and invalid numeric variable names are:

Valid	Invalid
A	/X
B	9
Z	4A
PR	$B
S9	#A

Although PR and S9 are shown as valid variable names, they may not be valid on some systems. Invalid field names cause syntax or usage errors when used in programs.

2. String variables—The first character of the variable name must be alphabetic and it must be followed by the $ symbol. Some systems accept two or more alphabetic characters followed by the $ symbol. When used as a suffix, the $ symbol defines a string variable name. Blank spaces are not recommended in variable names. Examples of valid and invalid string variable names are:

Valid	Invalid
N$	$
A$	$A
C$	9$
STATE$	$8

Although STATE$ is shown as a valid name, it may not be valid on some systems.

Record the variable name rules for the particular computer system used in Exercise 1–1.

**EXERCISE
1–1**

Numeric variable names _____

_____

String variable names _____

_____

The following additional rules apply to both numeric and string variable names.

1. Do not use BASIC reserved key words as variable names. Such reserved words as AT, FOR, GR, and TO cause particular problems. BASIC key words may not be imbedded within variable names on some systems. For example, the words RATE and FORM would not be acceptable on some systems because they contain the key words AT and FOR.
2. Relate variable field names to the type or purpose of the data being described. For example, rate of pay could be called variable R.
3. Keep variable field names short. Some organizations prefer variable names that readily identify the purpose of the data field. This is done for program documentation purposes.

**SELF-TEST
1–1**

A. Identify and correct the errors in the following BASIC program statements:
  1. 47.5 LET A = B   4. READ 100 A
  2. −100 PRINT A   5. 49.0 READ A
  3. REM Help Me

B. Identify the valid and/or invalid variable names. Explain why the invalid names are wrong. Assume the system permits a maximum of five characters plus the $ suffix in the field names.
  1. TE   6. $CITY
  2. TO   7. STATE$
  3. HAT   8. RATE
  4. F$ 9. X
  5. NAME$ 10. LET

**Answers for
Self-Test
1–1**

A. 1. 47.5 LET A = B
     Statement number must be a positive integer.
     Correction: 47 LET A = B
   2. −100 PRINT A
     Statement number must be a positive integer.
     Correction: 100 PRINT A
   3. REM Help Me
     Each statement must be numbered.
     Correction: 100 REM Help Me
   4. READ 100 A
     Statement number must be first.
     Correction: 100 READ A
   5. 49.0 READ A
     Statement numbers must be positive integers.
     Correction: 49 READ A

B. 1. TE—Valid
   2. TO—Invalid—BASIC key word
   3. HAT—Valid (Invalid on some—imbedded key word)
   4. F$—Valid
   5. NAME$—Valid

6. $City—Invalid—$ symbol must be suffix
7. STATE$—Valid
8. RATE—Valid (Invalid on some—imbedded key word)
9. X—Valid
10. LET—Invalid—BASIC key word

IMMEDIATE EXECUTION MODE (DIRECT PROGRAMMING)

Using the computer as a calculator is called direct programming or immediate execution. In this mode, it is not necessary to prepare a complete program to obtain an immediate response from the system. This is particularly helpful when solving calculations and formulas.

Immediate mode format differs from BASIC statement format in that it does not use statement numbers. Like the BASIC statement though, it does contain the key word and the parameter. The following is an immediate execution statement and its result.

] PRINT "BASIC"
BASIC

The PRINT key word is preceded by a prompting character, which varies with the system. Some systems display the word OK or READY instead of using a prompt.

The key word PRINT is used to print or display output. Most BASIC systems allow the use of the ? symbol to replace keying the word PRINT.

The string value "BASIC" is defined through the use of quotation marks. The computer returns the data shown on the next line, in this case, BASIC. The quotation marks used to delimit string values are not displayed at output.

Both numeric and string data can be used in direct execution. String data is defined through the use of quotation marks; numeric data is not so enclosed. The following are examples of direct execution statements and their results.

] PRINT "150"
150
] PRINT 150
150
] PRINT "ANOTHER ONE BITES THE DUST!"
ANOTHER ONE BITES THE DUST!
] PRINT 5 + 5
10

The immediate execution line PRINT 5 + 5 is a calculation operation that results in the display of the answer 10. Calculations can be done in PRINT statements as shown.

The process of placing a value in a numeric or string variable is known as an *assignment operation*. The following assignment statement causes the value 47 to be placed in the storage location known as variable P.

LET P = 47

LET is the BASIC key word that is used in assignment statements. Use of the key word LET is optional on some systems.

Calculation operations can be performed in the direct execution mode through the use of more than one statement. A combination of PRINT, assignment, and calculation statements is shown in figure 1–9. The information that the computer returns is also shown in the example.

The statement LET P = 47 assigns the value 47 to the variable P. Although no output results from this statement, the memory location known as P now contains the value 47.

PRINT "P" causes the string value P to be printed on the next line. P is identified

```
]  LET  P  =  47
]  PRINT  "P"
P
]  LET  P  =  P  +  50
]  PRINT  P
97
```

FIGURE 1–9
Immediate execution
mode

as a string variable by the quotation marks. There is no effect upon the numeric variable known as P.

The next line entered is an assignment statement that causes the value in P to become equal to the old value plus 50. Variable P will be valued at 97 after the assignment statement is executed. This type of statement, in which the value of a variable is increased by another value, is called an *accumulation statement*.

Finally, the statement PRINT P results in the value stored in variable P being printed. The value 97 is displayed on the next line.

PROBLEM 1–1

A. Enter the following statements into the computer and record the results.

1. PRINT "QUEEN"   RESULT _____

2. PRINT Q   RESULT _____

3. PRINT "150"   RESULT _____

4. PRINT 150   RESULT _____

5. PRINT 47 + 47   RESULT _____

6. PRINT 125 − 55   RESULT _____

B. Enter the following statements into the computer and record the result.

LET B = 128   RESULT _____

PRINT "B"   _____

LET B = B + 128   _____

PRINT B   _____

    _____

BASIC PROGRAM COMPONENTS

The BASIC program in figure 1–10 illustrates major program segments without being concerned with the individual parts. This structured BASIC program prints the company name. It uses sequential structured methodology, which means that the statements are executed in sequence.

Lines 100–150 are program documentation statements in which the author, date, and purpose are recorded. Separate program modules are identified in lines 200 and 300. The data to be processed is identified in lines 400–410.

The mainline module controls execution of the program. In the process module the data is entered and printed. When the READ statement is executed, the data is stored in the variable known as A\$ and when the LPRINT line is executed, the data is printed. Some systems use PRINT rather than LPRINT.

```
100                                                              REM
110        REM   FIGURE  1-10   WRITTEN BY LARRY FRY  1/1/83
120        REM    This program prints the company name
130                                                              REM
140        REM ***** Variable Identification
150        REM        A$ ........    Company Name
160                                                              REM
200        REM *****   Mainline Module
210  LPRINT
220  GOSUB  310
230  END
240                                                              REM
300        REM *****    Process  Module
310  READ    A$
320  LPRINT    A$
330  RETURN
340                                                              REM
400        REM *****    Data to be processed
410  DATA "PORT-EX  COMPANY"
420                                                              REM
430  STOP

PORT-EX  COMPANY
```

FIGURE 1—10
Structured sequential
BASIC program

CURRENT, OR TEMPORARY, PROGRAM STORAGE

When a program is being entered into the system or worked on, it is kept in the main memory, or the work space area, of computer storage. This is referred to as temporary, or current, memory. In mainframe computers a portion of primary computer memory located in the central processing unit is allocated to the user. Microcomputer main memory, known as random access memory (RAM), usually holds one program at a time. Microcomputer main memory is volatile—the contents are erased when the computer is turned off. Memory can also be cleared, or erased, through the use of the NEW command or its equivalent.

Before entering a program for the first time, the NEW command should be entered to clear microcomputer RAM areas. On a mainframe computer the SCRATCH or CLEAR command is used to perform an equivalent procedure.

After the memory has been cleared, statements for the new program are entered line by line. Program statements may be entered in any sequence. The computer automatically places them in the correct sequence when the program is executed or listed.

After all of the program statements have been entered, the program should be tested for correct execution. Programs in temporary memory are executed by entering the RUN command. When the RUN command is entered, the program stored in current memory is executed and the results are displayed. If there is a syntax or usage error in the program, the computer will stop execution.

The LIST command enables the user to view any of the program statements in current storage. When the LIST command is entered, the program statements are displayed upon the monitor or printer as indicated by the programmer. Because various systems offer different options with the LIST command, the computer reference manual should be checked. Two examples of options offered with the LIST command are: LIST may also be used as a program statement on some systems; and, when LIST is placed in the beginning of a program on some systems, the program is displayed whenever the RUN command is entered. Enter the system options for the LIST command in Exercise 1–2.

System List Commands			EXERCISE 1–2
Display entire program	LIST or	_____	
Display one line (200)	LIST 200 or	_____	

Display lines 1–100	LIST 1–100 or	_____
Display lines 100–200	LIST 100–200 or	_____
Display lines 400 to end	LIST 400– or	_____

A variety of procedures is offered by the different computer systems to revise program statements in current storage. In the interactive mode on a terminal, cursor or pointer movement is used for editing. On some systems a combination of the CONTROL (CTRL) and ESCAPE (ESC) key operations is used to produce cursor movement in the edit mode; on others, the EDIT command is used. Check the system manual for proper editing procedures and summarize them in Exercise 1–3.

EXERCISE 1–3

System Editing Procedures

Edit command _____

_____

_____

Cursor movement (up) _____

(down) _____

(left) _____

(right) _____

_____

Delete last character _____

Delete current line _____

Other _____

_____

Sometimes it is easiest to reenter the line. Statements are reentered by keying the line number that is to be replaced and adding the key word and the parameters. The new line automatically replaces the old line when it is entered in this manner.

Individual statements may be deleted by entering the line number followed by RETURN. This act cancels the referenced line. Some systems offer various combinations of the DELETE (DEL) command particularly when a large block of statements is deleted. The RUBOUT key is used by some systems to delete the last character entered.

The RESET or BREAK key is used to halt or cancel current operations. It can be used to return program execution to the beginning of the program. CONTROL C is used on some systems for a program break. Check the system manual for the proper use of these keys; if they are misused, the results can be disastrous.

PERMANENT PROGRAM STORAGE

Main computer memory is volatile—the contents are erased when the computer is turned off—therefore, auxiliary storage is used to save programs and data. Information necessary for the day-to-day operation of a business is recorded on permanent media such as cassettes, diskettes, and disks. Each of these methods of auxiliary storage is capable of storing many programs or data files. One diskette can store 70 or more files. The very large disk files associated with mainframe computers or minicomputers may hold thousands of files. The procedures for saving and retrieving programs from permanent storage are summarized in Appendix C.

There are rules for naming files. Generally, the same rules apply to file names as to variable names. On most systems the first character must be alphabetic and it can be followed by a maximum of thirty characters. Blank spaces usually may be included in file names. File names should be kept short and they should correspond to the intended use of the program. Summarize system file name rules in Exercise 1–4.

File Name Rules and Procedures

EXERCISE 1–4

Rules _____

_____

Procedures _____

_____

_____

Certain system commands are necessary to store and/or recall program files to/from auxiliary storage. These commands vary from system to system, but the following are the most commonly used.

1. CATALOG (DIRECTORY, FILES, or LIBRARY)—Displays an inventory of the program or data files stored on the disk. On some systems, the display includes the type of file and the amount of space consumed on the disk by each file.
2. DELETE (KILL or UNSAVE)—Erases program file name from auxiliary storage.
3. LOAD (OLD on time-sharing computers)—Transfers a file from auxiliary (permanent) storage to main (temporary) memory. Anything previously held in temporary memory is replaced by the transferred program. The operator can either LIST or RUN the program after entering the LOAD command.
4. LOCK—Prevents accidental deletion of a program. The program can be deleted by using the UNLOCK command. Since this requires a conscious two-step operation, it helps to eliminate accidental deletions.
5. NEW—Creates a new file name when used on time-sharing systems. Clears main memory (RAM) when used on microcomputers.
6. RENAME—Changes file names.
7. REPLACE (UNSAVE followed by SAVE on time-sharing systems)—Creates a new file and deletes an existing file with the same name.
8. RUN—Executes program in temporary memory. On some microcomputer systems when the RUN command is entered with a file name, as in RUN PAY, the file named, in this case PAY, is transferred from permanent to temporary storage and is immediately executed.
9. SAVE—Transfers the file in temporary memory to permanent storage. When a file name is specified, as in SAVE PAY, the program is stored under the specified

name, in this case, PAY. The program PAY is still available for use in main memory. The file name is automatically added to the CATALOG.

10. SCRATCH—Clears the temporary work space on time-sharing computers.

List the commands designated to perform the referenced system functions for the computer being used in Exercise 1–5.

EXERCISE 1–5

System Commands

Clear work space _____

Inventory of file names _____

Save file name _____

Delete file name _____

Load file name _____

Change file name _____

Safeguard file name _____

Load file name with

    immediate execution _____

Other _____

PROGRAM ERRORS

Two types of errors can exist in computer programs: usage errors, which are known as *syntax errors;* and *logic errors,* which are mistakes in implementation or in logic flow. In the BASIC language the program will not execute if it contains a syntax error. When the system encounters a syntax error, it displays a message that presents the line number and the error type. Some systems display the statement that contains the error, rather than the line number. An example of program termination caused by a syntax error is shown in figure 1–11. The error in this illustration is actually caused by a mismatch between the READ and DATA statement variable types.

If an interpreter is used, the process of eliminating errors may require several passes through the program. As the interpreter checks the program line by line, it is able to detect only one error at a time. Multiple errors in the program will not be detected on the first pass through the program. Corrections should be made on each pass.

If a compiler is used, multiple passes are not required. The compiler scans the entire program and lists all errors detected after the first pass.

The computer does not detect logic errors; they must be found by the programmer. This is accomplished by using a wide range of data to test the program as it is to be used operationally. Test data should be designed to examine all of the program options, or branches.

To thoroughly test the program, the programmer must know what the result of the program should look like. This is done by a pencil and paper simulation of the execution of the program. The procedure is known as a hand trace. All variables must be monitored and the values recorded as the program proceeds. The variable memory locations will contain different values as the program is executed and monitoring should simulate this.

```
100                                                              REM
110        REM    FIGURE  1-11    WRITTEN BY LARRY FRY  1/1/83
120        REM    This program prints the company name
130                                                              REM
140        REM ***** Variable Identification
150        REM        A$  .......   Company Name
160                                                              REM
200        REM *****   Mainline Module
210   LPRINT
220   GOSUB   310
230   END
240                                                              REM
300        REM *****   Process   Module
310   READ A
320   LPRINT  A$
330   RETURN
340                                                              REM
400        REM *****   Data to be processed
410   DATA "PORT-EX   COMPANY"
420                                                              REM
430   STOP
```

```
RUN
Syntax error in 410
OK
410   DATA  "PORT-EX   COMPANY"
```

FIGURE 1–11
BASIC program
termination by syntax
error

Likewise, any output should be recorded. Tracing should be done independently of program execution on the computer. The trace and the result of computer execution should then be compared to determine if there are any differences.

Through the use of a liberal number of PRINT statements program execution can be traced on the computer. When this method is used, the value of each variable is printed each time the contents of the memory location change during program execution. This results in a record of how the variables change, which is extremely valuable in detecting an error.

The act of removing syntax and logic errors is known as *debugging*. Some computer systems include built-in debugging tools to assist programmers in the location of errors. One such feature is the TRACE (TRON) command. When this command is used, the computer displays statement numbers and variable values as the program executes. This command is most useful if there is a logic error involving a program loop. Generally, the TRACE command must be cancelled by the programmer. TRACE (TRON) is cancelled by the NOTRACE (TROFF) command.

Debugging suggestions are included in the following chapters as appropriate. Although the debugging process is frustrating, it is important to learn what caused the error and to avoid repeating it. Do not be afraid to experiment and try new approaches. Errors may result, but this is perhaps the best way to learn. And remember: debugging is a skill that improves with experience.

SUMMARY

Computer systems have evolved from the huge mainframes of thirty years ago to the microcomputers used today. The development of the microcomputer has made owning a computer affordable for individuals and businesses that could not have afforded a mainframe or minicomputer.

BASIC is the dominant language supported by microcomputers. It is also used on other types of systems.

An essential part of program construction is identifying and classifying data. A single fact, or data field, is called a variable. A collection of related variables is called a record and a collection of related records is called a file. The most important thing to remember regarding data is that the variables within related records must be arranged in the same order.

Program documentation is another important aspect of program construction. It provides a complete record of the development, objective, and expected output for the program. This record helps the user during program maintenance and computer failure.

Structured BASIC programming uses the top-down, or stepwise refinement, methodology to develop programs. The programs are divided into major processing tasks which are called modules. Step-by-step instructions are then developed for each module.

Flowcharts are graphic solutions to problems. There are two types of flowcharts: the top-level flowchart, which depicts the program modules; and the detailed logic flowchart, which depicts the step-by-step flow for each module.

Three program control structures are used in BASIC programs. They are the simple sequential, the program branch, and the program loop.

The American National Standards Institute (ANSI) established 26 standard key words that must be operational on computers supporting the Minimal BASIC Standard. Computer manufacturers have added many additional key words to the standard set.

Interpreters and compilers are used on computers to translate the BASIC programs into binary form, called machine language, and to monitor the program for errors. Interpreters read the program line by line, while compilers read the program as a whole. Compiled programs usually execute faster than interpreted programs.

The BASIC statement consists of the line number, the key word, and the parameter.

Two types of variables are used in BASIC programs: numeric variables, which contain integer or real data; and, string variables, which contain alphabetic or alphanumeric data.

It is not always necessary to prepare a complete program to obtain a response from the computer. When the immediate execution format is used, the computer responds immediately to the statement entered.

Programs being entered into the system or worked on are held in the computer's temporary, or current, memory. The contents of this memory are erased when the computer is turned off. Programs can be entered, erased, or edited through the use of a variety of commands which are specified by the manufacturer.

Because the contents are erased from current memory when the system is turned off, the programs and data must be stored on permanent media such as cassettes, diskettes, and disks. A variety of system commands is used to store and/or recall program files to/from auxiliary storage.

Two types of errors can exist in programs: syntax errors, which are usage errors; and, logic errors, which are mistakes in implementation or in logic flow. The process of removing syntax and logic errors is called debugging.

BASIC Key Words/Commands Learned

AUTO	Automatically numbers statements.
BREAK	Interrupts program.
CATALOG	Creates inventory of file names.
CLEAR	Clears current memory or variables.
CONTROL (CTRL)	System command key for editing or interrupting program.
DELETE	Deletes file names or statement numbers.
DIRECTORY (DIR)	Inventory of file names.
EDIT	Edits or alters program statements in current memory.

END	Terminates program.
ESCAPE	System command key for editing or interrupting procedures.
FILES	Creates inventory of file names.
FORMAT	Diskette initialization of unformatted disks.
GO TO	Nonconditional program branch.
HOME	Clears screen and positions cursor at top left.
INITIALIZE	Diskette initialization of unformatted disks.
KILL	Deletes file name.
LET	Assignment key word.
LIBRARY	Creates inventory of file names.
LIST	Displays referenced program statements.
LOAD	Transfers program from permanent storage to current memory.
LOCK	Safeguards file name.
NAME	Alters file name.
NEW	Clears microcomputer current memory or assigns new file name on time-sharing system.
NOTRACE	Terminates TRACE.
OLD	Time-sharing command to LOAD file name from permanent memory.
PRINT	Displays or prints output.
REMARK (REM)	Program documentation or remark key word.
RENAME	Alters file name.
RENUMBER	Command or utility program to alter statement numbers.
REPLACE	Time-sharing statement equivalent to UNSAVE followed by SAVE.
RESET	Command key for interrupting program.
RETURN (ENTER)	Marks end of BASIC statement/command and enters it into system.
RUBOUT	Deletes last character/line.
RUN	Executes program in current memory.
SAVE	Transfers program file from current memory to permanent storage.
SCRATCH	Clears time-sharing work space.
STOP	Interrupts program and provides a BREAK message.
TRACE	Begins program trace, which monitors statement execution and variable values.

TROFF	Terminates TRON.
TRON	Begins program trace on some systems.
UNLOCK	Terminates file name safeguard.
UNSAVE	Deletes file name on time-sharing systems.

PROBLEM 1—1

Complete the following questions as appropriate for the system being used. See the glossary for definition of terms.

1. What type of computer will be utilized? _____

2. What is the type of processing unit (mainframe, minicomputer, or microcomputer)?

   _____

3. If using a mainframe or minicomputer:

   a. What is the size of main memory? _____

   b. What is the size of the central processing unit in bytes? _____

   c. What type of terminal will be used? _____

   d. What is the data transmission rate (baud)? _____

   e. What type of auxiliary storage does the computer have? _____

   f. What form of BASIC does the computer use? _____

   g. Does the machine use a BASIC interpreter or compiler? _____

   h. What sign-on and sign-off procedures are to be followed (see Appendix C)?

   (Password) _____

   _____

   _____

   _____

   _____

   _____

4. If using a microcomputer:

   a. What type of microprocessor does the machine have? _____

   b. What is the size of the microprocessor in bits? _____

   c. How much read-only memory capacity does the computer have? _____

   d. How much random access memory does the machine have? _____

e. What type of auxiliary storage does the computer have? _____

f. If it uses a diskette, what are the technical characteristics of the diskette, i.e.,

the amount of storage or density? _____

_____

_____

g. What brand or type of diskette is recommended? _____

h. What type of operating system does the computer use? _____

i. What form of BASIC does the computer use? _____

j. Does the machine use a BASIC interpreter or compiler? _____

k. What are the system start-up or boot procedures (see Appendix C)? _____

_____

_____

READ AND DATA STATEMENTS

2

OBJECTIVES

At the end of this chapter you should be able to perform the following tasks:

- Write structured BASIC programs using READ and DATA statements to enter data.
- Identify three ways to enter data using the BASIC language.
- Construct a data list and data pointer.

SERIAL DATA ENTRY—READ AND DATA STATEMENTS

In the BASIC programming language three types of statements are used to enter data into a computer: assignment statements, READ and DATA statements, and INPUT statements. Assignment statements are used to enter data values. READ and DATA statements are used to enter data in a series, which is referred to as batch or *serial processing*. Finally, INPUT statements are used to enter data in an interactive mode, which is referred to as *transaction processing*.

The simplest type of computer program is the input/output listing. The purpose of the program is to enter data and list it in a printed report. Listing programs can be used to provide a list of clients, customers, accounts, club members, or new prospects. READ and DATA statements are used to enter data and the PRINT statement, which was explained before in the section on immediate execution, is used to produce output. Following is the format for READ and DATA statements.

```
100 READ ⟨Parameter⟩
300 DATA ⟨Parameter⟩
```

The READ statement is placed in BASIC programs wherever it is necessary to give new values to specific variables. The DATA statement may be located anywhere in the program, but the conventional procedure in structured BASIC is to place it near the end. Programs that contain a READ statement must also contain one or more DATA statements. In BASIC the READ statement comprises a data record that is made up of one or more valid variable names. Remember: READ and DATA statements must correspond in sequence and type of variable names and data values.

In the following example variable A is defined as a numeric variable field in the READ statement.

```
100 READ A
    .
    .
300 DATA 49
```

The READ and DATA statements correspond in the sequence and type of data. After statement 100 is executed, variable A contains a value of 49. Numeric variables may be either integers or real numbers. Some systems permit the use of different suffixes for integer and real data. These will be described in Chapter 5.

READ and DATA statements may contain more than one variable, but the variable names must always be separated by commas. Following is the format for READ and DATA statements that contain more than one variable.

```
100 READ ⟨Parameter⟩, [Parameter], ⟨Parameter⟩
500 DATA ⟨Parameter⟩, ⟨Parameter⟩, ⟨Parameter⟩
```

Following are READ and DATA statements that contain more than one variable.

150 READ X, X$

.

.

600 DATA 35.50, "March"

The numeric variable X and the string variable X$ are defined in the READ statement. Notice that the sequence and type of variables are the same in the READ and DATA statements. String data values should be enclosed within quotation marks on most systems. The quotation marks are used by the programmer to set string value boundaries. The computer eliminates the quotation marks internally and does not display them in output. After line 150 is executed, the variable X contains the real value 35.50 and X$ contains the value "March" (the quotation marks are not part of the internal data value).

A mixture of integer, real, and string variables is contained in the following example.

250 READ N, N$, C$, A
500 DATA 111, "ACME CO", "CANTON, OH", 397.24

The order in which the types of fields are listed is not mandated; it is the programmer's option, but the READ and DATA statements must correspond in the sequence and type of variable fields. When commas, semicolons, or other symbols are used to separate information within a string value, that value must be enclosed in quotation marks, e.g., "Canton, OH". The quotation marks are used to set the boundaries of the string value. If they were not used, the computer would misinterpret the comma shown in the data value "Canton, OH" as a separator, which would result in syntax or logic errors.

The placement of blank spaces (symbol ƀ) within string values in DATA statements can be a programming aid as in the following statement.

300 DATA "SmithƀA", "SmithƀƀƀAƀ", 99

The computer begins storing the data as soon as the first quotation mark or first character (not ƀ) is detected after the word DATA or after a comma. Field 1 is stored in the computer's memory as SmithƀA with one blank space between the word Smith and the letter A. Field 2 is stored in the computer's memory as SmithƀƀƀAƀ with three blank spaces between the word Smith and the letter A and with one blank space after the character A. Field 3 is stored as 99. Variation in the number of blank spaces in string data within DATA statements is helpful in establishing output format.

To summarize, the computer begins storing data upon detecting quotation marks or the first character (not ƀ) after the word DATA or after a comma. All characters and blank spaces that follow are stored in that respective variable memory location until the next quotation mark, comma, or RETURN is encountered.

A. Identify and correct errors in the following READ-DATA statements:
  1. 100 READ X
     300 DATA "Spencer, A"
  2. 100 READ N, N$
     200 DATA 43 "Spencer, A"
  3. 100 READ X, Y, Z
     400 32, .05 97
  4. 400 READ A$, A
     600 DATA 15.00, "Pot-O-Gold"
  5. 200 READ X, A$, Y
     500 DATA 15, "K-Y"
  6. 300 READ X Y
     900 DATA 97.5, 100.4
  7. 400 READ Z, A, B
     1000 DATA 45, 90, 135, "INVOICE"

SELF-TEST
2–1

B. What is the value of the referenced variables after execution of the READ statement?
   1. 100 READ A, B
      200 DATA 30, .05
   2. 300 READ N$, B
      600 DATA "Shope-Rite", 1917.50
   3. 200 READ A, B, C, D$, O
      400 DATA 49, .05, .03, "Discount", 575.15
   4. 300 READ L$, N$, B$
      700 DATA "Heatherβ̸β̸A", "Rit̸β,D", "Sim̸β,R"
   5. 200 READ A
      300 READ B, C, D, X$
      900 DATA 3
      910 DATA 75, 90, 15, "CURRENT"

Answers for
Self-Test
2–1

A. 1. X is a numeric variable.
      Correction—100 READ X$
   2. DATA values are not separated by a comma.
      Correction—200 DATA 43, "Spencer, A"
   3. The word DATA is missing and a comma should appear after .05.
      Correction—400 DATA 32, .05, 97
   4. Variables in READ and DATA statements do not correspond.
      Correction—400 READ A, A$
   5. Out of data error will result because there is no data for Y.
      Correction—500 DATA 15, "K-Y", 1.98
   6. Variable names are not separated by commas in the READ statement.
      Correction—300 READ X, Y
   7. Variable name is not included for the string value.
      Correction—400 READ Z, A, B, C$
B. 1. A = 30   B = .05
   2. N$ = Shope-Rite   B = 1917.50
   3. A = 49   B = .05   C = .03   D$ = Discount
      O = 575.15
   4. L$ = Heatherβ̸β̸A   N$ = Rit̸β,D
      B$ = Sim̸β,R
   5. A = 3   B = 75   C = 90
      D = 15   X$ = CURRENT

DATA LIST

It appears that the sequence and type of data do not correspond in the following READ and DATA statements.

    200 READ D$, L
    600 DATA "Syay, Inc", 1200.00, "Acme Co", 5000.00
    610 DATA "BB Co", 4700.00, "A-Z Co", 3500.00

This format is acceptable, however, because the data being entered is placed in a *data list,* which is an internal storage area. Although multiple records have been placed in the same DATA statement, the READ and DATA statements still conform in the sequence and type of data. As programs are compiled/interpreted, they are scanned for DATA statements. Data statements are not executed; the contents are placed in the data list.

At the beginning of execution, the data list is established in the following manner and the *data pointer,* which indicates the beginning of a set of variable values, is located at the top of the data list. Execution of statement 200 results in the first two items in the data list being placed into the variable fields D$ and L. The variable D$ then contains the value Syay, Inc. and variable L contains 1200.00. The following is the data list.

Data List

Syay, Inc
1200.00
Acme Co
5000.00
BB Co
4700.00
A-Z Co
3500.00

Assume that this example is part of a program that contains a loop. A *program loop* is a statement or group of statements that is executed repeatedly. The number of times the loop is executed is a programmable option. Repeated execution of the READ statement would result in the remaining values in the data list becoming available for use.

After execution of line 200, the data pointer moves a specified number of values down the data list. This is determined by the number of variable names contained in the READ statement. The READ statement in line 200 contains two variable names; therefore, the data pointer moves down two values in the data list as in the following example.

Syay, Inc   <- - -   *Data Pointer*
1200.00
Acme Co   <- - -
5000.00
BB Co   <- - -
4700.00
.
.

Subsequent execution of the READ statement will, in turn, result in the data pointer moving down a corresponding number of values each time the loop is performed. Notice

```
GROUP 1

    100   READ   L, B$, C

    500   DATA   437

    510   DATA   "Mower"

    520   DATA   275.50

    530   DATA   54

    540   DATA   "Tiller"

    550   DATA   399.99


GROUP  2

    100   READ   L, B$, C

    500   DATA   437, "Mower",  275.50

    510   DATA   54, "Tiller", 399.99

GROUP  3

    100   READ L, B$, C

    500   DATA 437,"Mower",275.50,54,"Tiller",399.99
```

FIGURE 2–1
Equivalent READ and
DATA statements

that the items in the data list do correspond to the READ statement even though more than one record is included in each DATA statement.

In summary, the READ and DATA statement groups contained in figure 2–1 are equivalent with respect to the values assigned to each variable as the program is executed. A loop is assumed to be present in the program.

SELF-TEST 2–2

A. What is the value of the variables after execution of the following READ statements?

1. 100 READ X, Y, Z, A$
   300 DATA 57.55, 31, 18.75, "Brake"
2. 100 READ X, Y, Z, A$
   500 DATA 99.99
   510 DATA 17
   520 DATA 33.33
   530 DATA "Clutch"

B. Construct a data list from the following READ and DATA statements. Place a data pointer where appropriate. Assume that a program loop is present.

   100 READ I, N$, G, D, N
   400 DATA 327, "Quik-Stop", 47.50, 4.50, 43.00
   410 DATA 404, "D-Way", 6.50, 0, 6.50
   420 DATA 441, "Serv-U", 50, 5, 45

Answers for Self-Test 2–2

A. 1. X = 57.55   Y = 31   Z = 18.75
      A$ = Brake
   2. X = 99.99   Y = 17   Z = 33.33
      A$ = Clutch

B. DATA LIST
   327   <– – –   DATA POINTER
   Quik-Stop
   47.50
    4.50
   43.00
   404   <– – –
   D-Way
   6.50
   0
   6.50
   441   <– – –
   Serv-U
   50
   5
   45

SUMMARY

Three methods are used in BASIC to enter data. They are READ and DATA statements, INPUT statements, and assignment statements. The most important rule to remember regarding the construction of READ and DATA statements is that the sequence and type of data must correspond between the statements.

It is acceptable to place more than one variable in READ and DATA statements, but the variable names must be separated by commas. When a string value containing commas, semicolons, or other symbols is one of multiple variables in READ and DATA statements, it must be enclosed in quotation marks. If it is not enclosed in quotation marks, it will cause logic or syntax errors because it will be misread by the computer as a separator.

A DATA statement can hold more than one set of values for the variables named in the corresponding READ statement as long as the values match the sequence and type of data established for the variables. When the computer scans the program, it places the values in the DATA statement in a storage area called a data list. As the program is executed, the data pointer moves down the data list indicating the beginning of each group of variable values. A program loop in which a statement or group of statements is executed repeatedly is used to process the values in the data list.

BASIC Key Words/Operations Learned

DATA

> Data to be processed. Must be paired with a READ statement.

READ

> Data record entered. Programs with READ statements must also have DATA statements.

OUTPUT OPERATIONS—PRINT

OBJECTIVES

At the end of this chapter you should be able to perform the following operations:

- Write structured BASIC programs using the PRINT statement with print zones to output data.
- Identify the cause of wraparound in output.
- Code and execute structured input/output listing programs.
- Construct flowcharts for input/output listing programs.
- Use FOR/NEXT statements to control loop execution.
- Utilize GOSUB-RETURN for subroutine operations.
- Trace the results of an operational listing program.
- Center report headings using the TAB statement.
- Recognize common errors in BASIC listing programs.

PRINT—PRINT ZONES

The PRINT statement is used to provide output. PRINT, or LPRINT on some systems, is the key word that causes output to be displayed upon the monitor or the printer. It is also the statement used to record output on magnetic media, such as disks on some systems.

On most computer systems the print lines, or available horizontal space, on the monitor or the printer are divided into groups of columns, which are called *print zones*. System print zone width varies from 5 to 16 columns. Print zones are utilized through the use of commas in the PRINT statements. Whenever the computer detects a comma in a PRINT statement, the output device automatically skips to the next print zone. The following is the format for a PRINT statement that uses print zones.

400 PRINT ⟨Parameter⟩, ⟨Parameter⟩, ⟨Parameter⟩

The total number of characters available on one line on the monitor or printer is divided into separate print zones. If the monitor has 40 columns available per line, the print zones may be defined as follows.

```
          ZONE 1      ZONE 2   ZONE 3
      |----------------|----------------|------------|
      Col. 1           17               33          40
```

There are two print zones of 16 columns each plus one zone of 8 columns.

Printers with 132 columns may be divided into eight print zones of 16 columns each plus one zone of 4 columns. Because system differences will alter the preceding examples, it is important to study the system manual and experiment with the computer being used to obtain the best results.

Obviously, with 40 columns available on some monitors, the amount of data shown on one line is limited. BASIC enables the system to print more than is first evident, though, because any excess data is automatically carried to the next line. This feature is referred to as *wraparound* (see figure 3–1).

REMARK line 110 is entered as a statement. The number of characters in the statement exceeds 40, so the excess is automatically carried, or wrapped around, to the next line. In statement 130, the four variables separated by commas establish four print zones when only three are available on one line. It appears that variables A, B, C, and D in

```
100   REM   LARRY FRY      1/25/83
110   REM   THIS  PROGRAM  EXHIBITS  WRAP-
      AROUND   IN OUTPUT
120   PRINT
130   READ A, B, C, D
140   PRINT A, B, C, D
150   DATA 1111, 2222, 3333, 4444
160   END


1111              2222            3333
4444
```

FIGURE 3–1
Wraparound in output

PRINT statement 140 will be printed on one line; however, since there are only three print zones, variable D (value 4444) is wrapped around to the next line. Although this example is from the printer, the monitor would display the same effect. Many of the new systems use monitors with a capacity of 80 or more columns which helps to eliminate wraparound.

When commas are used in PRINT statements, output is placed in print zone format. For example, if variable names are separated by a comma as in the following READ-DATA-PRINT statement combination, the output will be separated into the print zones provided by the system.

```
150 READ A, L$
400 PRINT A, L$
500 DATA 43.75, "BASIC"
```

Printed result after execution:

```
43.75      BASIC
|          |
Col. 1     Col. 17
```

The sequence in which variable names are listed in PRINT statements is determined by the desired output format. The desired output should be considered before the PRINT statement is developed. Variables listed in the READ statement do not necessarily have to be printed. Any variables used in PRINT statements should have been previously defined (in READ statements, calculations, or assignment statements). If they have not been defined, syntax or logic errors may result.

There may be a system limit on the number of adjacent commas allowed in PRINT statements. Some systems permit only two consecutive commas as in the following statement.

```
600 PRINT A, , S, Y
```

It is acceptable to end a PRINT statement with a comma. This procedure is called a *hanging comma*. Hanging commas may cause erratic results on some systems. When they are used, the computer fills all available print zones on the display unit with data values and automatically advances to the next line to continue printing.

One result of a hanging comma is exhibited in the following example. Assume that a 40-column display is being used and that a program loop is present.

```
300 READ C, A$
500 PRINT C, A$,
900 DATA 147, "MOWER", 39, "RAKE"
910 DATA 14, "SHOVEL", 25, "HOSE"
```

Printed result after execution (40-column display):

147	MOWER	39
RAKE	14	SHOVEL
25	HOSE	

A. Identify and correct the errors present in the following READ-DATA-PRINT groups:

1. 100 READ I, J, N$
   300 PRINT I, J, N$
   600 DATA , 4.00, .10, "JC Hafen"

2. 200 READ A, B,
   300 PRINT B, A
   400 DATA 47, 99

3. 100 READ E, F$, G
   300 PRINT X, F$, G
   400 DATA 11, "Plug", 2.98

B. 1. Trace the results of the following READ-DATA-PRINT statements. Assume that there are 10 columns per print zone.

   100 READ L, L$, M
   300 PRINT L$, M, L
   500 DATA 45, "Jones", 375

2. Trace the results of the following READ-DATA-PRINT statements. Assume that there are 40 columns with 10 columns per print zone. Also, assume that a program loop is present.

   300 READ N$, B
   400 PRINT B, N$,
   900 DATA "JONES", 43.75, "SMITH", 15.55
   910 DATA "HARRIS", 29.99, "BAKER", 11.33

A. 1. There should not be a comma after DATA.
      Correction—600 DATA 4.00, .10, "JC Hafen"
   2. There is a comma at the end of the READ statement.
      Correction—200 READ A, B
   3. Variable X in the PRINT line was not defined.
      Correction—300 PRINT E, F$, G

B. 1. TRACE

Jones	375	45

   2. TRACE

43.75	JONES	15.55	SMITH
29.99	HARRIS	11.33	BAKER

INPUT/OUTPUT LISTING PROGRAM

At this point, an input/output listing program and flowchart can be examined. The flowchart shown in figure 3–2 was discussed in Chapter 1. To review, the top-level flowchart consists of three modules: the mainline, read, and output blocks. The detailed logic flowchart provides the logic flow for writing program instructions. Step-by-step instructions are presented for each of the modules identified in the top-level flowchart. The detailed logic flowchart is used to code the program instructions.

The mainline module uses a FOR/NEXT loop structure to control execution of the read and output subroutines. When the read subroutine is executed, the data values are entered into the system. When the output subroutine is executed, the information is printed.

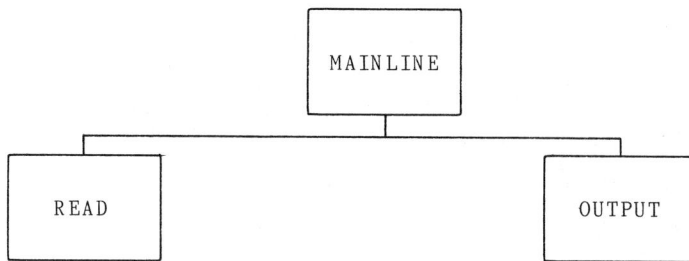

TOP-LEVEL FLOWCHART

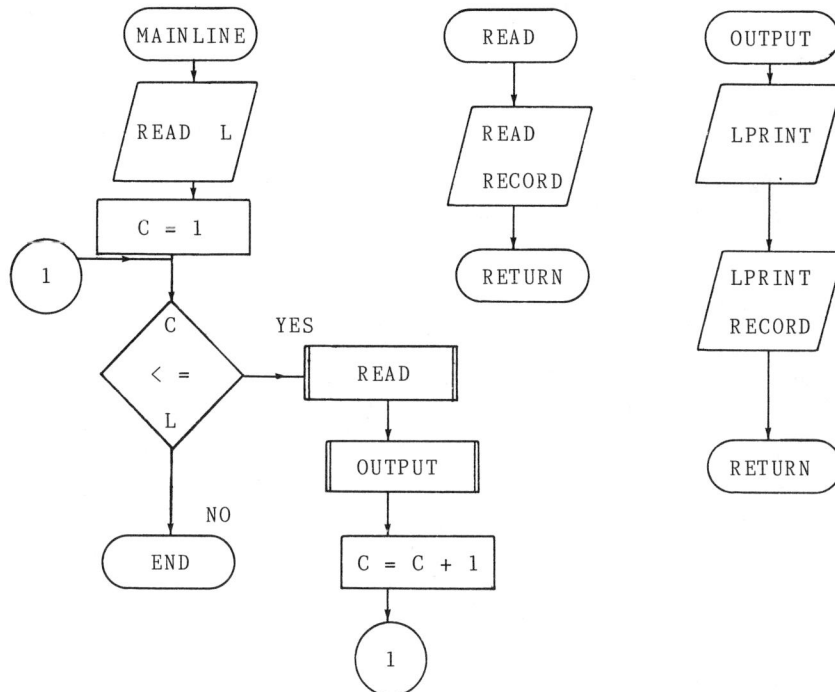

DETAILED LOGIC FLOWCHART

FIGURE 3–2
Top-level and detailed
logic flowcharts for
serial listing program

The BASIC program shown in figure 3–3 provides a listing of the gross national product for selected years. Most of the program elements have been individually discussed. The next step is to combine these individual steps into a functioning program that produces the desired results.

BASIC program execution begins with the lowest numbered line and proceeds through the program line by line to the highest numbered line unless a BASIC statement, such as FOR/NEXT or IF-THEN, alters the sequential path. Certain program elements, such as REM and DATA statements, are not executed. That is, these statements have no direct effect upon the output. In this example, program control begins with line 100 and proceeds through the program line by line. Program branches, when present, alter the direct sequential execution.

A system statement usually must be added to access the printer. Since the statement varies from system to system, it is virtually impossible to produce a standard for reference. The system used for this textbook uses the LPRINT statement. Other systems use PR# 1 (Slot # 1), or LPT1 (Line Printer 1). The instructor, owner's manual, or the purchase store should provide these system commands (see Appendix C). List printer access commands and print line length statements in Exercise 3–1.

```
100                                                                    REM
110      REM        FIGURE  3-3      WRITTEN BY LARRY FRY    1/2/83
120      REM This program prints the U.S. population and
130      REM    Gross National Product for selected years
140      REM       1960  -  1980  (Current Dollars)
150      REM  Source--STATISTICAL ABSTRACT OF THE UNITED STATES
160      REM  Population  -  Hundred Millions              REM
170      REM *****  Variable Identification
180      REM        Y  .....    YEAR
190      REM        P  .....    POPULATION
200      REM        G  .....    GROSS NATIONAL PRODUCT   (BILLION  $)
210      REM        L  .....    LOOP CONTROL
220      REM        C  .....    LOOP COUNTER
230                                                                    REM
300      REM *****  Mainline Module
310 READ  L
320 FOR  C  =  1  TO  L
330          GOSUB  410
340          GOSUB  440
350 NEXT  C
360 END
370                                                                    REM
400      REM *****  Read Module
410 READ Y, P, G
420 RETURN
430      REM *****  Output Module
440 LPRINT
450 LPRINT  Y, P, G
460 RETURN
470                                                                    REM
500      REM *****  Data to be processed
510 DATA  5
520 DATA  1960, 180.7, 506
530 DATA  1965, 194.3, 688
540 DATA  1970, 204.9, 982
550 DATA  1975, 213.6, 1529
560 DATA  1980, 222.3, 2629
600                                                                    REM
610 STOP
```

1960	180.7	506
1965	194.3	688
1970	204.9	982
1975	213.6	1529
1980	222.3	2629

FIGURE 3–3
BASIC input/output
listing program

**EXERCISE
3–1**

Printer Access Commands

Printer access statement   _____

_____

Print line length control statement   _____

_____

Program documentation statements are usually listed first in structured BASIC programs. REMARK statements (REM) are used for program documentation and clarification purposes. After reading them, a user should understand the program's objective, function, and logic flow. The following format is used for REMARK lines.

100 REM ⟨Parameter⟩

The quantity and location of REM lines are the programmer's option. Minimum documentation should include the author's name, the date, the program objective, variable name identification, and module identification. Large programs may call for frugal use of REM lines. REM lines should be distinguished from regular program lines if possible. This can be done by varying spacing on most systems.

In figure 3–3, REM statements are used in lines 110 through 220 to provide the program's author, date, objective, and variable identification. They are also used in statements 230, 370, 470, and 600 to separate modules. Program modules should be separated within the program. In these statements, the REM is placed at the extreme right to give the appearance of a blank line. This is especially helpful on systems that do not permit the use of numbered blank lines.

The results of program execution should be separated from the program listing by one or more blank lines. A blank line is created by a PRINT statement without a parameter. The LPRINT statement in line 440 causes one blank line to be printed after statement 610. This separates the body of the program from the output. Statement 440 is actually the first program line to produce output. The blank LPRINT line is within the program loop and will be executed each time the output subroutine is performed. This will cause double spacing of output.

The mainline module contains a FOR/NEXT loop control structure. Line 310 is a READ statement—when this is executed, the value in the first DATA line will be entered into the system. Variable L will then contain the value of 5, which is the number of records to be processed by the program. This variable controls the number of times the FOR/NEXT loop is executed.

The number of records to be processed in business data processing applications obviously exceeds the number illustrated in the textbook figures. Furthermore, it is possible that the precise number of records may not be known. In this case, a reasonably accurate number of the quantity of records to be processed can be obtained from the source document or organization records. This number is used for loop control purposes.

Although the number of records used at this level of programming is small, it is sufficient to test the program for syntax and logic errors. The number of records used to test programs in business exceeds the number used here.

Most business data processing organizations use disk files for storing and processing data. The loop structure used for disk files is controlled by the number of records contained in the file. More sophisticated techniques are used with disk files for loop control purposes. These are presented in Chapters 18–20.

FOR/NEXT loop control structures have the following format.

```
200 FOR ⟨Counter Variable⟩ = ⟨Parameter⟩ TO ⟨Parameter⟩
        ·
            Loop Elements
        ·

        ·
300 NEXT ⟨Counter Variable⟩
```

The FOR/NEXT loop segment from the example program is shown in figure 3–4.

The key word FOR begins the loop operation. Variable C serves as the loop counter; it is incremented each time the loop is performed by the NEXT statement. The counter is initialized with the value that follows the equal sign, in this case, 1. Beginning with the value of 1, the counter is incremented by + 1 each time the statement NEXT C is executed.

```
320   FOR   C   =   1   TO   L
330              GOSUB   410
340              GOSUB   440
350   NEXT   C
360   END
```

FIGURE 3–4
FOR/NEXT loop control segment

PASS	VARIABLE C	VARIABLE L	RESULT
1	2	5	Continue
2	3	5	Continue
3	4	5	Continue
4	5	5	Continue
5	6	5	Terminate

FIGURE 3–5
FOR/NEXT loop
parameter trace

There are five data records to be processed by this program. This is the value that is contained in variable L after line 310 is executed. Variable L follows the TO portion of the FOR/NEXT loop, setting the upper limit for the loop. The program loop, which consists of all operations between the FOR and the NEXT statements, is executed the number of times specified by the loop limit.

In this example, the loop contains GOSUB 410 and GOSUB 440. If the system allows it, loop elements should be indented. This makes the program easier to understand.

Loop execution is determined by the FOR statement parameters. NEXT C marks the end of the loop and increments the loop counter.

In figure 3–5 the values of variables C and L and the result after each pass through the FOR/NEXT loop are shown. Variable C begins with a value of 1 and contains a value of 2 after the first pass.

Execution of the FOR/NEXT loop continues as long as the counter variable is less than or equal to the limit parameter. When the counter variable is equal to the limit parameter, the loop is executed one last time. When the counter is initialized with a value that exceeds the limit, the loop is bypassed.

The counter exceeds the loop limit after the fifth pass. At this point, execution of the loop is terminated. Program control shifts to the line following the NEXT statement, in this case, END.

FOR/NEXT loops can also contain a STEP parameter if an increment other than + 1 is desired. The STEP parameter will be presented in Chapter 11.

PROBLEM 3–1

Trace the results of the following FOR/NEXT loops. Monitor the variables and record the results. Construct flowcharts to correspond to the loops.

```
1. 200 READ Z
   210 FOR X = 1 TO Z
   220     LET A = X * Z
   230     PRINT X, Z, A
   240 NEXT X
   250 END
   300 DATA 3
2. 400 READ K
   410 FOR J = 1 TO K
   420     LET I = J * J
   430     PRINT J, K, I
   440 NEXT J
   450 END
   500 DATA 5
3. 600 READ A
   700 FOR B = 4 TO A
   710     LET C = A * B
   720     PRINT A, B, C
   730 NEXT B
   800 PRINT A, B, C
   810 END
   900 DATA 1
```

```
330          GOSUB  410

340          GOSUB  440

400      REM  *****  Read Module

410   READ  Y,  P,  G

420   RETURN
```

FIGURE 3—6
GOSUB-RETURN
segment

GOSUB·RETURN is the BASIC language procedure for subroutine operations. The following is the format for GOSUB-RETURN.

330 GOSUB ⟨Statement Number Parameter⟩
.
.
.

420 RETURN

The program segment that illustrates a subroutine is shown in figure 3–6.

Line 330 is a subroutine call statement which shifts program control to the read module in line 410. Execution of the subroutine continues line by line until RETURN, in this case statement 420, is encountered. Program control then shifts back to the statement following the GOSUB which called the subroutine. Statement 340 is executed next in this segment.

REMARK statements are in programs for documentation purposes. They should not be referenced in GOSUB operations.

Line 360 (fig. 3–3) is the statement that terminates the program. END is the BASIC key word that is used for program termination. The key word END may be included at more than one place in a program, and it can appear in IF-THEN statements. In this case, END will be the next statement to be executed when the program loop terminates because it is on the line following NEXT C.

The data values are entered into the system in the READ module. The data record contains three variables as shown in line 410. The variables are the year (Y), population (P), and Gross National Product (G). The type and sequence of data corresponds between the READ and DATA statements. There are five data records.

The output for this program is shown in figure 3–3. The output module results in five printed lines which are known as *detail* or data lines. Each detail line printed contains the year, population, and Gross National Product. The values are printed in print zone format because of the commas. In this example there are 14 columns per print zone. The report is double-spaced as a result of the blank print line in statement 440.

The data to be processed is listed in lines 510–560. Statement 510 is the limit parameter that is used in the FOR/NEXT loop. Five data records are listed in the remaining statements.

The final program statement is line 610. When the STOP command is processed, program execution is halted and a BREAK message is printed on most systems. The BREAK message follows.

BREAK IN 610

STOP, rather than END, is used at this point to assure program validity. If the program is free of errors, this statement will not be executed. If there is an error, this statement will be executed, and on most systems the BREAK message will be printed. This message serves as an alert to the programmer that a logic or implementation error exists in the program. If the END statement were used in line 610, the program would terminate with no message.

Although all syntax errors may have been eliminated in a program, logic errors may still exist. The best way to test for logic errors is to provide a sample of test data that considers all possible variations.

To assist in logic error detection, the programmer prepares a *program trace*. A trace is a hand sketch analysis of the expected results of the program. Each variable in the pro-

OUTPUT ANALYSIS

	Blank Line	
1960	180.7	506
	Blank Line	
1965	194.3	688
	Blank Line	
1970	204.9	982
	Blank Line	
1975	213.6	1529
	Blank Line	
1980	222.3	2629
!	!	!
Col. 1	Col. 15	Col. 29

VARIABLES MONITORED

Y	P	G	C	L
			1	5
1960	180.7	506	2	5
1965	194.3	688	3	5
1970	204.9	982	4	5
1975	213.6	1529	5	5
1980	222.3	2629	6	5

FIGURE 3–7
Trace of listing program

gram is monitored as the program executes. That is, the value of each variable is recorded and changes in value are noted.

The trace is prepared separately from the program solution and is compared with the actual computer output to determine if there is a close match.

Monitoring variables through the trace can be of great value in debugging if an error is detected when comparing the trace with the printout. The possibility of internal rounding errors within the computer may result in slight differences between the trace and output. Programmers should be aware of this possibility and anticipate this result when working with real data.

A trace of the sample program includes a sketch analysis of output. The variables were monitored as the program executed. The trace is shown in figure 3–7.

SUMMARY PROGRAM

The primary objective of Chapter 3 is to develop the ability to write an input/output listing program. The summary program reviews the steps necessary to prepare a listing of accounts and to print report headings. READ and DATA statements are used to enter the data; notice that they correspond in sequence and type of variables. The same variables are printed as detail or data lines in print zone format.

As previously discussed, the organization may not know the exact number of records to be processed. If this is the case, a program loop termination procedure that is not dependent upon the user providing the precise number of records to be processed is required. If the number of records is known, the loop limit can be entered in a READ statement as in figure 3–3, line 310. The procedure used when the number of records is

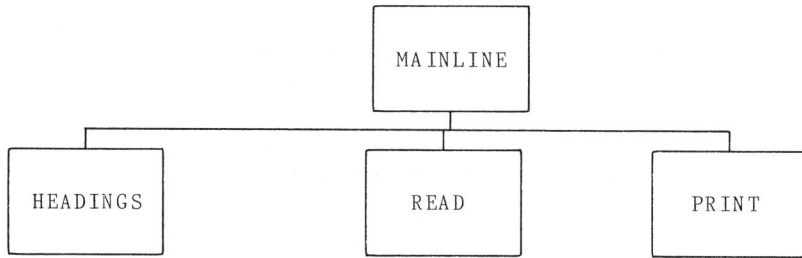

FIGURE 3–8
Top-level flowchart

not available is to insert a *termination DATA statement* after the significant DATA statements. An example of a termination DATA statement is figure 3–10, line 760. This statement is commonly referred to as a *trailer* or *dummy data* because it is not used in processing; its sole purpose is to stop execution of the program.

The top-level flowchart is shown in figure 3–8. The mainline routine controls the headings, read, and print subroutines.

The detailed logic flowchart is shown in figure 3–9. Headings are printed as a result of the headings block. A FOR/NEXT control structure is used in the mainline block to

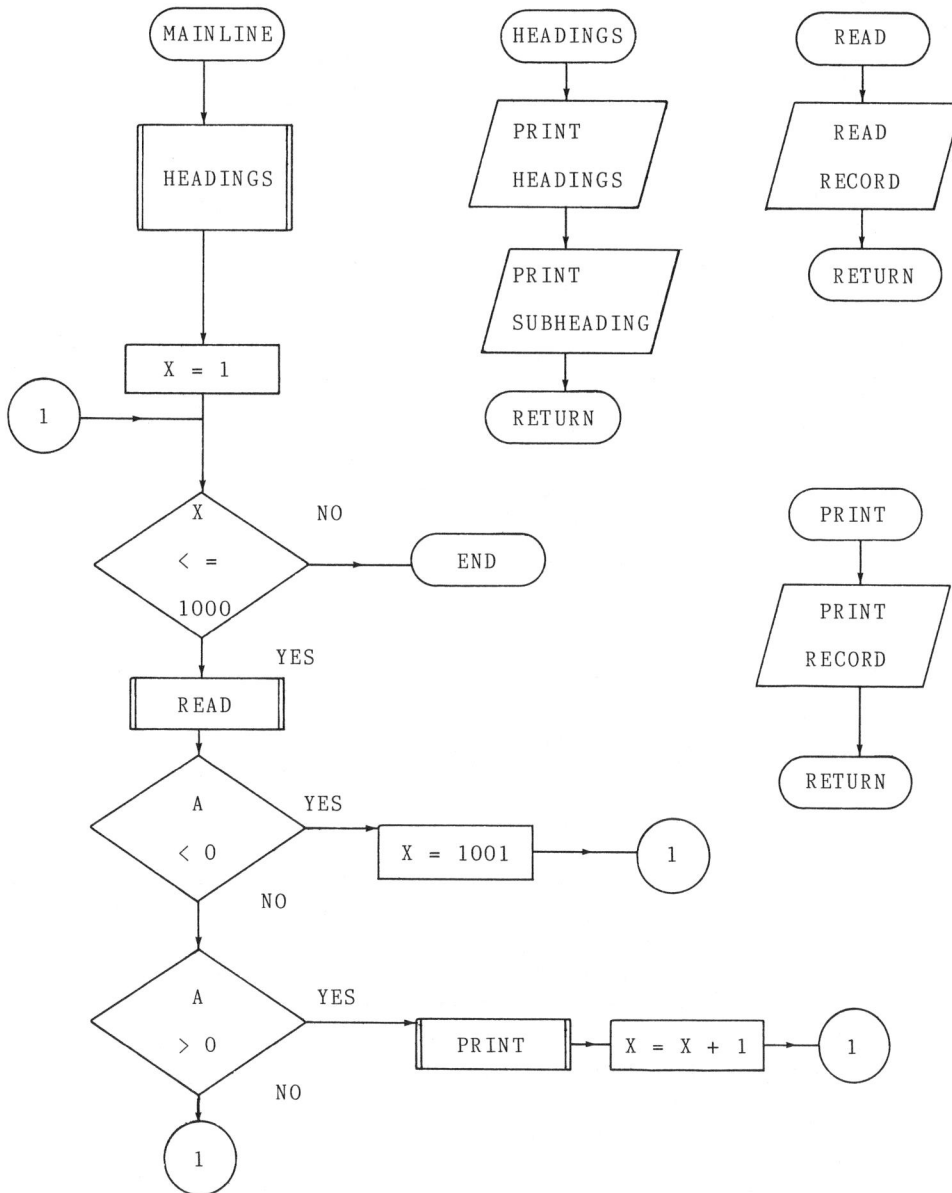

FIGURE 3–9
Detailed logic flowchart

```
100        REM    FIGURE 3-10   WRITTEN  BY  LARRY FRY      1/3/83
110        REM  This program prepares a chart of accounts
120        REM         for the Port-Ex Company
130                                                                  REM
140        REM *****   Variable Identification
150        REM         A  .....  Account Number
160        REM         C$ .....  Classification
170        REM         T$ .....  Title
180        REM         N$ .....  Balance Side
190        REM         B  .....  Account Balance
200        REM         L  .....  Loop Control
210        REM         X  .....  Loop Counter
220                                                                  REM
300        REM *****   Mainline Module
310   GOSUB 410
320   FOR  X  =  1  TO  1000
330        GOSUB  510
340              IF  A < 0 THEN LET X = 1001
350              IF  A > 0 THEN GOSUB 610
360   NEXT  X
370   END
380                                                                  REM
400        REM *****   Headings Module
410   LPRINT
420   LPRINT TAB(23); "PORT-EX COMPANY"
430   LPRINT
440   LPRINT TAB(22); "Chart of Accounts"
450   LPRINT
460   RETURN
470                                                                  REM
500        REM *****   Read Module
510   READ A, C$, T$, N$, B
520   RETURN
530                                                                  REM
600        REM *****   Print Module
610   LPRINT  T$, B, A, C$, N$
620   RETURN
630                                                                  REM
700        REM *****  Data to be Processed
710   DATA   110, "Asset", "CASH", "Debit", 5143.00
720   DATA   120, "Asset", "ACCOUNTS REC", "Debit", 6150.00
730   DATA   130, "Asset", "EQUIPMENT", "Debit", 12500.00
740   DATA   210, "Liability", "ACCOUNTS PAY", "Credit", 8793.00
750   DATA   310, "Capital", "CAPITAL", "Credit", 15000.00
760   DATA   -5, "END", "END", "END", -5
770                                                                  REM
780   STOP
```

PORT-EX COMPANY

Chart of Accounts

CASH	5143	110	Asset	Debit
ACCOUNTS REC	6150	120	Asset	Debit
EQUIPMENT	12500	130	Asset	Debit
ACCOUNTS PAY	8793	210	Liability	Credit
CAPITAL	15000	310	Capital	Credit

FIGURE 3–10
Serial input/output
program

execute the program loop. The loop limit parameter is set at a high number, 1000 in this program, to allow consideration of any possible number of records. The read subroutine is executed as part of the loop.

Variable A is used for program termination purposes. Program decision, or branch, procedures are used to test variable A for positive or negative values. The program loop is executed as long as the counter is less than or equal to the limit parameter. When variable A contains a positive value, the print subroutine is executed. When variable A contains a negative value, the dummy record has been read and the loop counter (X) is assigned a value of 1001. This terminates the loop.

The summary program prepares a listing of accounts (see figure 3–10). The mainline module controls program execution. Report headings are printed by the headings module. Since this module is not within the program loop, the headings are printed only once.

A FOR/NEXT structure controls the program loop, as in the following.

```
320 FOR X = 1 TO 1000
330     GOSUB 510
340             IF A < 0 THEN LET X = 1001
350             IF A > 0 THEN GOSUB 610
360 NEXT X
```

In statement 320 the loop limit parameter is set at 1000 to allow processing of any possible set of data. The read subroutine is called in line 330. In lines 340 and 350, the account number (A) controls loop execution. As long as variable A contains a positive value the print subroutine (line 610) is executed. This results in the output of all significant data records. When variable A contains a negative value, the trailer data record has been read. Negative values are used for illustration purposes. At this point, the loop counter is assigned a value of 1001 which terminates the FOR/NEXT loop.

Five significant data records (lines 710 through 750) are processed by this program. Statement 760 is the trailer data line. Variable A is assigned the value of −5 after this statement is read. This terminates the program loop.

The BASIC control structure for a branch operation in a program is the IF-THEN statement. Relational operators such as equal to (=), less than (<), or greater than (>) are used to test conditions in the program. The following is the format of an IF-THEN statement.

IF ⟨Condition Parameter⟩ THEN ⟨Parameter⟩

The program branch statements in lines 340 and 350 follow.

```
340 IF A < 0 THEN LET X = 1001
350 IF A > 0 THEN GOSUB 610
```

When evaluation of an IF statement gives a TRUE response, the THEN portion of the statement is executed. A FALSE result causes program control to shift to the next line. If variable A contains a value which is less than zero, the loop counter (X) is assigned the value 1001. If variable A contains a positive value, the print subroutine is executed. Therefore, when A is positive, the print subroutine is executed. When the value of A is negative, the program loop is terminated.

The headings module contains several blank print lines as shown in lines 410, 430, and 450. These blank lines are used to separate the headings when they are printed.

The TAB statement is used to center heading lines. The TAB function is equivalent to the tabulator key on a typewriter. The following is the format for a TAB statement.

420 LPRINT TAB(TAB Parameter); ⟨Parameter⟩

The TAB parameter, which is enclosed in parentheses, causes the system to skip to that column. A semicolon follows the right parenthesis. The system prints the parameter beginning at the referenced column. When the following statement is executed, the printer skips to column 23 before printing the string PORT-EX COMPANY.

420 LPRINT TAB(23); "PORT-EX COMPANY"

TAB can be used for centering report headings and subheadings. It can also be used to space between column headings or columns of data. Some systems have different interpretations of the TAB function, so careful review of the specifications is necessary.

The SPC key word is used to insert a specific number of spaces between printed values. The following is the format of a statement using the SPC key word.

4100 LPRINT ⟨Parameter⟩; SPC(15); ⟨Parameter⟩

In the following example the SPC key word is used to insert 15 blank spaces between

TITLE and BALANCE. Check the system manual for instructions on the use of the SPC key word as it is implemented differently on various systems.

    4100 LPRINT "TITLE"; SPC(15); "BALANCE"

The values are entered into the variable storage locations in the read module. Variables used in this program are the account number (A), classification (C$), title (T$), normal balance side (N$), and the account balance (B). The read subroutine is executed according to the FOR/NEXT loop parameters. As shown in this program, the loop could be executed a maximum of 1000 times.

Output is generated through the print module. Five variable values are printed as detail or data lines in print zone format. Single spacing is used in this program. The output is shown in figure 3–10.

The data to be processed is shown in lines 710 to 760. There are five significant records to be processed. Statement 760 is the dummy data line that causes loop termination.

PROGRAM DEVELOPMENT CHECKLIST

Serial input/output listing programs follow the general pattern exhibited in figures 3–3 and 3–10. Use the following checklist to ensure that all necessary components are included.

_____ Flowcharts

_____ REMARK lines for documentation

_____ Report headings

_____ Loop control (FOR/NEXT)

_____ READ and DATA statements

_____ Detail PRINT lines

_____ Single or double-spacing

_____ END/STOP

_____ Program trace

PROGRAM DEBUGGING

Some common listing program errors and methods of correcting them are:

1. SYNTAX ERROR	Check the key word for proper spelling, punctuation, and/or match of type and sequence of data in READ and DATA statements.
2. OUT OF DATA IN 240	(when 240 is the READ statement) Check all DATA statements for correct number of values. READ and DATA lines must correspond in sequence and type of data.
3. TYPE MISMATCH IN 160	Check the READ and DATA statements for proper sequence and type of data. When string data is used in an IF statement, check the test

field to be sure that it is enclosed in quotation marks, as in:

IF N\$ = "FIN" THEN END.

4. UNDEFINED STATEMENT IN 410

Check the statement to be sure that the line referenced in IF or GOSUB is listed in the program, as in:

410 IF A = 40 THEN GOSUB 1000.

Line 1000 must be listed in the program.

5. RETURN WITHOUT GOSUB

The number of GOSUB and RETURN statements must match. Some systems do not display an error message if GOSUB is listed without a corresponding RETURN.

6. NEXT WITHOUT FOR

Check the number of FOR and NEXT statements. They must correspond.

SUMMARY

The PRINT or LPRINT key word is used to generate output from the computer. Output is displayed on the monitor or the printer in print zones that range in size from 5 to 16 columns. Commas are used in PRINT statements to access the print zone format. When the computer detects a comma, the output device automatically skips to the next print zone. Wraparound occurs when the length of the data exceeds the space allotted to one line. A hanging comma causes the computer to fill all available print zones on one line and to automatically advance to the next line to continue printing.

BASIC programs are executed line by line unless a program loop or branch, such as the FOR/NEXT or IF-THEN statement, is encountered. The FOR/NEXT structure is used to control execution of the subroutines. There are two methods of limiting execution of the FOR/NEXT loop: the user can enter the number of records to be processed; or, if the exact number of records is unknown, a dummy DATA statement can be inserted in the program following the significant DATA records. The dummy DATA record is not executed; its sole function is to stop execution of the program.

GOSUB-RETURN is the BASIC language procedure used to access subroutine operations. When it is used, control of the program is shifted to the referenced line.

The hand trace is used to validate program execution. It is a hand sketch analysis of the expected results of the program.

BASIC Key Words/Operations Learned

BREAK	Program termination message returned by system.
END	Program termination.
FOR	BASIC loop control structure.
GOSUB	Subroutine operations.
IF	Program branch or decision.
LPRINT (with comma)	Enables print zone output.
NEXT	Marks end of FOR/NEXT loop and increments loop counter.

PRINT (with comma)	Enables print zone output.
REMARK	Program documentation.
RETURN	Marks end of subroutine.
SPC	Inserts blank spaces.
STEP	FOR/NEXT loop incrementation usually other than + 1.
STOP	Program termination with BREAK message.
TAB	Output spacing equivalent to tabulator.
THEN	Program decision parameter.

PROBLEM 3–2

Prepare a program trace and flowchart for the following program. Correct the program so that DATA line 560 will not print.

```
100   REM   UNIT 3 - PROBLEM 2   BY  LARRY FRY    1/3/83
110   REM   This program prepares a listing of
120   REM        Accounts Receivable
140                                                    REM
200   REM   ****    Mainline Module      *****
210   IF N = 999 THEN 250
220        GOSUB 310
230        GOSUB 410
240   GOTO 210
250   END
260                                                    REM
300   REM   ****    Read Module       *****
310   READ N, A$, S$, B
320   RETURN
330                                                    REM
400   REM   ****    Print Module       *****
410   LPRINT
420   LPRINT  A$, S$, B
430   RETURN
440                                                    REM
500   REM   ****    Data to be Processed    *****
510   DATA  131, "BRO-KEMP", "Current", 1917.20
520   DATA  132, "SPACE AIR", "Current", 597.50
530   DATA  133, "OFFICE MOD", "PAST DUE", 475.00
540   DATA  134, "PHIL DIRT CO", "Current", 115.75
550   DATA  135, "PETE MOSS A", "Inactive", 0
560   DATA  999, 9, 9, 9
570                                                    REM
580   STOP
```

PROGRAM ASSIGNMENT 3–1

Instructions

Prepare the flowcharts and structured BASIC program to list the area code and zip code for selected cities. Prepare a hand trace to verify output. Input records consist of the city, zip code, and area code. Use the following data.

Data

ZIP AND AREA CODE DIRECTORY

City	Zip Code	Area Code
Boston, MA	02101	617
New York, NY	10001	212
Baltimore, MD	21201	301
Washington, DC	20001	202
Miami, FL	33101	305

Output

Include report and column headings. Double-space detail line printing. Print the zip code first followed by the city and the area code. Use standard print zones in spacing.

Instructions

Prepare the flowcharts and structured BASIC program to list fixed assets. Prepare a hand trace to verify output. Input records consist of the serial number, machine type, manufacturer, year purchased, and purchase cost. Define purchase cost as a numeric field. Use the following data.

Data

PORT-EX COMPANY FIXED ASSETS

Serial	Machine	Manufacturer	Year	Cost
41379	DRILL PRESS	HI-TECH	1979	$11,971.50
L-3371	LATHE	MT INC	1980	$15,816.75
8711-NC	N C LATHE	HI-TECH	1978	$33,000.00
R-991	ROBOT WELDER	ROBOTICS	1983	$115,000.00
PP754	PUNCH PRESS	S-W CO	1981	6,755.55

Output

Include report and column headings in the printout. Double-space output and include machine type, manufacturer, year purchased, and the purchase cost, in that order. Use standard print zones in spacing.

Instructions

Prepare the flowcharts and structured BASIC program to produce an inventory report. Prepare a trace to verify output. Input records consist of the Universal Product Code (UPC) number, description, bin number, reorder point, quantity on hand, and cost per unit. Use the following data.

Data

FOOD CIRCUS GROCERIES

Inventory Report

Product No	Description	Bin	Reorder	On Hand	Cost
380541	MUNCHKINS	D12	500	790	$20.99
430034	NUMBER-0	D12	500	450	$19.97
512222	SWEET PEAS	S27	900	999	$14.70
530000	CORN NIB	S28	900	750	$13.00
111001	EXCESS TOWEL	A40	300	150	$22.00
755555	FROZEN CORN	F91	75	50	$10.00

Output

Include report heading, subheading, and column headings. Double-space detail line printing and include product description, reorder point, quantity on hand, and unit cost, in that order. Use standard print zones.

PROGRAM ASSIGNMENT 3–2

PROGRAM ASSIGNMENT 3–3

INTERACTIVE PROCESSING

OBJECTIVES

At the end of this chapter you should be able to perform the following tasks:

- Write structured BASIC programs using INPUT statements to enter data.
- Write programs using the PRINT or LPRINT statement with output packing.
- Code and execute word processing programs.
- Construct flowcharts for word processing programs.
- Trace the results of programs that use INPUT statements and non-zone printing.

INPUT STATEMENTS

The INPUT statement is used in an interactive environment where the operator responds to questions posed by the computer. The following is the format for a simple INPUT statement.

100 INPUT ⟨Parameter⟩

The operator's interaction with the computer has helped to eliminate some of the drudgery in data entry operations. It is seen as an improvement over straight keying of data with no interaction between the person and the machine.

Although the system used in the writing of this textbook does not require the use of a specific statement to access the keyboard and monitor to enter data using INPUT statements, some systems do use one. Statements such as PRINT, PR# 0, or slot designations may have to be placed in the program. A slot designation is an input/output device or system port designation. The APPLE uses slot PR# 0 to access the monitor, and PR# 1 to designate the printer. LPRINT statements are used to access the printer and PRINT returns output to the monitor. Check the system manual for instructions regarding INPUT statements. Summarize system access commands in Exercise 4–1.

EXERCISE 4–1

Device Access Statements

Access keyboard _____

Access monitor _____

Access printer _____

Access disk _____

Access other devices _____

_____

There are four general types of INPUT statements: the simple, multiple, combination, and prompting. The simple and multiple are explained briefly here, but their use is not recommended because neither provides the operator with much information.

The following simple INPUT statement consists of the word INPUT plus one variable field name.

150 INPUT D

When the program is executed, the computer returns one question mark ? on the screen. This means that the computer is waiting for a value to be entered, but there is no other prompt message identifying the type of data to be entered or the number of values.

The multiple INPUT statement allows more than one variable value to be entered into the computer. The following format is used with multiple INPUT statements.

150 INPUT ⟨Parameter⟩, ⟨Parameter⟩, ⟨Parameter⟩

An example of a multiple INPUT statement follows.

150 INPUT D, D$, A

As with the simple INPUT statement, when the program is executed, the computer returns one question mark. The operator enters the appropriate values, separating them with commas as shown in the INPUT statement. No other prompt is given by the computer. If the operator does not enter enough data, the computer responds with two question marks ??. The computer is waiting for data, but the type and number of data values are not identified for the operator. For this reason, the use of simple and multiple INPUT statements is not encouraged.

Some systems use a combination of PRINT-INPUT statements to enter data. In this case, a prompting message is given to the operator. The prompting message is triggered by the PRINT statement. It cues the operator to enter the appropriate data. The following is an example of a combination statement.

100 PRINT "ENTER Employee Number"
110 INPUT N

When the prompting message is displayed on the monitor, the operator enters the data.

Prompting INPUT statements are recommended because they give the operator explicit directions regarding the number, sequence, and type of variable values to be entered. The following format is used for prompting INPUT statements.

100 INPUT "⟨Prompt Message⟩"; ⟨Variable Parameter⟩

INPUT is followed by the literal message to the operator, and the variable field or fields to be entered. The following is an example of a prompting INPUT statement.

150 INPUT "ENTER Name, Hours, Rate"; E$, H, R

The prompting message to the user is enclosed in quotation marks and is followed by a semicolon. (It is a string value.) The word ENTER is included in the message to signify that the computer is waiting for the user to respond. Some systems automatically provide a question mark at the end of the prompt message. The semicolon separates the prompting message from the variable field names. Variable field names are separated by commas when more than one is included in the same INPUT statement. The computer returns the string message to the monitor. The correct user response is to enter three values, each separated by a comma. In the following example, operator response is underlined following the prompting message.

ENTER Name, Hours, Rate ?
"Smith, J", 40, 8.75

The preceding INPUT statement format works, but user confusion or the omission of commas could result in the entering of invalid data. To avoid confusion, it is advisable to limit INPUT statements to one variable. Since the following INPUT statements would achieve the best results, this is the format that is recommended.

150 INPUT "ENTER Employee Name "; N$
160 INPUT "ENTER Hours Worked "; H
170 INPUT "ENTER Pay Rate "; R

When the program is executed, the computer returns the following prompting messages on the monitor. The user's response is shown in the underlined space following the prompts. Each user response is followed by keying RETURN or ENTER (symbol ⟨).

ENTER Employee Name ? "Smith, J" ⟨
ENTER Hours Worked ? 40 ⟨
ENTER Pay Rate ? 8.75 ⟨

When a string data value containing a comma is entered, the value must be enclosed in quotation marks as shown in the preceding example.

SELF-TEST

4–1

A. Identify and correct the errors in the following INPUT statements. The operator's response is in the underlined area followed by ⟨.
   1. 100 INPUT A, A$
      ? "Baker", 49.75 ⟨
      REENTER (message returned by computer)
   2. 300 INPUT C C$
      SYNTAX ERROR IN 300 (message returned by computer)
   3. 100 INPUT Y, X$
      ? 33.33 "Alpha-Omega" ⟨
      REENTER (message returned by computer)
   4. 300 INPUT J$, Y
      ? "Heat-Co" 43.15 ⟨
      ?? (or NOT ENOUGH DATA) (message returned)
   5. 250 INPUT "ENTER Customer Balance"; B
      ENTER Customer Balance ? 69.99, 33.34 ⟨
      EXTRA IGNORED (message returned)

B. List the value of each variable after execution of the following INPUT statements. Operator response is underlined followed by ⟨.
   1. 100 INPUT C, D, E
      ? 47, 39.65, 37.75 ⟨
   2. 400 INPUT D$
      ? "6/30/83" ⟨
   3. 600 PRINT "ENTER ACCOUNT NUMBER"
      610 INPUT N
      ENTER ACCOUNT NUMBER
      ?1411 ⟨
   4. 200 INPUT "ENTER Account Number "; A
      210 INPUT "ENTER Account Name "; N$
      220 INPUT "ENTER Account Balance "; B
      230 INPUT "ENTER Account Status "; S$
      ENTER Account Number ? 1213 ⟨
      ENTER Account Name ? "CONSOLIDATED SHIPPERS" ⟨
      ENTER Account Balance ? 5714.97 ⟨
      ENTER Account Status ? "30–60 PAST DUE" ⟨

A. 1. Data values are switched.
Correction—? <u>49.75, "Baker"</u> ⟨
2. The comma is missing in the INPUT statement.
Correction—300 INPUT C, C$
3. The comma is missing between the data values.
Correction—? <u>33.33, "Alpha-Omega"</u> ⟨
4. The comma is missing between the data values.
Correction—? <u>"Heat-Co", 43.15</u> ⟨
5. Two values should not be entered.
Correction—ENTER Customer Balance ? <u>69.99</u> ⟨
B. 1. C = 47   D = 39.65   E = 37.75
2. D$ = 6/30/83
3. N = 1411
4. A = 1213   N$ = CONSOLIDATED SHIPPERS
B = 5714.97   S$ = 30–60 PAST DUE

NON-ZONE OR PACKED PRINTING IN OUTPUT

In BASIC, output can be printed in column or text format. Separation of output into columns is accomplished through the use of print zones as discussed earlier. *Non-zone* or packed printing is used to print output in text format.

To produce non-zone printing, semicolons are used in PRINT statements as shown in the following format.

100 PRINT ⟨Parameter⟩; ⟨Parameter⟩; ⟨Parameter⟩

Print packing can be done on the monitor or the printer. Use of semicolons in effect freezes or stops the print device immediately after it prints the last character preceding the semicolon in the PRINT statement. The printer resumes printing immediately after the semicoloned print position.

The following is an example of a PRINT statement.

400 PRINT "Dear "; D$; ":"

This PRINT statement would produce the following output if D$ contained the value "Jones & Sons".

Dear Jones & Sons:

Blank spaces (symbol ƀ) must be built into strings in the PRINT statements if they are desired in output. The print device is frozen immediately after the last referenced character before the semicolon on most systems and printing is resumed immediately after the semicoloned position.

Packing output also permits editing of output. For example, $ or % signs can be inserted in the values printed as follows. Variable B is equal to 333.33 and P is equal to 33.

400 PRINT "$"; B; " Is "; P; "%"
Output Results:
$333.33 Is 33%

Commas, which produce print zones, and semicolons, which produce packed or non-zone printing, can be freely mixed in PRINT statements. The following example demonstrates the combination of commas and semicolons. Variable E is equal to 34 and P is equal to 3617.15. Assume that there are 16 characters per print zone.

100 PRINT "Total Employees "; E, "Total Payroll $"; P
Output Results:

Total Employees 34	Total Payroll $3617.15
│	│
Col. 18	Col. 33

A semicolon is sometimes left hanging at the end of a PRINT statement. A *hanging semicolon* causes the print device to freeze immediately after the last referenced character printed before the semicolon rather than advancing to the next print line. This is especially helpful in programs that involve calculations. The following is an application of a hanging semicolon.

150 INPUT "ENTER Current CPI "; C
160 PRINT "The latest CPI increase of ";
170 PRINT C; "%"; " will cause"

The computer returns:

ENTER Current CPI ? 3 ⟨

Output results:

The latest CPI increase of 3% will cause

SELF-TEST
4–2

Trace the results of the following PRINT statements. Assume that there are 15 columns per print zone and that PRINT accesses the printer.
  1. 400 PRINT "Customer Name", , "Account Balance"
  2. 450 PRINT "Final Average = "; 47
  3. 500 PRINT "FICA Contributions ";
     510 PRINT "exceeding ";
     520 PRINT 7.35; "%"
  4. 600 PRINT "ҌҌҌMr. Jones:ҌҌ";
     610 PRINT "Please return the report"
  5. 700 PRINT "The snow depth of ";
     710 PRINT 36;
     720 PRINT " inches helped replenish"
  6. 800 PRINT "THE PRIME INTEREST RATE OF ";
     810 PRINT 15;
     820 PRINT "%"

Answers for
Self-Test
4–2

1. Customer Name	Account Balance
│	│
Col. 13	Col. 31

  2. Final Average = 47
  3. FICA Contributions exceeding 7.35%
  4. ҌҌҌMr. Jones: Please return the report
  5. The snow depth of 36 inches helped replenish
  6. THE PRIME INTEREST RATE OF 15%

WORD PROCESSING PROGRAM USING INPUT STATEMENTS AND PRINT PACKING

The sample BASIC program, figure 4–2, uses the computer in a word processing mode. Word processing is the use of computer technology and magnetic storage media to process text.

In business, word processing is used to prepare copies of correspondence that is used repeatedly. A program and data files are created for the correspondence and they are stored on a disk or diskette where they can be accessed as needed. This application of word processing saves time because it eliminates the retyping of correspondence used every day.

The flowcharts for a word processing program are shown in figure 4–1. Three blocks are identified in the top-level flowchart. The mainline block controls program execution. The input and print blocks contain the processing steps.

The mainline module contains a FOR/NEXT loop control structure, which is controlled by variable X. An INPUT statement is used to enter variable T, which is the limit parameter.

All variables are entered in the input subroutine. INPUT statements are used to enter variable values.

The print subroutine causes the heading, salutation, body and close of the letter to be printed. Variable data and strings are included in these items.

The word processing program is shown in figure 4–2.

A FOR/NEXT control structure is used in the mainline module to limit execution

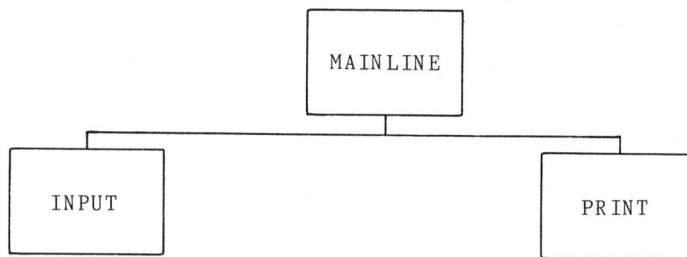

TOP-LEVEL FLOWCHART

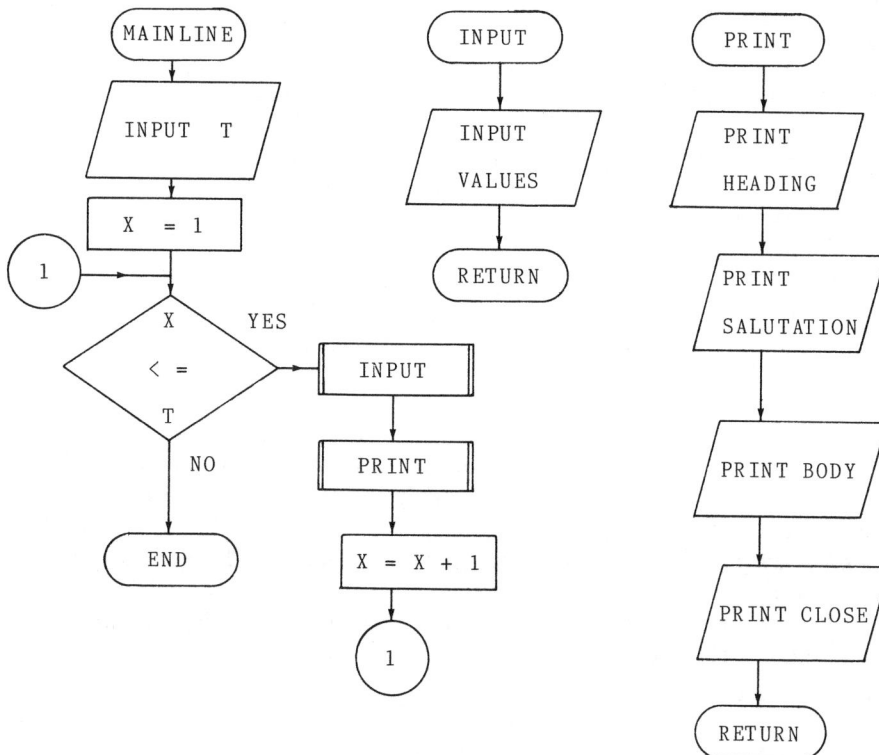

DETAILED LOGIC FLOWCHART

FIGURE 4–1
Flowcharts for word processing program

```
100       REM     FIGURE  4-2   WRITTEN BY LARRY FRY    1/1/83
110       REM      This program demonstrates computer use
120       REM         in the text processing mode
130                                                          REM
140       REM *****  Variable Identification
150       REM         D$  ....  DATE
160       REM         N$  ....  CLIENT'S NAME
170       REM         S$  ....  STREET ADDRESS
180       REM         C$  ....  CITY ADDRESS
190       REM         A$  ....  ASSOCIATE'S NAME
200       REM         T   ....  TERMINATION FIELD
210       REM         X   ....  COUNTER
220                                                          REM
300       REM *****  Mainline Module
310 INPUT  "ENTER the number of letters to be printed  "; T
320 FOR  X  =  1  TO  T
330          GOSUB  410
340          GOSUB  510
350 NEXT  X
360 END
370                                                          REM
400       REM *****  Input Module
410 INPUT  "ENTER Date ";  D$
420 INPUT  "ENTER Client's Name  ";  N$
430 INPUT  "ENTER Client's Street Address  ";  S$
440 INPUT  "ENTER City, State and ZIP ";  C$
450 INPUT  "ENTER Associate's Name  ";  A$
460 RETURN
470                                                          REM
500       REM *****  Print Module
510 LPRINT : LPRINT
520 LPRINT TAB(15); D$
530 LPRINT
540 LPRINT N$
550 LPRINT S$
560 LPRINT C$
570 LPRINT
580 LPRINT "DEAR SIR:"
590 LPRINT
600 LPRINT  "        ANNOUNCING  --  BASIC PROGRAMMING FOR BUSINESS"
610 LPRINT
620 LPRINT  "       DELMAR PUBLISHERS  takes pride in introducing"
630 LPRINT "a textbook on business BASIC programming to assist students"
640 LPRINT "in solving  business/home  data processing tasks."
650 LPRINT
660 LPRINT  "       The book entitled  BASIC PROGRAMMING FOR BUSINESS"
670 LPRINT "by Larry Fry is now available ";
680 LPRINT "from our"
690 LPRINT "representative, ";  A$;  "(card enclosed)."
700 LPRINT
710 LPRINT  "       We are sure you will be pleased!"
720 LPRINT TAB(15);  "DELMAR PUBLISHERS"
730 RETURN
740                                                          REM
750 STOP
```

FIGURE 4–2
Word processing
program

of the program loop. In the INPUT statement, line 310, variable T is entered. This sets the upper limit for the program loop. As long as the counter is less than or equal to this limit parameter the loop will be executed.

The program loop consists of the input and print modules. These two subroutines will be executed until the counter is greater than the limit parameter.

Data values are entered in the input module. The following is the program segment that contains the INPUT statements.

```
410 INPUT "ENTER Date "; D$
420 INPUT "ENTER Client's Name "; N$
430 INPUT "ENTER Client's Street Address ": S$
440 INPUT "ENTER City, State and ZIP "; C$
450 INPUT "ENTER Associate's Name "; A$
460 RETURN
```

These statements cause the date (D$), client's name (N$), street address (S$), city address (C$), and associate's name (A$) to be entered. Notice that prompting INPUT statements are used, and that only one value is entered on each line. The operator enters the appropriate values following the prompting messages and output automatically follows.

Output is generated in the print module. The LPRINT statements contained in lines 510–720 produce the business letter shown in figure 4–3. Line 510, which follows, contains two statements separated by a colon on the same line.

510 LPRINT:LPRINT

This is a valid BASIC feature. Two or more statements may be placed on the same line. When this is done, the statements must be separated by colons. Line 510 is used to advance two print lines for proper letter separation.

Proper separation of the date, address, salutation, letter body, and close is achieved through the use of blank LPRINT lines. Lines 520 and 720 center the date and company name through the use of TAB statements.

String values are used to print most of the letter. Variable values are entered through INPUT statements. Print packing or non-zone printing is used in lines 670, 680, and 690, which follow, to obtain text format.

670 LPRINT "by Larry Fry is now available ";
680 LPRINT "from our"
690 LPRINT "representative, "; A$; "(card enclosed.)"

The letter can be sent to different addresses as a result of the FOR/NEXT loop

```
                   JANUARY 2, 1984

     MR. SAM HARRIS
     345 EAST MARKET
     MUNCY,  PA   17735

     DEAR SIR:

          ANNOUNCING  --  BASIC PROGRAMMING FOR BUSINESS

          DELMAR PUBLISHERS  takes pride in introducing
     a textbook on business BASIC programming to assist students
     in solving  business/home  data processing tasks.

          The book entitled  BASIC PROGRAMMING FOR BUSINESS
     by Larry Fry is now available from our
     representative, R. A. PIERCE(card enclosed).

          We are sure you will be pleased!
               DELMAR PUBLISHERS


                   JANUARY 2, 1984

     LYCOMING COMMUNITY COLLEGE
     WEST THIRD STREET
     WILLIAMSPORT, PA   17701

     DEAR SIR:

          ANNOUNCING  --  BASIC PROGRAMMING FOR BUSINESS

          DELMAR PUBLISHERS  takes pride in introducing
     a textbook on business BASIC programming to assist students
     in solving  business/home  data processing tasks.

          The book entitled  BASIC PROGRAMMING FOR BUSINESS
     by Larry Fry is now available from our
     representative, R. A. PIERCE(card enclosed).

          We are sure you will be pleased!
               DELMAR PUBLISHERS
```

FIGURE 4–3
Output from word
processing program

contained in the program. The message in the letter or any of its parts can be changed by altering the appropriate LPRINT line or lines.

Program traces are used to validate and verify program implementation. A correct trace of the program shown in figure 4–2 would be identical to the output shown in figure 4–3.

PROGRAM DEVELOPMENT CHECKLIST

Transaction-oriented programs follow the same pattern as the example program in figure 4–2. Use the following checklist to ensure that all necessary components are included in the program.

_____ Flowcharts

_____ REMARK lines

_____ Loop control (FOR/NEXT)

_____ INPUT statements (one variable per statement)

_____ Detail print lines (strings and variable values)

_____ END/STOP

_____ Program trace

PROGRAM DEBUGGING

Errors commonly encountered when using INPUT statements are:

1. ??
The normal computer prompt when using IN-PUT statements is a single ?. Return of ?? means that insufficient data was entered. Entering more than one variable per INPUT statement can easily create this error.

2. REENTER
A mistake was made when the data was entered. String data entered for a numeric variable can result in this error.

3. EXTRA IGNORED
Excess data values were entered. The operator entered too many values given the number of variable names listed.

The easiest way to avoid errors when using INPUT statements is to provide prompting messages for the operator and to limit the number of variable values entered to one per statement.

SUMMARY

INPUT statements are used to enter data in an interactive, or transaction-oriented mode in which the user responds to questions posed by the computer. There are four types of INPUT statements: simple, multiple, combination, and prompt. The use of prompting INPUT statements is recommended over the use of simple and multiple statements.

Computer systems are capable of providing output in text format. This is known as non-zone or packed printing. Semicolons are used in PRINT or LPRINT statements to produce non-zone printing.

Word processing is the use of computer technology and magnetic media to process text. It is helpful in business where masters can be kept of correspondence that is used regularly, eliminating the need to retype individual letters. INPUT statements are used in word processing programs to enter the variable data.

BASIC Key Words/Operations Learned

INPUT	Interactive data entry.
PRINT or LPRINT (with ;)	Print packing or non-zone printing.

Trace the results for the following interactive program. Assume that the following variable values are entered by the INPUT statements shown in lines 210 and 310 to 380.

PROBLEM 4–1

```
100   REM   UNIT 4  -  PROBLEM  1         BY LARRY FRY        1/4/83
110   REM      This program prepares a marketing letter
120   REM        for a new product
130                                                               REM
200   REM   ****      Mainline Control      *****
210   INPUT  "ENTER the number of letters to be printed "; T
220   FOR X  =  1 TO T
230        GOSUB 310
240        GOSUB 410
250   NEXT X
260   END
270                                                               REM
300   REM   ****      Input Module      *****
310   INPUT  "ENTER Date "; D$
320   INPUT  "ENTER Company Name ";  C$
330   INPUT  "ENTER Contact's Name ";  N$
340   INPUT  "ENTER Street Address ";  S$
350   INPUT  "ENTER City,  State    ZIP ";  Z$
360   INPUT  "ENTER Product Name ";  P$
370   INPUT  "ENTER Price ";  P
380   INPUT  "ENTER Associate   ";  A$
390   RETURN
400   REM   ****      Print Module      *****
410   LPRINT
420   LPRINT TAB(15); D$
430   LPRINT
440   LPRINT C$
450   LPRINT N$
460   LPRINT S$
470   LPRINT Z$
480   LPRINT
490   LPRINT TAB(10); "NEW PRODUCT ANNOUNCEMENT"
500   LPRINT
510   LPRINT "ATTENTION  : "; N$
520   LPRINT
530   LPRINT  "     SOFT-TECH  wishes to announce  ";  P$;
540   LPRINT  ",  a new software"
550   LPRINT  "package to ease the paperwork burden in your office."
560   LPRINT
570   LPRINT  TAB(5); P$; "  is a complete inventory system designed"
580   LPRINT  "for companies of your sales volume."
590   LPRINT
600   LPRINT  TAB(5); A$;  ",  our Associate (card enclosed) will demonstrate"
610   LPRINT  P$; "  in your office.  The introductory price is  $"; P; "."
620   LPRINT
630   LPRINT  TAB(20); "Sincerely,"
640   LPRINT  TAB(20); "SOFT-TECH"
650   RETURN
660                                                               REM
670   STOP
```

T = 1	D$ = January 4, 1984
C$ = Food Circus Groceries	N$ = Ms. Sarah Simpson
S$ = 9200 Pratt Street	Z$ = Baltimore, MD 21005
P$ = BASE-INV	P = 750.00
A$ = Mr. Rap Think	

PROGRAM ASSIGNMENT 4–1

Instructions

Prepare the flowcharts and a structured BASIC program to print address labels for mailing envelopes. Prepare a hand trace to verify program results. Use INPUT statements to enter the data. Input records consist of the company name, contact person's name, street address, and city address. Following is the data to be processed.

Data

Company	Contact	Street	City
Hi-Tech	Saul Radnor	99 Tech Circle	Milford, NH 03055
M-T INC	Slim Pikin	49 Industry	Hartford, CT 06101
ROBOTICS	Marta Han	11 Robot Way	Boston, MA 02109
S-W Inc	Sue Flew	6 South High	Denver, CO 80202
Comp-Tech	Alison Man	8 Silicon Dr	Palo Alto, CA 94302

Output

Use standard address label format and single space each address label in output. Indent print lines ten spaces from the left edge of the paper. Separate the individual address labels with five blank lines.

PROGRAM ASSIGNMENT 4–2

Instructions

Prepare the flowcharts and a structured BASIC program to produce purchase orders for ordering grocery products. Prepare a hand trace to verify output results. Use INPUT statements to enter the data. Input records consist of the vendor, product description, quantity, unit cost, and total amount. Following is the data to be processed.

Data

Vendor	Description	Quantity	Cost	Total
Jolly-Giant	Sweet Peas	100	$14.99	$1499.00
Tasty Dairy	Peach Sherbet	50	$52.00	$2600.00
Pine Paper	Excess Towels	100	$22.00	$2200.00

Output

Use the following purchase order format to prepare the output.

FOOD CIRCUS GROCERIES　　**PURCHASE ORDER NO.**
9200 Pratt Street　　**Date**
Baltimore, MD 21005

Vendor: Jolly-Giant

Quantity	Description	Cost	Total
100	Sweet Peas	14.99	$1499.00

CALCULATION OPERATIONS

OBJECTIVES

At the end of this chapter you should be able to perform the following operations:

- Describe the BASIC calculation symbols.
- Utilize the BASIC calculation symbols in computations.
- Identify the order of operations in BASIC calculation statements.
- Determine system capabilities concerning the size of real and integer values.
- Utilize scientific notation or E format correctly.

BASIC CALCULATION SYMBOLS

The symbols used in BASIC calculation operations relate to the mathematical function being executed. In figure 5–1 the symbol, the BASIC operation, and the relative priority of each are illustrated.

In BASIC calculation statements, operations are performed in order from the highest to the lowest priority. Exponentiation (raising to a power) is performed first, followed by multiplication and division, which are middle priority, and addition and subtraction, which are low priority. When statements contain operations that have equal priority, the calculations are performed from left to right. For example, a statement containing a mixture of addition and subtraction operations is calculated from left to right. In a statement containing a mixture of multiplication and addition steps, the multiplication tasks are calculated first because they have higher priority.

The following examples illustrate the results of PRINT statements that include calculations. Variable A has a value of 50 and B has a value of 10.

```
10 PRINT A + B
Result: 60
20 PRINT A − B
Result: 40
30 PRINT A * B
Result: 500
40 PRINT A / B
Result: 5
50 PRINT A + B * 2
Result: 70
```

SYMBOL	OPERATION	PRIORITY
+	Addition	Low
−	Subtraction	Low
*	Multiplication	Middle
/	Division	Middle
∧	Exponential (Some systems use **)	High

FIGURE 5–1
Calculation symbols

The calculation operation shown in line 50 yields a result of 70. This statement contains a mixture of addition and multiplication operations, so evaluation does not progress from left to right. The multiplication step is performed first because it has higher priority.

70 PRINT A + 3.1416 * 4 ∧ 2
Result: 100.2656

Raising 4 to a power of 2 (resulting in 16) has the highest priority. Next, 16 is multiplied by 3.1416 and that result is added to variable A (50). The final result is 100.2656.

There are times when performing operations in a specific order is essential to obtaining a correct answer. When this is the case, parentheses are used to override *precedence* in the normal order of operations.

The following calculation statement appears to calculate the mean average of three variables.

80 PRINT P + T + R / 3

At first glance this statement seems to add the three variable values and then divide them by 3. When this statement is processed, however, the first operation performed is the division of variable R by 3 because the division operation has a higher priority than the addition steps. Variables P and T are then added.

The addition of parentheses to this statement results in the correct processing procedure by altering the normal order of evaluation. Parentheses have the highest priority in calculation statements.

100 PRINT (P + T + R) / 3

The relative priority of calculation operations after parentheses have been added is shown in figure 5–2.

Parentheses may be set inside each other. This is known in programming as *nesting*. In the following example, evaluation begins with the innermost set of parentheses and works out.

110 PRINT (A + (A − B * 4))
Result: 60

The innermost set of parentheses, 50 − 10 * 4, is evaluated first. The result 10 is then added to variable A, 50. The answer is 60. The following example also shows evaluation of nested parentheses.

120 PRINT (100 / (25 − 5 * 3))
Result: 10

Calculation of the inner set of parentheses produces the answer 10. One hundred is then divided by 10 and the result is 10.

Numeric data is assumed to be positive unless the value is preceded by a minus sign. The following PRINT statement would produce an answer of −50.

130 PRINT 100 − 75 * 2
Result: −50

SYMBOL	OPERATION	PRIORITY
( )	Precedence	Highest
∧	Exponential	High
*	Multiplication	Middle
/	Division	Middle
+	Addition	Low
−	Subtraction	Low

FIGURE 5–2
Calculation precedence

To summarize, in a case of equal priority, evaluation of calculation statements proceeds from left to right. Normal precedence can be overcome through the use of parentheses.

A. Record the results of the following assignment and PRINT statements. Assume variable A = 15, B = 5, and C = 6.
   1. 10 LET X = 5 + 12 / 3
   2. 20 LET X = 12 * 9 − 4
   3. 30 LET X = C + A / B
   4. 40 LET X = (B + A) / B
   5. 50 LET X = (32 + C) * C − B
   6. 60 LET X = A + 3.141593 * 5 $\wedge$ 2
   7. 70 PRINT (21 + 6) / (A − C)
   8. 80 PRINT A * 2 / (A − 3)
   9. 90 PRINT A $\wedge$ 2 − A * B * C
   10. 100 PRINT C + ((A − C) * 3)
B. Write the BASIC calculation statements to print the following:
   1. Area of triangle = 1/2 times base times height
   2. Perimeter of rectangle = 2 times length plus width
   3. Average collection time = $\dfrac{\dfrac{\text{Accounts receivable}}{\text{Net sales}}}{360}$
   4. Inventory turnover = $\dfrac{\text{Net sales}}{\text{Inventory}}$
   5. Book value of common stock = $\dfrac{\text{Value of common stock} + \text{Surplus} + \text{Reserves}}{\text{Shares of common stock outstanding}}$
   6. Current ratio = $\dfrac{\text{Current assets}}{\text{Current liabilities}}$

SELF-TEST
5–1

A. 1. X = 9
   2. X = 104
   3. X = 9
   4. X = 4
   5. X = 223
   6. X = 93.539825
   7. 3
   8. 2.5
   9. − 225
   10. 33
B. 1. A = .5 * B * H
   2. P = 2 * (L + H)
   3. T = A / (N / 360)
   4. T = N / I
   5. B = (V + S + R) / U
   6. C = A / L

Answers for
Self-Test
5–1

REAL DATA

Computers can use real data, but there is usually a limit on the total number of digits that the system can store or display. The total number of digits accepted may range from 7 to 16 or more depending upon the system. An easy way to determine the system's limitations is to enter calculations in immediate mode. The examples that follow would quickly determine system characteristics.

PRINT 100 / 6
Result: 16.66667

The result discloses the system's limitations. It also determines whether or not the computer will automatically round the least significant digit, which is referred to as the *low-order* position. In the preceding example, a total of 7 digits was printed and the least significant digit was rounded.

The following example shows the result of multiplying 9999 by 1000.

PRINT 9999 * 1000
Result: 9999000

This establishes the upper range for integer values for the system.

Variations of the preceding immediate mode calculations will reveal the maximum number of integer or real values the system will store and/or print. For instance, the following tests will establish the integer and decimal limitations.

PRINT 1000000 / 6
Result: 166666.7
PRINT 1 / 6
Result: .1666667
PRINT 10000 * 9999.999999999999
Result: 99999999.99999999

The largest decimal number that this system will compute, has 16 digits of real data.

Computer systems have additional precision capabilities. Variables may be described as integer or real with *single-precision* or *double-precision* values. Precision relates the exactness of a value. Single-precision real data values usually consist of seven digits. Double-precision values can extend to 16 or more digits. On some systems integer variables are declared with the % suffix. The following example assigns the integer value to variable Y%.

LET Y% = 1983

System limitations concerning integer values usually permit ranges from -32768 to 32767. Integer variables are usually processed fastest.

Real data (also known as floating-point) can be divided into single-precision or double-precision variables on some systems. Single-precision variables are often defined by the ! suffix. They are processed internally with 7 (or possibly more) digits, but depending on the system only a certain number of digits are displayed. A single-precision declaration is illustrated in the following example.

LET P! = 3.141593

Double-precision computations produce answers with a higher accuracy than do single-precision or integer computations, but double-precision operations usually require more time for processing. The 16-bit microcomputers have the capacity to perform double-precision computations, which generate values with 16 (or more) digits. On some systems double-precision variables are declared by the # suffix. The following examples are double-precision computations.

PRINT 100000# / 6
Result: 16666.66666666667
PRINT 100000# * 9999.999999999999#
Result: 999999999.9999999

Check the system manual for specific guidelines regarding single-precision and double-precision data values and summarize them in Exercise 5–1.

System Variable Declarations

Integer variable declaration   _____

Smallest integer value possible   _____

Largest integer value possible   _____

Real variable declaration   _____

Single-precision declaration   _____

Double-precision declaration   _____

Other   _____

BASIC will generally truncate all nonsignificant zeros on the left and right sides of the value. *Truncation* means that a portion of a data value is dropped. Truncation of a numeric value usually does not include rounding. The value 7.4599 truncated to the nearest tenth is 7.4. The far right side is known as the low-order side and the far left side is known as the *high-order* side. Low-order and high-order truncation of nonsignificant zeros is a standard BASIC language feature. The decimal point is also truncated if all decimal positions are zeros when using real data. The following example illustrates low-order truncation in immediate mode.

PRINT 9147.000
Result: 9147

SCIENTIFIC NOTATION OR E FORMAT

The computer may have a limit on the largest or smallest size data it can accept. This does not mean that the system cannot hold larger or smaller data. The machine can do so, but the numbers must be expressed in terms of *scientific notation* or *E format*. The following examples illustrate E format operations.

PRINT 10000 * 10000
Result: 1 E + 08

Basically, when positive E format is used, the decimal is moved to the right the number of times specified in the value following the E. In the preceding illustration the decimal would be moved 8 places to the right, giving an answer of 100000000.

The following example is in negative E format.

PRINT .1 / 6
Result: 1.6666667 E − 02

The decimal is moved to the left the number of times specified by the number following the E. In this case, the decimal would be moved 2 places to the left, giving an answer of .016666667.

When very large or small numbers are used, the computer rounds the values internally. In the following example the computer automatically rounds the values entered.

PRINT 10000 * 9999.9999999999999
Result: 100000000

The size of the preceding value exceeds the system's ability to handle real data, so the computer rounds it to 1000 and then performs the multiplication. This may result in insignificant errors in computations, which are known as internal rounding errors.

**PROBLEM
5–1**

Enter the following in immediate mode to determine system characteristics. Use the printer if a hard copy is desired.

1. PRINT .1 / 6
2. PRINT 1 / 6
3. PRINT 100 / 6
4. PRINT 1000000 / 6
5. PRINT 100 * 100
6. PRINT 100 * 1000
7. PRINT 1000 * 1000
8. PRINT 1000 * 10000
9. PRINT 10000 * 10000
10. PRINT 100 * 9999
11. PRINT 1000 * 9999
12. PRINT 10000 * 9999
13. PRINT 100000 * 9999
14. PRINT 1000 * 9999.999999
15. PRINT 1000 * 9999.99999999
16. PRINT 1000 * 9999.9999999999
17. PRINT 10000 * 9999.999999
18. PRINT 10000 * 9999.9999999999
19. PRINT 10000 * 9999.999999999999
20. PRINT 10000 * 9999.9999999999999
21. What is the smallest number the system will display before switching to scientific

    notation?_____
22. What is the largest number the system will display before switching to scientific

    notation?_____

SUMMARY

The BASIC symbols used in computation operations are addition (+), subtraction (−), multiplication (*), division (/), and exponentiation (∧ or **). The order of precedence for processing BASIC computations, from highest to lowest priority, is exponentiation, multiplication, division, addition, and subtraction. Normal precedence can be overcome through the use of parentheses.

Integer or real data variable names can use various suffixes. The % suffix is used by most systems to declare integer data variables. Single-precision variables use the ! suffix and double-precision variables use the # symbol as the suffix.

Scientific notation, or E-format, is used by computer systems when the data value exceeds the capacity or when specified.

SERIAL
CALCULATION
OPERATIONS

6

OBJECTIVES

At the end of this chapter you should be able to perform the following operations:

- Write structured BASIC programs that use READ and DATA statements and include calculation operations.
- Prepare flowcharts for programs that contain calculation operations.
- Code program statements that include the BASIC INT function.
- Trace the output and monitor variables for programs involving calculations.

ENTERING DATA—READ AND DATA STATEMENTS

To review, BASIC uses three methods to enter data: READ and DATA statements, which are used in a serial or batch mode; INPUT statements, which are used in an interactive environment; and assignment statements, which are used to enter constants or variable values. At this point, one or more processing modules and a summary or total output module are added in the structured approach.

The example program for this chapter uses READ and DATA statements to enter data and it includes calculations. The program's objective is to calculate and print per capita gross national product (G.N.P.) and to provide summary operations. The summary operations are used to compute and print percentage increases in the population and gross national product.

The top-level flowchart is shown in figure 6–1. Four main blocks are used for headings, entering data, processing and output, and for printing summary information.

The detailed logic flowchart is shown in figure 6–2. The control block results in the headings subroutine being executed only one time. The input and process subroutines are contained in the FOR/NEXT loop. Variable L controls the number of times the loop is executed. The summary subroutine is executed at the termination of the FOR/NEXT loop.

The headings subroutine causes the report and column headings to be printed. Data is entered in the READ routine and the year, population, gross national product, and per capita gross national product are printed in the process routine. The per capita amount is computed by dividing the population into the G.N.P.

A program branch, or decision block, in the process subroutine causes the initial population and G.N.P. to be stored for summary processing. The decision block is necessary because data for the initial year must be retained for summary calculations. The summary routine prints the percentage increases in population and G.N.P.

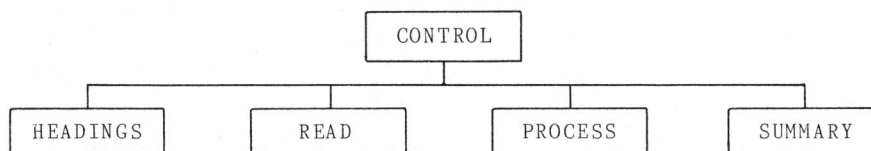

FIGURE 6–1
Top-level flowchart

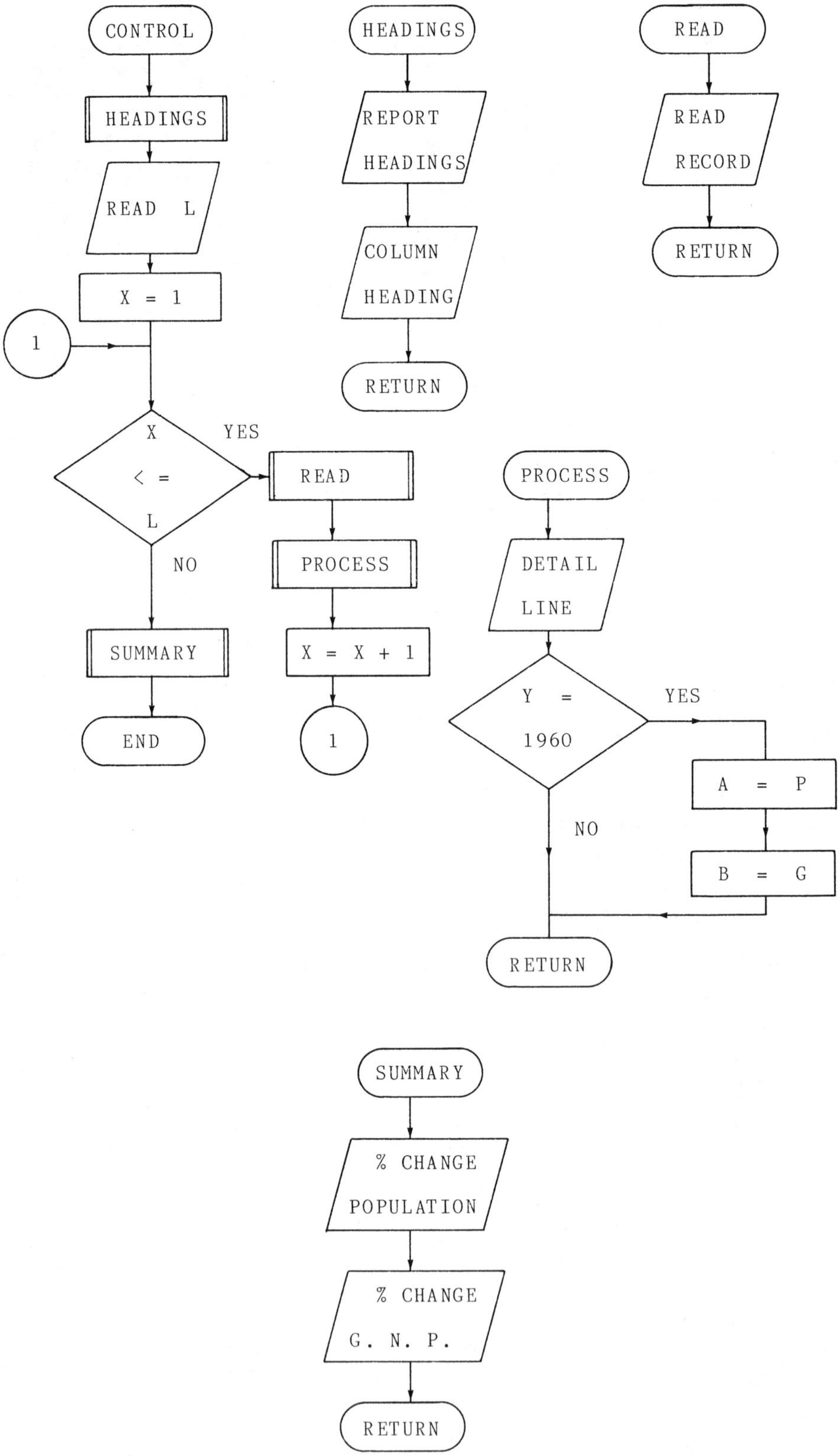

FIGURE 6–2
Calculation operations
with READ-DATA
statements

The BASIC program for this example is shown in figure 6–3. The variables used in this program are the year (Y), population (P), gross national product (G), initial population (A), and beginning G.N.P. (B). Per capita G.N.P. and summary computations are calculated in PRINT statements, so variable names are not necessary.

The mainline module controls execution of the program. The headings module is

```
100      REM       FIGURE  6-3    WRITTEN BY LARRY FRY    1/15/83
110      REM       This  program calculates the per capita Gross
120      REM             National Product and summarizes increases
130                                                                  REM
140      REM *****  Variable Identification
150      REM        Y  .....  Year
160      REM        P  .....  Population
170      REM        G  .....  Gross National Product
180      REM        A  .....  Beginning Population
190      REM        B  .....  Beginning G. N. P.
200      REM        L  .....  Loop Control
210      REM        X  .....  Loop Counter
220                                                                  REM
300      REM *****  Control Module
310   GOSUB 410
320   READ  L
330   FOR  X  =  1  TO  L
340          GOSUB 510
350          GOSUB 610
360   NEXT  X
370   GOSUB  710
380   END
390                                                                  REM
400      REM *****  Headings Module
410   LPRINT
420   LPRINT TAB(25); "PER CAPITA G. N. P."
430   LPRINT
440   LPRINT  "YEAR"; TAB(12); "POPULATION"; TAB(28); "G. N. P.";
450   LPRINT  TAB(42); "PER CAPITA"
460   LPRINT
470   RETURN
480                                                                  REM
500      REM *****  Read  Module
510   READ Y, P, G
520   RETURN
530                                                                  REM
600      REM *****  Process-Output Module
610   IF Y = 1960 THEN LET A = P  :  LET  B = G
620   LPRINT Y, P, G, G / P
630   RETURN
640                                                                  REM
700      REM *****  Summary Module
710   LPRINT
720   LPRINT "1960 - 1980 POPULATION PERCENTAGE INCREASE  = ";
730   LPRINT INT((P - A) / A * 100)
740   LPRINT "1960 - 1980 G. N. P. PERCENTAGE INCREASE     = ";
750   LPRINT INT((G - B) / B * 100)
760   RETURN
770                                                                  REM
800      REM *****  Data to be Processed
810   DATA  3
820   DATA 1960, 180.7, 506000
830   DATA 1970, 204.9, 982000
840   DATA 1980, 222.3, 2629000
850                                                                  REM
860   STOP
```

FIGURE 6-3
Serial data calculation program

executed on only the first pass through the program because it is not in the program loop.

The FOR/NEXT loop limit parameter is entered in the READ statement in line 320. This value is contained in the DATA statement in line 810. The program loop includes the read and process modules. It is performed until the counter variable X is greater than the limit parameter L. In this case, the loop will be executed three times followed by the summary module and program termination.

The headings module in lines 400–460 causes the report and column headings to be printed. TAB statements are used to center the headings. Blank lines are included for proper spacing.

The data record is entered in the read subroutine, lines 500–520. Variables Y, P, and G are entered each time the program loop is executed.

The process-output module, lines 600–630, controls calculations and detail printing.

Generally, modules should be limited to one function. In this case, however, the process and print functions are closely related. Calculations and detail printing are combined because they are part of the same operation. The detail line is printed and the per capita G.N.P. is calculated in the LPRINT statement in line 620, which follows.

620 LPRINT Y, P, G, G / P

Variables Y, P, and G are printed in the first three print zones. The G.N.P. value is then divided by the population and the result is printed in the fourth print zone. The result is a seven-digit real number with a maximum of three decimal places. Per capita G.N.P. for 1960 is computed at 2800.222, for 1980 the result is 11826.36.

Statement 610 contains a program decision operation. One of the BASIC language control structures for decision operations is the IF-THEN statement. The following format is used to write IF-THEN statements.

IF ⟨Condition Parameter⟩ THEN ⟨Parameter⟩

Line 610, which follows, is the program branch statement.

610 IF Y = 1960 THEN LET A = P : LET B = G

When variable Y contains the value 1960, evaluation of the IF statement gives a TRUE result and the THEN portion of the IF statement is executed. In this case, the assignment statements LET A = P and LET B = G will be performed. When evaluation of the IF statement gives a FALSE result, program control drops to the next line.

More than one operation may be contained on the same line through the use of a colon, as in the following example.

IF ⟨Condition Parameter⟩ THEN ⟨Parameter⟩ : ⟨Parameter⟩

Line 610 provides an example of this BASIC feature. When IF-THEN statements are used, it is possible to include several statements after the THEN. In the same manner, the IF-THEN-ELSE statement can contain more than one operation following the ELSE. More details on comparison operations and the IF-THEN-ELSE statement will be presented in Chapter 8.

The summary module in lines 700–760 calculates and prints the percentage increases in population and G.N.P. Computations are contained in LPRINT statements 730 and 750. The percentage increase in population between the years 1960 and 1980 is calculated in line 730, which follows.

730 LPRINT INT((P − A) / A * 100)

INT is the BASIC *system-defined function* that returns the integer part of a parameter. BASIC system-defined functions are internal calculation operations that are provided by the computer. Other system-defined functions are random number generators and trigonometric operations such as sine and tangent. The following format is used for the INT function.

INT (⟨Variable or Parameter⟩)

The INT function is enclosed in parentheses. INT returns the integer part of a variable or a parameter. Most systems return the integer that is closest to, but less than, the original value. INT does not produce a rounded answer. It truncates the decimal portion of the parameter and returns the integer value.

The parentheses enclosing the function are used to establish the boundaries of the function. They are not part of the calculation order of operations. All calculations within the function parentheses are evaluated before the INT operation is executed. When nested parentheses occur within the function, they are evaluated following precedence procedures.

In line 730 the operation contained in the nested parentheses, P − A, is performed first. The resulting value is then divided by A, the base year. This division computation produces a real number that is converted to a percentage when it is multiplied by 100. Finally, the INT function returns the integer portion of the parameter—23.

```
                      PER CAPITA G. N. P.

    YEAR        POPULATION       G. N. P.      PER CAPITA

    1960          180.7           506000        2800.222
    1970          204.9           982000        4792.582
    1980          222.3          2629000       11826.36

    1960 - 1980 POPULATION PERCENTAGE INCREASE   =   23
    1960 - 1980 G. N. P. PERCENTAGE INCREASE     =   419
```

FIGURE 6-4
Output from serial calculation program

The percentage increase in G.N.P. is calculated similarly in statement 750. The result is 419.

The data to be processed is contained in lines 810–840. Statement 810 contains the limit parameter of the FOR/NEXT loop. Data for the years 1960, 1970, and 1980 is contained in lines 820–840. The population and G.N.P. are expressed in terms of hundred millions.

A hand trace of this program should resemble the output shown in figure 6–4. There may be a slight difference in the values returned from the division operation due to system internal rounding errors. The hand trace for this program is shown in figure 6–5. System parameters call for a result with a maximum of seven digits. The hand trace reflects the fact that a single-precision computation is being used in this program. A comparison with the output reveals identical results.

PROGRAM DEVELOPMENT CHECKLIST

Serial calculation programs follow the general pattern exhibited in the chapter illustration. Use the following checklist to ensure that all necessary components are included in the program.

_____ Flowcharts

_____ REMARK lines for documentation

_____ Report headings

_____ Loop control (FOR/NEXT)

_____ READ and DATA statements

_____ Calculation operations

_____ Detail print lines

_____ Summary printing

_____ END/STOP

_____ Program trace

PROGRAM DEBUGGING

Following are common errors that occur with the use of calculation operations and suggested corrections.

1. DIVISION BY 0   The variable or parameter listed as the divisor has a value of zero. Check the formula or parameter.

2. TYPE MISMATCH   The variable field type and value are not consistent. Check the IF statements carefully.

PER CAPITA G. N. P.

YEAR	POPULATION	G. N. P.	PER CAPITA
1960	180.7	506000	2800.222
1970	204.9	982000	4792.582
1980	222.3	2629000	11826.36

1960 – 1980 POPULATION PERCENTAGE INCREASE   =   23

1960 – 1980 G. N. P. PERCENTAGE INCREASE   =   419

OUTPUT TRACE

Y	P	G	A	B	X	L
					1	3
1960	180.7	506000	180.7	506000	2	3
1970	204.9	982000			3	3
1980	222.3	2626000			4	3

VARIABLES MONITORED

FIGURE 6–5
Hand trace of calculation operations

SUMMARY

BASIC programs can be written to enter data in a series and to perform computations.

The BASIC IF statement is used for program branches, or decisions. It can contain more than one operation.

The INT function is a system-supplied function that truncates the decimal portion of the parameter and returns the integer value. Rounding procedures can be accomplished in calculation operations by using the INT function.

BASIC Key Words/Operations Learned

IF-THEN	Program decision, or branch, operations.
INT	Returns integer value.

PROBLEM 6-1

Prepare the flowcharts and hand trace for the following program. Monitor the variable values.

```
220 GOSUB 350
230 READ T
240 FOR A = 1 TO T
250     GOSUB 410
260     GOSUB 550
270 NEXT A
280 GOSUB 600
290 END
```

```
350 LPRINT
360 LPRINT "Machine", "Beginning", "Depreciation", ;
370 LPRINT "Ending"
380 RETURN
410 READ M$, B, D
500 LET E = B − D : LET TB = TB + E
510 RETURN
550 LPRINT
560 LPRINT M$, B, D, E
570 RETURN
600 LPRINT
610 LPRINT "TOTAL ENDING BOOK VALUE $"; TB
620 RETURN
690 DATA 4
700 DATA LATHE, 25000, 12500, DRILL, 6750, 4299
710 DATA WELDER, 3500, 1500, PRESS, 12750, 6999
```

Instructions

Prepare the flowcharts and a structured BASIC program to print a current account balance report. Prepare a hand trace to verify the output and monitor all variable values. Use READ and DATA statements to enter the data. The data includes the account number, beginning balance, purchases, and payments. The ending account balance is calculated by adding the purchases to the beginning balance and then subtracting the payments. Following is the data to be processed.

Data

Account Number	Beginning Balance	Purchases	Payments
1357	437.50	195.00	150.00
2648	1917.75	234.00	750.00
1438	350.00	0	100.00
3579	467.99	100.00	0

Output Format

Print the headings and detail lines using the following output format.

PORT-EX COMPANY

Account Balances

Account	Beginning	Purchases	Payments	Ending
XXXX	XXX.XX	XXX.XX	XXX.XX	XXX.XX
XXXX	XXX.XX	XXX.XX	XXX.XX	XXX.XX

Instructions

Prepare the flowcharts and a structured BASIC program to print an inventory report. Prepare a hand trace to verify output and monitor the variables. Use READ and DATA statements to enter the data. Data records consist of the product description, unit quantity, and the cost per unit. Multiply the unit quantity by the cost per unit to obtain the value of inventory for each item. Following is the data to be processed.

Data

Description	Unit Quantity	Cost per Unit
Munchkins	790	20.99
Number-0	450	19.97
Sweet Peas	999	14.70
Corn Nib	750	13.00
Excess Towel	150	22.00
Frozen Corn	50	10.00

Output Format

Print the headings and detail lines using the following output format.

**FOOD CIRCUS
GROCERIES**

Inventory Report

Description	Units	Cost
XXXXXX	XXX	XXX.XX
XXXXXX	XXX	XXX.XX

INTERACTIVE CALCULATION OPERATIONS

OBJECTIVES

At the end of this chapter you should be able to perform the following operations:
- Develop nested FOR/NEXT loops.
- Write structured BASIC programs that include calculation operations and utilize interactive data entry.
- Code parameters to round values to the nearest integer, tenth, hundredth, and so on.
- Execute programs that accumulate summary totals.
- Construct interactive calculation operation flowcharts.
- Trace the results of interactive calculation programs.

7

NESTED FOR/NEXT LOOPS

In some programs it may be necessary to develop a control structure that contains a loop within a loop. This is called *loop nesting*. For example, a processing loop may have to be nested within a program loop when a set of calculations must be executed repeatedly, as in the calculation of compound interest or depreciation. Following is the format used for nested loops.

```
100 FOR ⟨Counter Parameter X⟩ = ⟨Parameter⟩ TO ⟨Parameter⟩
          .   OUTER LOOP STATEMENTS
          .
200       FOR ⟨Counter Parameter Y⟩ = ⟨Parameter⟩ TO ⟨Parameter⟩
              .
              .   INNER LOOP BODY
              .
300       NEXT Y
400 NEXT X
```

FOR/NEXT structures are used to control execution of the loops. The nested loop elements should be indented if this is possible on the system being used. The counter parameters and the NEXT statements must correspond in a nested loop. The correct format for a nested loop follows.

```
– – – –> 100 FOR X = 1 TO 3
  .                    OUTER LOOP STATEMENTS
  .               .
  .
  .               .
  .
  .         200        – – – –> FOR Y = 1 TO 3
  .               .     .
  .               .     .
  .                     .
```

```
.                    .              .     INNER LOOP BODY
.                    .
.                    .              .
.                    .
.         300              – – – –> NEXT Y
.
– – – –> 400 NEXT X
```

The dotted lines, which are included in the example for illustration purposes only, must not cross. If the dotted lines do cross in nested loops, there is an error. Following are invalid loop parameters. Notice that the lines cross.

```
. – – – – –> 300 FOR X = 1 TO 3
.                          .
.                          .
.    400        . – – – –> FOR Y = 1 TO 3
.           .              .
.           .              .
.                          .
.           .        .
.           .  .
.                .
.    500   – – – –> NEXT X
.
– – – –>      510 NEXT Y
```

The loop parameters do not match; therefore, the dotted lines do cross in this illustration. This will cause an error.

Following are examples of nested FOR/NEXT loop statements.

```
100 FOR X = 1 TO 3
110     LPRINT "X = "; X
200         FOR Y = 1 TO 3
210             LPRINT "Y = "; Y
300         NEXT Y
400 NEXT X
```

The counter variable X is initialized at one, which is printed as a result of line 110. Control is then shifted to the nested loop contained in statements 200–300, where it remains until all of the parameters have been executed. Since the limit parameter is set at three, the inner loop is executed three times. After execution of the inner loop has been

```
X  =  1
Y  =  1
Y  =  2
Y  =  3
X  =  2
Y  =  1
Y  =  2
Y  =  3
X  =  3
Y  =  1
Y  =  2
Y  =  3
```

FIGURE 7–1
Nested FOR/NEXT loop
trace

completed, control is shifted to statement 400 which increments the outer loop. Execution of lines 100–400 is then repeated until all parameters in the outer loop have been satisfied.

A trace of this nested loop is shown in figure 7–1.

Trace the following nested FOR/NEXT loop. Monitor all variables and prepare a detailed logic flowchart.

```
200 FOR I = 1 TO 4
210     PRINT "I = "; I
300         FOR J = 1 TO 3
310             PRINT "J = "; J
400         NEXT J
500 NEXT I
```

I = 1
J = 1
J = 2
J = 3
I = 2
J = 1
J = 2
J = 3
I = 3
J = 1
J = 2
J = 3
I = 4
J = 1
J = 2
J = 3

TRANSACTION PROCESSING WITH CALCULATION OPERATIONS

The example program for this chapter calculates simple interest due on aged accounts receivable. INPUT statements are used to enter the variable values.

The top-level flowchart is shown in figure 7–2. The mainline block controls execution of the heading, input, process-output, and summary subroutines.

Detailed processing steps are shown in figure 7–3. Report and column headings are printed in the heading subroutine. This subroutine is executed only once because it is not part of the program loop.

Three accumulating summary values are initialized at zero. Summary totals summarize the processing that has taken place by providing final totals.

The FOR/NEXT loop controls execution of the processing subroutines. The loop limit parameter is set at 1000 because the exact number of records to be processed is not known. With this parameter the loop can be executed 1000 times.

Program branch statements are used to test for program continuation or termination.

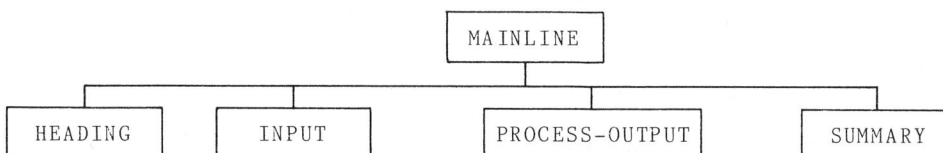

```
                    ┌──────────┐
                    │ MAINLINE │
                    └──────────┘
        ┌──────────────┬──────────────┬──────────────┐
┌─────────────┐ ┌─────────────┐ ┌─────────────────┐ ┌─────────────┐
│   HEADING   │ │    INPUT    │ │ PROCESS-OUTPUT  │ │   SUMMARY   │
└─────────────┘ └─────────────┘ └─────────────────┘ └─────────────┘
```

FIGURE 7–2
Top-level flowchart

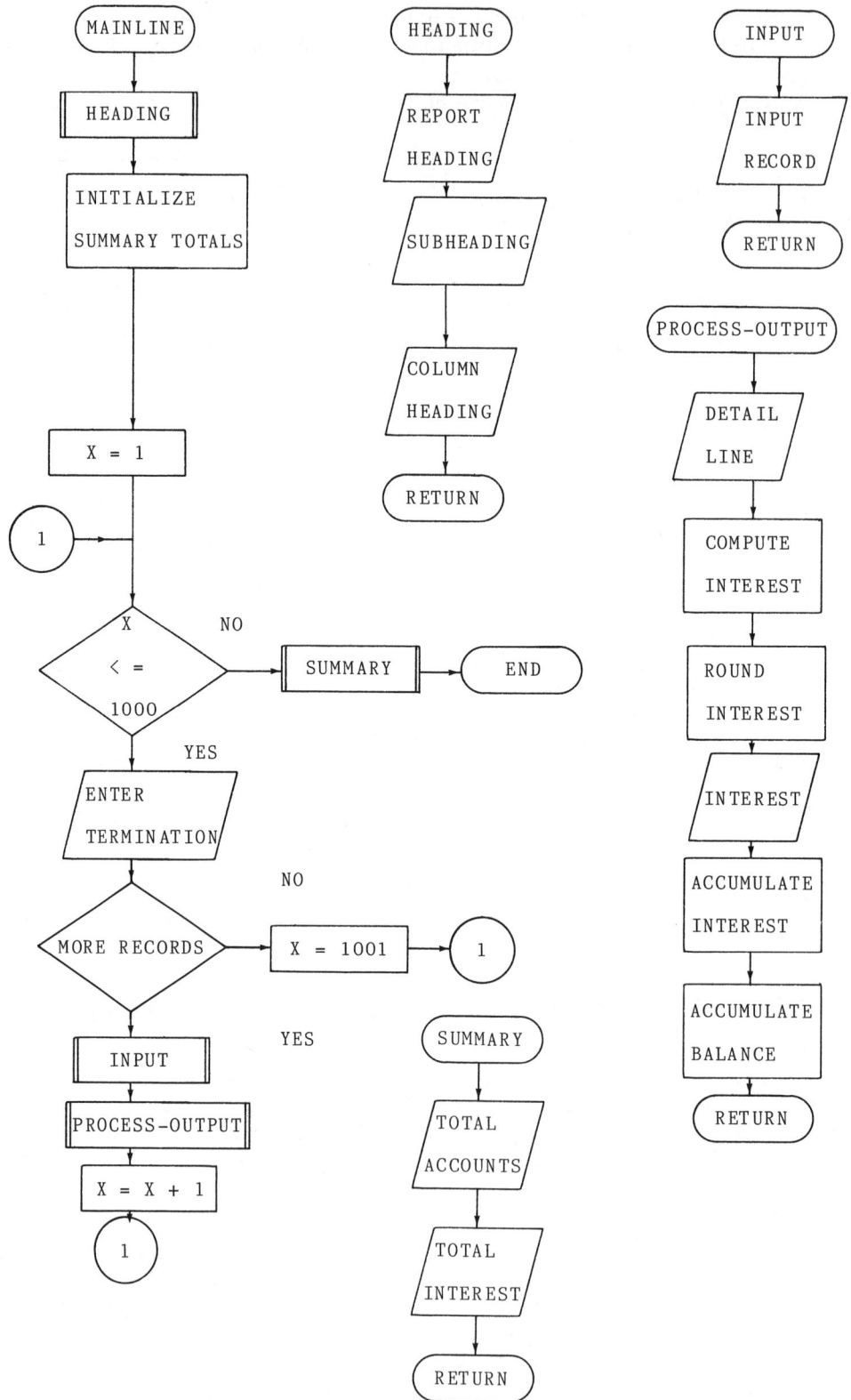

FIGURE 7-3
Detailed logic flowchart

When the user enters Y, indicating that there are more records to be processed, the input and process-output subroutines are executed. When the user enters N, the loop counter is assigned the value 1001 which terminates the loop.

After termination of the loop, the summary routine is executed.

The variable data is entered in the INPUT statements.

Processing and printing operations are combined into one routine because they are closely related. The amount of simple interest is calculated and rounded to the nearest cent. The detail lines printed include the amount of interest.

In the summary block, totals are computed for the number of aged accounts, the balance, and the interest due. They are added using accumulation computations. These totals, which summarize the report findings, are then printed.

The example program is shown in figure 7–4. The mainline module, lines 310–410,

```
100     REM     FIGURE   7-4    WRITTEN BY LARRY FRY    1/15/83
110     REM       This program calculates interest   due   on
120     REM          aged accounts receivable
130                                                           REM
140     REM *****  Variable Identification
150     REM       C$ .....  Customer Name
160     REM       N  .....  Invoice Number
170     REM       B  .....  Aged Invoice Balance
180     REM       R  .....  Interest Rate (annual simple)
190     REM       D  .....  Days Past Due
200     REM       I  .....  Interest Due
210     REM       X  .....  Loop Counter
220     REM       L$ .....  Loop Termination
230     REM       TB .....  Summary Total - Balance       REM
240     REM       TI .....  Summary Total - Interest
250     REM       TR .....  Summary Total - Accounts
260                                                           REM
300     REM *****  Mainline Module
310 GOSUB  510
320 TB  =  0
330 TI  =  0
340 TR = 0
350 FOR  X  =  1  TO  1000
360         INPUT "ARE THERE MORE RECORDS TO PROCESS  (Y/N) "; L$
370         IF L$ = "N"  THEN  LET X = 1001
380         IF L$ = "Y"  THEN GOSUB 610 : GOSUB 710
390 NEXT  X
400 GOSUB  910
410 END
500     REM *****  Headings Module
510 LPRINT
520 LPRINT TAB(22); "PORT-EX COMPANY"
530 LPRINT
540 LPRINT TAB(17); "INTEREST RECEIVABLE REPORT"
550 LPRINT
560 LPRINT  "INVOICE", "BALANCE", "RATE", "DAYS OVERDUE", "INTEREST"
570 RETURN
580                                                           REM
600     REM *****  Input Module
610 INPUT "ENTER Customer Name ";  C$
620 INPUT "ENTER Invoice Number ";  N
630 INPUT "ENTER Balance Past Due ";  B
640 INPUT "ENTER Interest Rate ";  R
650 INPUT "ENTER Days Past Due ";  D
660 RETURN
670                                                           REM
700     REM *****  Process - Output Module
710 LPRINT  N, B, R, D;
720 LET I  =  B  *  (D / 360) * (R / 100)
730 LET I  =  INT(I  *  100  +  .5)  /  100
740 LPRINT  ,  I
750 LET  TB  =  TB  +  B
760 LET  TI  =  TI  +  I
770 LET  TR  =  TR  +  1
780 RETURN
790                                                           REM
900     REM *****  Summary Module
910 LPRINT
920 LPRINT "NUMBER OF  ACCOUNTS PAST DUE  =  "; TR
930 LPRINT "TOTAL AMOUNT PAST DUE        = $"; TB
940 LPRINT "TOTAL AMOUNT OF INTEREST DUE = $"; TI
950 RETURN
960                                                           REM
970 STOP
```

FIGURE 7–4
Transaction-oriented
computation program

controls execution of the subroutines. In statement 310 the mainline module calls the heading module which is executed one time.

The three accumulating variables—for the account balances (TB), the amount of interest due (TI), and the number of records (TR)—are initialized at zero in lines 320–340. On some systems all numeric variables are automatically set at zero at run time, but it is good programming practice to initialize accumulating variables at zero. This act confirms that the variables have been initialized and eliminates the risk of obtaining faulty data from the memory if the system fails to perform automatic initialization.

A FOR/NEXT structure is used to control execution of the program loop. The loop limit parameter is set at 1000. This enables processing of any practical data set. The program loop follows.

```
350 FOR X = 1 TO 1000
360          INPUT "ARE THERE MORE RECORDS TO PROCESS
             (Y/N)"; L$
370          IF L$ = "N" THEN LET X = 1001
380          IF L$ = "Y" THEN GOSUB 610 : GOSUB 710
390 NEXT X
```

Each time the program loop is executed, the user receives the prompting message, ARE THERE MORE RECORDS TO PROCESS (Y/N). The user then enters Y or N, which determines program continuation or termination. When the user enters N, the loop counter is set at 1001, which terminates the loop. If the user enters Y, the program loop is executed.

The program loop consists of the input and process-output subroutines. It continues to execute as long as the user enters Y to a maximum of 1000 times as shown.

The headings module in statements 510–560 results in the report, subheading, and column headings being printed. TAB statements are used to center the report and sub-headings. The column headings are in print zone format.

INPUT statements are used in the input module, lines 610–650, to enter variable values. The variables are the customer name (C$), invoice number (N), aged invoice balance (B), interest rate (R), and days past due (D).

Processing and printing are executed in lines 710–770. These two operations are combined here because they are closely related. Line 710 results in detail line printing for the input variables. Variables N, B, R, and D are printed in print zone format to match the column headings. Simple interest is computed in line 720 by using the following formula.

Interest = Principal × Time × Rate

Line 720, which follows, calculates the simple interest due.

720 LET I = B * (D / 360) * (R / 100)

The calculation is evaluated using precedence procedures. The number of days past due is divided by 360 (banker's year is 360 days) to determine the decimal fraction for the time. The interest rate is divided by 100 to obtain the real number. The balance is then multiplied by the real numbers representing the time and rate. The result is the amount of interest.

Following is a hand trace through the first data record. Variable B equals 1000, D equals 30, and R equals 18. As dictated by the order of operations, the division operations are performed first.

```
I = 1000 * (30 / 360) * (18 / 100)
I = 1000 * .0833333 * .18
I = 14.99999
```

At this point, variable I equals 14.99999. The next operation rounds the amount of interest to the nearest cent. The BASIC language does not have a built-in rounding function, but a rounding procedure can be constructed using the INT function. Another function that is used for rounding is the output editing function PRINT USING. This

```
ROUND TO NEAREST INTEGER:

    LET  I  =  INT(I * 1  +  .5)  /  1



ROUND TO NEAREST TENTH:

    LET  I  =  INT(I * 10  +  .5)  /  10



ROUND TO NEAREST HUNDREDTH:

    LET  I  =  INT(I * 100  +  .5)  /  100



ROUND TO NEAREST THOUSANDTH:

    LET  I  =  INT(I * 1000  +  .5)  /  1000
```

FIGURE 7–5
Rounding functions

function is presented in Chapter 11. Recently, the CINT function, which simplifies the rounding process, has been added on some systems. CINT is a system-defined function that is also explained in Chapter 11. Statement 730 uses the INT function to produce the rounding operation as follows.

730 LET I = INT(I * 100 + .5) / 100

A hand trace of the rounding statement operation follows.

I = INT(14.99999 * 100 + .5) / 100
I = INT(1499.999 + .5) / 100
I = INT(1500.499) / 100
I = 1500 / 100
I = 15.00

Following the order of operations, variable I is first multiplied by 100. The result, 1499.999, is then added to .5, which determines whether or not the final result is rounded up. If the first digit to the right of the decimal in the variable is five or more, the final result is rounded up because when .5 is added to the value, the figure to the left of the decimal is raised. If it is four or less, the result is not rounded up because the figure to the left of the decimal is not affected. Remember: the INT function does not round the number; it truncates it.

In the following trace the answer is not rounded up.

I = INT(14.33333 * 100 + .5) / 100
I = INT(1433.333 + .5) / 100
I = INT(1433.833) / 100
I = 1433 / 100
I = 14.33

The statements shown in figure 7–5 produce rounding as indicated.

The operations shown in figure 7–5 can be used as program statements or as user-defined functions. *User-defined functions* are computations that are supplied by the programmer. They are described in Chapter 11.

After the interest has been rounded, it is printed as a result of the LPRINT statement in line 740. The comma causes the value to skip to the proper print zone.

There are three *summary,* or accumulating, variables in this program. They are used to summarize the report and are referred to as summary lines when printed. These variables were initialized at zero in the mainline module. Their function is to accumulate a sum each time the program passes through the loop. These values are referred to as summary, or final, totals. A general rule is that all accumulating variables should be initialized before loop execution. The following flow diagram outlines general procedures used in accumulating variables through loops.

```
INITIALIZE
     . . . . . . . .>     INCREMENT VARIABLE
     .
     .                         LOOP
     .
     .                              .
     . . . . . . . . . . . . . . . . .
          AT END
          - - - - -> PRINT SUMMARY LINE
```

The accumulating variables are TB, TI, and TR. Following are the calculation statements used to add the totals.

```
750 LET TB = TB + B
760 LET TI = TI + I
770 LET TR = TR + 1
```

Line 750 could be read as follows. The value TB becomes equal to the old value of TB plus the current value of B. Each time the loop is performed the old value in TB is incremented by the current value of B, which is entered through the INPUT statement in line 630.

In the same manner, the computation in line 760 accumulates the variable TI, which is the summary value for the amount of interest due. Each time the loop is executed, variable TI is incremented by the current value of I.

Variable TR accumulates the number of records processed. This type of summary process is called a tally because the incrementation is by +1.

Finally, the summary totals are printed. The summary module prints the number of records processed, the total of all aged accounts, and the total amount of interest due.

The output is shown in figure 7–6. Five records are processed in the example program. The headings, detail lines, and summary lines are shown. The summary totals are 5 for the number of records, 3901.08 for the account balances, and 150.21 for the interest due.

PROGRAM DEVELOPMENT CHECKLIST

Transaction processing with calculations follows the general pattern exhibited in figure 7–4. Use the following checklist to ensure that all necessary components are included in the program.

_____ Flowcharts

_____ REMARK lines for documentation

_____ Report headings

_____ Loop control (FOR/NEXT)

_____ INPUT statements

_____ Calculation operations

_____ Summary calculations

_____ Detail print lines

_____ Summary printing

_____ END/STOP

_____ Program trace

```
                    PORT-EX COMPANY

                 INTEREST RECEIVABLE REPORT

     INVOICE       BALANCE       RATE        DAYS OVERDUE   INTEREST
      1123          1000          18             30            15
      1134          1500          24             60            60
      1237          500           18             90            22.5
      1247          567.75        24             60            22.71
      1222          333.33        18             180           30

     NUMBER OF  ACCOUNTS PAST DUE  =   5
     TOTAL AMOUNT PAST DUE         = $ 3901.08
     TOTAL AMOUNT OF INTEREST DUE  = $ 150.21
```

FIGURE 7–6
**Output from
transaction-oriented
computation program**

SUMMARY

BASIC programs can be written to enter data in an interactive mode and to perform computations.

Nested FOR/NEXT loops are used to control processing operations when a loop is required within another loop. The counter parameters and the NEXT statements must correspond in nested loops.

The INT function can be used in BASIC to round numbers. BASIC also includes procedures for initializing accumulating, or summary, totals.

Instructions

Prepare the flowcharts and a structured BASIC program to print a present value report. Prepare a hand trace to verify the output and monitor all variables. Present value calculates the amount of money that must be invested now at certain interest rates to collect a given dollar amount in the future. For example, the procedure computes the amount that must be deposited now at 12% interest to collect $25,000 in five years.

Use INPUT statements to enter the data. Data records include the account name, amount desired, interest rate, and the number of years before maturity. Accumulate a summary total for the present value.

**PROGRAM
ASSIGNMENT
7–1**

Processing

Use the following formula to compute present value.

$$\text{PRESENT VALUE} = \frac{\text{Future Amount}}{(1 + I)^N}$$

Where: PRESENT VALUE = Amount deposited now
          Future Amount = Future amount to be collected
          I = Interest rate—decimal value
          N = Number of years until maturity
              or until future amount is collected

Data

Name	Future Amount	Interest	Years
Sinking Fund A	25,000	12%	5
Sinking Fund B	50,000	15%	5
Sinking Fund C	100,000	12%	3
Sinking Fund D	100,000	15%	5

Output Format

Print headings, detail lines, and summary lines. The detail lines should print the fund name, amount, interest, years, and present value. Print the summary total for the present value.

PORT-EX COMPANY

Sinking Fund Present Value

Name	Amount	Interest	Years	Present Value
xxxxxxxxxxxxxxx	xxxxx	xx%	x	xxxxxx.xx
xxxxxxxxxxxxxxx	xxxxx	xx%	x	xxxxxx.xx

TOTAL PRESENT VALUE $xxxxxx.xx

PROGRAM ASSIGNMENT 7–2

Instructions

Prepare the flowcharts and the structured BASIC program to produce a compound interest report. Prepare a hand trace to verify output and monitor all variables. Use INPUT statements to enter the data and a nested FOR/NEXT loop to calculate compound interest for each month.

Processing

The amount of principal plus all accumulated interest is used as the base when calculating the monthly interest. The principal plus all accumulated interest is multiplied by the monthly compounding rate. The monthly compounding rate is computed by dividing the annual rate by 12 and then by 100 to obtain the real number. Use the following formula.

MONTHLY INTEREST = Accumulated Principal * R / 12 / 100

Round the amount of monthly interest to the nearest cent. Calculate summary totals for the amount of interest and the ending account balances.

Data

Name	Principal	Rate	Months
Muck Raker	1000	12%	12
Doom Sayer	5000	15%	12

Output Format

Print headings, detail lines, and summary lines. Print the account name and the beginning principal on separate lines. Then print detail lines for each month's interest. Include the interest amount and the new accumulated principal in the monthly detail lines.

LAUNDRY SCAM NATIONAL BANK

Compound Interest Report

Name xxxxxxxxxxxxxx

Beginning Balance $xxxxxx.xx

| | *Accumulated* |
Monthly Interest	*Principal*
xxx.xx	xxxxx.xx
xxx.xx	xxxxx.xx
xxx.xx	xxxxx.xx
xxx.xx	xxxxx.xx

TOTAL INTEREST PAID $XXXXXX.XX
SUMMARY BALANCE $XXXXXX.XX

COMPARISON OPERATIONS

OBJECTIVES

At the end of this chapter you should be able to perform the following operations:
- Identify and describe relational operators.
- Identify and describe logical operators.
- Describe a Boolean, or logical, truth table.
- Utilize proper syntax for IF-THEN statements.
- Utilize proper syntax for IF-THEN-ELSE statements.
- Use numeric and string comparison operations.

RELATIONAL AND LOGICAL OPERATORS

The BASIC control structure for a decision operation in a program is the IF-THEN or the IF-THEN-ELSE statement. The IF-THEN statement was introduced in Chapter 6, but more details are necessary to gain total utilization of the operation.

BASIC uses the relational operators shown in figure 8–1 for comparison operations. These symbols are used as part of IF-THEN or IF-THEN-ELSE statements to execute comparison or relational operations.

When used in IF statements, relational operators give either a TRUE or FALSE result. Most systems represent these TRUE or FALSE conditions internally with either a −1 or a zero. Thus, a TRUE statement is represented by a relational operator of −1 and a FALSE condition is represented by a zero.

Logical, or Boolean (named after the mathematician credited with developing the technique), operations are used when multiple tests are necessary. Logical, or Boolean, operators commonly used in BASIC systems are shown in figure 8–2.

A Boolean truth table as shown in figure 8–3 graphically depicts the relationship of these operations.

To summarize, the AND operation must have TRUE responses in both conditions for the IF statement to be judged TRUE. The OR operation must have one TRUE response for the IF statement to be evaluated as TRUE. The NOT operation reverses the value and is sometimes referred to as the logical complement. Statements that are NOT TRUE are evaluated as FALSE and those that are NOT FALSE are TRUE. See page 86 for an example of the NOT logical operator.

IF-THEN AND IF-THEN-ELSE STATEMENTS

As discussed in Chapter 6 the following format is used with the IF-THEN statement.

IF ⟨Condition Parameter⟩ THEN ⟨Parameter⟩ : ⟨Parameter⟩

The branch in the statement results in a TRUE or FALSE condition. The THEN portion of the statement is executed only when a TRUE condition exists. The parameter or parameters following the THEN can consist of any valid BASIC expression, such as assignment, PRINT, GOSUB, or GO TO statements.

Structured programming does not use GO TO statements; however, they may have to be used with some systems. In the BASIC statement IF A = B THEN GO TO 700 control is shifted to line 700 if the condition is judged to be TRUE. GO TO statements do not provide the same results as GOSUB because control is not automatically returned.

```
SYMBOL              CONDITION

  =                 EQUAL TO

  >                 GREATER THAN

  <                 LESS THAN

  > =               GREATER THAN or EQUAL TO

  < =               LESS THAN or EQUAL TO

  < >               NOT EQUAL TO
```

FIGURE 8–1
Relational operators

There are three methods of wording IF-THEN statements. Some systems require the use of the key word THEN; others require the use of GO TO. Execution of the following statements would produce equivalent results on most systems.

500 IF A = B THEN GO TO 900
500 IF A = B GO TO 900
500 IF A = B THEN 900

When a FALSE condition exists, the THEN portion is not executed and control is shifted to the following statement. This is referred to as dropping through the IF statement. Examples of IF-THEN statements and their results follow. Assume that A = 50, B = 60, and C = 60.

300 IF A = B THEN GOSUB 1000
310 GOSUB 400

A is not equal to B, so the THEN portion of the IF statement is not performed. Control drops through the IF statement to line 310 which causes subroutine 400 to be executed.

500 IF B = C THEN LET A = C : GOSUB 700
510 GOSUB 900

B is equal to C, so the THEN portion of the IF statement is executed. A is assigned the value of C and subroutine 700 is executed. The computer then performs subroutine 900.

One or more parameters can be listed in the THEN portion of the statement, but each operation must be separated by a colon. The total number of characters allowed by the system in each BASIC statement determines the limit for each statement. Most systems permit 200 characters or more in one BASIC program statement.

100 IF A ⟨ ⟩ C AND A ⟨ ⟩ B THEN GOSUB 400
110 GOSUB 600

Evaluation of these statements results in a TRUE condition for the IF branch. Variable A is not equal to B or C, so the logical test is TRUE. When both portions of the Boolean operation are TRUE, the THEN portion of the IF statement is executed.

300 IF A = B OR B = C THEN GOSUB 800
310 GOSUB 900

Statement 300 results in an overall TRUE condition. The first operation is judged FALSE because variable A is not equal to B. The second condition is judged TRUE, however, so a TRUE condition exists.

```
OPERATOR            CONDITION

  AND               Both of the conditions must be true

  OR                One of the conditions must be true

  NOT               The reverse of the stated condition
```

FIGURE 8–2
Logical, or Boolean, operators

AND OPERATION

CONDITION	RESULT
TRUE and TRUE	TRUE
TRUE and FALSE	FALSE
FALSE and TRUE	FALSE
FALSE and FALSE	FALSE

OR OPERATION

CONDITION	RESULT
TRUE or TRUE	TRUE
TRUE or FALSE	TRUE
FALSE or TRUE	TRUE
FALSE or FALSE	FALSE

NOT CONDITION

CONDITION	RESULT
NOT TRUE	FALSE
NOT FALSE	TRUE

FIGURE 8–3
Logical, or Boolean,
truth table

The key word **NOT** reverses the condition of the IF-THEN statement. It is referred to as the logical complement. The NOT operation is illustrated in the following example.

500 IF NOT F = 1 THEN PRINT "ERROR" : GOSUB 700
510 GOSUB 800

If variable F is equal to one, the statement is judged NOT TRUE and the THEN portion is ignored. If variable F is not equal to one, the evaluation is NOT FALSE (or TRUE), and the THEN portion is executed.

Comparisons involving string values must include quotation marks which enclose the conditional parameter as in the following example.

300 IF A$ = " ⟨Parameter⟩ " THEN GOSUB 900

The following example of a comparison statement involves string values.

300 IF D$ = "DEPT A" THEN LET F = F + S

The relational operators (equal to, less than, greater than, and not equal to) can be used with string comparisons.

**SELF-TEST
8–1**

Trace the results of the following IF-THEN statements. Assume that X = 39.9, Y = 40, Z = 45, H = 5, and P = 0. GO TO statements are included for exercise purposes.
1. 400 IF X ⟨= 40 THEN P = X * H : GO TO 420
   410 P = (X − 40) * (H * 1.5) + H * 40
   420 PRINT P
2. 500 IF Z ⟨= 40 THEN P = Z * H : GO TO 520
   510 P = (Z − 40) * (H * 1.5) + H * 40
   520 PRINT P

3. 700 IF X > Z THEN P = X * H : PRINT P : GO TO 720
   710 P = Z * H : PRINT P
   720 PRINT X, Z, H
4. Assume A\$ = "SMITH CO", and B = 714.00
   800 IF A\$ = "JONES & SON" THEN 830
   810 P = B * .01
   820 PRINT P
   830 PRINT A\$

Answers for Self-Test
8–1

1. X = 39.9 and H = 5
   PRINTED RESULT = 199.5
2. Z = 45 and H = 5
   PRINTED RESULT = 237.5
3. X = 39.9, Z = 45, and H = 5
   PRINTED RESULT = 225
               39.9   45   5
4. A\$ = SMITH CO and B = 714.00
   PRINTED RESULT =   7.14
                     SMITH CO

All BASIC dialects utilize the IF-THEN statement. The majority of computer systems now also support the IF-THEN-ELSE function. Those systems that do not include IF-THEN-ELSE can be used for structured programming; however, well documented GO TO statements must be used. Although structured methodology calls for the elimination of GO TO, it is acceptable to use it when the IF-THEN-ELSE function is not available.

Following is the format of the IF-THEN-ELSE statement.

IF ⟨Condition⟩ THEN ⟨Parameter⟩ ELSE ⟨Parameter⟩

The THEN portion of this statement usually is limited to one parameter, but the ELSE segment may include one or more parameters. Multiple parameters must be separated by colons. Following is an example.

400 IF A ⟨ ⟩ B THEN PRINT "OK" ELSE PRINT "ERROR" : GOSUB 500
410 GOSUB 900

When variable A is not equal to B, a TRUE condition results and the THEN portion of the statement is executed. In this case, the program prints OK and control shifts to line 410. If variable A is equal to B, a FALSE condition exists and the ELSE portion of the statement is executed. In this case, the computer prints ERROR, the subroutine at line 500 is executed, and control shifts to line 410. The ELSE portion of such statements is commonly placed on a separate line when allowed by the system.

For those systems that do not offer the IF-THEN-ELSE function, the following statements are equivalent to the preceding IF-THEN-ELSE statement.

400 IF A ⟨ ⟩ B THEN PRINT "OK" : GO TO 430
410 PRINT "ERROR"
420 GOSUB 500
430 GOSUB 900

If A is not equal to B, the computer prints OK and skips to line 430. Lines 410 and 420 correspond to the ELSE portion of the IF-THEN-ELSE statement. When GO TO statements are used, the program should be well documented.

SELF-TEST
8—2

Trace the results of the following problems. Assume that D = 25, B = 300, R = .015, and I = 0.

1. 300 IF D < = 30 THEN PRINT "NOT PAST DUE"
   ELSE LET I = B * R : PRINT I
2. Assume D = 45.
   400 IF D < = 30 THEN PRINT "NOT PAST DUE"
   ELSE LET I = B * R : PRINT I

Answers for
Self-Test
8—2

1. D = 25, B = 300, R = .015, and I = 0.
   PRINTED RESULT = NOT PAST DUE
2. D = 45, B = 300, R = .015, and I = 0.
   PRINTED RESULT = 4.5

SUMMARY

The BASIC language contains procedures for executing comparisons. Comparisons are used for program decision, or branch, operations. The IF-THEN statement is the control structure used by the BASIC language for comparison operations. The IF-THEN-ELSE statement, which is available on most systems, adds additional processing power.

Relational operators are used in the IF-THEN statements to test for conditions of equality or inequality. Relational operators include equal to, less than, greater than, and not equal to.

Logical operators give program branches additional power. They include the key words AND, OR, and NOT.

BASIC Key Words/Operators Learned

AND	Program logical operator. All IF statement conditions must be TRUE.
GO TO	Program branch. System control branches to referenced line number.
IF-THEN	Program branch structure.
IF-THEN-ELSE	Program branch structure. More powerful than IF-THEN structure.
NOT	Program logical operator. Reverses logic pattern. Logical complement.
OR	Program logical operator. One of the listed conditions must be TRUE.

SERIAL COMPARISON OPERATIONS

9

OBJECTIVES

At the end of this chapter you should be able to perform the following operations:
- Utilize IF-THEN statements in a serial program.
- Construct a flowchart for a serial comparison program.
- Utilize test data to evaluate break points.

SERIAL COMPARISON OPERATIONS

The primary objective of this chapter is to demonstrate comparison operations in a serial BASIC program. Comparison operations are used in business data processing applications for decision making purposes. They are particularly helpful in the preparation of hourly payrolls, piecework payrolls, commission payments, and sales quota analyses. Comparison procedures are also used to prepare *exceptions reports,* which identify deviations from the norm, or standard.

The example program prepares a piecework payroll for the Flat Head Bolt Company and demonstrates the use of comparisons with serial, or batch, data. READ and DATA statements are used to enter the data for this chapter.

Workers are paid a certain rate for each piece produced. A bonus is usually paid when production exceeds a certain quantity. In this example, workers are paid at the base rate given for the first 400 units. A 55% bonus is paid for each unit produced in excess of 400.

FLOWCHARTS—SERIAL COMPARISONS

The flowcharts for the sample program are shown in figures 9–1 and 9–2. In the top-level flowchart, figure 9–1, the mainline routine controls execution of the program which consists of the headings, read, process, output, and summary blocks.

The detailed logic flowchart, figure 9–2, exhibits the step-by-step flow of the subroutines.

A FOR/NEXT loop is used to control execution of the routines. The loop limit is set at 5000, which allows processing of any practical data set. The data records are entered in the read routine, which is part of the loop.

The employee number variable (E) is used to test for program loop termination. As long as the employee number variable contains a positive value processing continues. When the value assigned to variable E is negative, the loop counter is assigned the value 5001 which terminates the loop. The program loop consists of the process and output routines. There are nine significant data records to be processed.

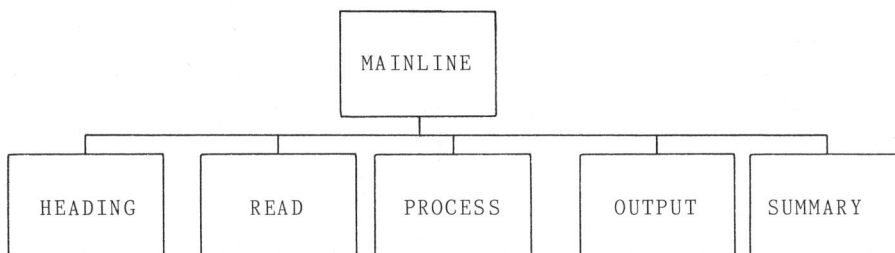

```
                        ┌──────────────┐
                        │   MAINLINE   │
                        └──────┬───────┘
        ┌──────────┬──────────┼──────────┬──────────┐
   ┌────┴───┐ ┌────┴───┐ ┌────┴────┐ ┌───┴────┐ ┌───┴─────┐
   │HEADING │ │  READ  │ │ PROCESS │ │ OUTPUT │ │ SUMMARY │
   └────────┘ └────────┘ └─────────┘ └────────┘ └─────────┘
```

FIGURE 9–1
Top-level flowchart

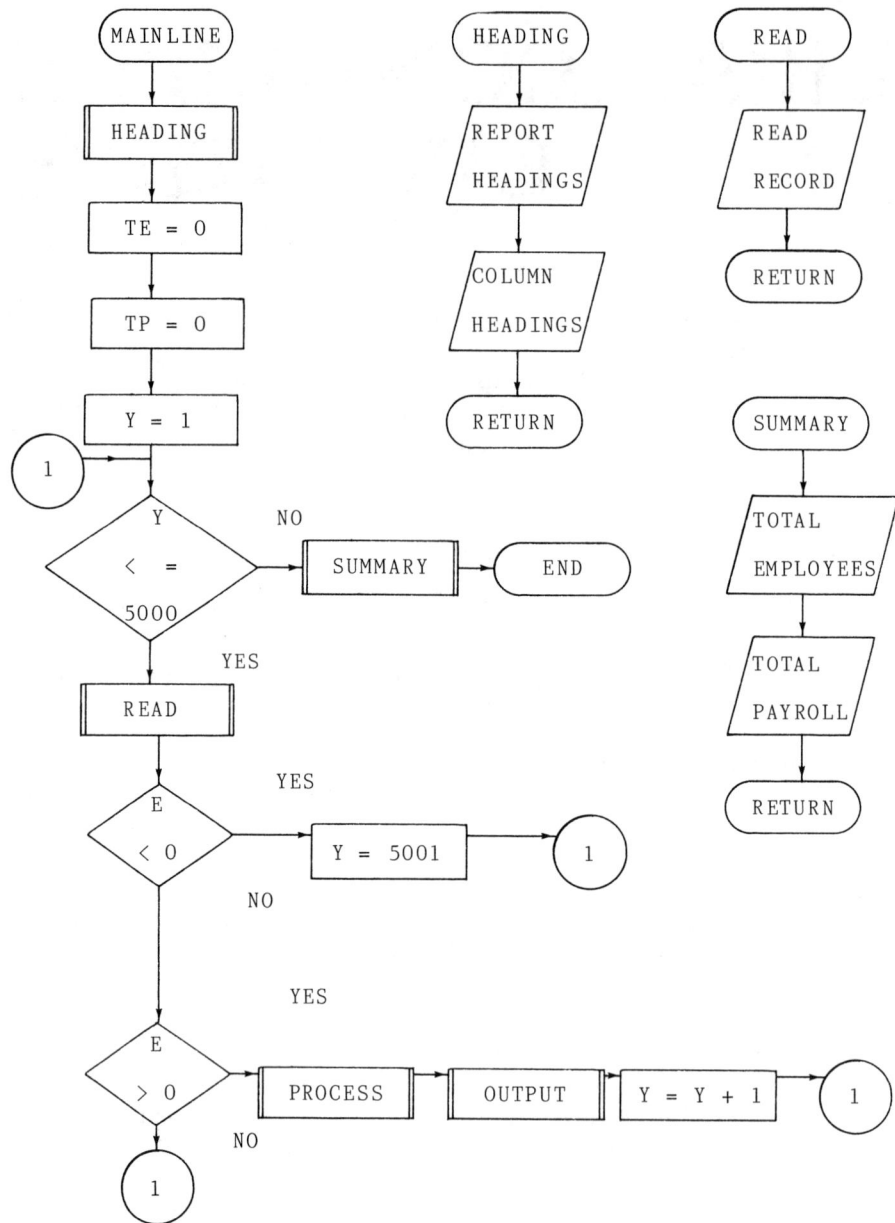

FIGURE 9–2
Detailed logic flowchart

The heading subroutine produces the report and column headings. Two report head ings and one column heading are printed as a result of this block.

The read routine causes the data records to be entered. Four variable values are entered each time the routine is executed.

The process subroutine contains two program branch statements that are used to compute regular and bonus earnings. The production of 400 units or less is paid at the regular rate per piece. A bonus rate of 55% is paid for all items produced in excess of 400. When used in a program branch structure such as this, the number of items is known as the break point.

If there is a TRUE response in the first block, the bonus earnings are assigned a value of zero. This cancels any value stored in that variable from previous processing. Failure to set the bonus pay at zero at this point could result in the program assigning an incorrect value from storage. Regular earnings based upon the number of items pro duced and the pay rate are then computed. If there is a FALSE response in the first block, control drops to the next decision block.

The second decision block determines whether the production exceeds 400 units. If

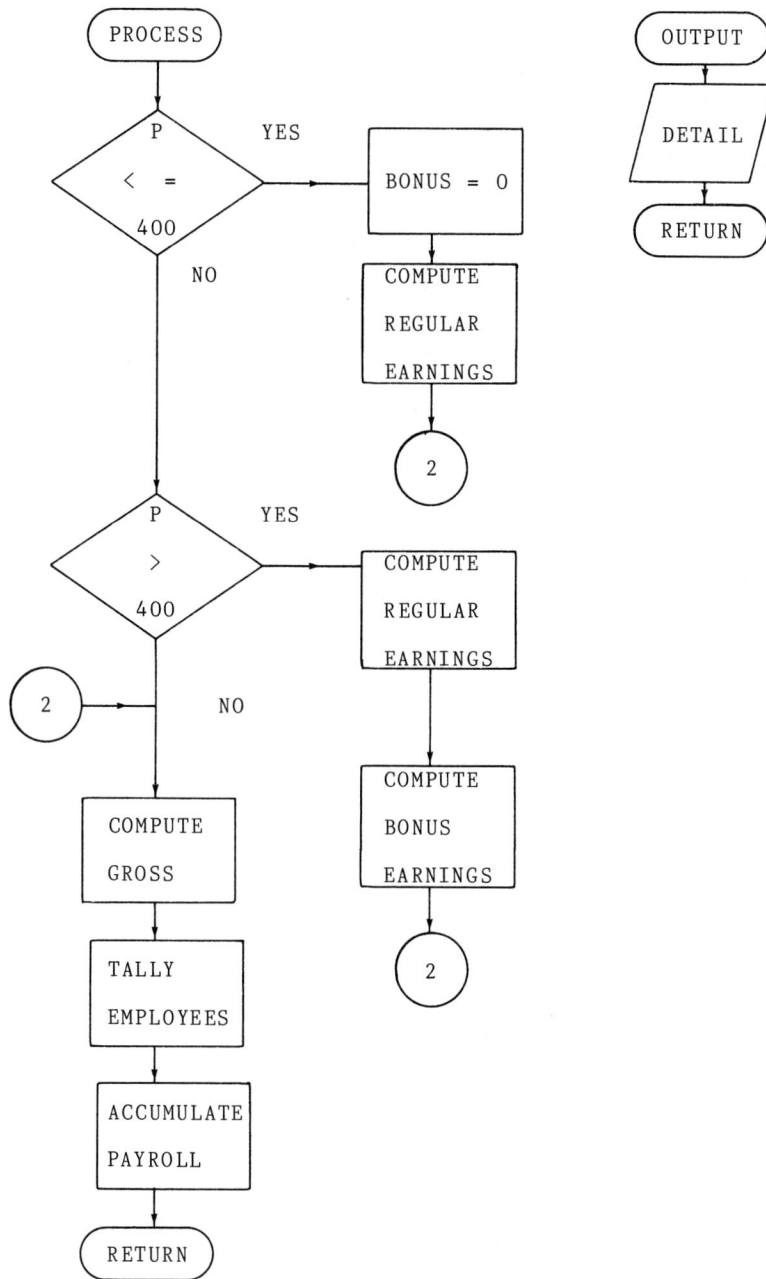

FIGURE 9–2
(Continued)

there is a TRUE response, the regular pay is computed for the first 400 units. The bonus pay is computed as base pay plus a 55% bonus for each item exceeding 400 units.

Gross earnings are computed by adding the regular pay to the bonus earnings. Summary totals are then added for the number of employees and the amount of payroll.

Detail printing is accomplished in the output routine. The report is double-spaced.

The summary block prints the totals for the number of employees and the payroll and the program ends.

EXAMPLE PROGRAM—SERIAL COMPARISONS

The sample program for this chapter is exhibited in figure 9–3. Program documentation and variable identification are shown in lines 200 through 360.

The mainline module is the command unit that controls execution of the program subroutines. Line 410 calls the headings subroutine. The report and column headings are

```
200     REM     FIGURE   9-3    WRITTEN BY LARRY FRY   1/18/83
210     REM        This program prepares the   piecework payroll
220     REM        for the Flat Head Bolt  Company.    A   55%
230     REM        bonus is paid for each unit produced in excess
240     REM        of 400.
250     REM   *****   Variable Identification
260     REM           E  .....  Employee Number
270     REM           E$  .....  Employee Name
280     REM           P  .....  Number of Units
290     REM           R  .....  Rate of Pay Per Unit
300     REM           B  .....  Bonus Rate Per Piece
310     REM           RE  .....  Regular Earnings
320     REM           BE  .....  Bonus Earnings
330     REM           GE  .....  Gross Earnings
340     REM           TE  .....  Total Employees
350     REM           TP  .....  Total Payroll
360     REM           Y  .....  Loop Counter
370                                                              REM
400     REM   *****   Mainline Control
410  GOSUB  610
420  LET  TE  =  0
430  LET  TP  =  0
440  FOR  Y  =  1  TO 5000
450          GOSUB  810
460          IF E = -1  THEN LET Y = 5001
470          IF E > O THEN GOSUB 910 : GOSUB 1010
480  NEXT Y
490  GOSUB  1110
500  END
510                                                              REM
520                                                              REM
600     REM   *****   Headings Module
610  LPRINT
620  LPRINT  TAB(27); "FLAT HEAD BOLT  COMPANY"
630  LPRINT
640  LPRINT  TAB(29);  "PIECEWORK  PAYROLL"
650  LPRINT
660  LPRINT  " Name", "Units"; TAB(24); "Rate";
670  LPRINT TAB(34); "Regular", "Bonus", "Total"
680  LPRINT
690  RETURN
700                                                              REM
800     REM   *****   Read Module
810  READ  E, E$, P, R
820  RETURN
830                                                              REM
900     REM   *****   Process Module
910  IF P < = 400   THEN LET BE = O : LET RE = P * R
920  IF P  > 400 THEN LET RE = 400 * R : LET BE = (P - 400) * (R * 1.55) :
              LET BE = INT(BE * 100 + .5) / 100
930  LET GE  =  RE  +  BE
940  LET TE  =  TE  +  1
950  LET TP  =  TP  +  GE
960  RETURN
970                                                              REM
1010    REM   *****   Output Module
1020  LPRINT  E$, P; TAB(23); R; TAB(33); RE, BE, GE
1030  LPRINT
1040  RETURN
1050                                                             REM
1100    REM   *****   Summary Module
1110  LPRINT
1120  LPRINT   "TOTAL EMPLOYEES  ";  TE
1130  LPRINT   "TOTAL PAYROLL    $";  TP
1140  LPRINT   TAB(16); "=========="
1150  RETURN
1160                                                             REM
1200    REM   *****   Data to be Processed
1210  DATA  111, "Rider,   J", 399, .52, 222, "Fuller, C",400, .55
1220  DATA  333, "Martina, A",401, .57, 444, "Marcen, S",450, .59
1230  DATA  555, "Cashin, R", 390, .55, 666, "Rinkle, J",450, .57
1240  DATA  777, "Campela, R", 0, .55, 888, "Sones, C", 425, .63
1250  DATA  999, "Chevez, E", 200, .55
1260  DATA  -1, "END", -1, -1
1270                                                             REM
1280  STOP
```

FIGURE 9–3
Serial comparison
program

printed as a result of the headings module. Blank lines are used to produce proper spacing. TAB statements are used to center the report heading lines horizontally. In lines 660 and 670 they are used to center the column headings above the data to be printed. TAB statements can be used in this type of situation to compress the total number of columns necessary in printing. The full width of a print zone is not used, so the amount of space required to print the report is reduced. This procedure can be used when a large number of columns is going to be printed.

Two summary variables are initialized at zero in lines 420 and 430. The summary totals for the number of employees (TE) and the amount of payroll (TP) are both assigned a value of zero. Numeric variable names of more than one character may not be allowed on some systems.

A FOR/NEXT structure is used in the mainline module to control execution of the program loop. There are nine significant data records to be processed.

The data values are entered in the read module. The variables are the employee number (E), the employee name (E$), the units produced (P), and the rate of pay per unit (R).

Program loop execution is determined by the employee number variable. As long as variable E contains a positive value, the process and output subroutines are executed. When E contains a negative value, the loop is terminated. Program branch statements are used to test variable E for positive or negative values. The program loop is shown in the following statements.

```
440 FOR Y = 1 TO 5000
450        GOSUB 810
460        IF E = -1 THEN Y = 5001
470        If E > 0 THEN GOSUB 910 : GOSUB 1010
480 NEXT Y
```

A key part of the program is the process module which contains the branch and calculation operations. The process module contains the two decision blocks that test for the break point of 400 units. The break point of 400 is tested with a wide range of data. The following are the program branch statements.

```
910 IF P <= 400 THEN LET BE = 0 : LET RE = P * R
920 IF P > 400 THEN LET RE = 400 * R :
                  LET BE = (P - 400) * (R * 1.55) :
                  LET BE = INT(BE * 100 + .5) / 100
```

Line 910 contains the program branch structure that tests for production of 400 units or less. Two program statements separated by colons follow the THEN. Both of these statements are executed when the result of the branch evaluation is TRUE. If the result of the decision is TRUE, the bonus earnings variable (BE) is set at zero to clear the memory. This eliminates the possibility of processing a data value previously stored in memory. In cases such as this where a variable may or may not contain significant data depending upon program branches, the variable memory location must be cleared or set at zero. Regular earnings (RE) are then calculated by multiplying the number of units by the rate.

When the IF-THEN statement produces a TRUE response, the calculations are executed. Control then shifts to line 920. Obviously, a TRUE response to statement 910 produces a FALSE response to line 920. Likewise, a FALSE answer in line 910 produces a TRUE result in statement 920.

When the IF-THEN statement in line 910 produces a FALSE result, program control drops to statement 920. The IF-THEN statement in line 920 computes bonus earnings when production exceeds 400 units. Several program statements separated by colons follow the THEN. Each computation is placed on a separate line for illustration purposes. All of these statements are executed when the branch is TRUE. Regular pay is calculated for the first 400 units. The next segment, which follows, calculates bonus earnings.

```
LET BE = (P - 400) * (R * 1.55) :
```

Bonus earnings are calculated by subtracting 400 from the number of units produced. Following the order of operations, this is done first. Next, the base rate of pay per unit is multiplied by 1.55 to compute the bonus pay per unit. Multiplying by 1.55 produces the same result as multiplying .55 by the base rate and adding the answer to the base.

It is possible to extend line 920 to the right margin when using a print line of 132 columns. The statement is dropped down to the next line in this case for illustration purposes. This procedure is made possible on some systems by the CONTROL-RETURN (CTRL-RETURN) combination, which continues the referenced program statement on the next line. The practice is used in structured programming to give the program a neater appearance. The same statement can be continued on the third line by using the same procedure. Bonus earnings are rounded to the nearest cent in the last line of the IF statement.

Gross earnings (GE) are calculated in statement 930. The regular and bonus earnings are added together to obtain gross earnings.

There are two summary calculations in the program. Line 940 tallies the number of employees. A tally is a variable that is incremented by one. Programs that count employees or customers use a tally procedure in the program loop. Each time the loop is executed the variable is incremented by one. Statement 950 accumulates the total payroll (TP).

The output module produces detail printing. Six values are printed on each line. TAB statements are used to center the detail values printed under the column headings.

The summary module prints the two accumulating variables. The total employees and total payroll are printed followed by a double underline (= symbol). The double underline is commonly used to mark the end of a business report.

The data to be processed is contained in lines 1210 to 1260. Statements 1210 through 1250 contain the nine significant data records. Line 1260 contains the trailer, or dummy, data record.

Output from this program is shown in figure 9–4. The headings, detail lines, and summary lines are printed as a result of the program. A hand trace of the program verifies that the results as printed are correct.

FLAT HEAD BOLT COMPANY

PIECEWORK PAYROLL

Name	Units	Rate	Regular	Bonus	Total
Rider, J	399	.52	207.48	0	207.48
Fuller, C	400	.55	220	0	220
Martina, A	401	.57	228	.88	228.88
Marcen, S	450	.59	236	45.73	281.73
Cashin, R	390	.55	214.5	0	214.5
Rinkle, J	450	.57	228	44.18	272.18
Campela, R	0	.55	0	0	0
Sones, C	425	.63	252	24.41	276.41
Chevez, E	200	.55	110	0	110

FIGURE 9–4

Serial comparison program output

TOTAL EMPLOYEES   9
TOTAL PAYROLL $ 1811.18
=========

PROGRAM DEVELOPMENT CHECKLIST

Use the following checklist to ensure that all components are included in the program.

_____ Flowchart

_____ Documentation

_____ Program control

_____ Headings

_____ READ-DATA statements

_____ Program branch structure

_____ Detail calculations

_____ Summary calculations

_____ Detail printing

_____ Summary printing

SUMMARY

The BASIC language contains procedures for conducting comparison operations with serial data. IF-THEN statements are used for comparison purposes to test for break points in data values. Summary variables are used to accumulate and print total amounts.

BASIC Key Words/Operators Learned

IF-THEN   Program branch structure.

Keyboard Operations Learned

CTRL-RETURN   Advances to next line while continuing BASIC statement.

Instructions

PROGRAM ASSIGNMENT 9–1

Prepare the flowcharts and a structured BASIC program to calculate and print the service charge for bank checking accounts. A service charge is made if the savings account balance is less than $500 or if the number of transactions exceeds 50. If the savings account balance is less than $500, a service fee of 24% of the amount less than $500 is charged. When the number of transactions exceeds 50, a service fee of 25 cents per item in excess of 50 is charged. There is no service fee if the savings account balance is equal to or greater than $500 or if the number of transactions is 50 or less. Round the service charge to the nearest cent.

Compute summary totals for the number of accounts processed, the number of transactions, and the service charges made.

Data records consist of the account number, account name, savings account balance, and the number of transactions. Use READ and DATA statements to enter the data. The data to be processed follows.

Data

Number	Name	Savings Balance	Transactions
1111	Martin, J	$550	40
2222	Francies, C	525	50
3333	Baker, R	510	40
4444	Fernandez, D	500	50
5555	Under, C	400	50
6666	Renn, C	500	60
7777	Eduardo, B	499	49
8888	Alfen, I	500	51
9999	Atler, J	501	55
2111	Smythe, M	500	49
3111	Martinez, J	400	60

Output Format

Print headings, detail lines and summary lines using standard print zones.

SILAS MARNER NATIONAL BANK

Service Charge Report

Account Number	Savings Balance	Transactions	Fee
XXXX	XXX	XX	X.XX
XXXX	XXX	XX	X.XX
SUMMARY TOTALS		XXXX	XXX.XX
ACCOUNTS	XXX		

PROGRAM ASSIGNMENT 9–2

Instructions

Prepare the flowcharts and a structured BASIC program to compute and print an hourly payroll. Compute regular earnings for all employees who work 40 hours or less (regular earnings = hours * rate). Employees who work more than 40 hours must be paid for the regular hours of work plus overtime for all hours that exceed 40. The overtime pay rate is calculated by multiplying 1.5 by the regular pay rate. This amount is then multiplied by the number of hours in excess of 40 to obtain overtime earnings. Gross earnings are calculated by adding regular and overtime pay. Round all computed results to the nearest cent.

Compute and print summary totals for the number of employees, regular earnings, overtime earnings, and gross earnings.

Data records consist of the employee name, the rate of pay, and the hours worked. Use READ and DATA statements to enter the data. Following is the data to be processed.

Data

Name	Rate	Hours
Grimm, J	5.75	39.9
Spicer, P	6.00	40.0
Lynch, J	9.99	40
Griffin, D	11.75	40.1
Hampton, F	7.75	30
Cash, R	8.33	45
Gross, R	6.67	23.5
Decker, R	4.45	0
Zimmerman, D	8.25	47.5
Brooks, M	7.77	40
Poage, J	9.13	44.5

Output Format

Print headings, detail lines, and summary totals using standard print zones.

SLIPT DISC RECORD STOP

Payroll Report

Name	Hours	Rate	Regular	Overtime	Gross
XXXXX,XX	XX.X	XX.XX	XXX.XX	XX.XX	XXX.XX
XXXXX,XX	XX.X	XX.XX	XXX.XX	XX.XX	XXX.XX
SUMMARY	EMPLOYEES XX		XXXX.XX	XXX.XX	XXXX.XX

INTERACTIVE COMPARISON OPERATIONS

OBJECTIVES

At the end of this chapter you should be able to perform the following operations:
- Access the computer operating system for the current date and time.
- Develop error handling routines.
- Execute programs with interactive comparison operations.
- Utilize proper syntax for nested IF-THEN-ELSE statements.
- Generate sound (beep) from the computer system.

INTERACTIVE COMPARISONS

The primary objective of this chapter is to demonstrate the BASIC language features used in interactive comparison operations. The example program prepares a salary cost analysis for salespeople. Salespeople are expected to generate a sales volume sufficient to pay their own salary plus other overhead costs. Salary cost is generally a specific percentage of expenses. This percentage, which varies with the store type, can be obtained from trade organizations or from National Cash Register (NCR), which also publishes an excellent resource.* The salary can be divided by the referenced percentage to determine the expected sales volume, or the sales volume can be multiplied by the percentage to compute salary range.

Two salary ranges are used to prepare the report in the example program. The salary cost percentage is 6.51%. Employees earning less than $200 in salary are expected to sell at least $2,923 in merchandise each pay period. Those earning $200 or more are expected to sell at least $3,460 in merchandise. These levels of sales cover the salesperson's salary and contribute to overhead costs. Comparison statements must be developed to consider these two situations.

FLOWCHARTS—INTERACTIVE COMPARISONS

The flowcharts for the example program are shown in figures 10–1 and 10–2. Figure 10–1 is the top-level flowchart. The top-level flowchart contains a mainline routine which controls execution of the subroutines. The program subroutines include the headings, input, error handling, process, and summary blocks.

The detailed logic flowchart is shown in figure 10–2. The mainline routine is used as the driver module to control execution of the subroutines.

Report headings, subheadings, and column headings are printed as a result of the heading routine. The current date is obtained from the computer operating system for printing the subheading.

Two summary totals are then initialized at zero. These summary totals are accumulated in the process block.

*National Cash Register Company. *Expenses in Retail Business.* Dayton, OH: National Cash Register Company, 1973.

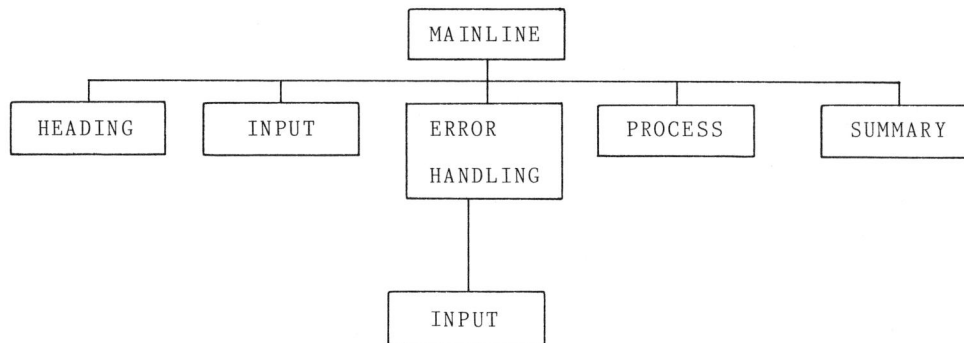

FIGURE 10–1
Top-level flowchart

The program loop is controlled by a FOR/NEXT structure. The program body is executed according to the loop parameters. The loop limit parameter is initialized at 500, which means that the program loop could be executed a maximum of 500 times. The program provides a prompt to the user to determine whether or not the loop should be executed. When the user indicates that there are more records, the program loop, consisting of the input, error, and process blocks is executed. If there are no more records to process, the loop counter is set at 501, which terminates the loop.

Data records are entered in the input subroutine. There are four variable values to be entered by INPUT statements.

The error handling routine is used to check the data that is entered and to verify that it is within reasonable range. In the example, salespeople should not receive less than $180 or more than $250. The logical operator OR is used in this program for the error handling branch. The verification procedure is used to insure that the data is within reasonable range. If the data is out of range, an error message is displayed upon the monitor screen and a bell is sounded. At this point, the input module is called for data reentry.

The process-output routine combines process and output operations because they are closely related. Although modules are usually limited to one function, there are times when it is necessary to combine them. The combination of functions, in this case, makes the program more efficient. Detail printing is double-spaced and the data record is printed first.

Program branches are created by two nested IF statements. If the salary is less than $200, the amount of sales is checked to determine if it exceeds $2,923. A TRUE response to both conditions causes the message "STATUS OK" to be printed. Control then drops to the RETURN block. When the salary is less than $200 and the sales are less than $2,923, there is a sales deficiency. This situation is considered in the ELSE portion of the statement: a message is printed; the amount of shortfall is calculated, printed, and accumulated; and the flag variable is tallied.

In the same manner, when the salary is greater than or equal to $200, the sales volume is checked to determine if it exceeds $3,460. If the response is TRUE, the message "STATUS OK" is printed. When the sales volume is less than $3,460, there is a FALSE result. This activates the ELSE portion of the statement: a warning message is printed; the sales shortfall is calculated, printed, and accumulated; and the flag variable is tallied.

The total sales shortfall and the number of flagged deficiencies are printed in the summary subroutine.

EXAMPLE PROGRAM—INTERACTIVE COMPARISONS

The example program for this chapter is shown in figure 10–3. The program objective is to generate a sales deficiency report. The salary amount and the amount of sales are compared with certain range values to determine if there is a deficiency.

The mainline module controls execution of all subroutines.

The headings module is executed before the program loop is entered. The print

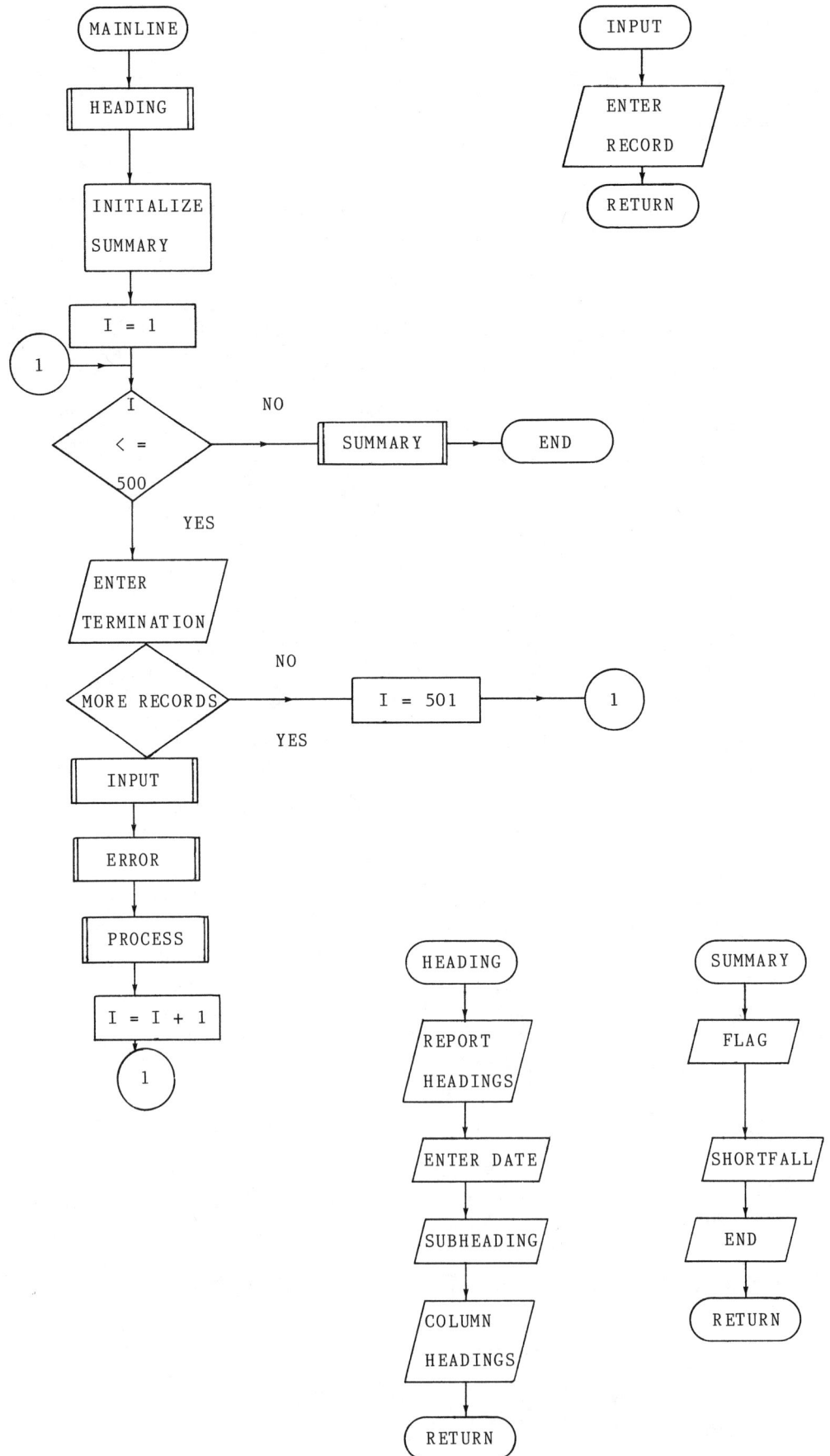

FIGURE 10–2
Detailed logic flowchart

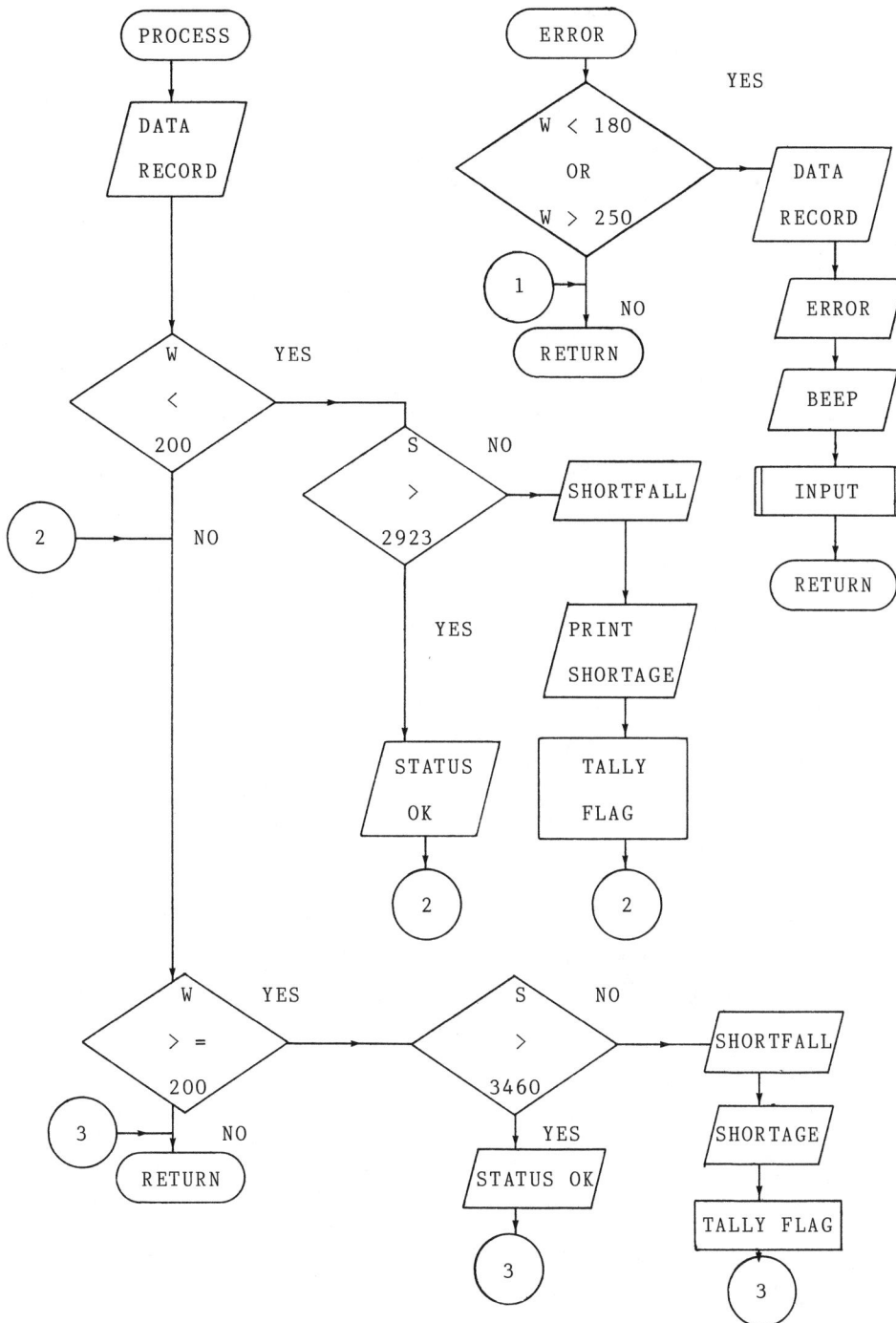

FIGURE 10–2
(Continued)

statements in the headings module are preceded by a *control statement* that causes the printer to advance to a clean page. This procedure is commonly referred to as a *formfeed*. Formfeed causes the paper to advance to the next sheet. The results of program execution are then separated from the program listing and the report is printed beginning at the top of the sheet.

Control statements such as this are used for a variety of purposes, such as programming the printer and accessing disk data files, in the BASIC language. The control statement formats for the monitor screen and the printer follow.

```
1010 PRINT CHR$(⟨Parameter⟩)
1010 LPRINT CHR$(⟨Parameter⟩)
```

```
200      REM     FIGURE   10-3   WRITTEN BY LARRY FRY   1/20/83
210      REM     This program prepares a salary cost analysis for
220      REM     the Soiled Form Office Supply Company.
230      REM     Salary Cost Percentage  =  6.51%
240      REM   *****  Variable Identification
250      REM         N   .....  Employee Number
260      REM         N$  .....  Employee Name
270      REM         W   .....  Weekly Salary
280      REM         S   .....  Weekly Sales
290      REM         F   .....  Number Flagged
300      REM         D   .....  Sales Deficiency
310      REM         I   .....  Loop Counter
320      REM         L$  .....  Loop Limit Control
330                                                            REM
400      REM   *****  Mainline Module
410   GOSUB 1010
420   F = 0  :  D = 0
430   FOR  I  =  1  TO  500
440          INPUT "ARE THERE MORE RECORDS TO PROCESS  (Y/N) "; L$
450          IF L$ = "N"  THEN  LET I = 501
460          IF L$ = "Y"  THEN GOSUB 1210 : GOSUB 1310 : GOSUB 1410
470   NEXT I
480   GOSUB   1610
490   END
500                                                            REM
510                                                            REM
1000     REM   *****  Headings Module
1010  LPRINT CHR$(12)       :       REM   FORMFEED
1020  LPRINT TAB(21); "SOILED FORM OFFICE SUPPLY CO."
1030  LPRINT
1040  LPRINT TAB(25); "SALARY COST ANALYSIS"
1050  LPRINT
1060  LPRINT TAB(21); "For Week Ending "; DATE$
1070  LPRINT
1080  LPRINT TAB(5); "Name", "Salary", "  Sales",  , "Remarks"
1090  LPRINT
1100  RETURN
1110                                                           REM
1200     REM   *****  Input Module
1210  INPUT "ENTER Salesperson's Number  ";  N
1220  INPUT "ENTER Salesperson's Name ";  N$
1230  INPUT "ENTER Weekly Salary ";   W
1240  INPUT "ENTER Sales Amount ";  S
1250  RETURN
1260                                                           REM
1300     REM   *****  Error-Handling Routine
1310  IF W < 180 OR W > 250 THEN   PRINT N$, W, S, "ERROR IN DATA" :
                            PRINT CHR$(7) : GOSUB 1210
1320  RETURN
1330                                                           REM
1400     REM   *****  Process - Output Module
1410  LPRINT
1420  LPRINT  N$, W, S; TAB(50);
1430  IF W < 200  THEN      IF S > 2923 THEN LPRINT "STATUS   OK" :
                            ELSE LPRINT "SHORTFALL OF $"; : LPRINT 2923 - S :
                            LET D = D + (2923 - S) : LET F = F + 1
1440  IF W = > 200 THEN     IF S > 3460 THEN LPRINT "STATUS   OK"
                            ELSE LPRINT "SHORTFALL OF $"; : LPRINT 3460 - S :
                            LET D = D + (3460 - S) : LET F = F + 1
1450  RETURN
1460                                                           REM
1600     REM   *****  Summary Module
1610  LPRINT
1620  LPRINT "Number of Deficiencies   ";  F
1630  LPRINT "Total Sales Shortfall   ";  D
1640  LPRINT
1650  LPRINT  "END OF REPORT"
1660  RETURN
1670                                                           REM
1680  STOP
```

FIGURE 10–3
Transaction comparison program

The command PRINT CHR$ or LPRINT CHR$ is a BASIC control statement that causes a specified action on the monitor screen, printer, disk file, or the central processing unit. Following is the command that causes the printer to execute a formfeed.

1010 LPRINT CHR$(12)

Variations of this control statement can be used to program the printer for margins, tabulator stops, and print enhancement. The control statements used to program printers vary from system to system. The printer manual should be checked for the proper code and switch settings before the printer is programmed.

Report headings, subheadings, and column headings are printed as a result of the headings module. Line 1060 causes the current date, which is obtained from the computer operating system, to be printed. Following is the BASIC statement format to accomplish this.

1060 LPRINT DATE$

Line 1060 follows.

1060 LPRINT TAB(21); "For Week Ending"; DATE$

Following is the printed result of line 1060.

For Week Ending 09–20–1984

The DATE$ key word produces a ten-character string as in the preceding example. This is a valuable feature when printing business reports. It is available on mainframe and minicomputers and many microcomputer systems now support it. On some systems the user provides the current date to the computer operating system, while on others an internal clock is included or can be added with a plug-in circuit board.

The current time can also be printed with many systems. This value is also obtained from the computer operating system. Following is the statement format used to print the current time.

1100 LPRINT TIME$

The TIME$ command produces an eight-character string. This feature is required when preparing time-critical or perishable reports.

Two summary totals are initialized at zero in statement 420. Variable F is used to tally the number of deficiencies and D is used to accumulate the amount of shortfall.

A FOR/NEXT structure is used to control execution of the input, error handling, and process-output modules. The loop limit parameter, which is initialized at 500, determines the maximum number of times that the program loop will be executed. Following is the program loop.

```
430 FOR I = 1 TO 500
440     INPUT "ARE THERE MORE RECORDS TO PROCESS (Y/N)"; L$
450     IF L$ = "N" THEN LET I = 501
460     IF L$ = "Y" THEN GOSUB 1210 : GOSUB 1310 :
                GOSUB 1410
470 NEXT I
```

Statement 440 prompts the user to enter the loop control variable (L$). When variable L$ is equal to "N", the loop counter is assigned the value 501 which terminates the loop. If L$ is equal to "Y", the program loop is executed. The program loop consists of the input, error, and process-output subroutines.

Data is entered in the input module. The INPUT statements in lines 1210 through 1240 cause the salesperson's number (N), the salesperson's name (N$), weekly salary (W), and sales amount (S) to be entered.

An *error handling* subroutine is contained in statement 1310. This procedure is used to validate data and to ensure that the data is within the correct range. The following program statement is used to accomplish this.

1310 IF W < 180 or W > 250 THEN PRINT N$, W, S,
"ERROR IN DATA" : PRINT CHR$(7) : GOSUB 1210

The company has determined that all salespeople are paid from $180 to $250. If the data entered falls within this range, it is valid. Data that falls outside of that range is invalid. The logical operator OR is used to accomplish this routine. If W is less than $180 or greater than $250, an error is present. Since the IF statement is TRUE, the THEN portion of the statement is executed: the values are displayed on the monitor screen; an error message is printed on the screen; a warning bell is sounded; and, the input module is executed to reenter the data. The BASIC control statement, which follows, is used to produce the warning bell.

PRINT CHR$(7)

On most systems the statement PRINT CHR$(7) causes the bell or beep to sound. Keying CTRL - G produces the same result. The key word BEEP has been added to some systems to accomplish the same task.

The warning beep and an error message tell the user that an error has been made. The input module is executed at this point so the user can enter the correct data.

The program branches, computations, and detail printing are executed in the process-output module. Detail lines are printed as a result of lines 1420 through 1440. The report is double-spaced.

Two *nested IF* statements are used to implement program branch logic. Program branch nesting is developed in two levels in these statements. There is an IF-THEN-ELSE statement nested within an IF-THEN statement. Some systems permit nesting of IF statements to several levels. Statement 1430, which follows, is an example of a nested IF statement.

1430 IF W < 200 THEN IF S > 2923 THEN LPRINT "STATUS OK" :
ELSE LPRINT "SHORTFALL OF $"; :
LPRINT 2923 − S:
LET D = D + (2923 − S) :
LET F = F + 1

Each statement segment is shown on a separate line for illustration purposes (see figure 10–3 for actual statement configuration).

The top level of the nested IF statement is a branch to determine if the weekly salary is less than $200. If the answer is FALSE, control drops to statement 1440 which is another nested IF statement. When the weekly salary is less than $200 (but more than $180 which is taken care of in the error handling module), the THEN portion of the statement, the IF-THEN-ELSE procedure, is executed. The inner branch is an IF-THEN-ELSE statement that determines if the amount of sales exceeds $2,923. A TRUE response results in the THEN portion of the statement, which prints the message "STATUS OK," being executed.

Sales less than $2,923 result in a FALSE response which causes the ELSE portion of the statement to be executed. When the ELSE portion is executed, the message "SHORTFALL OF $" is printed, the amount of shortfall is computed and printed, and the number of deficiencies is tallied.

This type of data processing operation is known as an exceptions report. The objective of this program is to generate a list of salespeople who do not meet sales expectations. Those salespeople who have not met the goal are exceptions to the standard, or accepted, sales amount.

Statement 1440 is another nested IF statement. It checks those salespeople whose salaries are equal to or greater than $200 (but less than $250). For these employees, sales should exceed $3,460. The nested IF statement in line 1440 performs the exceptions processing for these salespeople.

The total amount of shortfall and the number of deficient salespeople are printed in the summary module.

```
                    SOILED FORM OFFICE SUPPLY CO.

                      SALARY COST ANALYSIS

                   For Week Ending 09-20-1984

       Name       Salary        Sales              Remarks


    FRY            195           3000        STATUS   OK

    HILL           195           2800        SHORTFALL OF $ 123

    GRAY           225           3500        STATUS   OK

    BOWER          245           3200        SHORTFALL OF $ 260

    SHANER         199           2900        SHORTFALL OF $ 23

    REESE          205           3475        STATUS   OK


    Number of Deficiencies    3
    Total Sales Shortfall    406

    END OF REPORT
```

FIGURE 10–4
Transaction comparison
program output

Figure 10–4 exhibits the output generated by this program. Six records are processed and the detail lines are printed. The summary lines are then printed followed by "END OF REPORT"

PROGRAM DEVELOPMENT CHECKLIST

Use the following checklist to ensure that all components are included in the program.

_____ Flowcharts and documentation

_____ Program control

_____ Headings

_____ Data entry

_____ Program branch structure

_____ Detail calculations

_____ Detail printing

_____ Summary calculations

_____ Summary printing

SUMMARY

The BASIC language contains procedures for conducting comparison operations in the transaction mode. IF-THEN statements are used for comparison purposes to control processing and to check for errors in the data.

The current date and time is accessed from the computer operating system and printed as appropriate.

The BASIC control statement PRINT CHR$ is used to control or access various system components.

BASIC Key Words/Operators Learned

BEEP	Generates bell or beep.
CTRL - G	Generates bell or beep.
DATE$	Returns current date from computer operating system.
LPRINT CHR$( )	BASIC control statement for programming printer.
PRINT CHR$( )	BASIC control statement for accessing monitor, disk files, or central processing unit.
TIME$	Returns current time from computer operating system.

PROGRAM ASSIGNMENT 10–1

Instructions

Prepare the flowcharts and a structured BASIC program to process bank checking account transactions. The total amount of deposits is added to the beginning balance. The total amount of checks returned is subtracted. If the amount of the returned check exceeds the account balance, a warning message should be printed and a service fee of $20 should be charged. Negative balances should be processed as such.

Compute summary totals for the number of accounts, amount of deposits, returned checks, service fees, and the ending balance.

Data records consist of the account number, account name, beginning balance, total deposits, and total returned checks. Use prompting INPUT statements to enter the data.

Data

Number	Name	Balance	Deposits	Checks
1111	Osouna, S	$1,397.40	$250.00	$673.91
2222	Heline, L	417.53	0.00	125.60
3333	Martinez, E	175.00	100.00	295.00
4444	Confer, J	560.50	275.00	0.00
5555	Campbell, P	845.75	323.13	540.75
6666	Feigles, E	0.00	150.00	45.55

Output Format

Print the report date, headings, detail lines, and summary lines using standard print zones.

SILAS MARNER NATIONAL BANK

Account Balance Report Month Ending xx-xx-xx

Name	Balance	Deposits	Checks	Ending
XXXXX,XX	XXXX.XX	XXX.XX	XXX.XX	XXXX.XX
XXXXX,XX	XXXX.XX	XXX.XX	XXX.XX	XXXX.XX
SUMMARY ACCOUNTS xx		XXXX.XX	XXXX.XX	XXXX.XX
SERVICE FEES XXX.XX				

Instructions

Prepare the flowcharts and a structured BASIC program to process and print journal entries. Use prompting INPUT statements to enter the entries. Use program branches to provide proper printing format for the debit and credit entries.

Accumulate summary totals for the number of transactions, the debit amount, and the credit amount.

Data records consist of the entry type (DB or CR), the date, the account name, the source document, the debit amount, and the credit amount. The current date may be used for journal entries.

Data

Type	Date	Account	Source	Debit	Credit
DB	7/1	Office Equip	c-149	197.00	0.00
CR	7/1	Cash	c-149	0.00	197.00
DB	7/1	A/R - Spicer	I-457	200.00	0.00
CR	7/1	Sales	I-457	0.00	200.00
DB	7/1	Misc Exp	PO-94	35.55	0.00
CR	7/1	Cash	PO-94	0.00	35.55
DB	7/1	Salary Exp	c-150	225.45	0.00
CR	7/1	Cash	c-150	0.00	225.45
DB	7/1	Cash	CR-63	475.75	0.00
CR	7/1	Sales	CR-63	0.00	475.55

Output Format

Print the report date, the headings, the detail lines, and the summary lines. The current date may be used in the journal entries. Indent the account name for credit entries.

PORT-EX COMPANY

Journal Entries for xx-xx-xx

Date	Account	Source	Debit	Credit
7/1	Office Equip	c-149	197.00	
	Cash	c-149		197.00
7/1	A/R—Spicer	I-457	200.00	
	Sales	I-457		200.00

SUMMARY ENTRIES xx   xxxx.xx   xxxx.xx

Instructions

Prepare the flowcharts and a structured BASIC program to compute and print a monthly sales bonus report. Use prompting INPUT statements to enter the data. The PORT-EX COMPANY employs full-time and part-time salespeople to market electronic components. Use nested IF-THEN-ELSE statements when possible. The bonus for full-time salespeople is calculated at 4.5% for all sales up to $10,000 and 9.5% for all sales exceeding $10,000. Part-time salespeople are paid 2.5% for all sales up to $5,000 and 5.5% for all sales exceeding $5,000. Include an error handling routine for data validation purposes.

Calculate summary totals for the bonus amount paid to full-time salespeople and for the bonus amount paid to part-time salespeople.

Data records consist of the salesperson's name, sales district, employment status, and amount of sales.

Data

Name	District	Status	Sales
Smith	NE	F	$ 8,577.93
Fores	SE	F	12,917.47
Hawes	NE	P	4,333.33
Zenfor	SW	P	7,666.66
Flynn	NE	P	5,000.00
Rastor	SW	F	10,000.00
Hadin	SE	F	9,999.99

Output Format

Print the report date, the headings, the detail lines, and the summary lines using standard print zones.

PORT-EX COMPANY

Sales Bonus Report

Sales Month Ending xx-xx-xx

Name	Status	Sales	Bonus
XXXXXX, XX	F	XXXXX.XX	XXX.XX
XXXXXX, XX	P	XXXXX.XX	XXX.XX

SUMMARY   FULL-TIME BONUS $XXXXX.XX
                 PART-TIME BONUS $XXXXX.XX

END OF REPORT

FUNCTIONS AND APPLICATIONS PROGRAMMING

OBJECTIVES

At the end of this chapter you should be able to perform the following operations:
- Clear the monitor screen.
- Set printer width using program statements.
- Center headings and other output.
- Edit output.
- Develop user-defined functions.
- Write user-defined rounding statements.

NESTED PROGRAM LOOPS

Nested FOR/NEXT loops were presented in Chapter 7. To review, it may be necessary to repeat certain processing steps as the program is executed. This can be done by using nested FOR/NEXT loops. The example program in this chapter provides an illustration of nested loops.

The objective of the example program is to produce a depreciation report using the sum-of-year's-digits method. Depreciation is the accounting procedure used to spread the cost of an asset over its useful life by expensing a portion of the cost each year. The method used in the example program is one of several available.

Several new BASIC features are exhibited in this program. They include user-defined functions, heading placement, loop nesting, and output editing.

FLOWCHARTS—FUNCTIONS

The flowcharts for the example program are shown in figures 11–1 and 11–2. In the top-level flowchart, figure 11–1, program execution is controlled by the mainline routine. The mainline routine controls execution of the heading, input, and process-output subroutines.

The detailed logic flowchart is shown in figure 11–2. Certain system initialization tasks are accomplished in the program. These procedures, such as formatting output, clearing the system, and defining user functions, are commonly referred to as *housekeeping tasks*. They are usually located near the beginning of the program listing. It is assumed that these tasks are included in all programs, so the common practice is to omit references to the procedures in the flowcharts. The organization's policies concerning the inclusion/exclusion of these tasks in flowcharts should be followed. The housekeeping tasks performed in this program include declaring the user-defined function and formatting several output lines.

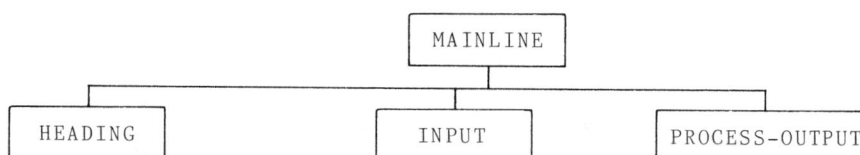

FIGURE 11–1
Top-level flowchart

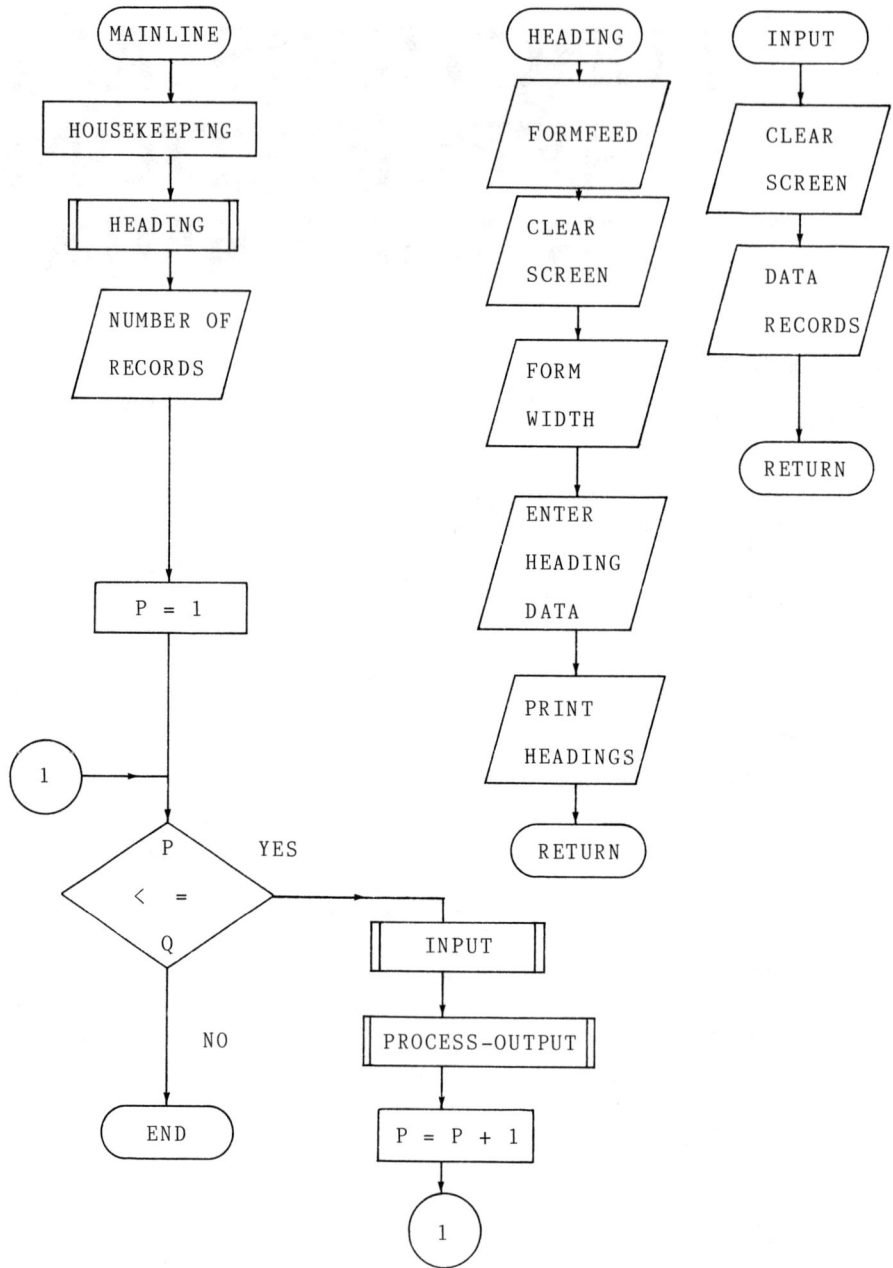

FIGURE 11–2
Detailed logic flowchart

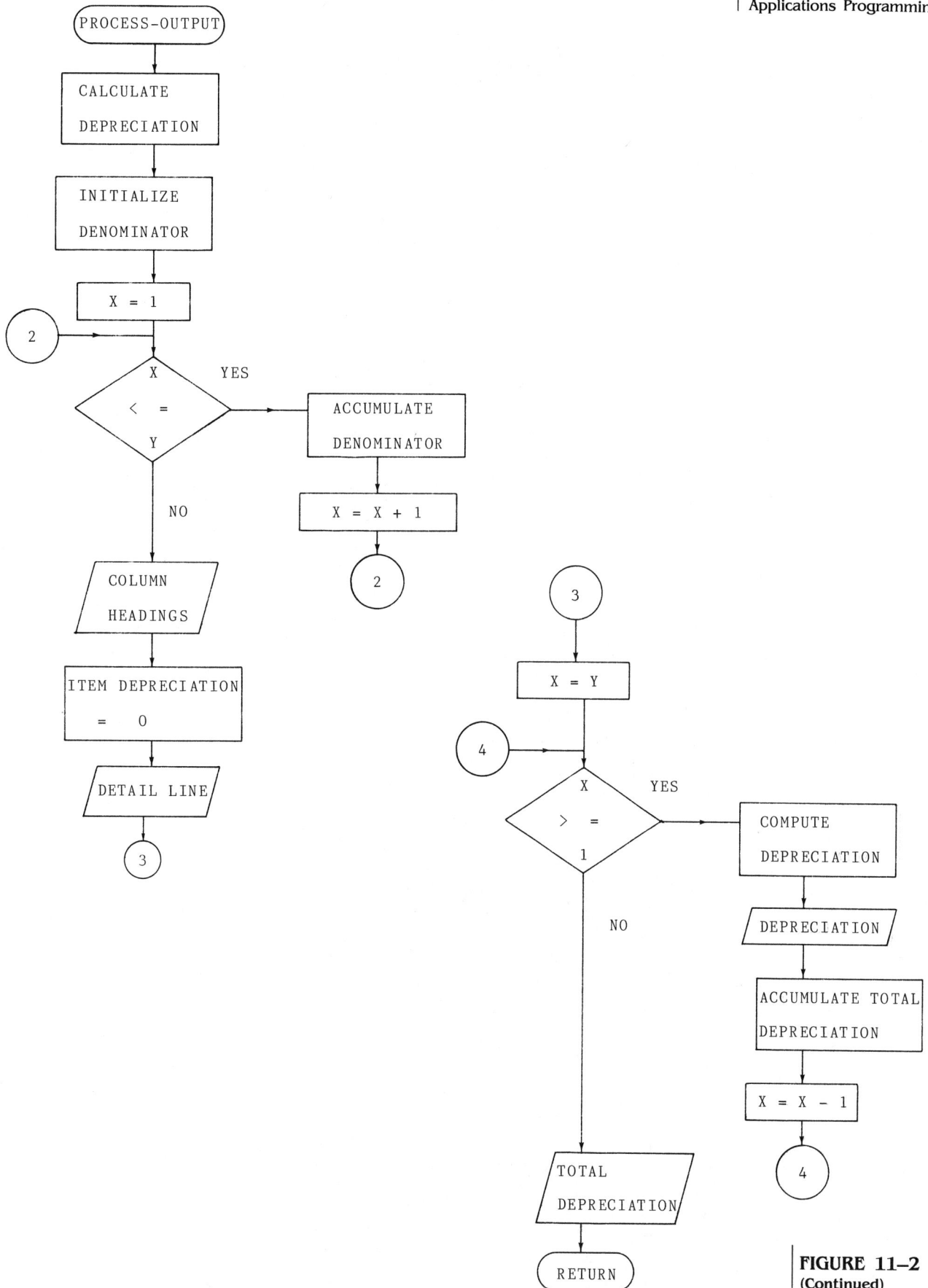

FIGURE 11–2
(Continued)

```
100     REM       FIGURE  11-3    WRITTEN BY LARRY FRY  2/24/83
110     REM       This program prepares a depreciation report for
120     REM       the Breakfast Machine Tool Company.  The sum
130     REM       of years digits (S-Y-D)  method is used.
140     REM       *****  Variable  Identification
150     REM              C$   .....  Company Name
160     REM              S$   .....  Report  Subheading
170     REM              A$   .....  Asset Type
180     REM              C    .....  Asset Cost
190     REM              Y    ....   Useful Years
200     REM              V    .....  Salvage Value
210     REM              D    .....  Annual Depreciation function
220     REM              A    .....  Amount to be Depreciated
230     REM              TD   .....  Total Depreciation
240     REM              P    .....  Program Loop Counter
250     REM              Q    .....  Program Loop Limit
260     REM              X    .....  Process Loop Counter
270     REM              Z    .....  S-Y-D  Denominator
280     REM              F    .....  Form Width for Report
290                                                                       REM
300     REM       *****  User-Defined Function
310  DEF  FND(N)  =  CINT(A  *  (X  /  Z))
320                                                                       REM
330     REM       *****  Output Format Lines for PRINT  USING
340  LET O1$ = "Asset              Cost          Salvage Value
Useful Years    Remaining Life   Annual Depreciation"
350  LET O2$ = " &              $$###,###          $$#,###
  ##"
360  LET O3$ = "
                    ##          $$###,###. "
370                                                                       REM
400     REM       *****  Mainline Module
410  GOSUB  610
420  INPUT "ENTER Number of Records to be Processed "; Q
430  FOR  P  =  1  TO  Q
440          GOSUB  810
450          GOSUB  1010
460  NEXT  P
470  END
480                                                                       REM
600     REM       *****  Headings Module
610  LPRINT CHR$(12)
620  CLS
630  INPUT "ENTER Form Width - Columns ";  F
640  WIDTH "LPT1:", F
650  INPUT "ENTER Company Name ";  C$
660  INPUT "ENTER  Subheading "; S$
670  LPRINT TAB(F / 2  -  LEN(C$) / 2);  C$
680  LPRINT
690  LPRINT TAB(F / 2  -  LEN(S$) / 2);  S$
700  RETURN
710                                                                       REM
800     REM       *****  Input Module
810  CLS
820  INPUT "ENTER Asset Type ";  A$
830  INPUT "ENTER Asset Cost ";  C
840  INPUT "ENTER Useful Years ";  Y
850  INPUT "ENTER Salvage Value ";  V
860  RETURN
870                                                                       REM
1000    REM       *****  Process-Output Module
1010 LET  A  =  C  -  V
1020 LET  Z  =  0
1030 FOR  X  =  1  TO  Y
1040          LET  Z  =  Z  +  X
1050 NEXT  X
1060 LPRINT
1070 LPRINT  O1$
1080 LPRINT
1090 LPRINT USING O2$; A$, C, V, Y
1100 TD  =  0
1110 FOR  X  =  Y  TO  1  STEP  -1
1120          LPRINT USING O3$;  X, FND(N)
1130          LET  TD  =  TD  +  FND(N)
1140 NEXT  X
1150 LPRINT
1160 LPRINT USING "TOTAL  DEPRECIATION  $$###,###";  TD
1170 LPRINT : LPRINT : LPRINT
1180 RETURN
1190                                                                       REM
1200 STOP
```

FIGURE 11-3
Functions program

Centering of the report headings is accomplished in the headings subroutine. A formfeed operation is used to cycle the printer paper to a new page. The monitor screen is then cleared for data entry. An INPUT statement is used to enter the form width needed to print the headings. The report heading and subheading are then entered and printed.

A FOR/NEXT structure is used to control execution of the program loop. An INPUT statement is used to enter the number of data records to be processed. This number controls execution of the loop.

The data records are entered in the input subroutine. The monitor screen is cleared each time the program loop is executed.

Detail processing and printing are performed in the process-output subroutine. The amount to be depreciated is calculated by subtracting the salvage value from the purchase cost. The sum-of-year's-digits procedure uses the aggregate value of the year's digits as the denominator in computations. This value must be initialized at zero each time the program loop is executed. A nested loop is used to calculate the sum-of-year's-digits. Column headings are then printed for each separate asset. A detail line is printed to provide relevant asset identification. Next, the total depreciation is initialized at zero for each asset. Annual depreciation is then computed in a nested loop. This value is computed and printed for each year of useful life. A user-defined function is used as part of the calculation. The total depreciation for each asset is accumulated within the nested loop and is printed upon termination of the loop. Several blank lines are printed to separate asset records.

EXAMPLE PROGRAM—FUNCTIONS

The primary objective of this chapter is to demonstrate the BASIC procedures for user-defined functions and for report editing. The example program is shown in figure 11–3.

Program documentation and variable identification are shown in lines 100 to 290. Statements 300 to 370 provide a user-defined calculation function and also output format lines for report editing. These are commonly referred to as housekeeping tasks. The function and format statements are discussed later in this chapter.

The mainline module is used to control execution of the program. Report headings and subheadings are printed as a result of the headings module, statements 600 to 700. Line 610 produces a formfeed operation.

Statement 620 clears the monitor screen. The monitor screen is cleared to eliminate previous printing which may distract the user. The command used to clear the monitor screen is CLS. Although many systems use the CLS command, the HOME command is also used to clear the monitor screen. Following is statement 620.

620 CLS

It is also a good idea to clear the screen at the beginning of program execution or when entering data to reduce clutter.

The number of columns to be used for the printed report is entered in the INPUT statement in line 630. Variable F is used to enter the value for form width. This value is used to center report headings and to program the printer for the number of characters to be printed on one line.

Line 640 is the statement that programs the printer. It causes the printer form width to be programmed (some printers may not be programmable).

Normally, systems are set at a specific number of print positions for one line. This is known as the *default value*. The default value for most printers is either 40 or 80 columns. It is set automatically each time the system is turned on. The default value on most systems is programmed in the circuits. It can be changed through the use of system program statements, such as the WIDTH statement which is used to program the print width. The statement format follows.

630 WIDTH "⟨Device⟩:", ⟨Parameter⟩

The WIDTH key word alters the default value for the specified device. The parameter sets the number of columns. WIDTH may be used to set the monitor screen, printers, disk files, or telecommunications. Statement 640, which follows, is used to alter the default value of the printer, device LPT1, from the value of 80 to 115.

640 WIDTH "LPT1:", F

The value for variable F is entered in the INPUT statement in line 630. In this program, the value is 115.

The statement used to alter printer width varies for the different systems. Many systems use the following control statement to alter printer width.

PRINT CHR$(Parameter)

Check the system manual for the proper statement to be used with programmable printers. Enter these statements in Exercise 11–1.

EXERCISE 11–1

Printer Programming Commands

Printer default value _____

Printer access _____

Program printer width _____

Other _____

The report heading and subheading are entered as a result of the INPUT statements in lines 650 and 660. Variable C$ is used to enter the string value for the company name and S$ is used to enter the subheading.

Statements 670 through 690 cause the headings to be centered horizontally in the output report. The TAB statement parameter is used to control the printing position.

The LEN($) function is used as part of the TAB statement. LEN($) is a system-supplied string processing function that returns or displays the number of characters/spaces contained in a string data value. The following format is used for the LEN($) statement.

LEN(⟨String Parameter⟩)

This function returns the number of characters in the string parameter. The statement LEN(C$) returns the number of characters contained in the string C$.

Print lines can be centered horizontally through the use of the following formula.

Centering = Form Center − Print Line Length / 2

For any print line to be centered, the horizontal center of the form must be determined by taking the width and dividing by 2. If the report width is 115, the center is 57. Next, the length of the string is determined through the use of the LEN($) function. This value is also divided by 2. The typewriting centering technique of backspacing one character for every two being typed is the procedure used. The following LPRINT statement results in the value C$ being centered when C$ contains the value "BREAKFAST MACHINE TOOLS".

670 LPRINT TAB(F / 2 − LEN(C$) / 2); C$

Variable F is divided by 2 to obtain the form center. The number of characters in C$ is determined by the LEN function, and this value is also divided by 2. The printer skips to the programmed position and prints the heading C$. In the same manner, the subheading is centered as a result of line 690.

1. What is the value of A after execution of the following statements?
   300 LET A$ = "THE YEAR OF THE CAT!"
   310 LET A = LEN(A$)
   320 PRINT A
2. Record the results of the following statements.
   600 LET S$ = "MESS"
   610 LET X = LEN(S$)
   620 FOR Y = 1 TO X
   630   PRINT S$
   640   PRINT
   650 NEXT Y
3. Record the results of the following statements.
   800 LET D$ = "DESCRIPTION"
   810 LET P$ = "COST"
   820 LET X = (30 − LEN(D$) − LEN(P$)) / 2
   830 PRINT TAB(X); D$; TAB(X + LEN(D$) + X); P$

1. A = 20
2. MESS
   MESS
   MESS
   MESS
3.   DESCRIPTION   COST
       Col. 7   Col. 25

The INPUT statement in line 420 is used to enter a value for variable Q, which is the number of records to be processed. This is the upper limit for the program loop. A FOR/NEXT structure is used to control execution of the program loop. The program loop consists of the input and process-output modules. Statement 460 increments variable P, which is the loop counter.

The input module contained in lines 800 through 860 causes the variable values to be entered. The monitor screen is cleared as a result of statement 810. INPUT statements are used to enter the data records. The variables are the asset type (A$), the asset cost (C), the useful years (Y), and the salvage value (V).

The process-output module is contained in lines 1000 through 1180. Processing and output functions are combined in this structured program because they are closely related. When the sum-of-year's-digits depreciation is calculated, the salvage value must first be subtracted from the asset cost to determine the dollar amount to be depreciated (A). This computation is shown in statement 1010. The sum-of-year's-digits is then calculated. This computation sums or integrates the digits for the years of useful life. When an asset has four years of useful life, the digits are summed as follows: 4 + 3 + 2 + 1. The sum-of-year's-digits is equal to 10. Before computing the sum, it is necessary to initialize the sum variable (Z) at zero. A FOR/NEXT loop is used to sum the digits. Line 1040 computes the sum. The loop is performed until the counter exceeds the number of years of useful life. Each time the loop is executed, the appropriate digit is added to the sum. Therefore, when the number of years of useful life is equal to four, the sum is equal to ten.

At this point in the program some print statements are executed. The program is capable of processing a number of separate assets, so the column headings are printed for each item. The LPRINT statement in line 1070 causes the string value O1$ to be printed. The string value for O1$ is assigned in the output format statement shown in line 340. It causes the column headings to be printed. All print format statements, such as this, are located in the housekeeping area of the program. The use of this procedure gives the program a tidier appearance.

Several new BASIC features are used in this program. These include report editing, the STEP parameter, and user-defined functions. These features are presented under separate headings.

Report Editing

The preparation of business reports to satisfy user requests usually requires *output editing*. Editing includes the insertion of such symbols as dollar signs, percentage symbols, commas, and decimals. If the system does not have built-in editing procedures, string values can be used in PRINT statements to produce the required symbols. Most systems, however, have the PRINT USING or LPRINT USING feature, which makes editing much easier. The PRINT and LPRINT USING functions require the use of specific symbols, which may vary with the system. Figure 11–4 shows the symbols used to edit string data on this system. The symbols used to edit numeric data are shown in figure 11–5. Se-

```
                        STRING EDITING

        Assume that   F$  =  "STRUCTURED BASIC"

             SYMBOL                              RESULT

               &                 Prints variable length string.

                                 All characters in string printed.


                                 EXAMPLE FORMAT:

                                 PRINT USING "OUTPUT = &";  F$

                                 RESULT:

                                 OUTPUT = STRUCTURED BASIC


          \       \              Prints the number of characters

                                 contained  between backslash

                                 symbols plus  2.

                                 EXAMPLE FORMAT:

                                 PRINT USING "OUTPUT = \       \"; F$

                                 RESULT:

                                 OUTPUT = STRUCTU


               !                 Prints only first character in

                                 the string.

                                 EXAMPLE FORMAT:

                                 PRINT USING "OUTPUT = !"; F$

                                 RESULT:

                                 OUTPUT = S
```

FIGURE 11–4
String editing symbols

lected editing examples are included for string and numeric data. The PRINT USING statement is explained in the pages that immediately follow figures 11–4 and 11–5.

The PRINT and LPRINT USING symbols may vary from system to system. Summarize the symbols appropriate for the system being used in Exercise 11–2.

String Editing Format

Symbol	Result
————	Prints entire string
————	Prints certain number of string characters
————	Prints first character
————	Other ————————————

Numeric Editing Symbols

Symbol	Result
————	Prints digit
————	Prints decimal
————	Prints sign (+ or −)
————	Prints floating dollar sign
————	Prints fixed dollar sign
————	Prints comma
————	Prints space filler (*)
————	Other ————————————

The LPRINT format assigned in lines 1090 and 1120 is one method that can be used when working with output editing. Another method is shown in line 1160. Both of these procedures are commonly used.

The output format strings identified as 02$ and 03$ assign editing and print location specifications. Following are the assignment statement and the print statement for 02$.

```
350 LET 02$ = " &     $$###,###     $$#,###
   ##"
1090 LPRINT USING 02$; A$, C, V, Y
```

These lines are interrelated. The LPRINT statement in line 1090 accesses the *output format statement* to be used and identifies the variables to be printed. LPRINT USING statements have the following format.

```
1090 LPRINT USING ⟨Format⟩; ⟨Parameter⟩, ⟨Parameter⟩
```

Line 1090, which follows, is the statement that actually calls for output editing.

```
1090 LPRINT USING 02$; A$, C, V, Y
```

Specifications for the layout and spacing of the printed output are contained in the format statement identified as 02$. The format variable to which the string value is assigned must follow the word USING. The format parameter is followed by a semicolon. Next, the variables to be printed as specified in the output format statement are listed.

NUMERIC EDITING

SYMBOL	RESULT
#	Prints number of digits specified. One digit printed for each # symbol. This symbol enables automatic zero suppression, zero fill-in, and rounding.
.	Prints decimal.

EXAMPLE FORMAT:

PRINT USING "OUTPUT = ####"; 09741

RESULT:

OUTPUT = 9741

EXAMPLE FORMAT:

PRINT USING "OUTPUT = ##.##"; 79.857

RESULT:

OUTPUT = 79.86

+	Prints the sign of the number (positive or negative). May be placed before or after the edit format.
-	Prints minus sign at end when placed on right side of format.
**	Prints asterisks in leading blank spaces. Used for filling numeric values in financial documents.
$$	Prints single dollar sign to left of first significant digit. Floating dollar sign.
*$$	Prints asterisks in leading blank spaces plus one dollar sign to left of first significant digit.
,	Prints commas to the left of every third digit when comma is formatted to the left of the decimal.

FIGURE 11–5
Numeric editing
symbols

```
EXAMPLE FORMAT:

PRINT USING "OUTPUT $$##,###.##"; 1437.957

RESULT:

OUTPUT =    $1,437.96



EXAMPLE FORMAT:

PRINT USING "OUTPUT = +*$$#,###.##"; -2347.66

RESULT:

OUTPUT =  -**$2,347.66
```

FIGURE 11–5
(Continued)

They must be listed in the correct sequence. The print format statement and the variables listed must correspond in the sequence and type of data.

The output format for this print line is contained in line 350 which follows.

350 LET 02$ = " & $$###,### $$#,###
##"

The format statement is a string value that is assigned to 02$. The first edit symbol is an ampersand. This symbol causes the complete value for variable A$ to be printed. The entire value is desired, so the ampersand is used. When only a certain number of characters in the value is to be printed, the \ \ symbols are used. A predetermined number of spaces can be printed when the backslashes are used. The backslash symbols are counted when figuring the number of characters on most systems. If only the first character of a string is to be printed, the exclamation symbol is used.

The next format group is a numeric value. The symbol $$###,### causes a dollar sign to be printed just to the left of the first significant digit. The dollar sign floats according to the number of significant digits. This feature is called a _floating dollar sign._

The ## symbols in the format cause the significant digits of the data value to be printed. All nonsignificant zeros are suppressed. This feature is called _zero suppression._

The comma symbol causes a comma to be placed every third digit to the left of the decimal. In this program the decimal is not being printed because only full dollar amounts are entered. Computation variables are rounded to the nearest dollar. This format also rounds to the nearest dollar. The next format group, which is for the salvage value, is similar. Finally, the last format group prints the integer value for the useful years.

The statement that causes 02$ to be printed is located outside the FOR/NEXT loop in statement 1110, so 02$ is printed only once for each asset. This feature is known as group printing. The statement that causes 03$ to be printed is contained within the loop, so 03$ is printed the specified number of times.

The statement in line 360 assigns an output format value to 03$. This format is used to print the annual depreciation and is called in line 1120. Statement 03$ is wrapped around in statement 360 because of the predetermined print line format.

Another method of editing output is shown in line 1160. Following is the format for this type of statement.

1160 LPRINT USING " ⟨String⟩ ⟨Format⟩ "; ⟨Parameter⟩

In this case, one variable is printed after a string message. Following is the print line.

1160 LPRINT USING "TOTAL DEPRECIATION $$###,###"; TD

The variable value for the total depreciation is printed according to the output specified in the edit format.

Two factors to consider when developing output edit statements are: the format of the output report, and the size of the variable values. When preprinted forms are being used, the format of the output must match the format of the form. Edit formats that are not large enough to contain the variable value may result in truncation of significant data.

A. Construct editing statements for the following problems using the symbols referenced in this textbook. The largest potential size of variable values is shown.

1. TOTAL EMPLOYEES ẋxx   TOTAL SALES $x,xxx.xx

2. DESCRIPTION   COST   QUANTITY   TOTAL

   xxxxxxxxxx   xxx.xx   x,xxx $x,xxx,xxx.xx

3.   NAME   HOURS   RATE   GROSS   NET

   xxxxxxxxxx   xx.x   xx.xx   x,xxx.xx   x,xxx.xx

B. Construct editing statements for the preceding problems using symbols for the computer system being used.

A. 1. 1000 PRINT USING "TOTAL EMPLOYEES ### TOTAL SALES
      $$###,###.##"; E, S

2. 400 LET H1$ = "DESCRIPTION COST QUANTITY TOTAL"
   410 LET H2$ = "&   ###.##   #,### $$###,###.##

3. 600 LET F1$ = "   NAME HOURS RATE   GROSS   NET"
   610 LET F2$ = "\   \ ##.# ##.## #,###.## #,###.##"

B. Answers vary due to system differences.

STEP Parameter

The FOR/NEXT loop control structure is executed in increments of +1 when the STEP parameter is not present. When increments other than +1 are desired, it is necessary to include the STEP parameter. Following is the STEP statement format.

FOR ⟨Counter⟩ = ⟨Parameter⟩ TO ⟨Limit⟩ STEP ⟨Parameter⟩

The following nested FOR/NEXT loop is used to control computations.

```
1110 FOR X = Y TO 1 STEP −1
1120     LPRINT USING 03$; X, FND(N)
1130     LET TD = TD + FND(N)
1140 NEXT X
```

The loop body includes statements 1120 and 1130. These lines are used for depreciation computations and printing. The user-defined function of FND(N) is presented in the next section.

The nested processing loop is controlled by the FOR/NEXT loop in statement 1110. The counter variable (X) is initialized with the value for the number of useful years (Y). If the number of useful years is four, X is initialized with that value. The counter is then incremented according to the STEP parameter. When a negative STEP clause is used, the loop is executed as long as the counter parameter is greater than or equal to the limit parameter. When a positive STEP clause is used, the loop is executed as long as the counter is less than or equal to the limit. In this case, the STEP is −1; therefore, every time the NEXT statement is executed, the counter variable is decreased by one. As soon as the counter is less than the limit parameter, the loop is terminated. The processing loop is executed four times if the number of years of useful life is four.

Record the value of C after the following statements have been executed. Assume that X = 10, Y = 0.25, and Z = 0.5.

1. 100 FOR A = 1 TO X
   110   LET C = C + 1
   120 NEXT A
   130 PRINT C
2. 200 FOR B = 0 TO X STEP Z
   210   LET C = C + 1
   220 NEXT B
   230 PRINT C
3. 300 FOR D = 0 TO 100 STEP X
   310   LET C = C + 1
   320 NEXT D
   330 PRINT C
4. 400 FOR E = Z TO Y STEP − .05
   .410   LET C = C + 1
   420 NEXT E
   430 PRINT C
5. 500 FOR F = X TO 0 STEP −1
   510   LET C = C + 1
   520 NEXT F
   530 PRINT C

1. C = 10
2. C = 11
3. C = 11
4. C = 6
5. C = 11

User-Defined Functions

A set of functions that can be used in a variety of applications is provided on computer systems. At certain times, however, a function not provided by the system may be required. In such cases, the programmer can develop user-defined functions. Generally, this is done when a specific function is required several times in the same program. Rounding is an example of a mathematic function that may be needed several times in the same program. User-defined functions are of small benefit if the routine is used only once. Following is the format for a user-defined function.

DEF FN ⟨Function Name⟩ (⟨Argument⟩) = ⟨Parameter⟩

The function statement must begin with the key word DEF, which is followed by FN. FN is followed by the function name, which is any valid variable name. Some systems also allow the use of string processing user-defined functions.

The *argument specification* is enclosed in parentheses which enable the function to be used at any point in the program to process any variable of the same type. The argument is referred to as the dummy specification. Any variable of the same type can be specified in the argument. For example, assume the program includes three different numeric variables each of which must be rounded to the nearest cent. The respective variable names are listed in the argument location when the user-defined function is called. Assume the program contains variables A, N, and P, and that these must be rounded to the nearest cent. This can be accomplished with one rounding statement. The appropriate variable name is placed in the argument location whenever rounding is needed.

The final portion of the user-defined function is the actual parameter, which is usually a computation. The following user-defined statement is a rounding statement.

300 DEF FNR(X) = INT(X * 100 + .5) / 100

This user-defined function can be called at any point in the program after it is defined. It can be used to round any numeric variable. If variables A, N, and P are to be rounded at different points in the program, the following statements will accomplish this purpose.

```
300 DEF FNR(X) = INT(X * 100 + .5) / 100
440 LET A = 143.763
450 PRINT FNR(A)
590 LET N = 23.375
600 PRINT FNR(N)
830 LET P = 16666.66666
840 PRINT FNR(P)
```

Printed result:

```
143.76
23.38
16666.67
```

Each of the respective variables are rounded to the nearest cent through the use of the user-defined function. When this procedure is used, the entire rounding statement does not have to be repeated.

The user-defined function in the example program is called in two separate lines. Statement 1120 results in the current year and the amount of depreciation being printed. The same function is used to accumulate total depreciation in line 1130. This saves having to repeat the entire computation.

The user-defined function in this program is contained in line 310 which follows.

310 DEF FND(N) = CINT(A * (X / Z))

The purpose of this statement is to compute the annual depreciation using the sum-of-year's-digits procedure and to round the result to the nearest dollar. The following formula is used to compute annual depreciation.

$$\text{DEPRECIATION} = \text{Amount to be depreciated} * \frac{\text{Current year}}{\text{Sum-of-year's-digits}}$$

The amount to be depreciated (A) is calculated by subtracting the salvage value (V) from the purchase cost (C). This amount is calculated in line 1010. The current year (X) is determined in the FOR/NEXT loop in statement 1110. The STEP of -1 causes the computation of the current year to begin with the year of purchase. The loop continues for the number of years of useful life (Y). The counter decreases by one each time the loop is executed thus giving the current year. The sum-of-year's-digits (Z) is computed in the FOR/NEXT loop in statements 1030 to 1050.

The system-defined function that rounds to the nearest integer is CINT. This function may not be available on some systems. The key word CINT results in rounding to the nearest integer or, in this case, to the nearest dollar.

The current year and the annual depreciation are printed as a result of statement 1120. Format statement 03$, which is declared in line 360, is used to control the output.

The program computes and prints the annual depreciation for each year of useful life. The total depreciation (TD) for each separate asset is accumulated in statement 1130.

Upon completion of the nested FOR/NEXT loop, which computes and prints the annual depreciation, the total depreciation for each separate asset is printed. Statement 1160 prints the total depreciation for each asset.

The output for this program is shown in figure 11–6. The annual depreciation and

BREAKFAST MACHINE TOOLS

S-Y-D DEPRECIATION REPORT

Asset	Cost	Salvage Value	Useful Years	Remaining Life	Annual Depreciation
TRUCK	$9,716	$1,000	3	3	$4,358
				2	$2,905
				1	$1,453

TOTAL DEPRECIATION $8,716

Asset	Cost	Salvage Value	Useful Years	Remaining Life	Annual Depreciation
ROBOT	$147,000	$7,000	10	10	$25,455
				9	$22,909
				8	$20,364
				7	$17,818
				6	$15,273
				5	$12,727
				4	$10,182
				3	$7,636
				2	$5,091
				1	$2,545

TOTAL DEPRECIATION $140,000

FIGURE 11–6
Function program
execution

123

total depreciation are computed for two assets. The first is a truck with a purchase cost of $9,716 and a salvage value of $1,000. The useful life is three years. Annual depreciation is computed at $4,358 for the first year, $2,905 for the second, and $1,453 for the third year respectively. The total depreciation is accumulated at $8,716.

The second asset is a robot with a purchase cost of $147,000, a salvage value of $7,000, and a useful life of ten years. Annual depreciation is computed for each of the ten years, resulting in total depreciation of $140,000.

PROGRAM DEVELOPMENT CHECKLIST

Use the following checklist to ensure that all necessary components are included in the program.

_____ Flowcharts and documentation

_____ Housekeeping tasks

_____ User-defined function

_____ Program control

_____ Headings

_____ Data entry

_____ Detail calculations

_____ Detail printing

_____ Summary calculations

_____ Summary printing

SUMMARY

The BASIC language contains procedures for developing nested loops, user-defined functions, and output editing. Nested FOR/NEXT loops are used in various business data processing applications, such as calculating sum-of-year's-digits depreciation, and sorting data values. The STEP parameter is included in FOR/NEXT statements when incrementation other than +1 is desired.

User-defined functions are an important procedure. They are commonly used when a mathematic or string processing function is to be used repeatedly in a program.

Output editing formats printed reports to include such features and symbols as dollar signs, commas, and zero suppression. Business reports commonly require the use of output editing.

BASIC Key Words/Operators Learned

CINT	Rounds to nearest integer.
CLS	Clears monitor screen.
DEF FNN	User-defined function.

HOME	Clears monitor screen.
LEN($)	String processing function. Returns number of characters in string.
LPRINT USING	Editing statement for printer.
PRINT CHR$( )	Control statement that programs printer width.
PRINT USING	Editing statement for monitor screen.
STEP	FOR/NEXT parameter for incrementation other than +1.
WIDTH	Programs printer width.

Instructions

PROGRAM ASSIGNMENT 11–1

Prepare the flowcharts and a structured BASIC program to print an Individual Retirement Account pay-out report for 24 months. Use prompting INPUT statements to enter the data. Use user-defined functions to compute the pay-out and interest, and to round numbers. The formula to be used and the processing steps follow.

MONTHLY INTEREST = (BALANCE − PAY-OUT) * (APR / 12)

Processing Steps

1. Subtract the amount of monthly pay-out from the previous balance.
2. Compute the interest on the remaining balance. The monthly interest is computed as follows:

   Interest = Balance * (APR /12).

   The APR must be entered as a decimal.
3. Add the amount of interest to the balance.

Data

Following is the data to be processed.

Account Name	Balance	Pay-out	APR
Miser, Lee	40,000	1,000	12%

Output Format

Print headings and detail lines. Print the monthly status for the first 24 months. Use report editing if available. Use group printing to print the account identification. Print detail lines for the monthly computations.

SLO-GRO FUND, INC.

IRA Pay-out

Name	Balance	Pay-out	Interest	Balance
Miser, Lee	$40,000	$1,000		
			xxx.xx	$xx,xxx.xx
			xxx.xx	$xx,xxx.xx

PROGRAM ASSIGNMENT 11–2

Instructions

Prepare the flowcharts and a structured BASIC program to print a present value table for different interest rates. Use prompting INPUT statements to enter the data. Use a nested FOR/NEXT loop to prepare the table for interest rates that range from 15% to 10% in increments of 1%.

Use user-defined functions to compute present value. The formula follows. (See Program Assignment 7–1 for present value discussion.)

$$\text{PRESENT VALUE} = \frac{F}{(1 + R)^Y}$$

Where:

$$F = \text{FUTURE AMOUNT}$$
$$R = \text{INTEREST RATE}$$
$$Y = \text{NUMBER OF YEARS}$$

Data

Following is the data to be processed. Data records include the future amount and the number of years.

Future Amount	Years
15,000	3
25,000	5
50,000	10

Output Format

Print headings and detail lines. Edit the output using report editing if available.

PORT-EX COMPANY

Sinking Fund Table

Present Value

Future Amount				Years	
	$15,000			3	
15%	14%	13%	12%	11%	10%
XX,XXX.XX	XX,XXX.XX	XX,XXX.XX	XX,XXX.XX	XX,XXX.XX	XX,XXX.XX

Future Amount				Years	
	$25,000			5	
15%	14%	13%	12%	11%	10%
XX,XXX.XX	XX,XXX.XX	XX,XXX.XX	XX,XXX.XX	XX,XXX.XX	XX,XXX.XX

SCREEN MANAGEMENT

OBJECTIVES

At the end of this chapter you should be able to perform the following tasks:

- Control program execution through the use of a menu.
- Locate printed output on the monitor screen.
- Control program execution through the use of WHILE loops.
- Utilize the LINE INPUT statement for data entry.
- Develop program branch techniques that utilize the ON statement.

12

SCREEN MANAGEMENT OPERATIONS

The growing use of computers with video display terminals (VDTs) or cathode ray tubes (CRTs) presents a new area of programming interest and skill. The programmer now must design monitor screen displays, so that the user can easily determine what needs to be done. In programs of this type the programmer usually provides the user with a greeting message that identifies the program and provides other pertinent information. The user then makes selections to accomplish his or her particular task.

The users may range from an inexperienced clerical worker to a master programmer. For this reason, the program must be designed to satisfy a diverse clientele. A summary of instructions and/or a detailed step-by-step list of procedures may have to be provided. The user can then select the level of instructions or background knowledge necessary for his or her purpose.

The user may also be provided with a list of possible operations that the program is capable of performing. This is commonly referred to as a MENU. Examples of business application programs that could use a menu are accounting operations, disk data file manipulation, and customer queries concerning account status. A typical menu for a program that creates, maintains, reads, or updates disk data files is shown in figure 12–1.

When the menu appears on the monitor screen, the user selects the option necessary to execute the task. Programs of this type commonly use the VDT for most processing steps. They may also include printed output. The format display upon the monitor screen should be designed so that the text, messages, and data are centered and easily read. Output format charts, templates, or overlays for this purpose can be designed or purchased.

FLOWCHARTS—MENU OPERATIONS

The example program, shown in figures 12–4 and 12–5, illustrates a program menu and user selection of options. The program computes compound interest for a savings account. Program components include user instructions, data entry, a menu, calculations, output display, and a loop.

The top-level flowchart, shown in figure 12–2, consists of seven blocks. The program is driven by the mainline routine. The processing blocks include the greeting, instruction, input, menu, 7.5% process, and 10.3% process subroutines.

The detailed logic flowchart in figure 12–3 provides the step-by-step logic for the program. The mainline routine acts as the driver module and controls program execution.

```
                        PORT-EX COMPANY

                 DATA FILE MANIPULATION PROGRAM

                             MENU


              OPTION                    DESCRIPTION

                1      .....      DETAILED INSTRUCTIONS

                2      .....      CREATE DATA FILE

                3      .....      UPDATE DATA FILE

                4      .....      DISPLAY DATA FILE

                5      .....      PRINT DATA FILE

                6      .....      DELETE DATA FILE

                7      .....      CREATE BACKUP FILE

                8      .....      QUIT

     ENTER OPTION   ...  ? _
```

FIGURE 12–1
Typical program menu

A WHILE-WEND control structure is used to control execution of the program loop. Program execution continues as long as the loop parameters are satisfied. The program loop consists of an input routine and a menu block that displays the options. Processing, computations, and termination of the program loop are dependent upon the user's selections.

The greetings subroutine causes the opening, or greeting message, to be displayed. This routine also enables the user to select whether detailed program instructions are desired.

Data is entered as a result of the input subroutine. The data to be entered consists of three variables.

Program options are displayed as a result of the menu subroutine. At this point, the user enters the appropriate option for the computation of compound interest. Messages that explain the options to the user are displayed. The user then selects the option that would accomplish the given task. In this section of the program, execution is controlled by user selection. Control is shifted to the appropriate processing subroutine based upon user selection.

There are two processing subroutines in this program: one is used to compute compound interest based upon a 7.5% rate; the other is used to compute compound interest based upon a 10.3% rate. The results are displayed upon the monitor screen after the computations are completed. Additional options can be included. Only two are processed here for the purposes of illustration.

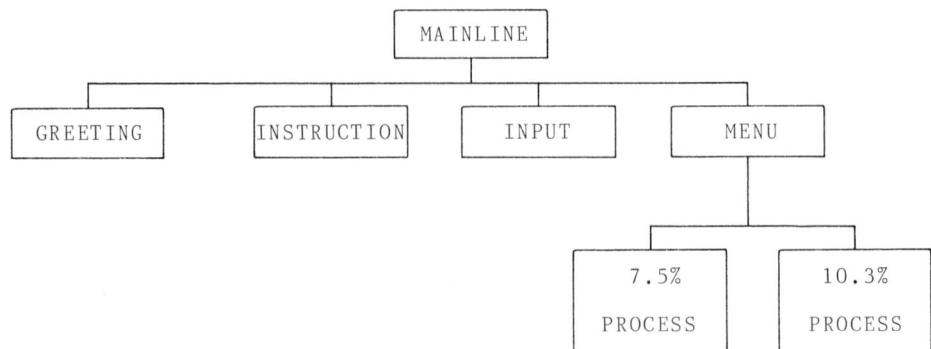

FIGURE 12–2
Top-level flowchart

EXAMPLE PROGRAM—COMPOUND INTEREST

The primary objective of this chapter is to illustrate the various BASIC statements used in screen set up and management. The example program calculates compound interest. A WHILE-WEND structure is used to control the program loop. A FOR/NEXT loop, which is used to compute and accumulate interest, is nested within the WHILE loop. A program menu is used to guide the user through the proper processing steps.

Figures 12–4 and 12–5 exhibit the example program for this chapter. Lines 100 through 860 are shown in figure 12–4. This portion of the program contains the program documentation, and the mainline control, greeting, and instruction modules. Lines 900 through 1640 are shown in figure 12–5. This portion of the program contains the input, menu, and process modules.

Program documentation and variable identification are shown in lines 100 to 240.

The mainline module in lines 300 to 400 is used as the command unit. Program output is displayed upon the monitor screen. There is no printed output from this program.

It is possible to set all numeric variables at zero and to initialize all strings as blank spaces, or null strings. This can be accomplished on most systems by using one command—CLEAR. The CLEAR command follows.

310 CLEAR

Use of the CLEAR command at the beginning of a program automatically initializes all numeric values at zero and all strings as null. Some systems automatically clear all variable values upon execution of the RUN command, but it is still a good idea to CLEAR them to be certain. By using the CLEAR command the programmer avoids having to initialize individual variables at zero.

CLEAR is also used as a program statement on some systems to reserve storage space for numeric or string variables. Following is the format used to reserve storage space.

510 CLEAR 25

This statement allows string variable values with a maximum length of 25 characters to be entered in this program.

The subroutine called in statement 320 is the greetings module. A greetings routine is used to inform the user about the general objectives of the program and to provide introductory information. Such facts as the program's purpose, version, the data files necessary, and the security classification can be included in the greetings module.

Statement 520 clears the monitor screen. The command CLS is used on this system. Other systems may use HOME to clear the screen.

The statement in line 530 is used to locate the cursor or printed output at a specific point on the screen. Several factors affect the programming of screen location. They are vertical and horizontal centering, available screen format, background and foreground color, and readability. Most monitor screens are 80 columns wide by 24 rows long, but some systems may have only 40 columns available. The format for the screen positioning statement follows.

530 LOCATE ⟨Row⟩, ⟨Column⟩, ⟨Cursor⟩

The row, or print line, parameter is the vertical position on the screen and the column is the horizontal location. The cursor parameter indicates whether the cursor is visible (1) or not (0). The following statement places a visible cursor at row 15 and column 20.

400 LOCATE 15, 20, 1

Program statements 520 through 540 follow.

520 CLS
530 LOCATE 10, 20
540 PRINT "SILAS MARNER NATIONAL BANK"

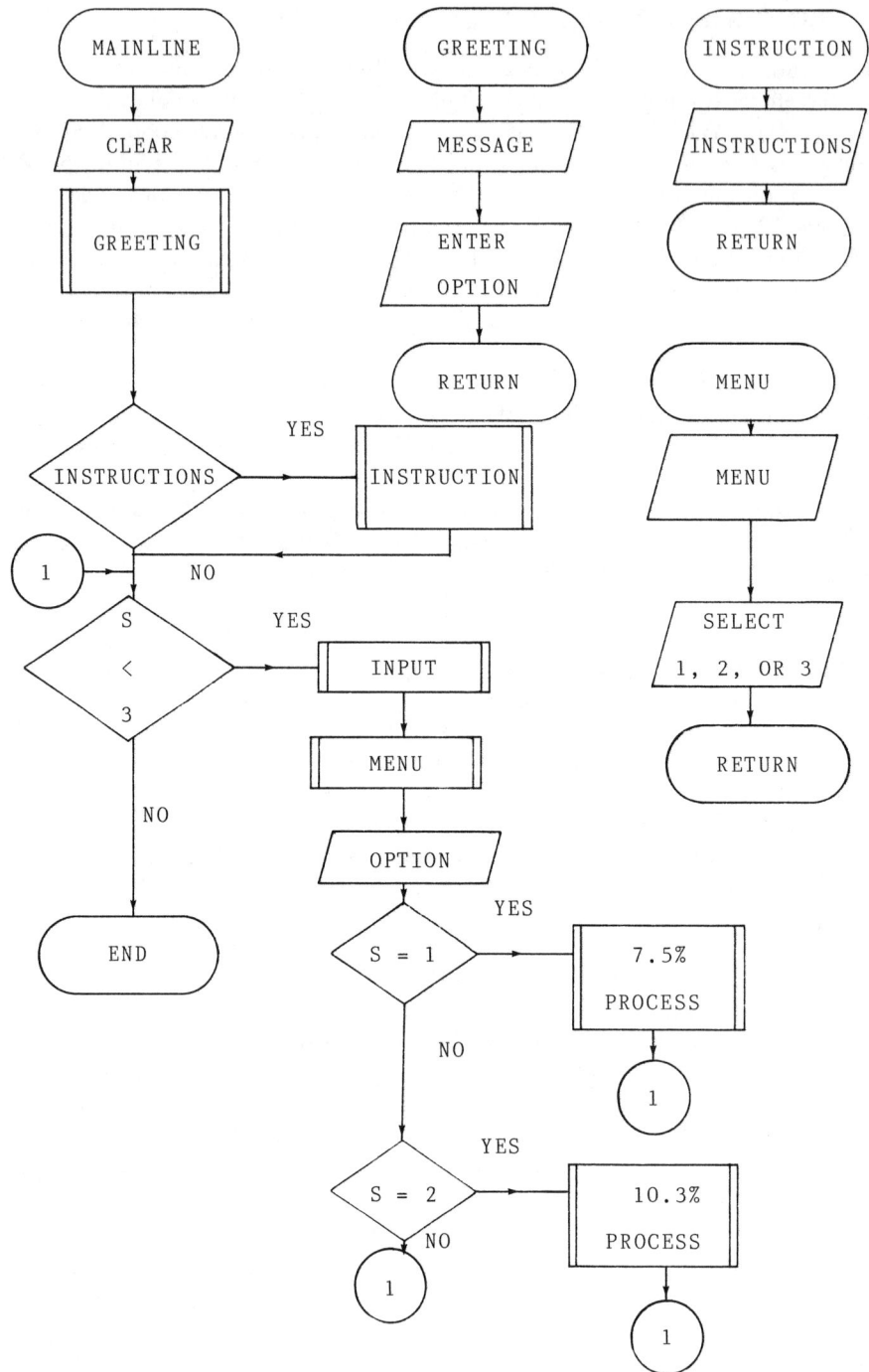

FIGURE 12–3
Detailed logic flowchart

The following message is displayed upon the screen as a result of statements 520 through 540.

SILAS MARNER NATIONAL BANK

Row 10, Column 20

The different systems use a variety of statements to locate output upon the monitor screen. The APPLE microcomputer, APPLESOFT BASIC, and MICROSOFT BASIC utilize the commands VTAB and HTAB to locate the cursor or print. VTAB is used for vertical print placement, and HTAB is used for horizontal or column placement. The APPLE monitor uses 40 or 80 columns depending upon hardware configuration, and 24

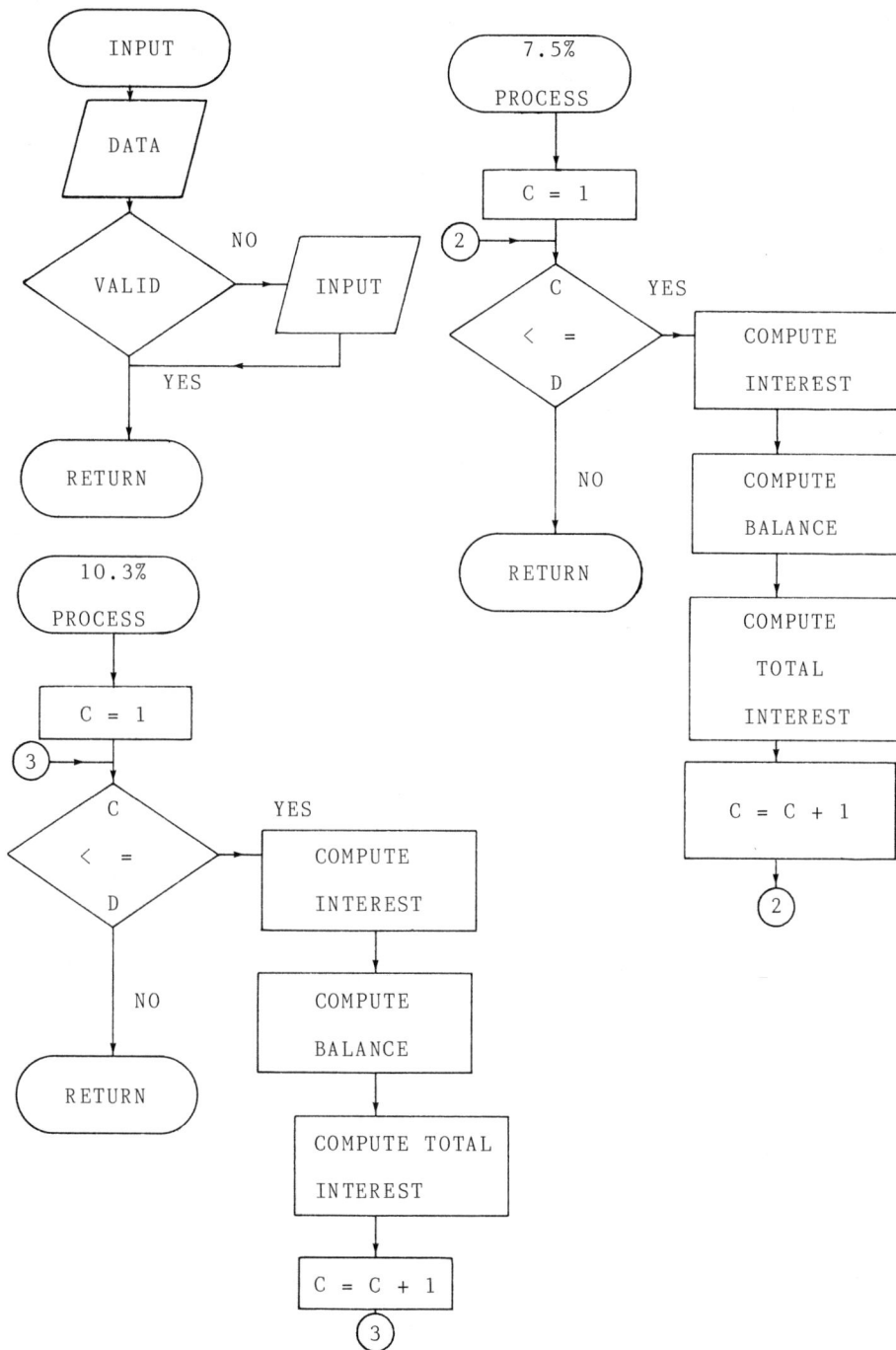

FIGURE 12–3
(Continued)

lines, or rows. The VTAB statement has a range of 1 to 24. The largest value for HTAB is 255—this produces wraparound.

The following statements are equivalent to program lines 520 through 540.

210 HOME
220 VTAB 10 : HTAB 20
230 PRINT "SILAS MARNER NATIONAL BANK"

TANDY-RADIO SHACK TRS-80 LEVEL II BASIC employs a different technique. There are 16 print lines, or rows, and 64 columns. This provides 16 times 64 or 1024 unique print locations. Vertical line 10 and column 20 in statement 220 would be print location 608 on the TRS-80. The TRS-80 system uses the PRINT @ statement to

```
100              REM   FIGURE   12-4      WRITTEN BY  LARRY FRY  4/19/83
110              REM   This program illustrates screen management.  It
120              REM   prepares compound interest for a variety of
130              REM   accounts.  A menu is provided for user selection.
140                                                                        REM
150              REM   *****  Variable Identification
160              REM          I$ .....  Instruction Call
170              REM          S  .....  User Selection
180              REM          N$ .....  Account Name
190              REM          B  .....  Account Balance
200              REM          D  .....  Days of Compounding
210              REM          C  .....  Loop Counter
220              REM          I  .....  Interest
230              REM          TI .....  Total Account Interest
240                                                                        REM
300              REM   *****  Mainline Control
310  CLEAR
320  GOSUB   510
330  IF LEFT$(I$,1) =  "Y" OR    LEFT$(I$,1) = "y" THEN GOSUB 710
340  WHILE   S < 3
350          GOSUB   910
360          GOSUB  1110
370          ON  S   GOSUB   1310,  1510
380  WEND
390  END
400                                                                        REM
510              REM   *****  Greetings Module
520  CLS
530  LOCATE   10, 20
540  PRINT "SILAS MARNER NATIONAL BANK"
550  LOCATE   14,20
560  PRINT "COMPOUND INTEREST PROGRAM"
570  LOCATE   20, 10
580  PRINT "PRESS RETURN  TO CONTINUE"
590  INPUT I$
600  CLS
610  LOCATE   20, 10
620  PRINT "DO YOU NEED PROGRAM INSTRUCTIONS (ENTER YES OR NO) ?"
630  LOCATE   22, 65, 1
640  INPUT  I$
650  RETURN
660                                                                        REM
700              REM   *****  Instructions Module
710  CLS
720  LOCATE   10, 20
730  PRINT "This program calculates compound interest."
740  PRINT
750  PRINT "A menu is used to describe processing steps."
760  PRINT
770  PRINT "Enter the listed option for the appropriate rate."
780  PRINT
790  PRINT "For example, enter  2  for the 10.3% rate."
800  PRINT
810  PRINT "The program can be terminated at any time by keying CTRL-BREAK."
820  PRINT
830  PRINT "PRESS RETURN  TO CONTINUE"
840  INPUT I$
850  RETURN
860                                                                        REM
```

FIGURE 12–4
Screen management program

locate output at specific screen positions. The following TRS-80 statements are equivalent to lines 520 through 540 in the program.

```
410 CLS
420 LET E$ = "SILAS MARNER NATIONAL BANK"
430 PRINT @ 608, E$
```

Some systems offer inverse display or output. This white-on-black or black-on-white display can be used on those systems that have the INVERSE command or its equivalent.

Enter the clear screen, cursor location, and monitor display commands for the system being used in Exercise 12–1.

```
900               REM  *****  Input and Verification Module
910   CLS  :  TI = 0
920   LOCATE  10, 10, 0
930   LINE INPUT  "Enter Account Name ";  N$
940   LOCATE  12, 10
950   INPUT  "Enter Account Balance ";  B
960   LOCATE  14, 10
970   INPUT  "Enter Number of Days ";  D
980   CLS
990   LOCATE  10, 10
1000  PRINT  "DATA  ENTRY VERIFICATION"
1010  PRINT :  PRINT
1020  PRINT  "ACCOUNT  NAME  =  ";  N$
1030  PRINT  "ACCOUNT BALANCE  =  ";  B
1040  PRINT  "NUMBER OF DAYS  =  ";  D
1050  PRINT :  PRINT
1060  INPUT "IS THE ABOVE DATA CORRECT (YES / NO)  "; I$
1070  IF LEFT$(I$,1) = "N" OR LEFT$(I$,1) = "n" THEN GOSUB 910
1080  RETURN
1090                                                              REM
1100               REM  *****  Menu Module
1110  CLS
1120  LOCATE  6, 38, 0
1130  PRINT  "M  E  N  U"
1140  LOCATE  10, 15
1150  PRINT  "OPTION                      DESCRIPTION"
1160  LOCATE  14, 17
1170  PRINT  "1     .........     PASSBOOK  -  7.5%  INTEREST"
1180  LOCATE  16, 17
1190  PRINT  "2     .........     I. R. A.  - 10.3%  INTEREST"
1200  LOCATE  18, 17
1210  PRINT  "3     .........     QUIT"
1220  LOCATE  22, 40, 1
1230  INPUT  "ENTER OPTION"; S
1240  RETURN
1250                                                              REM
1300               REM  *****  Process Module  -  7.5%
1310  FOR  C  =  1  TO  D
1320        LET I = INT(B * (.075 / 360)* 100 + .5) / 100
1330        LET B = B + I :  LET  TI = TI + I
1340  NEXT  C
1350  CLS
1360  LOCATE  15, 20, 0
1370  PRINT  "Name", "Days", "Interest", "New Balance"
1380  LOCATE  17, 5
1390  PRINT USING  "  &          ###        $$##,###.##     $$##,###.##"; N$, D, TI
1400  LOCATE  22, 20
1410  INPUT "PRESS RETURN TO CONTINUE ";  I$
1420  RETURN
1430                                                              REM
1500               REM  *****  Process Module  -  10.3%
1510  FOR  C  =  1  TO  D
1520        LET I = INT(B * (.103 / 360) * 100 + .5) / 100
1530        LET B = B + I :  LET TI = TI + I
1540  NEXT C
1550  CLS
1560  LOCATE  15, 20, 0
1570  PRINT  "Name", "Days", "Interest", "New Balance"
1580  LOCATE  17, 5
1590  PRINT USING  "  &          ###        $$##,###.##     $$##,###.##"; N$, D, TI
1600  LOCATE  22, 20
1610  INPUT "PRESS RETURN TO CONTINUE ";  I$
1620  RETURN
1630                                                              REM
1640  STOP
```

FIGURE 12–5
Screen management
program

**EXERCISE
12–1**

Monitor Screen Commands

Function	Textbook	System Command
Clear screen	CLS	_____
Vertical line	LOCATE	_____
Horizontal column	LOCATE	_____
Screen display	PRINT	_____
Inverse display		_____
Other		_____

The greetings module is shown in figure 12–6.

```
510                REM     *****    Greetings Module
520  CLS
530  LOCATE  10, 20
540  PRINT "SILAS MARNER NATIONAL BANK"
550  LOCATE 14, 20
560  PRINT "COMPOUND INTEREST PROGRAM"
570  LOCATE  20, 10
580  PRINT "PRESS RETURN TO CONTINUE"
590  INPUT I$
```

FIGURE 12–6
Greetings module

The screen display, which is a result of the program statements in the greetings module, is shown in figure 12–7. Three print lines are displayed. The user controls the amount of time that the screen is displayed. This gives the user as much time as is required to view the display and complete such tasks as loading data file disks. To move the program to the next screen, the user presses RETURN. In this program, the INPUT statement in line 580 is used to continue execution. Some systems use the INKEY command as follows.

```
580 PRINT "PRESS ANY KEY TO CONTINUE"
590 I$ = INKEY$
```

The INKEY$ command allows the user to depress any key to continue execution of the program. When INKEY$ is used, a one-character string is returned from the keyboard.

Other systems use GET, rather than INKEY$. The GET and INKEY$ statements

```
               SILAS MARNER NATIONAL BANK


               COMPOUND INTEREST PROGRAM
```

FIGURE 12–7
Greetings screen display

```
?              PRESS RETURN  TO CONTINUE
```

```
600  CLS

610  LOCATE  20, 10

620  PRINT "DO YOU NEED PROGRAM INSTRUCTIONS (ENTER YES OR NO)? "

630  LOCATE  22, 65, 1

640  INPUT I$

650  RETURN
```

FIGURE 12–8
Selection of instructions

are similar to an INPUT statement, except that only one character is entered and RE-TURN does not have to be pressed. INKEY$ and GET cause the character to be entered automatically without keying RETURN. The character entered may or may not appear on the screen.

The purpose of these commands is to halt program execution until the user is ready to proceed. INKEY and GET may not be available on all systems, or they may not produce full screen display. In such cases, INPUT may have to be used.

Lines 600 to 650 are used to provide the user with an option concerning the selection of program instructions. The instructions can be as brief or as detailed as necessary depending upon program clientele. The size and difficulty of the program as well as the user's level of experience determine the extent of instructions offered. The program statements shown in figure 12–8 are used to offer instructions.

The screen is cleared and the message is displayed upon line 20. The visible cursor is displayed upon line 22. The screen display from this program segment is shown in figure 12–9. The user selects instructions and/or the level of instructions necessary according to the program. If instructions are desired, the user enters YES or yes. If instructions are not needed, the user enters NO or no.

Program statement 330 in the mainline module is used to branch to the instruction module as follows.

330 IF LEFT$(I$,1) = "Y" OR LEFT$(I$,1) = "y" THEN GOSUB 710

If the user's response is YES or yes, the system branches to the instruction module. The program uses the string processing feature LEFT$, which checks to determine if the character on the far left of the variable I$ is equal to "Y" or "y". The logical operator OR is used to check the value. Following is the format for the string processing feature that evaluates the character on the far left of the variable.

LEFT$(⟨String Variable, Parameter⟩)

The statement LEFT$ means that the portion of the string on the far left is to be checked. The string variable identifies the string to be examined, and the parameter identifies the position, or positions, to be checked. The parameter can range from 1 to 255 on most systems. The following LEFT$ segment is used in the program.

LEFT$(I$,1)

In this example, the character on the extreme left of the string I$ is examined to determine if it is equal to "Y" or "y".

The characters can be displayed for the user through the use of the following statements. Assume X$ is equal to "STRUCTURED BASIC".

1000 A$ = LEFT$(X$, 5)
1010 PRINT A$

Following is the message printed as a result of this operation.

STRUC

```
       DO YOU NEED PROGRAM INSTRUCTIONS (ENTER YES OR NO) ?

                                                                ?
```

FIGURE 12–9
Instructions screen
display

The following string processing features are used to manipulate the middle and extreme right portions of strings.

MID$(⟨String⟩, ⟨Beginning Character⟩, ⟨Parameter⟩)

RIGHT$(⟨String⟩, ⟨Parameter⟩)

The RIGHT$ function is equivalent to LEFT$, except that the far right portion of the string is manipulated. The MID$ function processes the middle portion of the string beginning with the character specified and continuing the number of characters identified in the parameter.

Statement 330 results in the execution of the instruction module if "Y" or "y" is entered in the INPUT statement in line 640. Instructions contained in the module can be as brief or as detailed as necessary. For this example, a brief message, which outlines the major steps in the program, is displayed. The routine is shown in figure 12–10.

CLS is used to clear the screen. The first print line is located at row 10 beginning at column 20 in statement 720. In the rest of the module PRINT statements are used to control placement of the display. Statements that use LOCATE or its equivalent, as shown in the greetings module, can also be used to control the display.

There is an alternate method of terminating program execution—keying CTRL-BREAK. This combination of keys terminates execution of the program and shifts control back to the command, or BASIC system, level. Some systems use CTRL-RESET or similar combinations for this purpose.

The screen display that is produced by the instruction module is shown in figure 12–11. The instructions are displayed until the user presses the RETURN key.

Program execution is controlled by the WHILE-WEND statements shown in lines 340 through 380. Systems that do not support the WHILE structure use the FOR/NEXT structure to control program loop execution. The WHILE statement tests the parameters

```
700          REM      *****      INSTRUCTIONS MODULE

710   CLS

720   LOCATE  10,20

730   PRINT "This program calculates compound interest."

740   PRINT

750   PRINT "A menu is used to describe processing steps."

760   PRINT

770   PRINT "Enter the listed option for the appropriate
         rate."

780   PRINT

790   PRINT "For example, enter 2 for the  10.3% rate."

800   PRINT

810   PRINT "The program can be terminated at any time by
         keying CTRL-BREAK."

820   PRINT

830   PRINT "PRESS RETURN TO CONTINUE"

840   INPUT I$

850   RETURN
```

FIGURE 12–10
Instructions module

```
        This program calculates compound interest.

A menu is used to describe processing steps.

Enter the listed option for the appropriate rate.

For example, enter  2  for the 10.3%  rate.

The program can be terminated at any time by keying CTRL-BREAK.

PRESS RETURN  TO CONTINUE
?
```

FIGURE 12-11
Instructions

before the loop is executed. It is used extensively in structured programming, particularly with disk files. When a FOR/NEXT loop is used the general assumption is that the loop will be executed at least once and probably more than that. A WHILE loop is not necessarily executed; it depends upon the parameters. Following is the WHILE statement format.

WHILE ⟨Parameter⟩ ⟨Logical Operator⟩ ⟨Parameter⟩

        .
        .   Loop Body
        .

WEND

The WHILE loop is executed as long as the statement parameters are satisfied. If the parameters are not satisfied, the loop is not executed.

The WHILE-WEND loop in the example program is shown in figure 12–12.

The WHILE-WEND loop is executed as long as variable S is less than three. When this variable value is equal to or exceeds the parameter of three, the loop is terminated. Variable S is initialized at zero by the CLEAR statement in line 310. Therefore, the beginning value of S is less than three and the loop is executed on the first pass through the program.

```
340   WHILE   S < 3

350           GOSUB   910

360           GOSUB   1110

370           ON S GOSUB 1310, 1510

380   WEND
```

Figure 12–12
WHILE-WEND loop

Evaluate the following WHILE loops.
1. Assume that F = 0, A = 40, and R = 2.
   100 WHILE F = 0
   110   IF A <= 40 THEN B = B + A * R
   120   IF B > 100 THEN F = 1
   130   LET A = 30
   140 WEND
   150 PRINT "F = "; F, "A = "; A, "B = "; B
2. Assume that F = 1, A = 40, and R = 2. Evaluate the loop in question one.
3. Assume that X = 0, A = 0, and B = 1. Evaluate the following loop.
   200 WHILE X < 5
   210   IF A < B THEN A = A + 2 : X = X + 1
   220   IF A > = B THEN B + B + 1
   230 WEND
   240 PRINT "X = "; X, "A = "; A, "B = "; B

SELF-TEST
12–1

1. F = 1   A = 30   B = 140
2. The WHILE loop is not executed because F is greater than 0.
3. X = 5   A = 10   B = 10

The WHILE-WEND loop in the example includes GOSUB statements that call the input and menu modules, and a program branch. Line 350 calls the input module. This module, located in lines 900 through 980, contains statements used to enter the data records and to verify that the values entered are correct. Line 910 is used to clear the monitor screen and to reinitialize the total interest variable at zero. A LINE INPUT statement is used in line 930 to enter the account name. The following format is used for LINE INPUT statements.

930 LINE INPUT "⟨Prompt⟩"; ⟨Variable⟩

Following is statement 930.

930 LINE INPUT "Enter Account Name "; N$

An advantage of the LINE INPUT statement is that it accepts the entire value entered from the keyboard while ignoring delimiters such as commas. All characters entered are accepted as part of N$ until RETURN is pressed. RETURN terminates entry of the data value.

Lines 1000 through 1050 cause the values that have been entered to be displayed. Statement 1060 asks the user to verify that the values are correct. This is a *data verification* routine that should be provided to the user whenever possible. If the user determines that the values are incorrect, the branch statement in line 1070 recalls the data entry subroutine.

The menu module is called in statement 360. In this subroutine, the available functions are listed and the user is asked to select the proper option. The screen displayed is shown in figure 12–13. Three options are shown in the example for illustration purposes; however, more could be added. The user enters the appropriate option. If the QUIT option is entered, the program is terminated because variable S is then equal to three.

Statement 370 contains a program branch procedure called the ON-GOSUB statement that is commonly used in menu operations. The following format is used for the ON-GOSUB statement.

ON ⟨Variable⟩ GOSUB ⟨Parameter⟩, GOSUB ⟨Parameter⟩

This statement can also be used in the form GO TO. The ON-GOSUB statement is the BASIC language format for the *CASE OF* structure. Program execution branches to the subroutine indicated by the variable parameter. Following is the program branch statement.

370 ON S GOSUB 1310, GOSUB 1510

```
                          M  E  N  U


       OPTION                        DESCRIPTION



          1      . . . . . . . . .   PASSBOOK  -  7.5%  INTEREST

          2      . . . . . . . . .   I. R. A.  - 10.3%  INTEREST

          3      . . . . . . . . .   QUIT
```

FIGURE 12–13
Program menu

```
                                     ENTER OPTION?
```

Name	Days	Interest	New Balance
SIMPSON, SARAH	60	$12.60	$1,012.60

PRESS RETURN TO CONTINUE ?

FIGURE 12-14
Program execution

When variable S contains a value of one, the program branches to subroutine 1310. As the value of S increases in increments of one, the respective subroutine is called. Therefore, if S is valued at two, the program branches to line 1510. Although only two parameters are shown here, more could be added. For example, if variable S were valued at seven, the seventh subroutine listed would be called. However, the number of parameters and subroutines referenced in the ON-GOSUB statement should not be excessive.

The subroutine called when the first option is chosen calculates and prints compound interest at a 7.5% rate. Daily compounding is performed for the appropriate number of days in the nested FOR/NEXT loop as follows.

```
1310 FOR C = 1 TO D
1320     LET I = INT(B * (.075 / 360) * 100 + .5) / 100
1330     LET B = B + I : LET TI = TI + I
1340 NEXT C
```

The daily interest is computed and rounded for each day as a result of statement 1320. The daily interest is then added to the accumulated balance and interest in statement 1330. The loop is executed for the correct number of days. After the computations have been completed, statements 1350 to 1400 cause the output to be displayed on the screen. The monitor screen display shown in figure 12–14 is an example of program execution for the 7.5% rate.

In the same manner, the subroutine in statements 1510 to 1610 calculates and displays interest at the 10.3% rate. The second option is used to call this subroutine.

The program is terminated by the user entering the third option, QUIT, during the menu display. It can also be terminated by entering CTRL-BREAK or CTRL-RESET as described in the instructions to the program user.

PROGRAM DEVELOPMENT CHECKLIST

Use the following checklist to ensure that all necessary components are included in the program.

_____   Flowcharts and documentation

_____   Program control

_____   Greeting subroutine

_____   Instruction subroutine

_____   Menu subroutine

_____   Processing subroutine

SUMMARY

The BASIC language contains procedures for managing output display upon the monitor screen and for controlling program execution through the use of a menu. Subroutines are designed to greet the user and to prompt the user to perform tasks that control execution of the program. The presence of a menu in a program enables users of all levels of skill to use the program.

The WHILE-WEND structure is used to control execution of the program loop. It is used to test the parameters before a loop is executed.

Program branch procedures use the CASE OF structure. The ON statement is the BASIC language format for the CASE procedure.

BASIC Key Words/Operators Learned

CLEAR	Clears variables. Sets numeric variables at zero and string variables at null.
GET	Accepts one character from keyboard.
HTAB	Locates horizontal, or column, placement of output on screen.
INKEY$	Accepts one character from keyboard.
LEFT$	String processing function. Evaluates left-most characters of string value.
LINE INPUT	Accepts input line from keyboard.
LOCATE	Locates vertical and horizontal placement on screen.
MID$	String processing function. Evaluates middle segment of string value.
ON-GOSUB	CASE structure program branch.
PRINT @	Locates vertical and horizontal placement on screen.
RIGHT$	String processing function. Evaluates right-most portion of string value.
VTAB	Locates row, or vertical, placement on screen.
WEND	Marks end of WHILE loop.
WHILE	Program loop structure.

Keyboard Operations Learned

CTRL-BREAK	Terminates program execution and returns control to command level.
CTRL-RESET	Terminates program execution and returns control to command level.

PROGRAM ASSIGNMENT 12–1

Instructions

Prepare the flowcharts and a structured BASIC program to display and/or print an account status report. Use prompting INPUT statements to enter the data. When the system permits, use greetings, instructions, menu, and processing subroutines to display relevant information to the user on the monitor screen. Include the following options in the menu:

- Display current account balance.
- Display customer purchase.
- Display customer payment.
- Compute monthly interest (2% per month) on past due accounts.
- Print monthly statement.
- Quit.

Use FOR/NEXT or WHILE-WEND statements for program loop control. Use the ON-GOSUB statement for program branches.

Processing Steps

1. Add customer purchases to the account balance.
2. Subtract customer payments from the account balance.
3. Compute monthly interest for those accounts that are past due (no payment on balance since last statement), and add the interest to the balance.
4. Print a monthly statement for each data record.

Data

Following is the data to be processed. The variables are the account name, beginning balance, payments, purchases, and status.

Account Name	Beginning	Payments	Purchases	Status
Bro-Kemp	$1,137.94	$500.00	$100.00	OK
Space-Air	3,450.00	0	100.00	1 month
Office-Mod	750.00	250.00	400.00	OK
Hi-Tech	0	0	150.00	OK

Output Format

When it is possible, program the greeting, instruction, and menu subroutines to be displayed on the monitor screen. Use printed messages if a monitor screen is not available for the displays.

Print the monthly statements. Following is the output.

PORT-EX COMPANY

Monthly Statement for January, 1985

BEGINNING BALANCE	$X,XXX.XX
PAYMENTS	X,XXX.XX
PURCHASES	X,XXX.XX
SERVICE CHARGE	XX.XX
ENDING BALANCE	$X,XXX.XX

ACCOUNT STATUS (CURRENT OR PAST DUE)

SUBTOTALS AND FINAL TOTALS

OBJECTIVES

At the end of this chapter you should be able to perform the following tasks:
- Develop programs that prepare business reports with subtotals and final totals.
- Develop methodology for preparing summary reports.
- Utilize control break procedures to compute subtotals and final totals.
- Develop programs that reuse DATA statements.
- Develop methodology for exceptions reports.

SUBTOTAL AND FINAL TOTAL OPERATIONS

A common requirement of business data processing is the preparation of reports that include subtotals and final totals. Some examples of this type of report are plant production totals by operating division, store sales by department, customer distribution by zip code, and costs by project number.

The data processing procedure used in this type of report is to initialize the key, or test, variable with the value indicated in the first data record. As long as the key field and the data value being entered are the same, the subtotal (or subtotals) are accumulated. When the data value being entered differs from the key field, subtotal operations are performed. The data processing term associated with these subtotal operations is *control break*. A control break occurs when there is a difference between the key field and the data value entered. Upon detection of a control break the system prints a subtotal line. It also performs several other tasks. Following are the control break tasks.

1. Subtotal line is printed.
2. Final totals are accumulated.
3. Subtotal (or subtotals) is reinitialized at zero.
4. Value of key, or test, field is changed to reflect new data value.

These tasks are referred to as subtotal operations. They are performed each time there is a control break.

When a subtotal report is prepared, the data to be processed must be arranged in a predetermined sequence. The arrangement can be based upon the department number, the customer number, the sales region, the plant name, the salesperson's name, or other predetermined keys.

The key field must be determined in cooperation with the program user. Once the key field is determined the data must be arranged in sequence to correspond with the program. This can be accomplished at data entry or the data in existing data files can be sorted using a sort routine based upon the key field. Sort procedures are presented in Chapter 16.

Business reports may include more than one level of subtotals. A balance sheet contains totals for the account section and for the separate controlling accounts. Other reports may call for total company production by department within each separate plant. These programs may include two or more levels of subtotals or control breaks in addition to the final totals.

At times, programs are written to accomplish more than one processing task. The same set of data is reused instead of developing a new program. BASIC has the capability to accomplish this when READ-DATA statements are used in processing. In effect, the data pointer is restored to the top of the data list.

FLOWCHARTS—SUBTOTAL OPERATIONS

The example program for this chapter is designed to perform two tasks. The first task is to print a production report that includes subtotals by production plant and final totals for the company. The second is to examine plant production to determine if production quotas have been satisfied. The same set of DATA statements is used to accomplish both of the tasks.

The top-level flowchart is shown in figure 13–1. The mainline routine controls execution of the program. The headings, input, read, subtotal, control break, summary, and exceptions subroutines constitute the program body.

Housekeeping tasks are performed at the beginning of the program before the mainline routine takes control of program execution. The variables are cleared, the key field used to test for control breaks is initialized, and output statements are formatted. The value assigned to the key field should reflect the data contained in the first record. In this program, an assignment statement is used; however, READ-DATA or INPUT statements could also be utilized.

The detailed logic flowchart for the example is shown in figure 13–2. The mainline routine uses two separate FOR/NEXT loops to control execution of the subtotal and exception reports.

The heading routine prints the report and column headings. Three heading lines are printed.

Two INPUT statements are used in the input subroutine: one is used to enter the number of records for program loop control; the other is used to enter the production quota for the exceptions report.

A FOR/NEXT structure is used to control execution of the loops for the subtotal and exceptions reports. The subtotal loop consists of the read subroutine and two program branch statements. These branch statements are used to test for key field equality with the data being entered. If the fields are not equal, there is a break in control and the control break subroutine is executed. The control break subroutine executes the subtotal operations, which include printing the subtotal, accumulating the final total, reinitializing the subtotal, and resetting the key field. When the fields are equal, the subtotal routine is performed. The subtotal subroutine adds the summary totals.

After this loop is terminated, the subtotal for the last group is printed. The program loop is executed according to the number of data records, so the final subtotal is not

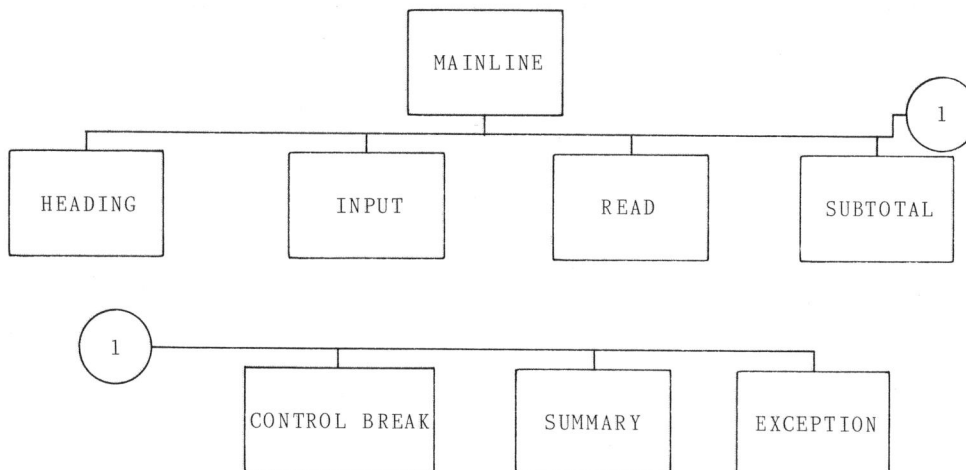

FIGURE 13–1
Top-level flowchart

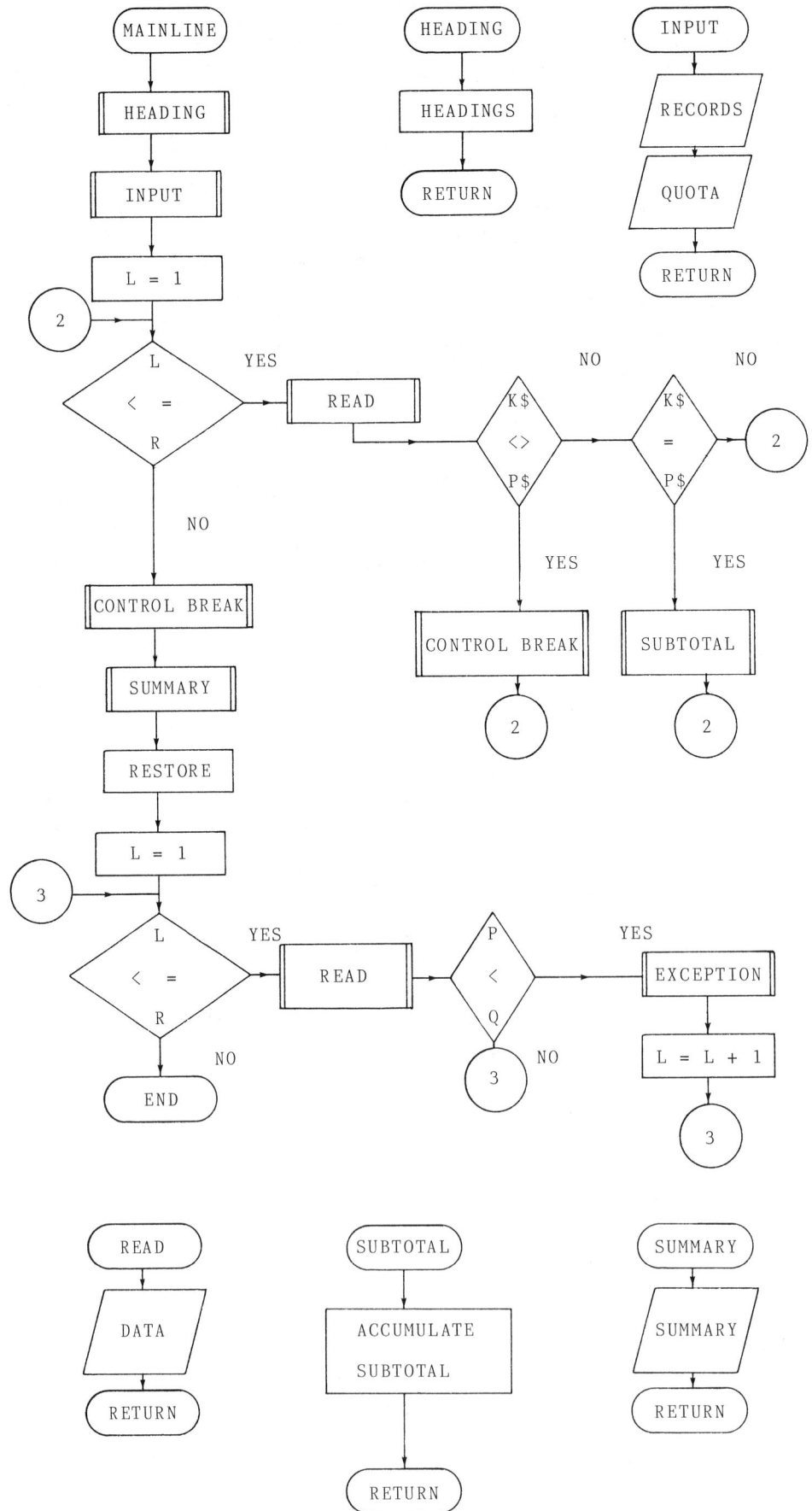

FIGURE 13–2
Detailed logic flowchart

CONTROL BREAK

SUBTOTAL

ACCUMULATE
FINAL TOTAL

REINITIALIZE
SUBTOTAL

RESET KEY
FIELD

RETURN

EXCEPTION

EXCEPTIONS

RETURN

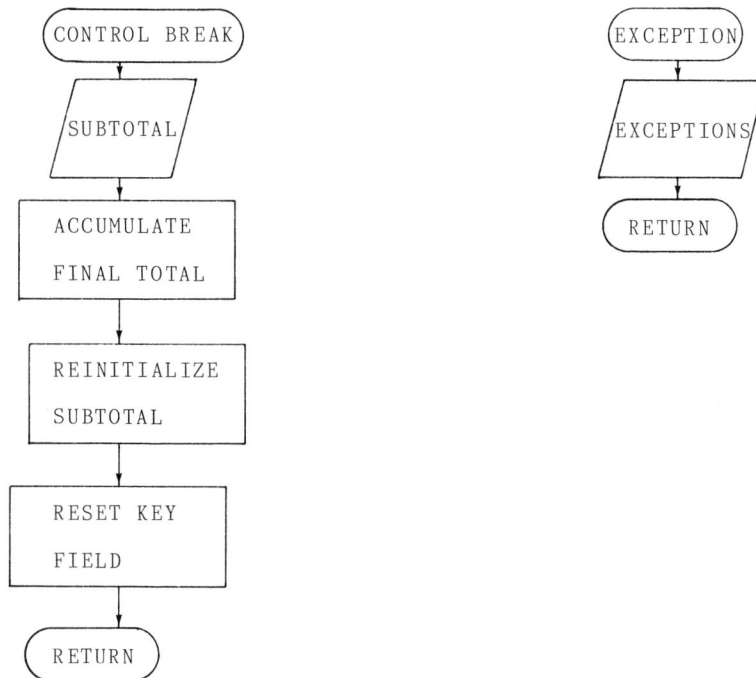

FIGURE 13–2
(Continued)

printed within the loop. This is taken care of by including the control break routine after the termination of the loop.

Summary totals are printed next. In this program, the final total production for all plants is printed.

The second phase of the program compares plant production by shift to the quota. This illustrates the use of the RESTORE statement, which resets the data pointer at the top of the data list. A FOR/NEXT structure is used to control loop execution. This loop includes the read routine and a program branch statement. If the production for that shift is less than the quota, the exceptions subroutine is performed. The program is terminated at the conclusion of this loop.

EXAMPLE PROGRAM—SUMMARY AND EXCEPTIONS REPORTS

The primary objective of this chapter is to demonstrate the BASIC language procedures used to produce reports that include subtotals and final totals. These are called summary reports because they summarize the data records. The example also shows the procedure necessary to reuse listed DATA statements to accomplish a secondary program objective. Two FOR/NEXT loops are used to control execution of the program's two phases.

The program for this chapter is exhibited in figures 13–3 and 13–4. Lines 100 through 790 are contained in figure 13–3 while 800 through 1610 are shown in figure 13–4. Figure 13–3 contains program documentation, program initialization, housekeeping, and the mainline and heading modules. The input, read, subtotal, control break, summary, and exceptions modules are shown in figure 13–4.

Program documentation and variable identification are contained in lines 100 through 250. Housekeeping tasks are detailed in statements 300 to 380. The system is cleared in line 310. In statement 330 the key field (K$) is initialized with the initial data value.

330 LET K$ = "Flint"

This assignment statement is used to initialize the key field with the plant name for the first data record. Although the plant name is used in the example, other variables, such as the plant number, could be used. The data should be arranged in some predeter-

```
100            REM      FIGURE  13-3  WRITTEN BY  LARRY FRY  4/20/83
110            REM      This program illustrates the accumulation
120            REM      and printing of subtotals and final totals
130            REM      in business reports.  The  RESTORE Command
140            REM      is used to check production quotas.
150                                                                      REM
160            REM      Variable Identification
170            REM      K$  .....  Key Field
180            REM      P$  .....  Plant Name
190            REM      S   .....  Production Shift Number
200            REM      P   .....  Production Amount
210            REM      Q   .....  Production Quota
220            REM      ST  .....  Plant Subtotal
230            REM      FT  .....  Final Total
240            REM      L   .....  Loop Counter
250            REM      R   .....  Loop Limit
260                                                                      REM
300            REM      Program Initialization
310   CLEAR
320            REM      Key variable initialization
330   LET K$ = "Flint"
340            REM      PRINT USING Format Statements
350   LET 01$ = "          PLANT                          PRODUCTION"
360   LET 02$ = "        \            \           $$###,###.##"
370   LET 03$ = "FINAL TOTAL PRODUCTION    $$###,###.##"
380                                                                      REM
500            REM  *****  Mainline Module
510   GOSUB  710
520   GOSUB  810
530   FOR  L  =  1  TO R
540           GOSUB  910
550           IF LEFT$(K$,3) <> LEFT$(P$,3) THEN GOSUB 1210
560           IF LEFT$(K$,3) =  LEFT$(P$,3) THEN GOSUB 1010
570   NEXT  L
580   GOSUB  1210
590   GOSUB  1310
600   RESTORE
610   FOR  L  =  1  TO R
620           GOSUB  910
630           IF P < Q THEN GOSUB 1410
640   NEXT   L
650   END
660                                                                      REM
700            REM  *****  Headings Module
710   LPRINT  :  LPRINT
720   LPRINT TAB(21);  "PORT-EX COMPANY"
730   LPRINT
740   LPRINT TAB(21);  "PRODUCTION REPORT"
750   LPRINT
760   LPRINT  01$
770   LPRINT
780   RETURN
790                                                                      REM
```

FIGURE 13–3

Subtotal program

mined sequence corresponding with the key field initialization. The first statements in the DATA module shown in figure 13–4 are records for the Flint plant.

An assignment statement is used in the example; however, INPUT or READ-DATA statements could be used equally as well for this purpose. INPUT statements could be used in an interactive subtotal program.

Statements 350 through 370 are used to provide the formats for printing the column headings and for printing edited summary lines. These format lines are identified as 01$, 02$, and 03$.

The mainline module is shown in statements 500 through 650. This routine is used to control program execution. The program is divided into two phases, each of which is controlled by a FOR/NEXT loop. The first phase computes and prints subtotals and final totals, and the second phase checks production against the quota. There are nine data records to be processed, so the loops are executed accordingly. The same set of data is used in both phases.

```
800                 REM  *****  Input Module
810   CLS
820   INPUT  "Enter Number of Data Records  ";  R
830   INPUT  "Enter Production Quota ";  Q
840   RETURN
850                                                            REM
900                 REM  *****  Read Module
910   READ P$, S, P
920   RETURN
930                                                            REM
1000                REM  *****  Subtotal Accumulation Module
1010  LET ST = ST + P
1020  RETURN
1030                                                           REM
1200                REM  *****  Control Break Module
1210  LPRINT : LPRINT USING 02$; K$, ST
1220  LET  FT = FT + ST
1230  LET  ST = 0
1240  LET  K$ = P$
1250  RETURN
1260                                                           REM
1300                REM  *****  Summary Module
1310  LPRINT : LPRINT USING 03$; FT
1320  RETURN
1330                                                           REM
1400                REM  *****  Exceptions Module
1410  LPRINT : LPRINT : LPRINT : LPRINT
1420  LPRINT USING "SHORTFALL-PLANT    &    SHIFT  #      AMOUNT $$#,###.##";
P$, S, Q-P
1430  RETURN
1440                                                           REM
1500                REM  *****  Data to be Processed
1510  DATA  "Flint",  1,   4975.75
1520  DATA  "Flint",  2,   4599.99
1530  DATA  "Flint",  3,   4405.70
1540  DATA  "Pontiac",1,  4666.67
1550  DATA  "Pontiac",2,  4584.33
1560  DATA  "Pontiac",3,  4702.21
1570  DATA  "Windsor",  1,   4888.88
1580  DATA  "Windsor",  2,   4576.77
1590  DATA  "Windsor",  3,   4407.00
1600                                                           REM
1610  STOP
```

FIGURE 13–4
Subtotal program

Line 510 calls the headings module which prints the report and column headings. The report headings are printed as a result of statements 720 and 740. The output format line identified as 01$ is used to print column headings.

Statement 520 calls the input module which is used to enter the loop parameter and the production quota. There are nine data records, so the loop limit is set at nine. The shift production quota is $4,500. This figure is used as the test value in the second phase of the program.

A FOR/NEXT structure is used to control execution of the program loop. The loop is executed according to the limit parameter entered in the input module. The first program loop consists of the read module and two program branch statements. The data to be entered in the read module includes the plant name (P$), the shift number (S), and the production amount (P).

The branch statements within the program loop are used to determine if a control break has occurred. The processing tasks performed depend upon the results of the branch statements that follow.

```
550     IF LEFT$(K$,3) <> LEFT$(P$,3) THEN GOSUB 1210
560     IF LEFT$(K$,3)  =  LEFT$(P$,3) THEN GOSUB 1010
```

Statement 550 compares the three characters on the far left of the key field with the three characters on the far left of the data value (P$). The LEFT$ function is used solely for illustration purposes. It is not necessary to use the LEFT$ function in a program such as this.

If the variables are not equal, the control break module is performed. There are several concepts to remember when working with control break methodology. First, when the key field and the data value entered are equal, there is no break in control. As long as the data value entered is equal to "Flint", there is no control break. The data processing tasks performed within the loop should be limited to accumulating the subtotal(s). There should be no printing at this time, unless detail print lines are desired. The procedure is to provide summary printing at the subtotal and final total levels, unless detail printing is required.

Secondly, when the key field and the data value are not equal, there is a break in control. For example, when the data value entered does not equal "Flint", a control break occurs. DATA lines 1510, 1520, and 1530 each contain the value "Flint" for the variable P$. Statement 1540, however, contains the value "Pontiac". When this statement is executed, there is a break in control. The same thing happens when DATA line 1570 is entered because the data value changes to "Windsor".

Finally, there are specific procedures that should be performed whenever there is a control break. Control break methodology calls for the execution of the following tasks when there is a break in control:

1. Print the subtotal summary line.
2. Accumulate final total(s) by adding subtotal(s).
3. Reinitialize subtotal(s).
4. Reset the key field to reflect the new data value.

A review of control break procedures reveals that it is logically correct to perform the not equal branch before executing the equal one. Therefore, statement 550 is the program branch that tests for not equal conditions, whereas line 560 is the branch that tests for equal values. When there is a break in control, it is necessary to print and reset the subtotal. Then, the subtotal value for the new item must be accumulated before the READ statement is executed again. Otherwise, the production amount for the new plant that was entered and caused the control break would be lost. These procedures are performed in the correct logical order when control break tests are arranged in the order shown in statements 550 and 560.

When the key field (K$) equals the data value entered, program control drops to statement 560. The evaluation of statement 560 results in a true response, so subroutine 1010 is called. This routine accumulates the subtotal. The following calculation is executed as long as the key field is equal to the data value.

1010 LET ST = ST + P

The production amount for the current plant is added to the subtotal. More than one subtotal can be accumulated at this point in the program.

When the key field does not equal the data value, statement 550 is evaluated as true. This causes the control break module to be called. The program segment shown in figure 13–5 is the control break subroutine.

Statement 1210 causes the subtotal line for the referenced plant to be printed. The output is edited through the use of LPRINT USING. The output format statement is contained in line 360. The output format is identified as 02$. Notice that the plant name printed in line 1210 is identified as K$. The value in the data field (P$) has already changed to something new. A control break has occurred because the values of K$ and P$ are not equal. This is the only format that can be used on line 1210. The value of P$ has changed, but K$ has not. This is the reason K$ is printed at this point.

```
1210    LPRINT : LPRINT USING 02$; K$, ST

1220    LET FT = FT + ST

1230    LET ST = 0

1240    LET K$ = P$

1250    RETURN
```

FIGURE 13–5
Control break
subroutine

Line 1220 accumulates the final total for all of the plants. Each time there is a break in control, the subtotal for each plant is added to the final total.

The subtotal is reinitialized at zero in line 1230. The value for each of the plants begins at zero. It is not correct to accumulate the production from one plant with that of another.

Finally, the value in the key field, K$, is reset to reflect the new plant name. Obviously, the value in P$ has changed, because this is the only way the control break module is performed. After statement 1240 is executed, K$ will contain the same value as P$. This procedure is used to change K$ from "Flint" to "Pontiac", and from "Pontiac" to "Windsor".

Program control then returns to statement 560 which is evaluated as true. The subtotal accumulation module is executed and the current value of P is added to the subtotal.

For those systems that support the IF-THEN-ELSE branch structure, the following statement is equivalent to lines 550 and 560.

550 IF LEFT$(K$,3) = LEFT$(P$,3) THEN GOSUB 1010
ELSE GOSUB 1210 : GOSUB 1010

If the key field is equal to the data value, the subtotal accumulation module (GO-SUB 1010) is performed. Otherwise, the control break module and the subtotal accumulation module are executed. The ELSE portion of the statement is GOSUB 1210 followed by GOSUB 1010.

Execution of the FOR/NEXT loop continues according to the limit parameter. There are nine data records. At the conclusion of the first program loop, it is necessary to print the subtotal for the last production plant. In this case, the Windsor subtotal has not yet been printed.

When the FOR/NEXT structure is used to control the program, the last subtotal is not printed within the loop. Therefore, it is necessary to call the control break module one additional time to print the last subtotal and to accumulate the final total. Statement 580, which is listed after the FOR/NEXT loop, performs these operations for the last plant.

The final total (FT) is printed as a result of line 590. This statement calls the summary module. Output format 03$, which is assigned in line 370, is used to print the final total.

The second phase of the program compares the production amount for each shift with the quota that is entered in line 830. The quota is $4,500. The original set of data is used in both phases of the program. This is accomplished through the use of the RE-STORE command, which is shown in line 600. RESTORE simply resets the data pointer at the top of the data list. This enables the program to reuse the DATA statements. The second phase of the program is added to illustrate the RESTORE command.

Another FOR/NEXT loop is used to control execution of the second phase of the program. The read subroutine is called in statement 620. This is an example of the benefit of program modularity where the same module is called from different points during execution. The same module is reused wherever possible in the program. This saves resources by avoiding duplication of the same function. The development of modules that can be recycled is one of the strengths of structured programming methodology.

Statement 630 is a program branch that compares the shift production amount with the quota. If the production amount is less than the quota, there is a shortfall. When evaluation of statement 630 yields a true result, the exceptions module is called.

The exceptions module causes a line that identifies the production plant, the shift, and the amount of shortfall to be printed. Line 1420 is used to format the printed line. The LPRINT USING statement edits the printing. The program is terminated following execution of the second phase.

The output from the program is shown in figure 13–6. The first part of the report lists the three subtotals for the production plants. This is followed by the total for all of the plants. The second phase output, which follows, produces two printed lines identifying those production shifts that have shortfalls.

```
                        PORT-EX COMPANY

                        PRODUCTION REPORT

              PLANT                          PRODUCTION


              Flint                        $13,981.44

              Pontiac                      $13,953.21

              Windsor                      $13,872.65

    FINAL TOTAL PRODUCTION        $41,807.30



    SHORTFALL-PLANT    Flint    SHIFT   3    AMOUNT   $94.30



    SHORTFALL-PLANT    Windsor  SHIFT   3    AMOUNT     $93.00
```

FIGURE 13–6
Subtotal program
execution

PROGRAM DEVELOPMENT CHECKLIST

Use the following checklist to ensure that all necessary components are included in the program.

_____ Flowcharts and documentation

_____ Program control

_____ Housekeeping tasks

_____ Key field initialization

_____ Control break tests

_____ Subtotal accumulation

Control break operations

_____ Print subtotal line

_____ Accumulate final total

_____ Reinitialize subtotal

_____ Reset key field

_____ Print summary lines

SUMMARY

The BASIC language contains procedures for preparing business reports that accumulate subtotals and final totals. Business data processing often requires the preparation of summary reports that accumulate subtotals and final totals. The data processing concept used to accumulate totals is the control break.

The RESTORE command is used to recycle values in DATA statements that have been used previously in a program.

Program branch procedures are used to prepare an exceptions report.

BASIC Key Words/Operators Learned

RESTORE   Places the data pointer at the top of the data list.

Instructions

PROGRAM
ASSIGNMENT
13–1

Prepare the flowcharts and a structured BASIC program to print a summary report that identifies the number of charge customers and the total amount charged by zip code. Accumulate and print subtotals for the total number of charge customers and the total amount charged for each zip code. Compute and print final totals for the store chain.

Following is the data to be processed. Use READ and DATA statements to enter the data. Data records include the zip code, the telephone exchange, the number of charge accounts, and the amount charged.

Data

Zip Code	Exchange	Charge Accounts	Amount
80226	836	235	$94,187.77
80226	838	192	62,339.05
80226	879	317	114,368.41
80215	452	112	39,879.40
80215	456	67	28,221.91
80228	357	271	87,510.65
80228	339	189	65,773.71
80210	573	48	17,805.93
80210	596	61	23,437.67

Output Format

Print headings and summary lines. Use report editing if available. Print one summary line for each zip code. Print a summary line for the final totals.

MILE-HIGH DEPARTMENT STORE

Charge Customer Distribution

Zip Code	Accounts	Amount
80226	x,xxx	$xxx,xxx.xx
80215	x,xxx	$xxx,xxx.xx
FINAL TOTALS	x,xxx	$xxx,xxx.xx

Instructions

PROGRAM
ASSIGNMENT
13–2

Prepare the flowcharts and a structured BASIC program to print a summary report that computes and prints the amount sold by salesperson and by region. Use two levels of control breaks. Calculate and print subtotals for each salesperson in the first level. In the second level, accumulate and print subtotals for each sales region. Include the number of salespeople and the amount sold in the sales region subtotals. Accumulate and print final company totals for the number of salespeople and the amount sold.

Following is the data to be processed. Use READ and DATA statements to enter the data. Data records include the salesperson's name, region, and amount of sales.

Data

Name	Region	Sales
Smith	NE	$23,457.97
Smith	NE	14,447.31
Smith	NE	11,811.94
Hawes	NE	16,667.41
Schoe	SE	10,551.11
Schoe	SE	12,237.99
Rit	SE	19,841.37
Fores	SE	9,875.05
Fores	SE	7,302.19

Output Format

Print headings and summary lines. Use report editing if available. Print one summary line for each salesperson. Print a separate summary line for each respective sales region and print a summary line for final totals.

PORT-EX COMPANY

Sales Summary

	Region	Salesperson	Amount
	NE	Smith	$xxx,xxx.xx
	NE	Hawes	$xxx,xxx.xx
NE REGION		xx SALESPERSONS	$xxx,xxx.xx SALES
FINAL TOTALS		XX SALESPERSONS	$XXX,XXX.XX SALES

PROGRAM ASSIGNMENT 13–3

Instructions

Prepare the flowcharts and a structured BASIC program to print a balance sheet. Include summary totals for each controlling account and for each account section in the balance sheet. Use two levels of control breaks. In the first level, calculate and print a subtotal for each controlling account. In the second level, accumulate and print subtotals by account section. Account section totals for assets and liabilities should be calculated as follows. The amount of capital is calculated by subtracting total liabilities from total assets.

Following is the data to be processed. Use READ and DATA statements to enter the data. Data records include the account section, the controlling account, the subsidiary account, and the subsidiary account balance.

Data

Account Section	Controlling Account	Subsidiary Account	Account Balance
Asset	Cash	Petty Cash	$ 75.00
Asset	Cash	Checking	675.00
Asset	Cash	Savings	750.00
Asset	Account Receivable	J. Jones	3,330.00
Asset	Account Receivable	A. Locke	2,475.00
Asset	Office Machines	Word Processor	5,000.00
Asset	Office Machines	Computer	4,565.00
Asset	Office Machines	Typewriter	1,000.00
Asset	Office Furniture	Desk	300.00
Asset	Office Furniture	Cabinet	700.00
Asset	Building	Building	25,000.00
Liability	Account Payable	Apex Supply	1,916.75
Liability	Account Payable	Super Dist	1,437.00
Liability	Note Payable	1st Bank	5,000.00

Output Format

Print headings and summary lines. Use report editing if available. Print one summary line for each individual controlling account. Print a separate summary line for each account section. Calculate and print the amount of capital (capital = assets − liabilities).

PORT-EX COMPANY

NORTHEAST SALES DIVISION

Balance Sheet for Period Ending December 31, 1984

Cash	$xxx,xxx.xx	
Account Receivable	$xxx,xxx.xx	
Office Machines	$xxx,xxx.xx	
Office Furniture	$xxx,xxx.xx	
Building	$xxx,xxx.xx	
TOTAL ASSETS		$XXX,XXX.XX
Account Payable	$xxx,xxx.xx	
Note Payable	$xxx,xxx.xx	
TOTAL LIABILITIES		$XXX,XXX.XX
CAPITAL		$XXX,XXX.XX

ONE-DIMENSIONAL TABLES

14

OBJECTIVES

At the end of this chapter you should be able to perform the following operations:
- Develop programs that use one-dimensional tables.
- Utilize proper procedures to reserve memory space for tables.
- Prepare programs that manipulate data through the use of subscripts.
- Identify common errors associated with tables and subscripts.

TABLES AND SUBSCRIPTS

This chapter introduces the data processing concept of *one-dimensional tables*. Business applications that can use one-dimensional tables include preparation of payrolls, customer account reports, and manipulation of inventory data. Sophisticated data processing operations, such as searching data lists for specified values and sorting data into a predetermined sequence, require additional BASIC features. Some of the BASIC operations presented earlier can be used to perform searches or sorts, but the tables are more efficient. Program execution, speed and efficiency become important as the problems and programs become larger and more rigorous.

The best program methodology for search or sort procedures, at this level, involves the use of one-dimensional tables. In a one-dimensional table the data values are arranged in a column giving each value a unique address. This allows access to each data value individually. The tables can contain string or numeric data. For example, the inventory for the Food Circus Groceries is arranged in a series of one-dimensional tables. One of the tables is for the product name and another is for the product number. Other tables cover the quantity on hand, the price, and the total value.

The values for the product number include the following: 1479, 4375, 9705, 6479, and 1622. The variable name should reflect the fact that the table is numeric. The data values are arranged in column, or table, form as follows. The table name for the product number variable is I.

PRODUCT NUMBER TABLE

I	
Element Number	*Data Value*
1	1479
2	4375
3	9705
4	6479
5	1622

The strength of handling data in table form is that it is possible to address each individual element with one variable name. There are five data values stored in Table I, and each has a separate element, or cell, number. The data processing procedure used to address individual elements in a table is the *subscript*. Subscripts allow individual data values to be addressed and accessed. BASIC subscripts use the form I(1). The table variable name I(1) references and addresses an individual data value in table I. In this example, the data value of I(1) is equal to 1479. Each of the other data values can also be accessed or addressed by its unique element number, or subscript.

The table variable known as I can contain more than one value. Therefore, I(X) can reference or access many separate and unique data values. Each data value has its own element number. A subscript is used to address each element.

Table I with appropriate subscripts follows.

Table Subscript	Element Value
I(1)	1479
I(2)	4375
I(3)	9705
I(4)	6479
I(5)	1622

The subscripts are shown here as integers. Subscripts may be integers, variables, or any valid BASIC expressions. The following examples are valid subscripts.

I(10)
A(I)
A$(4)
P(X)
P(X * 2)
P$(I + 1)

String values may be placed in table form. Subscripts are used to access each individual element. The product name table identified as P$ follows.

PRODUCT NAME TABLE

P$

Table Subscript	Element Value
P$(1)	Veg Juice
P$(2)	Pap Towels
P$(3)	Mushrooms
P$(4)	Ground Round
P$(5)	Orange Jui

Tables and subscripts enable relative identification of data values in separate tables. The preferred procedure is for each individual subscript to address the corresponding values in the separate tables. This means that the data must be arranged in a predetermined sequence in each table. Corresponding data values can then be addressed by the unique subscript. This procedure adds tremendous power and speed to programs. The two tables and their corresponding subscripts follow.

Table Subscript	Product Number	Product Name
X	I(X)	P$(X)
1	1479	Veg Juice
2	4375	Pap Towels
3	9705	Mushrooms
4	6479	Ground Round
5	1622	Orange Jui

The data is arranged to correspond between the tables. The relative position of the data in the product number table is arranged to correspond with the position of the data in the product name table. All other tables are arranged in the same manner. Therefore, subscript 3 refers to product number 9705 and to product name Mushrooms, respectively.

Additional tables and elements can be added. System memory is the ultimate limit upon the number of tables and/or element length.

Systems may require that memory space be reserved when working with tables. A general rule is that tables exceeding ten elements must be declared in a DIMENSION statement. Although tables with less than ten elements may not have to be declared for the particular system, it is usually recommended that space be reserved.

Be sure to check system characteristics regarding string tables. Some systems limit the number of characters permitted in each string element value. Other systems limit the number of characters, but offer the opportunity to increase the element value size through the use of certain system commands. Obviously, string tables that contain large data values consume a large portion of memory. System commands may have to be utilized when processing large string values.

Once data is arranged in a table, it is possible to perform sophisticated operations, such as searches or sorts. Table search procedures are presented in Chapter 15. Sort operations are discussed in Chapter 16.

Data can be arranged in two dimensions or more. Two-dimensional tables are used to arrange data in rows and columns. These are presented in Chapter 17.

FLOWCHARTS—ONE-DIMENSIONAL TABLES

The example program for this chapter reads data, places it in several one-dimensional tables, performs computations, and prints the results.

Figure 14–1 contains the top-level flowchart. Program execution is controlled by the mainline routine. The program body consists of the heading, read, calculation, print, and summary subroutines.

Housekeeping tasks are executed at the beginning of the program before the mainline module takes control of program execution. These include clearing the system, reserving memory for the data tables, and formatting output lines.

Figure 14–2 contains the detailed logic flowchart. The report and column headings are printed as a result of the headings subroutine before the program loop is executed.

A FOR/NEXT structure is used to control execution of the program loop. There are ten data records in the program, so the loop parameter is initialized at ten. The loop body consists of the read, calculation, and output subroutines. After the program loop is terminated, the totals are printed in the summary routine.

The read routine causes the data to be entered and loaded into the respective tables. Four separate tables are created as a result of the read block.

The calculation subroutine consists of two processing steps. The item price is calculated by multiplying the price by the quantity elements in the respective tables. The final total price is then accumulated.

Detail printing is controlled by the output routine. Data values from the fives tables are printed.

At the conclusion of the program loop the summary line is printed.

EXAMPLE PROGRAM—TABLE PROCESSING

The primary objective of this chapter is to illustrate the BASIC language procedures used to process and manipulate data that is arranged in one-dimensional tables. The data is entered, processed, and printed while in table form.

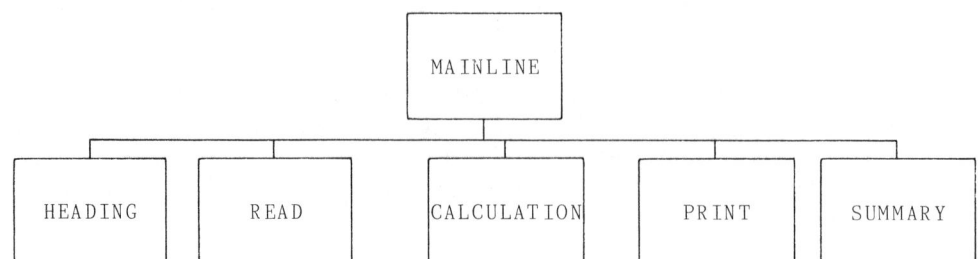

FIGURE 14–1
Top-level flowchart

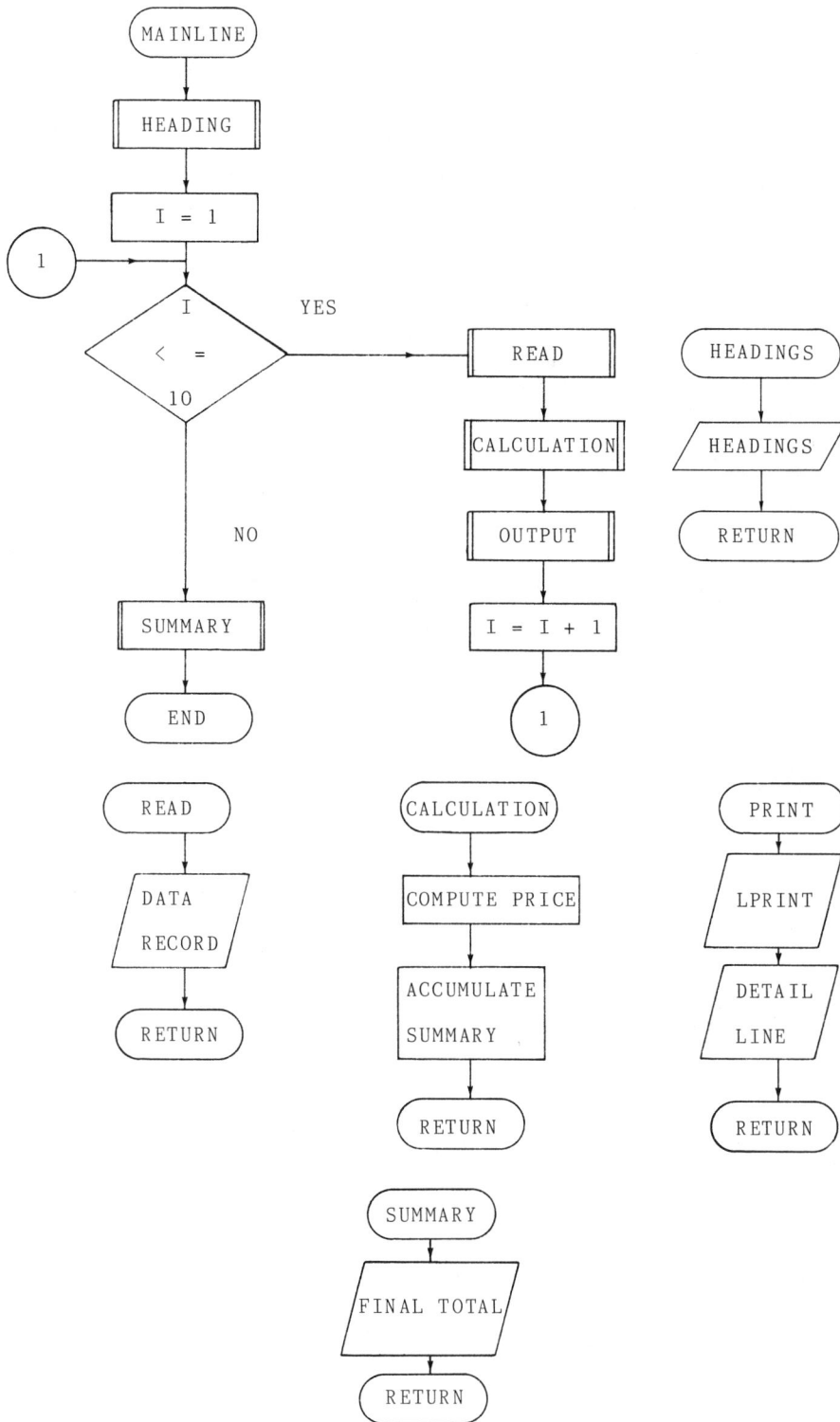

FIGURE 14-2
Detailed logic flowchart

The example program is exhibited in figure 14–3. Program documentation and variable identification are shown in lines 100 to 210. Program initialization and housekeeping tasks are contained in lines 300 through 380. The system is initialized in statement 310. The CLEAR command, if it is used, should be listed before the tables are declared.

System memory is reserved for the one-dimensional tables in statement 340. The BASIC key word used to declare tables and reserve memory on most systems is DIMENSION, or DIM. Following is the BASIC format for DIM.

340 DIM Variable (⟨Parameter⟩), Variable (⟨Parameter⟩)

```
100     REM         FIGURE  14-3     WRITTEN BY LARRY FRY     4/25/83
110     REM         This program prepares an inventory report from
120     REM         one-dimensional tables.
130     REM         *****       Variable Identification
140     REM         I      .....  Subscript Index
150     REM         I(I)   .....  Product   ID
160     REM         P$(I)  .....  Product Name
170     REM         Q(I)   .....  Quantity
180     REM         P(I)   .....  Item Price
190     REM         T(I)   .....  Total Price
200     REM         T(0)   .....  Final Total Price - Zero Subscript Element
210                                                                         REM
300     REM         *****       Program Initialization
310   CLEAR
320                                                                         REM
330     REM         *****       Dimension Tables
340   DIM  P$(10), I(10), P(10), Q(10), T(10)
350                                                                         REM
360     REM         *****       Output Format Statements
370   LET 01$ = "Identification        Name        Price      Quantity       Total"
380   LET 02$ = "     ####           \              \    ##.##         ###        ###.##"
390                                                                         REM
400     REM         *****       Mainline Control
410   GOSUB   510
420   FOR I  =  1   TO  10
430          GOSUB   610
440          GOSUB   710
450          GOSUB   810
460   NEXT   I
470   GOSUB   910
480   END
490                                                                         REM
500     REM         *****       Headings Module
510   LPRINT CHR$(12)
520   LPRINT TAB(25);   "FOOD CIRCUS GROCERIES"
530   LPRINT
540   LPRINT TAB(27);   "INVENTORY REPORT"
550   LPRINT
560   LPRINT   01$
570   LPRINT
580   RETURN
590                                                                         REM
600     REM         *****       Read Data and Load Tables
610   READ I(I), P$(I), P(I), Q(I)
620   RETURN
630                                                                         REM
700     REM         *****       Calculation Module
710   LET T(I) = P(I)  *   Q(I)
720   LET T(0) = T(0) + T(I) :   REM T(0) = ZERO SUBSCRIPT ELEMENT
730   RETURN
740                                                                         REM
800     REM         *****       Output Module
810   LPRINT
820   LPRINT USING 02$;   I(I), P$(I), P(I), Q(I), T(I)
830   RETURN
840                                                                         REM
900     REM         *****       Total Module
910   LPRINT
920   LPRINT USING "Final Total Price   $$###,###.##";   T(0)
930   RETURN
940                                                                         REM
1000    REM         *****       Data to be Processed
1010   DATA  1479, "Veg. Juice", 1.19, 55, 4375, "Pap. Towels", .57, 75
1020   DATA  9705, "Mushrooms", .95, 25, 6479, "Ground Round", 3.96, 60
1030   DATA  1622, "Orange J.", 1.11, 50, 5605, "Clean Det.", 1.60, 40
1040   DATA  6366, "Chicken", 4.50, 35, 9944, "Lettuce", .79, 50
1050   DATA  7777, "Cola Soda", 1.89, 35, 8411, "Frozen Corn", .67, 30
1060                                                                        REM
1070   STOP
```

FIGURE 14–3
Table processing
program

The variable name(s) declared in the DIM statement may be for numeric or string variables. On most systems parameters may be integers, variables, or valid BASIC expressions.

The DIM statement automatically initializes all numeric elements at zero and all string elements as blank on most systems. One or more tables may be declared in the DIMENSION statement. Each table declaration is separated by a comma. The DIMENSION statement must be listed early in the program before there are any references to the tables. Program line 340 follows.

340 DIM P$ (10), I(10), P(10), Q(10), T(10)

The number of table elements desired is enclosed in parentheses. The number of elements declared may exceed the number actually used in the program. The segment of the DIM statement used for the product name, P$(10), limits this string table to 11 elements on the system—P$(0) (zero subscript element) through P$(10). The OPTION BASE key words may be necessary to use the zero element on some systems. OPTION BASE is explained later in this chapter.

Five separate one-dimensional tables are declared in the DIM statement. They are the product name (P$), identification (I), price (P), quantity (Q), and total (T). Each of the tables can be declared in separate DIM statements, or they can be combined into one statement as shown. Tables may only be declared once. The declaration of the same table in more than one DIM statement can cause errors.

On most systems a DIMENSION statement is not required when the DIM size is ten or less; however, it is recommended that one always be included when tables are used. A SUBSCRIPT OUT OF RANGE or an UNDIMENSIONED TABLE error may result if tables are not declared.

Lines 370 and 380 contain output format statements that are used in printing the column headings and the detail lines. The output formats are assigned to strings 01$ and 02$.

The mainline module is shown in lines 400 to 490. This routine is used to control program execution. Line 410 calls the heading module. The report and column headings are printed as a result of this routine.

A FOR/NEXT structure is used to control the program loop and to set the subscripts for the various tables. There are ten data records to be processed in the program, so this number is used to set the loop limit parameter. The program loop body consists of the read, calculation, and output modules.

The FOR/NEXT loop counter variable is used for subscript purposes in the read, calculation, and output modules. There are ten data records; therefore, the table subscripts should range from one to ten. The use of a FOR/NEXT loop to vary the subscripts from one to ten is an expedient and efficient programming practice. One FOR/NEXT loop is used to read, process, and print the various tables. It is possible to use separate FOR/NEXT loops for each of these tasks. They are combined into one loop in this program for illustration purposes. The FOR/NEXT loop follows.

```
420 FOR I = 1 TO 10
430    GOSUB 610
440    GOSUB 710
450    GOSUB 810
460 NEXT I
```

The counter variable I varies according to the loop parameters. Variable I is also used as the subscript in the read, calculation, and print modules.

Execution of the read module is controlled in line 430. The READ statement in line 610 follows.

610 READ I(I), P$(I), P(I), Q(I)

Execution of the READ statement during the first pass through the program loop causes certain data values to be entered into the respective table elements.

Notice that there is a numeric table identified as variable I and a subscript identified by the same variable name. These are two separate variable names: one is the product identification table; the other is the loop counter and subscript. This is a valid procedure on most systems.

During the first pass through the loop, all table subscript references are valued at one. The first pass includes the read, calculation, and print module operations. After the first pass through the loop, the various table elements contain the following values.

I	I(I)	P$(I)	P(I)	Q(I)	T(I)
1	1479	Veg. Juice	1.19	55	65.45

Variable I contains a value of one during the first pass, so all such subscript references point to the preceding data values.

Following is a trace of the FOR/NEXT loop for the first three passes and comprehensive table element values.

I	I(I)	P$(I)	P(I)	Q(I)	T(I)
1	1479	Veg. Juice	1.19	55	65.45
2	4375	Pap. Towels	0.57	75	42.75
3	9705	Mushrooms	0.95	25	23.75

The loop is executed for a total of ten passes. The loop parameter serves as the subscript varying from one to ten. The respective element number, or subscript, is assigned to the data values as the loop is executed.

Line 440 calls the calculation module which follows.

710 LET T(I) = P(I) * Q(I)
720 LET T(0) = T(0) + T(I)

Variable T(I) is computed during each pass through the program loop. During the first pass through the loop, subscript I is equal to one. Subscript values during the first pass are as follows.

710 LET T(1) = P(1) * Q(1)
720 LET T(0) = T(0) + T(1)

T(1) is equal to the product of the first element in the price table and in the quantity table. T(1) is equal to the product of 55 and 1.19 or 65.45.

The final total price is accumulated in statement 720. Variable T(0) (zero subscript element) is used to accumulate the final total price during each pass through the loop. The zero subscript permits a separate variable element outside the range of the FOR/NEXT loop, which varies from one to ten. The zero element is available on most systems.

Some systems require the use of the OPTION BASE key word to use the zero element. The key word format follows.

300 OPTION BASE ⟨Parameter⟩

The OPTION BASE key word declares the minimum, or base, subscript value. The default value is zero on most systems. This means that the OPTION BASE key word does not have to be included in the program if subscript zero is used. When OPTION BASE is used, it must be listed like the DIM statement before any reference to the table. The OPTION BASE parameter may be a zero or one.

Technically, there are 11 elements in table T(I) because the DIM statement T(10) permits the use of T(0) (zero subscript element) automatically. There are 11 variables within the range of T(0) through T(10).

On each pass through the FOR/NEXT loop the appropriate values are placed in the T(I) table elements. The element values in the total table are the product of the respective elements in the price and quantity tables.

```
               FOOD CIRCUS GROCERIES

                INVENTORY REPORT

  Identification      Name       Price    Quantity     Total


       1479        Veg. Juice     1.19       55        65.45

       4375        Pap. Towels    0.57       75        42.75

       9705        Mushrooms      0.95       25        23.75

       6479        Ground Round   3.96       60       237.60

       1622        Orange J.      1.11       50        55.50

       5605        Clean Det.     1.60       40        64.00

       6366        Chicken        4.50       35       157.50

       9944        Lettuce        0.79       50        39.50

       7777        Cola Soda      1.89       35        66.15

       8411        Frozen Corn    0.67       30        20.10

  Final Total Price        $772.30
```

FIGURE 14–4
Table program output

Detail printing is produced by statement 820, which follows.

820 LPRINT USING 02$; I(I), P$(I), P(I), Q(I), T(I)

The output format assigned to 02$ in line 380 is used for detail printing. The FOR/NEXT loop parameter controls printing of the respective table elements. The table subscripts vary from one to ten according to loop parameters.

The summary module is performed at the conclusion of the FOR/NEXT loop. Output is edited according to the LPRINT USING statement in line 920. Variable T(0) (zero subscript element) is printed as the final total price.

The data to be processed is shown in lines 1000 to 1060. Two data records are combined in each DATA statement.

The report printed as a result of this program is shown in figure 14–4. Ten detail lines are printed, followed by the summary line.

Record the results of the following program segments.

SELF-TEST 14–1

```
1. 100 LET M = 5
   110 FOR L = 1 TO M
   120     LET A(L) = L * M
   130 NEXT L
   140 FOR L = 1 TO M
   150     PRINT A(L):PRINT
   160 NEXT L
   170 END
```

```
2. 200 FOR I = 1 TO 7
   210     LET T(I) = I * I
   220 NEXT I
   230 FOR I = 1 TO 7
   240     PRINT T(I):PRINT
   250 NEXT I
   260 END
```

```
3. 100 DIM U(16)
   300 LET R = 4:LET Z = 1
   310 FOR S = 1 TO R
   320     FOR T = 1 TO R
   330         LET U(Z) = S * T
   340         LET U(0) = U(0) + U(Z)
   350         LET Z = Z + 1
```

```
4. 500 LET J = 10
   510 FOR I = 1 TO J
   520     READ A$(I)
   530 NEXT I
   540 FOR I = J TO 1 STEP − 1
   550     PRINT A$(I):PRINT
   560 NEXT I
```

```
360     NEXT T
370 NEXT S
380 FOR V = 1 TO Z − 1
390     PRINT U(V):PRINT
400 NEXT V
410 PRINT
420 PRINT U(0)
430 END
```

```
570 DATA ALPHA, BRAVO,
        CHARLIE, DELTA, ECHO
580 DATA FOXTROT,
        GEORGE, HENRY, IN-
        DIGO, JANE
```

Answers for
Self-Test
14–1

1. 5
   10
   15
   20
   25

2. 1
   4
   9
   16
   25
   36
   49

3. 1
   2
   3
   4
   2
   4
   6
   8

3
6
9
12
4
8
12
16

100

4. JANE
   INDIGO
   HENRY
   GEORGE
   FOXTROT
   ECHO
   DELTA
   CHARLIE
   BRAVO
   ALPHA

CLEARING SYSTEM MEMORY

The use of a large number of tables and/or table elements may cause the program to exceed available system memory. This problem can sometimes be eliminated by erasing tables that are no longer needed in processing. The format for the ERASE key word follows.

700 ERASE Table Name

The table name to be erased is listed. The system memory that was reserved for the listed table is then free to be used for other purposes. Following is an example of an ERASE statement.

700 ERASE X, Y

Following execution of this statement, the space that was previously reserved for tables X and Y are available.

PROGRAM DEVELOPMENT CHECKLIST

Use the following checklist to ensure that all necessary components are included in the program.

_____ Flowcharts and documentation

_____ Program loop control

_____ Program housekeeping

_____ OPTION BASE

_____ DIMENSION statement

_____ Table subscripts

_____ Data entry

_____ Processing

_____ Output

PROGRAM DEBUGGING

There are several errors commonly encountered when manipulating data in table form. Following are the errors and suggested corrections.

1. BAD SUBSCRIPT ERROR — Table is not dimensioned correctly. Check DIM statement and compare with subscripts referenced.

2. ILLEGAL SUBSCRIPT (or QUANTITY) ERROR — Negative subscript value used in program. Check BASIC expression.

3. MEMORY EXCEEDED (or OUT OF MEMORY) — Table sizes referenced exceed available system memory. Check to see if tables previously used can be erased, restructure program, or start at beginning.

4. REDIMENSIONED ARRAY (or DUPLICATE DEFINITION) — Same table is referenced in two DIM statements. Check for duplicate definition.

5. SUBSCRIPT OUT OF RANGE — Table subscript exceeds DIM statement range. Check for proper dimension range.

These are the diagnostic messages commonly encountered when working with tables. System differences may result in variations in wording.

SUMMARY

Data can be processed using one-dimensional tables. One-dimensional tables result in a columnar arrangement of data somewhat similar to the data list explained previously.

It is necessary to reserve system memory when using tables. The DIMENSION, or DIM, statement is used to reserve memory for table processing. Generally, tables that exceed ten elements in length must be declared; however, it is best to declare all tables.

The data values stored in individual table elements, or cells, can be separately addressed or accessed through subscripts. BASIC subscripts are written in the form—B(J). Subscripts may be integers, variables, or valid BASIC expressions.

The zero element is available for table processing. The OPTION BASE key word may have to be used on some systems to enable use of the zero element.

System memory may be totally used when referencing large tables. The ERASE key word can be used on some systems to free memory that was previously reserved for a table that is no longer needed.

Common diagnostic messages encountered when processing data in table form are BAD SUBSCRIPT ERROR, ILLEGAL SUBSCRIPT, MEMORY EXCEEDED, RE-DIMENSIONED ARRAY, and SUBSCRIPT OUT OF RANGE.

BASIC Key Words Learned

DIMENSION (or DIM)	Reserves system memory for use in processing data in table form.
ERASE	Deletes tables that are no longer needed.
OPTION BASE	Enables use of the zero table element on most systems.

PROGRAM ASSIGNMENT 14–1

Instructions

Prepare the flowcharts and a structured BASIC program to print a sales commission report that uses tables to manipulate the data. Use a separate table for each of the following variables: salesperson's name, amount sold, commission rate (decimal), and amount of commission. Compute the amount of commission by multiplying the amount sold by the commission rate for each corresponding table element. Accumulate a summary total for the commission amount. Identify the highest individual commission amount paid and print the relevant data for that salesperson. (Program hint: assume that the first person in the table earned the highest commission. Compare the following elements and record the subscript for the highest commission.)

Following is the data to be processed. Use READ and DATA statements to enter the data. The data fields are the salesperson's name, the amount sold, and the commission rate.

Data

Salesperson's Name	Sales	Rate
Smith	23,475.97	.06
Hawes	16,667.41	.09
Schoe	10,551.11	.12
Rit	19,841.37	.09
Fores	9,875.05	.15
Savren	13,575.00	.12
McNab	18,493.81	.09
Aftner	17,997.81	.09

Output Format

Print headings, detail lines, and summary lines. Use report editing if available. Print the data tables for each salesperson. Identify the salesperson earning the highest commission and print the relevant data.

PORT-EX COMPANY

Commission Report

Salesperson	Sales	Rate	Commission
XXXXXXX	XX,XXX.XX	.XX	XX,XXX.XX
XXXXXXX	XX,XXX.XX	.XX	XX,XXX.XX
	TOTAL COMMISSION		$XX,XXX.XX

HIGHEST COMMISSION
NAME   XXXXXXXXXX   AMOUNT $XX,XXX.XX

**PROGRAM
ASSIGNMENT
14–2**

Instructions

Prepare the flowcharts and a structured BASIC program to print an income and expense distribution report. Use one-dimensional tables to enter and process the data. Use a separate table for each of the following variables: store name, sales income, selling expense, cost of goods sold, total expenses, and net profit. Net profit is calculated by subtracting the total expenses from the sales income for each corresponding table element.

Compute and print the average dollar amount of selling expenses, cost of goods sold, total expenses, and net profit for all stores. Also, compute and print the average percentage of sales for selling expense, cost of goods sold, total expenses, and net profit.

Following is the data to be processed. Use READ and DATA statements to enter the data. The data fields are the store name, the sales amount, the selling expense, the cost of goods, and the total expenses.

Data

Store Name	Sales	Selling Expense	Cost of Goods	Total Expenses
Austin	1,675,000	201,000	1,088,750	1,643,175
Allandale	1,342,575	159,776	836,424	1,316,529
Bergstrom	1,193,825	149,228	817,770	1,169,948
Oak Hill	1,411,750	197,645	940,225	1,384,926
University	1,921,335	288,200	1,250,981	1,882,716

Output Format

Print headings, detail lines, and summary lines. Use output editing if available.

HACKERS DELIGHT COMPUTER MART

Sales Analysis Report

Store	Sales	Sales Expense	Cost of Goods	Total Expenses	Net Profit
XXXXXXX	X,XXX,XXX	XXX,XXX	X,XXX,XXX	X,XXX,XXX	XXX,XXX
XXXXXXX	X,XXX,XXX	XXX,XXX	X,XXX,XXX	X,XXX,XXX	XXX,XXX
AVERAGE AMOUNT		XXX,XXX	X,XXX,XXX	X,XXX,XXX	XXX,XXX
AVERAGE PERCENTAGE		XX.X	XX.X	XX.X	XX.X

TABLE SEARCH OPERATIONS

OBJECTIVES

At the end of this chapter you should be able to perform the following operations:
- Develop programs that search one-dimensional tables for specified data.
- Use transaction processing as the search key.
- Utilize sequential table search procedures.

SEARCHING ONE-DIMENSIONAL TABLES

This chapter utilizes the one-dimensional tables introduced in Chapter 14 as the basis for searching the elements for specified data values. After a series of tables is established, transaction-oriented procedures are used to enter the search key. The search key is used to look in the appropriate table to determine if such data is present. The search is conducted element by element in sequential order. This procedure is known as a *sequential search*.

If the particular number or string value is located in the table, all the relevant data for that account, employee, or customer can be accessed. The subscript for the specified element is used to access corresponding cells in the other tables. The search procedure is the key to determining the appropriate subscript. Once the subscript is identified, it can be used to access and manipulate all necessary data values from the other corresponding elements.

An error handling procedure should be included in search routines in case an error is made in entering the key, or the data value is not present in the table. Error messages should be included to handle these possibilities.

The following example, figure 15–1, illustrates a table search routine. The table lists salespersons' names.

The data is loaded into the appropriate tables in predetermined sequence, and the name of the desired salesperson is then entered in transaction mode. A FOR/NEXT structure is used to search the table to determine if the specified name is present. Assume that the data for salesperson Fores is desired. That person's name is entered as the search

TABLE SUBSCRIPT	SALESPERSON'S NAME
X	S$(X)
1	Smith
2	Hawes
3	Schoe
4	Rit
5	Fores
6	Savren
7	McNab
8	Aftner

FIGURE 15–1
Salesperson's name table

166

key. The search routine scans the table until the element containing the proper name value is detected. In this table, element five contains the matching value. Subscript five can then be used to access all corresponding table data pertaining to salesperson Fores.

The table is searched element by element until the proper value is detected or the loop ends. It is searched in sequential order.

An error is present if the entire table is searched without detecting the specified key. For instance, if the search key were Fry, which is not in the table, an error message would be printed.

FLOWCHARTS—TABLE SEARCHES

The example program shown in figures 15–4 and 15–5 reads data, loads it in several one-dimensional tables, prints the tables, searches the specified table for the key value, and prints the result of the search.

Figure 15–2 contains the top-level flowchart. Program execution is controlled by the mainline routine. The program body consists of the read, print, heading, and search blocks.

Housekeeping tasks are executed at the beginning of the program. These include clearing the system, reserving memory for the various data tables, and formatting output lines.

The detailed logic flowchart is shown in figure 15–3. There are ten data records in the program, so the loop limit parameter is set at ten.

The read subroutine is used to read the data and load it into the respective tables. In this program, it loads the data into four tables.

A single heading line and the detail lines are printed as a result of the print routine. A FOR/NEXT loop is used to control printing of the detail lines. The ten data records are printed using output editing.

A heading line is printed as a result of the transaction heading block. This line separates the table listing and the transaction inquiries.

An INPUT statement is used to enter the number of search transactions desired. This figure is used to limit the transaction loop which controls the search subroutine.

The transaction search subroutine is used to enter the search key and print the results. The table searched in this program is the product identification number. INPUT statements are used to enter the search key. This number is echoed, or printed, so that the user can observe the number entered. A flag variable is initialized at zero before each search routine is executed. This variable records search hits and misses.

A nested FOR/NEXT loop produces a search of the ten table elements. A branch statement checks for a match, or hit, between the search key and the table element. If the search key matches a table element, the corresponding cells from the tables are printed and the flag variable is assigned a value of one. If the FOR/NEXT loop terminates with the flag variable still at zero, a match has not occurred. When a match has occurred, the flag is equal to one. When the flag equals zero, an error message should be printed.

The program ends when the transaction loop is terminated.

EXAMPLE PROGRAM—TABLE SEARCH

The objective of this chapter is to demonstrate the BASIC language procedures for executing a sequential search of a data table. This program searches the product identi-

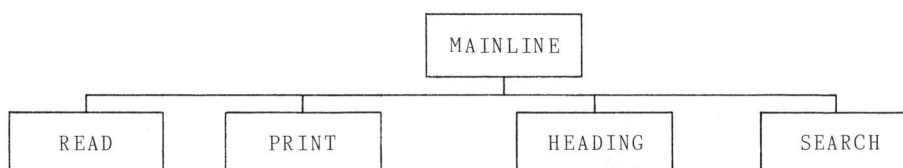

FIGURE 15–2
Top-level flowchart

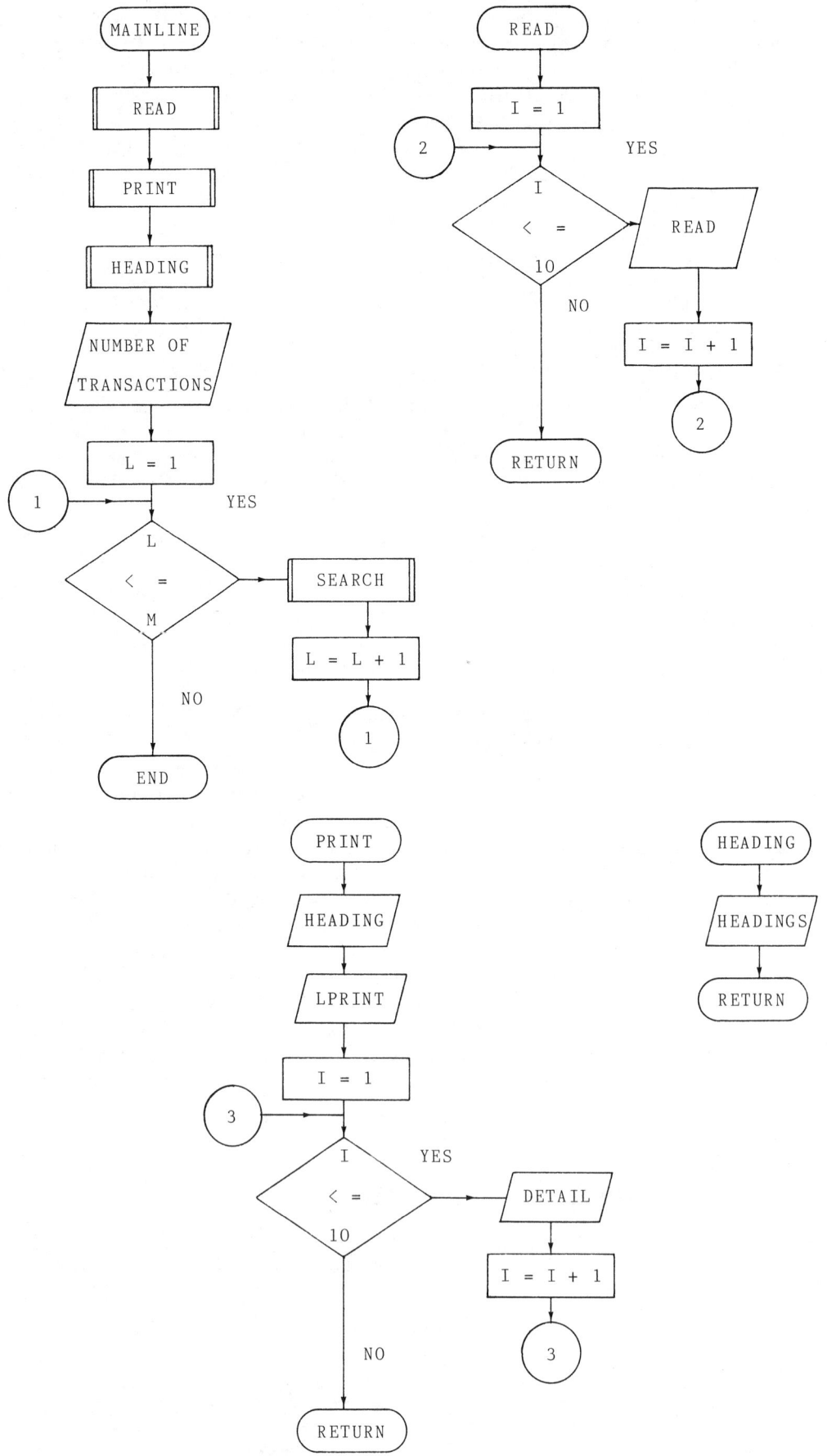

FIGURE 15-3
Detailed logic flowchart

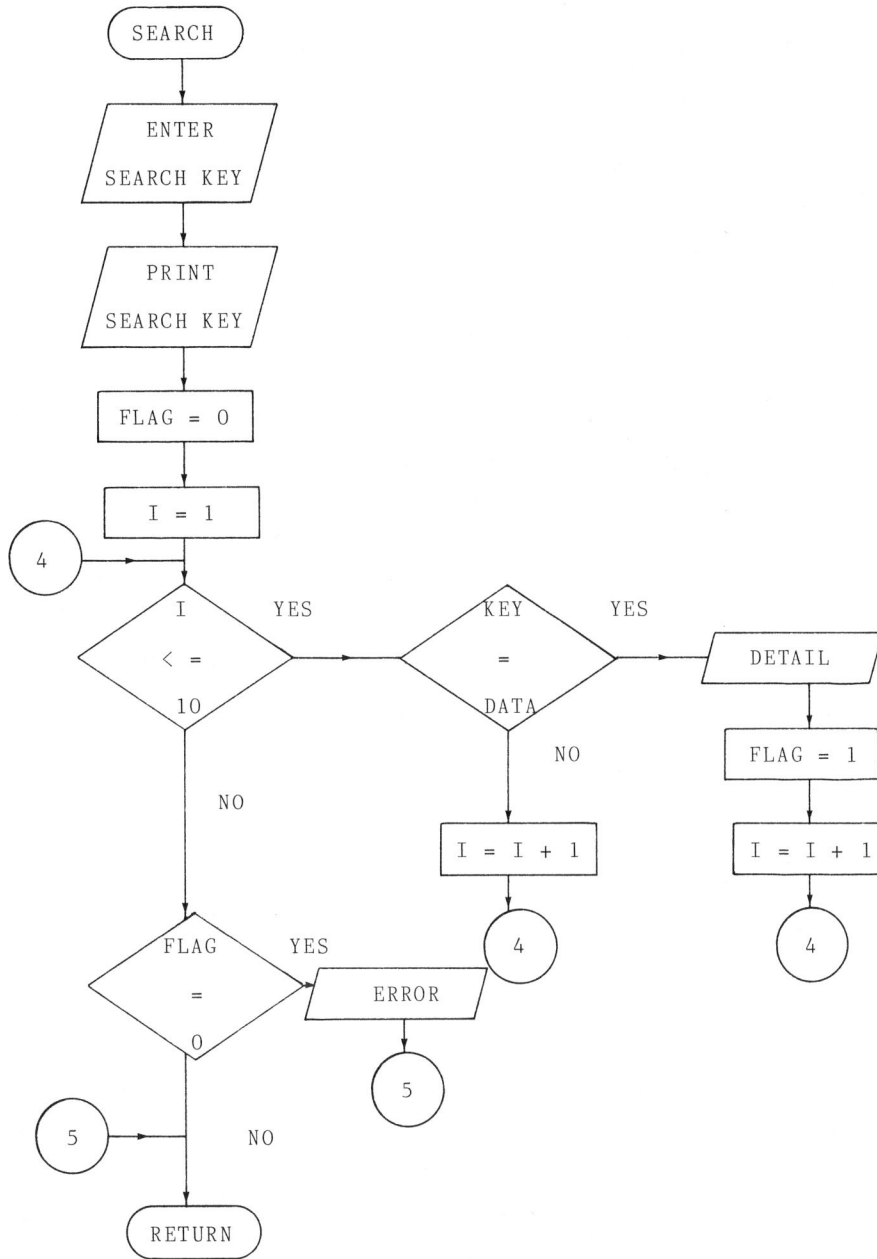

FIGURE 15–3
(Continued)

fication table. Each of the corresponding elements from the various tables is then printed. Data is loaded into four tables. The tables are printed and the identification table is searched for a specified value.

The example program is exhibited in figures 15–4 and 15–5. Figure 15–4 contains lines 100 through 650 and figure 15–5 contains lines 700 through 1170.

Program documentation and variable identification are shown in lines 100 to 240. Initialization and housekeeping tasks are contained in statements 300 to 390. The system is cleared in statement 310. The CLEAR command should be listed before the tables are dimensioned.

System memory is reserved for the one-dimensional tables in statement 340. The tables are dimensioned as having ten elements. One-dimensional tables are declared for the product identification number (ID), the product name (P$), the price (P), and the quantity (Q).

Lines 370 and 380 contain the output format statements. These statements are used

```
100     REM     FIGURE  15-4    WRITTEN BY LARRY FRY     4/30/83
110     REM     This program produces a product listing from
120     REM     one-dimensional tables.    A search routine is
130     REM     used to seek information for specific products.
140     REM     *****      Variable Identification
150     REM     I     ..... Subscript Index
160     REM     ID(I) ..... Product  ID
170     REM     P$(I) ..... Product Name
180     REM     Q(I)  ..... Quantity
190     REM     P(I)  ..... Price
200     REM     X     ..... Transaction Search Variable
210     REM     ID(0) ..... Search Flag - Zero Subscript Element
220     REM     L     ..... Transaction Loop Counter
230     REM     M     ..... Transaction Loop Limit
240                                                                   REM
300     REM     *****      System Initialization
310  CLEAR
320                                                                   REM
330     REM     *****      Dimension Tables
340  DIM ID(10), P$(10), P(10), Q(10)
350                                                                   REM
360     REM     *****      Output Format Lines
370  LET O1$ = "  ####        \           \        #.##       ###"
380  LET O2$ = "PRODUCT IS = \              \     PRICE IS = #.##     QUANTITY IS =
     ###"
390                                                                   REM
400     REM     *****      Mainline Control
410  GOSUB   610
420  GOSUB   710
430  GOSUB   810
440  PRINT  : CLS
450  INPUT  "Enter Number of Transaction Inquiries  ";  M
460  FOR  L = 1  TO  M
470        GOSUB  910
480  NEXT  L
490  END
500                                                                   REM
510                                                                   REM
600     REM     *****      Read Data and Load Tables
610  FOR  I = 1  TO  10
620        READ  ID(I), P$(I), P(I), Q(I)
630  NEXT I
640  RETURN
650                                                                   REM
```

FIGURE 15–4
Table search program

to print the tables and the search results. The output format statements are assigned to
O1$ and O2$.

The mainline module is shown in statements 400 to 510. This routine is used as the
driver module to control execution of the program subroutines.

Line 410 calls the read module. This routine causes the data to be entered into four
one-dimensional tables as declared in the DIMENSION statement. A FOR/NEXT structure in the read module results in ten data records being loaded into the various tables.
The read loop is executed ten times according to the limit parameter.

In this example, the variable values are arranged in random order in the DATA
statements. It is possible to arrange the DATA statements in ascending order based upon
the product identification number. This arrangement may make the search routine more
efficient, particularly in very large programs.

The print module is called in line 420. This subroutine causes one heading line and
the data in the various tables to be printed. Line 710 advances the printer to the top of
a new page. The heading line is printed as a result of statement 720. Two blank lines for
report separation are produced by line 730. A FOR/NEXT loop is used to print the data
that is contained in the four tables. The LPRINT USING statement uses the output
format assigned to O1$ to print the tables.

In normal day-to-day business operations, it is not necessary to print the data tables.
This is done occasionally to obtain a hard copy for archive purposes. The routine is
included in the example program and assignments for illustration and skill development.

```
700     REM     *****     Print Data in Tables
710   LPRINT CHR$(12)
720   LPRINT TAB(25);  "DATA IN TABLES"
730   LPRINT  :  LPRINT
740   FOR  I  =  1  TO  10
750          LPRINT USING O1$; ID(I), P$(I), P(I), Q(I)
760   NEXT  I
770   LPRINT :  LPRINT
780   RETURN
790                                                             REM
800     REM     *****     Transaction Report Heading
810   LPRINT  :  LPRINT
820   LPRINT TAB(10);  "TRANSACTION INQUIRIES"
830   LPRINT : LPRINT
840   RETURN
850                                                             REM
900     REM     *****     Transaction Inquiries  -  Search and Print
910   PRINT  :  CLS
920   INPUT  "Enter  Product  ID  Number  ";  X
930   LPRINT "PRODUCT  ID NUMBER INPUT WAS = ";  X
940   LET  ID(0) = 0
950   FOR  I  =  1  TO  10
960          IF ID(I) = X  THEN LPRINT USING O2$; P$(I), P(I), Q(I)   :
LET ID(0) = 1
970   NEXT  I
980   IF ID(0) = 0 THEN LPRINT  "Invalid ID No.  = "; X ; "   Reenter"
990   LPRINT  :  LPRINT
1000   RETURN
1010                                                            REM
1100    REM     *****     Data to be  Processed
1110  DATA  1479, "Veg. Juice", 1.19, 55, 4375, "Pap. Towels", .57, 75
1120  DATA  9705, "Mushrooms", .95, 50, 6497, "Ground Round", 3.96, 100
1130  DATA  1611, "Orange Juice", 1.11, 50, 5605, "Clean Det.", 1.60, 35
1140  DATA  6366, "Chicken", 4.50, 65, 9944, "Lettuce", .79, 45
1150  DATA  7777, "Cola Soda", 1.79, 75, 8411, "Frozen Corn", .67, 35
1160                                                            REM
1170  STOP
```

The next portion of the program processes the transaction inquiries. Statement 430 calls the transaction heading module which separates the data tables and the report search transactions. Several blank lines and the heading are printed as the result of this routine.

FIGURE 15–5
Table search program

Line 440 switches output from the printer to the monitor and also clears the screen. The number of transaction inquiries to be processed (M) is entered in the INPUT statement in line 450. This sets the transaction loop limit. Transaction processing is controlled by the FOR/NEXT loop in statements 460 through 480. The search routine is called in line 470.

Statement 910 returns output to the monitor and clears the screen. The search key (X) is entered in line 920. An INPUT statement is used to enter the desired product identification number. The search key entered is then printed in line 930, so the user can observe the number. This is a useful step if an error results from the search routine. The echoed input data helps to isolate the error type if one occurs.

In most BASIC forms, a flag variable is used in search routines to determine if there is an error in the transaction. Errors can result from entering incorrect data, or from the search key not being present in the table. The flag variable is initialized in line 940 which follows.

940 LET ID(0) = 0

The zero table element, which is available on most systems, was presented in Chapter 14. In this example, ID(0) (zero subscript element) is used as the flag variable. Some systems use another format—FLAG or F is the most commonly used. The flag variable ID(0) is initialized at zero to begin the search procedure.

A FOR/NEXT loop is used to search the identification number table. The loop parameter means that all elements will be searched sequentially. Following is the FOR/NEXT loop.

```
950 FOR I = 1 to 10
960     IF ID(I) = X THEN LPRINT USING 02$; P$(I), P(I), Q(I):
   LET ID(0) = 1
970 NEXT I
```

The loop scans all ten elements of the identification number table. Each table element is compared with variable X as a result of statement 960. If there is a match, or hit, between ID(I) and the search key X, the corresponding elements from the product name, price, and quantity tables are printed. P$(I), P(I), and Q(I) are printed according to the edit format 02$, which is assigned in line 380.

The appropriate subscript for the search key is established as a result of the branch statement in line 960. This subscript points to the corresponding elements in the other tables. The flag variable ID(0) (zero subscript element) is assigned the value one when ID(I) is equal to X.

The output for the example program is shown in figure 15–6. The data tables are printed first, and are followed by the transactions. As an example of the transaction search routine, assume that the value 6366 has been entered as the search key (X). This is illustrated in the first search transaction in figure 15–6. Following is the output produced by this search transaction.

PRODUCT ID NUMBER INPUT WAS = 6366
PRODUCT IS = Chicken   PRICE IS = 4.50   QUANTITY IS = 65

The first line of output echoes the data entered by the INPUT statement. Identification number 6366 is the seventh element in the table. I equals 7; therefore, the seventh

```
                      DATA  IN  TABLES


        1479        Veg. Juice          1.19          55
        4375        Pap. Towels         0.57          75
        9705        Mushrooms           0.95          50
        6497        Ground Round        3.96         100
        1611        Orange Juice        1.11          50
        5605        Clean Det.          1.60          35
        6366        Chicken             4.50          65
        9944        Lettuce             0.79          45
        7777        Cola Soda           1.79          75
        8411        Frozen Corn         0.67          35




          TRANSACTION  INQUIRIES


   PRODUCT  ID NUMBER INPUT WAS =   6366
   PRODUCT IS = Chicken           PRICE IS = 4.50        QUANTITY IS =  65


   PRODUCT  ID NUMBER INPUT WAS =   3291
   Invalid ID No.   =   3291      Reenter


   PRODUCT  ID NUMBER INPUT WAS =   8411
   PRODUCT IS = Frozen Corn       PRICE IS = 0.67        QUANTITY IS =  35


   PRODUCT  ID NUMBER INPUT WAS =   6666
   Invalid ID No.   =   6666      Reenter


   PRODUCT  ID NUMBER INPUT WAS =   1479
   PRODUCT IS = Veg. Juice        PRICE IS = 1.19        QUANTITY IS =  55


   PRODUCT  ID NUMBER INPUT WAS =   7777
   PRODUCT IS = Cola Soda         PRICE IS = 1.79        QUANTITY IS =  75
```

FIGURE 15–6
Table search output

element in the product name, price, and quantity tables is printed. The second line of output is produced by the LPRINT USING statement in line 960. Output format 02$ is used to edit the printing.

The FOR/NEXT loop is executed according to the parameters even if there is a match between the search key and the table element on the first pass. In this example, the match occurs on the seventh pass. The remainder of the loop is still executed.

The flag variable ID(0) (zero subscript element) is used to identify errors caused by the search procedure. Variable ID(0) is assigned a value of zero in statement 940. If a match occurs during execution of the loop, ID(0) is assigned a value of one. When there is no match between the search key and the table elements, ID(0) contains a value of zero at the end of the search loop. The branch statement in line 980, which follows, determines whether an error is present.

> 980 IF ID(0) = 0 THEN LPRINT "Invalid ID No. = "; X;" Reenter"

If ID(0) (zero subscript element) is equal to zero at the end of the loop, an error message is printed. The second search transaction in figure 15–6 records the result when the search key is equal to 3291. The output follows.

> PRODUCT ID NUMBER INPUT WAS = 3291
> Invalid ID No. = 3291   Reenter

Identification number 3291 is entered as a result of the INPUT statement, and this value is echoed. Number 3291 is not present in the table, so an error exists. The error causes the second line of output to be printed.

A mix of valid and invalid transactions is included in the report. The number of table elements and search transactions is used for illustration purposes only. The tables could be larger depending upon the system's capability.

The data to be processed is shown in statements 1100 to 1160. Ten data records are listed.

The data tables and the search transactions are exhibited in figure 15–6. There are ten elements in each of the four tables. Six search transactions are shown.

PROGRAM DEVELOPMENT CHECKLIST

Use the following checklist to ensure that all necessary components are included in the program.

_____ Flowcharts and documentation

_____ System initialization

_____ Housekeeping tasks

_____ Program loop control

_____ Dimension statement

_____ Table subscripts

_____ Data entry

_____ Print tables

_____ Search routine

_____ Error procedure

_____ Print transactions

SUMMARY

The BASIC language contains procedures for searching one-dimensional tables for a specified data value. The search key is entered in the transaction mode. When there is a match between the search key and an element in the table, the corresponding elements from other tables can be processed or printed. The table subscript is used to access corresponding elements in the tables.

An error handling procedure is included in searches in case there is no match between the search key and the table elements.

PROGRAM ASSIGNMENT 15–1

Instructions

Prepare the flowcharts and a structured BASIC program to convert from the calendar day to the numeric day of the month. Use one table for the calendar month and another for the number of days in that month (assume February = 28). Use INPUT statements to enter these tables and to print them. Include search transaction processing to enable the user to enter the calendar month and the day of the month. Use a search routine to match the search key with elements in the month table. Accumulate and print the number of days as the numeric day of the year. The system should echo the search key and print the numeric date.

Use two data tables: one for the calendar month; and the other for the number of days in each month. Use INPUT statements to enter the data.

Output Format

Print the headings and the data tables. Echo the search transaction month and day entered. On the third print line for each transaction print the numeric date. The program should process at least five transactions. Use output editing if available.

SILAS MARNER NATIONAL BANK

Calendar to Numeric Date

Data Tables

| JANUARY | 31 |
| FEBRUARY | 28 |

Search Transactions

CALENDAR MONTH FROM INPUT	= MARCH
DAY OF MONTH	= 19
MARCH, 19	= DAY XXX
CALENDAR MONTH FROM INPUT	= SEPTEMBER
DAY OF MONTH	= 3
SEPTEMBER, 3	= DAY XXX

PROGRAM ASSIGNMENT 15–2

Instructions

Prepare the flowcharts and a structured BASIC program to print a current depreciation status report. Use one-dimensional tables to enter and process the data. Create one table for each of the following variables: asset name, beginning book value, current year, annual depreciation, accumulated depreciation, and current book value. After the data is entered into the one-dimensional tables, print the tables.

Prepare the current depreciation status for those assets listed in the following table under transaction data. Use a search routine to update only these assets. The search key is the asset name. Add the annual depreciation to the accumulated depreciation. Then subtract the accumulated depreciation from the beginning book value to obtain current book value, and increment the current year by one. Next, prepare a current depreciation status report for those assets that have been updated. Include an error routine in the search procedure.

Following is the data to be included in the tables. Use READ and DATA statements to enter the data.

Table Data

Name	Beginning Book	Current Year	Annual Depreciation	Accumulated Depreciation
Calculator	600	1	200	200
VDT	875	3	292	875
Typewriter	1,000	2	333	666
Word Processor	5,000	2	1,000	3,000
Computer	6,395	1	1,279	1,279
Desk	300	2	100	200
Cabinet	700	1	233	466
Safe	1,500	3	500	1,500
Building	25,000	6	2,500	15,000

Transaction Data

Use the following data for search transaction purposes.

Asset Name
Calculator
Chair
Word processor
Computer
Work station
Building

Output Format

Print the headings and the data tables. Echo the transaction search key. In the second transaction detail line, print the updated depreciation status. Include an error routine. Use output editing if available.

PORT-EX COMPANY

NORTHEAST SALES DIVISION

Depreciation Report

Name	Beginning Book	Current Year	Annual Depreciation	Accumulated Depreciation
xxxxxxxx	x,xxx	x	x,xxx	x,xxx
xxxxxxxx	x,xxx	x	x,xxx	x,xxx

Transaction Processing

ASSET NAME FROM INPUT = Calculator

Name	Beginning Book	Current Year	Annual Depreciation	Accumulated Depreciation	Book Value
Calculator	600	2	200	400	200

ASSET NAME FROM INPUT = Chair

Chair   NOT PRESENT IN TABLE   REENTER

PROGRAM ASSIGNMENT 15–3

Instructions

Prepare the flowcharts and a structured BASIC program to print a customer account report. Use one-dimensional tables to enter and process the data. Create a separate table for each of the following variables: account number, account name, transactions to date, current balance, and account status. Enter the data into one-dimensional tables and print it.

Print a customer transaction report. Use the search routine to update the customer accounts according to the transactions. A program menu with various options is suggested. Possible transactions include the following:

1. Purchase
2. Payment
3. Purchase for overdue account—transaction not processed and message printed.
4. Change account status to past due—change account number.
5. Change account status to OK—change account number.

The search key is the account number. Additional purchases should not be processed when accounts are overdue. Print a warning message for overdue transactions. When payments are made on overdue accounts, the status is changed to OK.

For those transactions identified as purchases, add the amount charged to the corresponding current balance and increment the transactions-to-date variable by one.

For those transactions identified as payments, subtract the amount paid from the corresponding current balance and increment the transactions-to-date variable by one.

Accumulate and print the total payments, total purchases, and total current balance.

Include an error routine in the search procedure.

Following is the data to be included in the tables. Use READ and DATA statements to enter the data.

Table Data

Account Number	Account Name	Transactions to Date	Current Balance	Account Status
1570	Bro-Kemp	37	1,137.94	OK
3900	Space Air	10	3,450.00	Past due
2480	Office Mod	20	750.00	OK
1120	Phil Dirt Co	19	0	OK
1660	Pete Moss Assoc	23	2,450.00	OK
1220	Chuck Roast Ent	17	0	OK
1490	X-Y Games	9	497.15	OK
1270	A-Z Assoc	29	1,157.40	OK
1380	BYTO Computers	32	995.55	OK
3800	Hi Tech Comp	8	632.47	Past due
1470	Able Mable Ent	18	575.25	OK

Transaction Data

Account Number	Type	Amount
2480	Purchase	350.00
1270	Change to past due— change account number to 3600	
1120	Purchase	475.00
3900	Purchase	150.00
3800	Payment	200.00
3800	Change account number to 1770	
1280	Purchase	150.00
1660	Payment	500.00
1490	Purchase	225.00
2480	Payment	550.00
1380	Purchase	387.50

Output Format

Print the headings and the beginning data tables. Echo the transaction search key. Print the transaction type and amount. After all of the transactions have been processed, print the current data tables. The summary totals for purchases, payments, and the ending balance are printed at the end of the report. Use output editing if available.

PORT-EX COMPANY

Account Status Report

Account Number	Account Name	Transactions to Date	Beginning Balance	Account Status
XXXX	XXXXXXXXXX	XX	X,XXX.XX	XX
XXXX	XXXXXXXXXX	XX	X,XXX.XX	XX

Transactions

ACCOUNT NUMBER FROM INPUT = 2480
ACCOUNT NAME = Office Mod   TYPE = Purchase   AMOUNT = 350

Updated Tables

Account Number	Account Name	Transactions to Date	Current Balance	Account Status
XXXX	XXXXXXX	XX	X,XXX.XX	XX
XXXX	XXXXXXX	XX	X,XXX.XX	XX

TOTAL PURCHASES $XX,XXX.XX
TOTAL PAYMENTS $XX,XXX.XX
UPDATED BALANCE $XX,XXX.XX

TABLE SORT OPERATIONS

OBJECTIVES

At the end of this chapter you should be able to perform the following operations:
- Develop programs that sort one-dimensional tables into numeric order.
- Develop programs that sort one-dimensional tables into alphabetic order.

SORTING NUMERIC OR ALPHABETIC TABLES

This chapter utilizes one-dimensional tables to sort data into numeric or alphabetic order. The sort key can be ascending or descending for either data type.

The procedures used by the computer system to sort alphabetic or numeric data into ascending or descending order are basically the same. Each of the numeric or string characters is given a code that the computer system uses internally. These codes are compared during a sort procedure to place data into the proper sequence.

The American Standard Code for Information Interchange (ASCII) is the data code currently used by most computer systems when entering data. The computer system converts the ASCII code (or the system code use) into binary form for internal processing. Each of the separate characters in the set utilized has a unique internal code.

The ASCII code for data being sorted is used in this illustration. The system compares the values and arranges them in ascending sort. For example, the ASCII code for the character A (65) is less than that for the letter C (67). Therefore, character A is placed ahead of C because it has a lower ASCII code value.

A variety of sort procedures is available when using BASIC. This sort technique arranges data in the order specified by passing repeatedly through the data table. The data is arranged in the order specified at the conclusion of the nested loop. Data values in the table float or bubble into the correct sequence. Each pass through the loop places the data closer to the desired final arrangement.

This sort procedure is slow compared to advanced BASIC procedures or to procedures written in Assembly or Machine Language, but it is adequate for this level of programming.

Nested FOR/NEXT loops are used to implement the sort procedure. This causes the data to float as previously described. The relative slowness of the procedure is caused by the repeated passes through the loop.

Following is an illustration of the sort routine. The computer system names should be arranged in alphabetic order when the procedure is completed. The table elements are compared cell by cell. The first pass through the loop begins by comparing the first element with all other elements. The original data arrangement follows.

Element Number	System Name
1	Tech-System
2	Number Cruncher
3	Bit Master
4	Computech

The first table element is compared with all others beginning with the first two cells. The string value Tech-System is greater than Number Cruncher. Element two is less than element one in value, so the two elements are swapped. The new table arrangement follows.

Element Number	System Name
1	Number Cruncher
2	Tech-System
3	Bit Master
4	Computech

Elements one and three are then compared. Element three is less than element one in value, so the two are swapped. The new table arrangement follows.

Element Number	System Name
1	Bit Master
2	Tech-System
3	Number Cruncher
4	Computech

Elements one and four are compared next. Bit Master is less than Computech in value, so the elements remain in the same order.

This completes the first pass through the inner loop in the nested structure. The second pass through the inner loop compares the second element with all following elements. A second pass is required because the data is not yet in alphabetic order. The second pass begins by checking the second element with those that follow. Element two is greater than element three in value, so the two are swapped. The new arrangement follows.

Element Number·	System Name
1	Bit Master
2	Computech
3	Tech-System
4	Number Cruncher

Element two is then compared with element four. Computech is less than Number Cruncher, so the two elements are switched. The resulting table arrangement follows.

Element Number	System Name
1	Bit Master
2	Computech
3	Tech-System
4	Number Cruncher

One final pass through the table is required to place the elements in alphabetic order. Elements three and four are compared and switched. The final order follows.

Element Number	System Name
1	Bit Master
2	Computech
3	Number Cruncher
4	Tech-System

The procedures used in this type of sort cause the table elements to float, or bubble, into the proper sequence. The element being compared with those that follow increases by one with each pass through the inner loop. During the first pass through the inner loop, the first element is compared with all others. In the second pass through the inner loop, the second element is compared with all those that follow. The third pass compares the third element with all those that follow. The same pattern is executed regardless of the number of elements. The four sort guidelines that follow can be formulated from the preceding illustration.

1. Nested FOR/NEXT loops are required to sort one-dimensional tables.
2. The number of passes through a table required to arrange the data into proper sequence is determined by the number of elements minus one. When the table contains N elements, $N-1$ passes are required. For example, a table with four elements requires three passes through the inner loop to sort the data.
3. Table elements are compared cell by cell according to the nested loop parameters. The elements are switched, or swapped, as required according to the sort key.
4. During the first pass through the inner loop, the first element is compared with all others. On the second pass, the second element is compared with all that follow. The same procedure is used regardless of the number of elements.

These procedures should be used when constructing sort programs. Although this sort routine is not the fastest available in BASIC, it is adequate for this programming level.

Data tables can be arranged in numeric or alphabetic order in ascending or descending sequence. The sort key should be determined before designing the sort routine. Data values can be arranged in a predetermined sequence at data entry. If the arrangement of data values at data entry affects the efficiency of the sort routine, the sequence can be changed at any time through another sort routine.

FLOWCHARTS—TABLE SORT OPERATIONS

The example program for this chapter reads data, loads it in several one-dimensional tables, sorts the data by seniority, and sorts the data by department name. The tables are printed after each step.

Figure 16–1 contains the top-level flowchart. Program execution is controlled by the mainline routine. The program body consists of the heading, read, print, numeric sort, heading, print, restore, read, alphabetic sort, heading, and print subroutines.

Several subroutines are used more than once. This example illustrates one of the advantages of program modularity. The ability to reuse the subroutines saves resources because new routines do not have to be written for each function.

Housekeeping tasks are executed at the beginning of the program. These include clearing the system, reserving memory for the data tables, and formatting output lines.

The detailed logic flowchart is shown in figure 16–2. There are 11 data records to

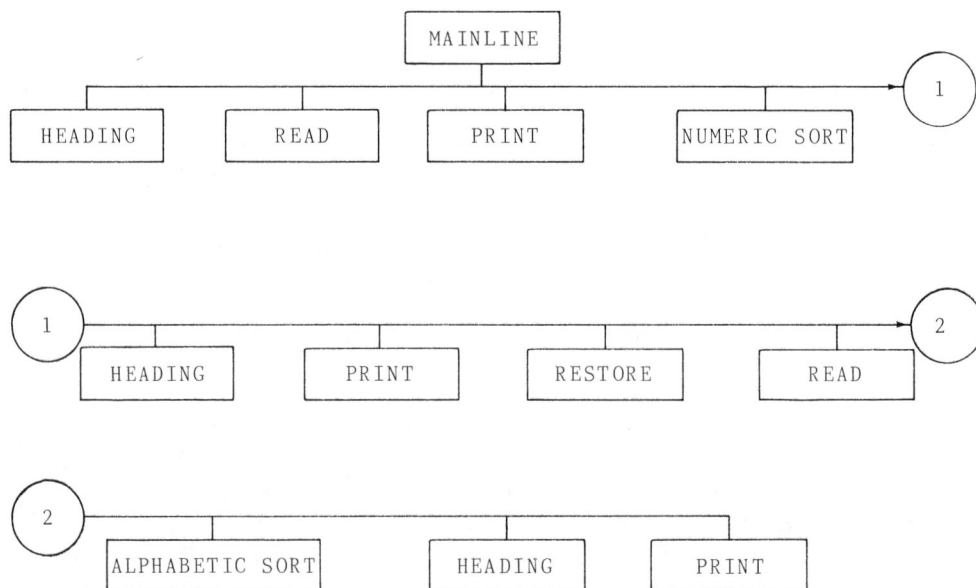

FIGURE 16–1
Top-level flowchart

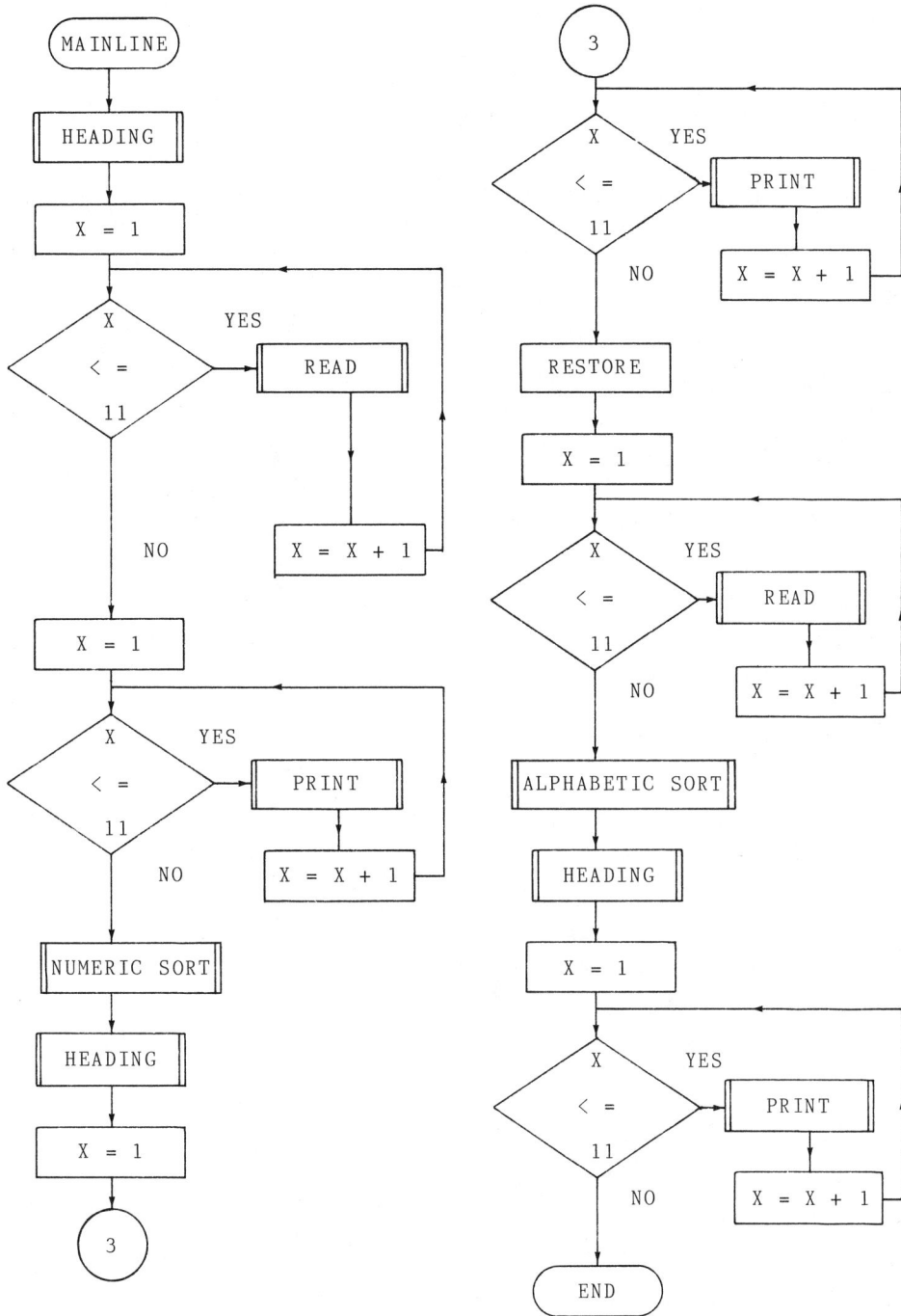

FIGURE 16–2
Detailed logic flowchart

be processed, so the DIMENSION statement and loop limit parameters are set accordingly.

The heading subroutine is executed first. This routine prints the report and column headings. The same routine is used to print the headings each time the tables are printed.

The read block enters the data and loads it into the respective tables. A FOR/NEXT loop in the mainline routine controls execution of the read subroutine. The read routine is used twice in the program.

Output is produced by the print subroutine. A FOR/NEXT loop in the mainline routine controls printing. The data tables are printed three separate times through the use of this subroutine.

The numeric sort routine sorts the three tables into descending order according to seniority. The seniority table is used as the sort key. Nested FOR/NEXT loops are used

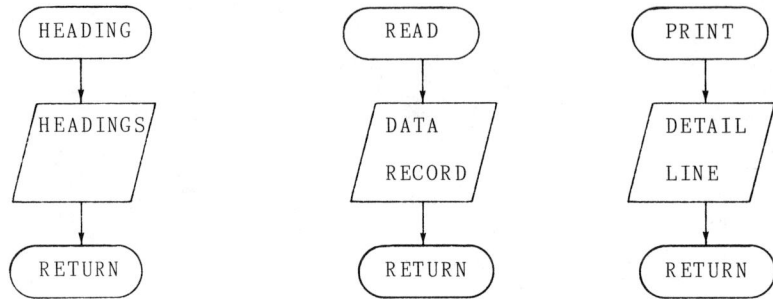

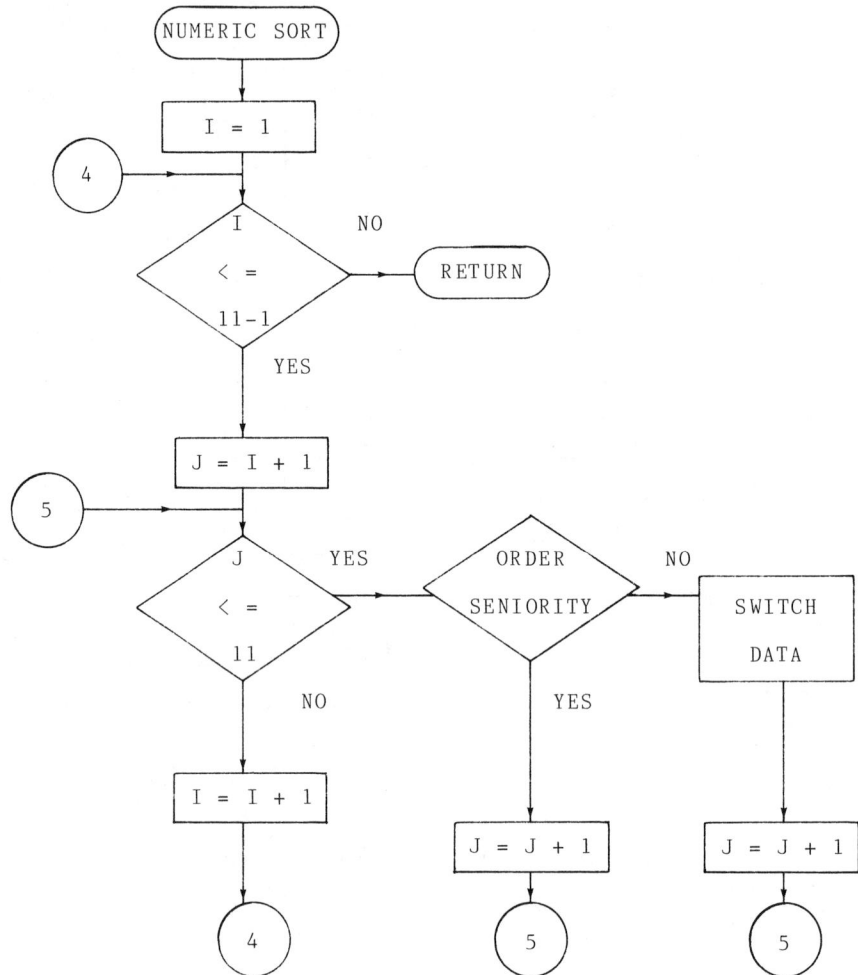

FIGURE 16–2
(Continued)

to control the sort operation. The outer loop controls the number of passes through the table. There are 11 data elements; therefore, the number of passes is equal to 11 − 1, or 10. The first pass compares element I, which is one, with all other elements.

The nested structure, which is the inner or J loop, compares the following elements with the first element. The elements specified are switched with the first element when the first element is less than those that follow. Switching each element is a three-step process. The corresponding values in each of the other tables must be switched. (Refer to the computer system sort example presented earlier in this chapter when studying the flowchart.) The three tables are printed upon conclusion of the sort procedure.

The alphabetic sort routine sorts the department name table into alphabetic order. Nested loops are used to control the sort procedure. The corresponding elements in the other tables are also switched. The three tables are printed upon conclusion of the sort routine.

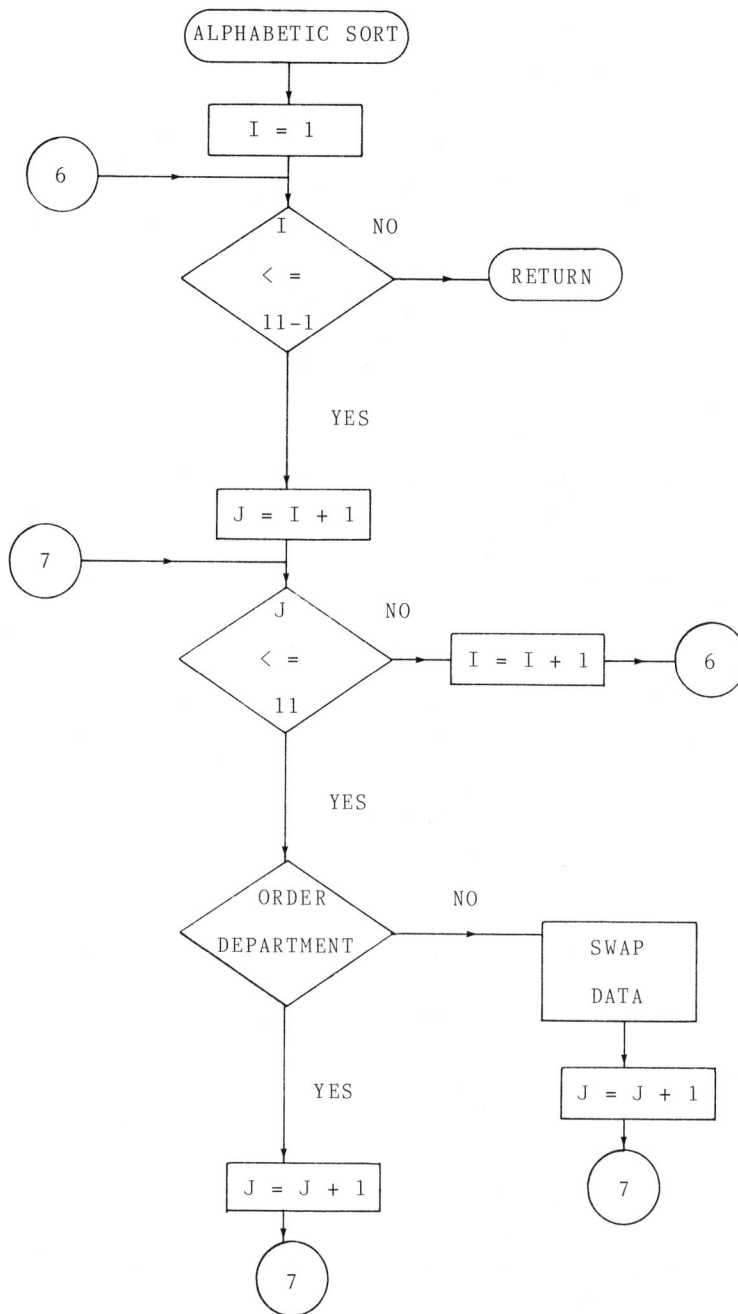

FIGURE 16–2
(Continued)

EXAMPLE PROGRAM—TABLE SORT OPERATIONS

The primary objective of this chapter is to illustrate the BASIC language procedures for sorting alphabetic and numeric tables. One-dimensional tables and nested FOR/NEXT loops are used to execute these operations. This program loads data into three tables, which are declared for the employee name, the department name, and seniority by months employed. The DATA statements are arranged in alphabetic order by employee name. A sort routine arranges the tables into descending order based upon the sort key, which is seniority. The tables are then sorted into alphabetic order based upon the department name. They are printed after each program phase.

The sample program is exhibited in figures 16–3 and 16–4. Figure 16–3 includes the program documentation, the housekeeping tasks, and the mainline module. Program statements 100 through 630 are included in this illustration. Figure 16–4 includes program lines 700 through 1570. The headings, read, numeric sort, print, and alphabetic

```
100          REM      FIGURE  16-3    WRITTEN BY LARRY FRY   6/20/83
110          REM      This program sorts data numerically and then
120          REM      alphabetically.  The sort keys are descending by
130          REM      seniority, and then alphabetical by department.
140                                                                      REM
150          REM      *****       Variable Identification
160          REM      X     .....  Subscript Index
170          REM      N$(X) ....  Employee Name Table
180          REM      D$(X) ....  Department Name Table
190          REM      S(X)  ....  Seniority Table
200          REM      I     ....  Sort Index (Outer Loop)
210          REM      J     ....  Sort Index (Inner Loop)
220          REM      N$(0) ....  Temporary String Variable
230          REM      S(0)  ....  Temporary Numeric Variable
240          REM      D$(0) ....  Temporary String Variable
250                                                                      REM
300          REM      *****       Program Initialization
310 CLEAR
320                                                                      REM
330          REM      *****       Dimension Tables
340 DIM N$(11), D$(11), S(11)
350                                                                      REM
360          REM      *****       Format Output Lines
370 LET 01$ = "    EMPLOYEE           DEPARTMENT          SENIORITY"
380 LET 02$ = "   \          \          \          \          ###"
390                                                                      REM
400          REM      *****       Mainline Module
410 GOSUB 710
420 FOR X = 1 TO 11
430       GOSUB 810
440 NEXT X
450 FOR X = 1 TO 11
460       GOSUB 1210
470 NEXT X
480 GOSUB 1010
490 GOSUB 710
500 FOR X = 1 TO 11
510       GOSUB 1210
520 NEXT X
530 RESTORE
540 FOR X = 1 TO 11
550       GOSUB 810
560 NEXT X
570 GOSUB 1410
580 GOSUB 710
590 FOR X = 1 TO 11
600       GOSUB 1210
610 NEXT X
620 END
630                                                                      REM
```

FIGURE 16–3
Table sort program

sort modules are contained in figure 16–4. This figure also includes the DATA statements.

Program documentation and variable identification are shown in lines 100 to 250. Program initialization and housekeeping tasks are contained in statements 300 to 390. The system is cleared in line 310.

System memory is reserved for the three tables in statement 340. The tables are dimensioned with 11 elements. One-dimensional tables are declared for the employee name (N$), the department name (D$), and seniority (S).

Lines 370 and 380 contain the output format statements to be used in printing the column headings and the tables. The output formats are assigned to 01$ and 02$.

The mainline module is shown in statements 400 to 630. This routine is used as the driver module to control execution of the program subroutines. Several subroutines are reused in this program.

The headings module is executed first. This module prints the report and column headings. The data tables are printed three times, and the same heading is used each time.

A FOR/NEXT loop is used to enter the data records. There are 11 data records, so

```
700                 REM     *****      Headings Module
710   LPRINT CHR$(12)
720   LPRINT TAB(22); "PORT-EX, INC"
730   LPRINT
740   LPRINT TAB(20); "EMPLOYEE LISTINGS"
750   LPRINT
760   LPRINT O1$
770   LPRINT
780   RETURN
790                                                                REM
800                 REM     *****      Read Module
810   READ N$(X), D$(X), S(X)
820   RETURN
830                                                                REM
1000                REM     *****      Numeric Sort Module
1010  FOR I = 1 TO 11 - 1
1020       FOR J = I + 1 TO 11
1030          IF S(I) < S(J) THEN N$(0) = N$(I) : N$(I) = N$(J) : N$(J) = N$(0) :
                              D$(0) = D$(I) : D$(I) = D$(J) : D$(J) = D$(0) :
                              S(0) = S(I)   : S(I) = S(J)   : S(J) = S(0)
1040       NEXT J
1050  NEXT I
1060  RETURN
1070                                                               REM
1200                REM     *****      Output Module
1210  LPRINT USING O2$; N$(X), D$(X), S(X)
1230  RETURN
1240                                                               REM
1400                REM     *****      Alphabetic Sort Module
1410  FOR I = 1 TO 11 - 1
1420       FOR J = I + 1 TO 11
1430              IF D$(I) > D$(J) THEN SWAP N$(I), N$(J) : SWAP D$(I), D$(J) :
                              SWAP S(I), S(J)
1440       NEXT J
1450  NEXT I
1460  RETURN
1470                                                               REM
1480  STOP
1500                REM     *****      Data to be Processed
1510  DATA    "Adams T", "Shipping", 46, "Baker R", "Receiving", 111
1520  DATA    "Chan C", "Testing", 24, "Drim L", "Components", 37
1530  DATA    "Elfor M", "Assembly", 65, "Fry J", "Design", 108
1540  DATA    "Fry L", "Office", 96, "George B", "Assembly", 21
1550  DATA    "Pulling B", "Office", 47, "Skar T", "Testing", 13
1560  DATA    "Sylvia L", "Design", 72
1570                                                               REM
```

FIGURE 16–4
Table sort program

the loop parameters are set accordingly. The read module loads the employee name, the department name, and the seniority tables. The DATA statements are arranged in alphabetic order based upon employee name.

The FOR/NEXT loop in statements 450 through 470 is used to print the data tables as entered. The LPRINT USING statement in line 1210 uses the output format assigned to 02$.

Line 480 calls the numeric sort module, which is shown in lines 1010 through 1060. This sort procedure arranges the tables in descending order based upon seniority. A nested loop is used to implement the sort. The outer loop uses variable I as the counter. The limit parameter for the outer loop is assigned the value of the number of table elements minus one. Variable I is also used as a table subscript in the sort procedure.

The inner loop uses variable J as the counter. Variable J is also used as a table subscript in the sort procedure. It is used to compare all elements following the I cell in the table. The J loop variable is assigned the value of I plus one because the J cell is compared with the I element; therefore, the J element must be at least one subscript greater than the I element. The limit parameter for the J loop is assigned the value of the table elements because all of the table elements must be checked.

The outer, or I, loop controls the number of times the sort procedure is executed and it identifies the comparison base element. The inner, or J, loop executes the comparison and switch operations.

Following is the sort routine. Each of the three data swapping steps is shown on a separate line for illustration purposes.

```
1010 FOR I = 1 TO 11 − 1
1020    FOR J = I + 1 TO 11
1030       IF S (I) < S(J) THEN
                N$(0) = N$(I) : N$(I) = N$(J) : N$(J) = N$(0) :
                D$(0) = D$(I) : D$(I) = D$(J) : D$(J) = D$(0) :
                S(0) = S(I)   : S(I) = S(J)   : S(J) = S(0)
1040    NEXT J
1050 NEXT I
```

The nested sort routine is evaluated using the following steps:

1. The parameters for the outer loop are set. In this case, I is assigned the value of 1. The outer loop is performed 11 − 1, or 10, times.
2. The inner loop parameters are set. Variable J is assigned the value of I + 1, or 2.
3. The inner loop is executed according to the parameters. In this program, the inner loop causes variable J to be assigned the values 2 through 11 as the program is executed. Therefore, the IF statement is executed 10 times. The value of the inner loop variable (J) varies faster than I does.
4. The IF statement causes element I (which is valued at 1) to be compared with all elements that follow (element J, or cells 2 through 11). If element I is less than element J, the two element values must be switched.
5. After the J loop parameters are satisfied, program control passes back to the outer loop. The outer loop variable is assigned the new value according to loop parameters. Control then shifts back to the inner loop.

To summarize, the inner loop is executed ten times during the first pass. Execution of the outer and inner loops is controlled by the FOR/NEXT statements. The variables are assigned values according to loop parameters. The loop body is executed many times, which is the reason for the slowness of bubble type sorts. This sort procedure is adequate for the vast majority of BASIC applications. This is particularly true when the slow speed of BASIC system printers is considered.

The body of the loop consists of an IF statement that compares the table elements and switches them when necessary. This branch statement also switches the corresponding elements in the other tables. The tables are sorted so that all three are in descending seniority order.

The sort procedure compares elements I and J. If element I is less than J, the values must be switched. The corresponding elements in the employee name and the department name tables must also be switched. Some BASIC systems now include the key word SWAP, which is illustrated in the alphabetic sort routine in this program. The temporary storage procedure shown in line 1030 is used on those systems that do not include SWAP.

The sort routine in statement 1030 follows. The actual switch operation is shown on separate lines for illustration purposes.

```
1030 IF S(I) < S(J) THEN
         N$(0) = N$(I) : N$(I) = N$(J) : N$(J) = N$(0) :
         D$(0) = D$(I) : D$(I) = D$(J) : D$(J) = D$(0) :
         S(0) = S(I)   : S(I) = S(J)   : S(J) = S(0)
```

Element I is compared with J in the seniority table. When element I is less than J, they must be switched. The procedure for switching the elements in the seniority table follows. Corresponding elements in the other tables are also switched as part of statement 1030.

```
S(0) = S(I) : S(I) = S(J) : S(J) = S(0)
```

Element S(0) (zero subscript element) is used as a temporary holding location to store the value of element S(I). The value contained in element S(J) is then assigned to S(I). Finally, S(J) is assigned the value of S(0). The temporary storage location S(0) is used to hold the value of the appropriate table element, so that the values contained in S(I) and S(J) can be switched. Some systems may not permit the use of S(0). When this is the case, any variable, such as TEMP$, T$, or T, can be used. Variable T$ is commonly used for string data and T for numeric data.

A portion of the sort execution follows to illustrate the procedure.

Element	Element Value
1	46
2	111
3	24
4	37
5	65
6	108

According to the sort specifications, element S(I) is compared with S(J). Variable I has an initial value of 1, and J contains the value 2. Therefore, S(1) is compared with S(2). If S(1) is less than S(2), the values are switched. In this case, S(1) is less than S(2). After these elements are switched, the table appears as follows.

Element	Element Value
1	111
2	46
3	24
4	37
5	65
6	108

The corresponding elements in the other two tables are also switched according to loop parameters.

The remainder of the inner loop is executed until the loop parameters are satisfied. Element one contains the value 111. Since this is the largest value in the table, the table elements are not switched again during this pass through the outer loop.

Control then shifts to the outer loop where variable I is assigned the value 2. The second element in the table is then compared with the following elements. Variable J is assigned the value of I + 1, or 3. Variable I contains a value of 2, and J has a value of 3; therefore, element two is compared with element three. In turn, all elements that follow are compared with the second element. Element two contains the value 46. This is greater than elements three and four, which are valued at 24 and 37 respectively. There is no switch during these comparisons.

Element five is greater than the second element, so the values are switched. The corresponding elements in the other tables are also switched. The seniority table then appears as follows.

Element	Element Value
1	111
2	65
3	24
4	37
5	46
6	108

Next, element six is compared with element two. The sixth element is greater, so the values are switched. Following is the table arrangement that results from the switch.

Element	Element Value
1	111
2	108
3	24
4	37
5	46
6	65

Execution of the nested loop continues until all parameters are satisfied. This means that the body of the loop is executed 55 times. When the nested loop is terminated, the seniority table appears as follows.

Element	Element Value
1	111
2	108
3	96
4	72
5	65
6	47
7	46
8	37
9	24
10	21
11	13

The final arrangement of the three tables when sorted in descending order is shown in the program output in figure 16–5. The first listing shows the original data, which is in alphabetic order by employee name. The second listing is by seniority. Finally, the data is shown in department name order.

The routine in statement 1030 sorts the data into descending numeric order. The tables can be sorted into ascending order by changing the relational operator from less than ($<$) to greater than ($>$).

After the numeric sort module is executed, the revised tables are printed. The headings module is called in statement 490. The FOR/NEXT loop in lines 500 to 520 prints the tables, which are arranged by seniority.

Statement 530 places the data pointer at the top of the data list. Although the RESTORE statement is not required, it is included here for illustration purposes. RESTORE, in effect, returns the program to the original data list which is in alphabetic order based upon employee name. The FOR/NEXT loop in lines 540 to 560 reloads the tables in the original alphabetic order.

Statement 570 calls the alphabetic sort module. The sort procedures used here are the same as previously described in the numeric sort. Nested FOR/NEXT loops are used to implement the sort routine. The sort key is the department name table. Line 1430, which follows, is the branch statement that compares and swaps the table elements as necessary. The only difference from the numeric sort is that this routine sorts string data.

```
1430 IF D$(I) > D$(J) THEN SWAP N$(I), N$(J) :
                        SWAP D$(I), D$(J) :
                        SWAP S(I), S(J)
```

The sort procedure is shown on separate lines for illustration purposes.

This routine compares two department name elements as specified. If element I is greater than J, the elements are swapped. The corresponding elements in the other tables are also switched. The SWAP key word is used to switch the elements. Following is the SWAP statement format.

SWAP ⟨ Parameter ⟩, ⟨ Parameter ⟩

```
                    PORT-EX, INC
              EMPLOYEE LISTINGS

    EMPLOYEE          DEPARTMENT        SENIORITY

    Adams T           Shipping             46
    Baker R           Receiving           111
    Chan C            Testing              24
    Drim L            Components           37
    Elfor M           Assembly             65
    Fry J             Design              108
    Fry L             Office               96
    George B          Assembly             21
    Pulling B         Office               47
    Skar T            Testing              13
    Sylvia L          Design               72

                    PORT-EX, INC
              EMPLOYEE LISTINGS

    EMPLOYEE          DEPARTMENT        SENIORITY

    Baker R           Receiving           111
    Fry J             Design              108
    Fry L             Office               96
    Sylvia L          Design               72
    Elfor M           Assembly             65
    Pulling B         Office               47
    Adams T           Shipping             46
    Drim L            Components           37
    Chan C            Testing              24
    George B          Assembly             21
    Skar T            Testing              13

                    PORT-EX, INC
              EMPLOYEE LISTINGS

    EMPLOYEE          DEPARTMENT        SENIORITY

    Elfor M           Assembly             65
    George B          Assembly             21
    Drim L            Components           37
    Fry J             Design              108
    Sylvia L          Design               72
    Pulling B         Office               47
    Fry L             Office               96
    Baker R           Receiving           111
    Adams T           Shipping             46
    Skar T            Testing              13
    Chan C            Testing              24
```

FIGURE 16–5
Table sort program output

The key word SWAP is followed by the two element parameters that are to be switched. The routine for switching the department name follows.

SWAP D$(I), D$(J) :

This procedure swaps the two elements automatically; the use of a temporary storage variable is not necessary. Some systems and/or forms of BASIC now include SWAP or the equivalent. Those systems that do not support SWAP must use the temporary storage routine as previously described.

The routine in line 1430 compares the I and J elements in the department name table. Nested loop procedures are used to execute this bubble sort routine. The two elements are swapped when the yalue of I is greater than J.

The final product of this sort routine is a table arranged in alphabetic order based upon department name. The final listing in figure 16–5 shows the printed result of this sort routine.

SELF-TEST

16-1

Using the original data table shown here, record the results of the sort routine that follows.

Element	Salesperson S$	Sales S
1	HAWES	23,475.97
2	SMITH	16,667.41
3	FORES	9,875.05
4	AFTNER	17,997.81

Sort Routine

```
1510 FOR X = 1 TO 4 − 1
1520        FOR Y = X + 1 TO 4
1530               IF S$(X) > S$(Y) THEN SWAP S$(X), S$(Y) :
                                       SWAP S(X), S(Y)
1540        NEXT Y
1550 NEXT X
```

Record the results after each pass.

Results After Pass 1

X = _____

Y = _____

Element	S$	S
1	_____	_____
2	_____	_____
3	_____	_____
4	_____	_____

Results After Pass 2

X = _____

Y = _____

Element	S$	S
1	_____	_____
2	_____	_____
3	_____	_____
4	_____	_____

Results After Pass 3

X = _____

Y = _____

Element	S$	S
1	_____	_____
2	_____	_____
3	_____	_____
4	_____	_____

Results After Pass 1				**Results After Pass 2**		
X = 2				X = 3		
Y = 5				Y = 5		
Element	*S$*	*S*		*Element*	*S$*	*S*
1	AFTNER	17997.81		1	AFTNER	17997.81
2	SMITH	23475.97		2	FORES	9875.05
3	HAWES	16667.41		3	SMITH	23475.97
4	FORES	9875.05		4	HAWES	16667.41

Results After Pass 3

X = 4		
Y = 5		
Element	*S$*	*S*
1	AFTNER	17997.81
2	FORES	9875.05
3	HAWES	16667.41
4	SMITH	23475.97

Line 580 causes the headings to be printed for the final listing. The loop shown in statements 590 to 610 prints the final table arrangement. The program is terminated after the sorted data tables have been printed.

The data to be processed is contained in lines 1500 to 1570. Eleven data records are processed in the program.

The printed results of the sort routines are exhibited in figure 16–5. In the first listing, the tables are arranged in original alphabetic order as entered by the READ-DATA statements. In the second listing, the tables are arranged in descending numeric order based upon seniority. Finally, the tables are arranged in department name order. The names of the employees are not arranged in alphabetic order by department. This change in order is a result of the bubble sort changes.

PROGRAM DEVELOPMENT CHECKLIST

Use the following checklist to ensure that all necessary components are included in the program.

_____ Flowcharts and documentation

_____ Housekeeping tasks

_____ Dimension statement

_____ Program loop

_____ Data entry

_____ Sort and switch routine

_____ Output

SUMMARY

The BASIC language includes procedures for sorting data contained in one-dimensional tables. Numeric or string data tables can be sorted. The sort key can be ascending or descending.

Nested FOR/NEXT loops are used in the sort routine to arrange the data according to the sort key. A program branch statement is used to arrange the tables into the correct sequence. Table subscripts are controlled by the nested loop parameters. The subscripts can be used to switch values in the specified table. Corresponding elements in other tables can also be swapped.

The SWAP key word or its equivalent is available on some systems to switch table elements. Those systems that do not support SWAP must use a temporary variable to switch the element values.

BASIC Key Word Learned

SWAP	Switches element values according to loop parameters.

PROGRAM ASSIGNMENT 16-1

Instructions

Prepare the flowcharts and a structured BASIC program to print a depreciation report. Use one-dimensional tables to enter and sort the data. Create one table for each of the following variables: asset name, beginning book value, and annual depreciation. Print the data tables in the original order. Then sort the tables into ascending order based upon the beginning book value. Use the SWAP key word or its equivalent if available. Otherwise, use the temporary storage routine. Print the tables after the sort procedure.

Following is the data to be processed. Use READ and DATA statements to enter the data.

Data

Asset Name	Beginning Book	Annual Depreciation
Calculator	600.00	200.00
Typewriter	1,000.00	333.33
Transcriber	75.00	25.00
VDT	875.00	291.67
Word processor	5,000.00	1,000.00
Computer	6,375.00	1,279.00
Desk	300.00	100.00
Cabinet	700.00	233.33
Display modules	960.00	320.00
Work station	1,000.00	333.33
Safe	1,500.00	500.00
Building	25,000.00	2,500.00

Output Format

Print report and column headings. Then print the original data tables, followed by the sorted tables. Use output editing if available.

PORT-EX COMPANY

NORTHEAST SALES DIVISION

Depreciation Status

Asset Name	Beginning Book	Annual Depreciation
Calculator	600.00	200.00
Typewriter	1,000.00	333.33

PORT-EX COMPANY

NORTHEAST SALES DIVISION

Depreciation Status

Asset Name	Beginning Book	Annual Depreciation
Transcriber	75.00	25.00
Desk	300.00	100.00

Instructions

PROGRAM ASSIGNMENT 16–2

Prepare the flowcharts and a structured BASIC program to print a list of participants at a new product conference. Use prompting INPUT statements to enter the data to be sorted. Use one-dimensional tables to process the data. Create separate tables for the participant's name and the company represented. Print the tables in the original order. Then, sort the tables into alphabetic order based upon the participant's name. Use the SWAP statement if available. Otherwise, use the temporary storage routine. Print the tables after the sort procedure.

Following is the data to be processed. Use prompting INPUT statements to enter the data.

Data

Name	Representing
Fathley, Ron	Precision Devices
Tarte, Susan	Tech-System Computers
Randy, Alice	Number Cruncher Computers
Sildette, Mike	Standard Test
Botwin, Teresa	Standard Test
Milan, Jacob	Precision Equipment
DeJesus, Sue	DOD
Zeller, Liz	DOD
Adams, Jan	Aircraft Arms
Witten, Debbie	COMMERCE
Cristoff, Tom	Chime Aircraft

Output Format

Print the report and column headings. Then print the original data tables, followed by the sorted data.

PORT-EX COMPANY

National Product Conference

Name	*Representing*
Fathley, Ron	Precision Devices
Tarte, Susan	Tech-System Computers

PORT-EX COMPANY

National Product Conference

Name	*Representing*
Adams, Jan	Aircraft Arms

PROGRAM ASSIGNMENT 16–3

Instructions

Prepare the flowcharts and a structured BASIC program to print a sales summary report that computes the amount sold by salesperson and by region. Use prompting IN-PUT statements to enter the data. Use one-dimensional tables to process the data. Create separate tables for the salesperson's name, the sales region, and the sales amount. First, print the tables in transaction order. Then, sort the tables into alphabetic order based upon the salesperson's name. Print the tables following the sort procedure. Use control break procedures to accumulate and print subtotals for each salesperson. Accumulate and print a summary total.

Next, sort the tables into alphabetic order based upon the sales region. Print the tables following the sort procedure. Use control break procedures to accumulate and print subtotals for each region. Accumulate and print a summary total.

Following is the data to be processed in transaction sequence. Use prompting IN-PUT statements to enter the data.

Data

Salesperson	*Region*	*Sales*
Smith	NE	3,455.70
Zenfor	SW	5,498.75
Smith	NE	2,677.33
Fores	SE	7,435.32
Hawes	NE	4,575.90
Zenfor	SW	3,666.67
Smith	NE	1,975.25
Fores	SE	3,276.75
Rastor	SW	8,999.99
Smith	NE	3,237.45
Zenfor	SW	4,475.55
Fores	SE	2,225.50
Hawes	NE	3,987.75
Rastor	SW	1,575.00

Output Format

Print the headings. Print the data tables as entered and also after each sort procedure. Use control break procedures to accumulate and print subtotals for the salespeople and the regions. Print the summary totals. Use output editing if available. See Chapter 17 for control break and subtotal procedures.

PORT-EX COMPANY

Sales Analysis Report

Original Tables

Tables Sorted by Name

Salesperson Subtotals

Summary Total

Tables Sorted by Region

Region Subtotals

Summary Total

TWO-DIMENSIONAL ARRAYS

17

OBJECTIVES

At the end of this chapter you should be able to perform the following operations:
- Utilize DIMENSION statements with double subscripts.
- Develop programs that use two-dimensional arrays to process data.

TABLES, ARRAYS, AND MATRICES

The procedures for processing data arranged in one-dimensional tables were developed in chapters 14 through 16. The objective of this chapter is to analyze the BASIC language procedures used to handle data arranged in two dimensions. The term array, or matrix, is used to describe a *two-dimensional* arrangement of data.

It is possible to arrange data in one-dimensional tables, two-dimensional arrays, three-dimensional matrices, or even in other dimensions. Most business data processing applications use either one or two-dimensional data arrangements. Advanced statistical simulation or business model development may require the use of more sophisticated data handling procedures.

Two-dimensional tables are commonly used when data must be arranged in rows and columns. In some situations a two-dimensional arrangement of data assists in perceiving solutions to problems. The location of items in storage bins in a warehouse is an example of a two-dimensional arrangement. The warehouse is divided into aisles, and a number of storage bins are located in each aisle. Each bin has a specific row and column location that corresponds with the bin and aisle. Following is an example of the use of an array to record the location of products stored in a warehouse.

Row	Column			
Bin Number	*Aisle 1*	*Aisle 2*	*Aisle 3*	*Aisle 4*
1	1111	2222	3333	4444
2	5555	6666	7777	8888
3	9999	1211	1222	1233
4	1244	1255	1266	1277

A search of the array for product number 2222 reveals that it is stored in bin 1, aisle 2. Product number 2222 is located in row 1, column 2. As another example, product number 1222 is located in bin 3, aisle 3. Therefore, product 1222 is located in row 3, column 3.

The BASIC procedure used to declare and manipulate an array is the *double subscript*. Following is the double subscript format.

P(R,C)

Array P consists of two dimensions. The first character (R) refers to the number of rows, and the second (C) refers to the number of columns. Array P, as declared in the following statement is a 4 by 4 matrix.

DIM P(4,4)

There are 4 rows and 4 columns in array P. This means that 16 separate elements, or cells, are contained in the array. Each element can be individually accessed. Product number 2222 is in row 1, column 2; therefore, the BASIC subscript reference that identifies this element is P(1,2). In the same manner, the subscript for product number 1222 is P(3,3).

A simple rule to follow when using double subscripts is that the row is listed first followed by the column. Or, more simply, RC.

Nested FOR/NEXT loops are commonly used to process arrays. The example program demonstrates the use of nested loops and double subscripts.

FLOWCHARTS—ARRAYS

The top-level flowchart for the example program is shown in figure 17–1. The program is controlled by the mainline routine. This routine controls execution of the read, calculation, heading, output, and summary subroutines.

The detailed logic flowchart is shown in figure 17–2. The mainline routine controls execution of the program. INPUT statements are used to enter the number of rows and columns in the arrays. Processing subroutines include the read, calculation, heading, output, and summary blocks.

The read subroutine causes the data records to be entered. Nested FOR/NEXT loops are used to enter the data into the pay rate and hours worked arrays. The outer FOR/NEXT loop controls the row (R) variable. The loop limit (X) is entered in an INPUT statement in the mainline block. The inner loop is used to control the column (C) variable. An INPUT statement in the mainline routine enters the inner loop limit (Y).

When nested FOR/NEXT loops are used in a program, the inner loop is executed faster than the outer loop. A review of the detailed logic flowchart in figure 17–2 shows that loop counter C changes in value much faster than R. Therefore, data is entered row by row. Each time the outer loop is executed the row being processed is incremented. One row is completely loaded with data each time the outer loop is executed according to parameters.

The calculation routine includes a nested FOR/NEXT loop. The same loop procedures are used as in the read block. The processing is accomplished row by row. Gross pay is computed by multiplying the appropriate elements in the pay rate and hours worked arrays. Elements in the gross pay, pay rate, and hours worked arrays correspond according to loop parameters.

A summary total is accumulated for gross pay each time the loop is executed. Each element in the gross pay array is added to the summary total.

The output subroutine prints the data values contained in the pay rate, hours worked, and gross pay arrays. Nested loops are used to print each of the arrays. The pay rate array is printed first followed by the hours worked and gross pay arrays.

Finally, the summary routine prints the accumulated total for gross pay. The program is terminated at this point.

EXAMPLE PROGRAM—ARRAY PROCESSING

The objective of this chapter is to demonstrate the BASIC language procedures for processing data in two-dimensional arrays. Two-dimensional arrays, or matrices, arrange the data in rows and columns. Arrays should be declared in DIMENSION statements.

The sample program for this chapter is exhibited in figures 17–3 and 17–4. Statements 100 through 880 are contained in figure 17–3, and statements 1000 through 1660

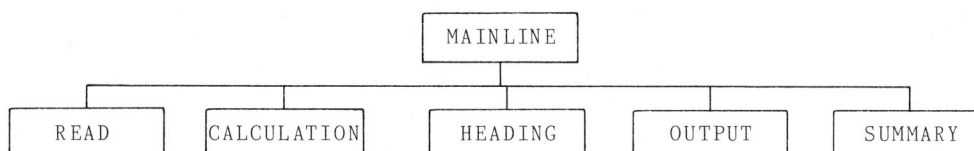

FIGURE 17–1
Top-level flowchart

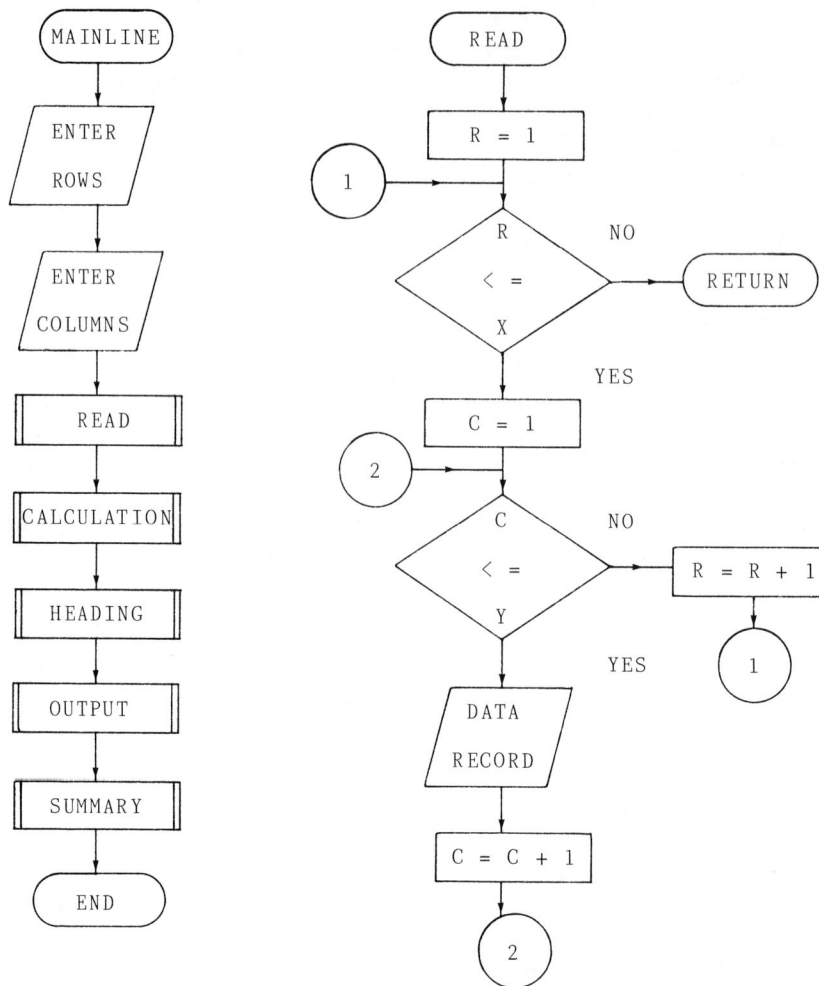

FIGURE 17–2
Detailed logic flowchart

are shown in Figure 17–4. Program documentation and variable identification are contained in lines 100 to 240.

System initialization and housekeeping tasks are contained in statements 300 to 390. The system is cleared in line 310.

Statement 340, which follows, declares the arrays to be used.

340 DIM P(10,10), H(10,10), G(10,10)

Three arrays are declared. They are the pay rate (P), the hours worked (H), and the gross pay (G). Each matrix is dimensioned as having 10 rows and 10 columns. Arrays may be dimensioned as integers, variables, or as valid BASIC expressions. The rows are listed first and are followed by the number of columns. A DIMENSION statement that declares a 10 by 10 matrix reserves memory for 100 elements. The number of rows is multiplied by the number of columns to determine the number of elements. The size of the arrays as dimensioned can exceed the number of elements actually used in the program.

Caution should be exercised when dimensioning arrays to declare only the amount of memory actually needed to execute the program. It is easy to reserve much memory very quickly. An array declared as being 100 by 10 reserves 1,000 elements. This may consume all of the available memory on a small system.

The system may display memory available when booted. BASIC systems usually include a key word to display the amount of available memory. The format follows. The argument is a dummy variable that may not be required on some systems.

PRINT FRE(Argument)

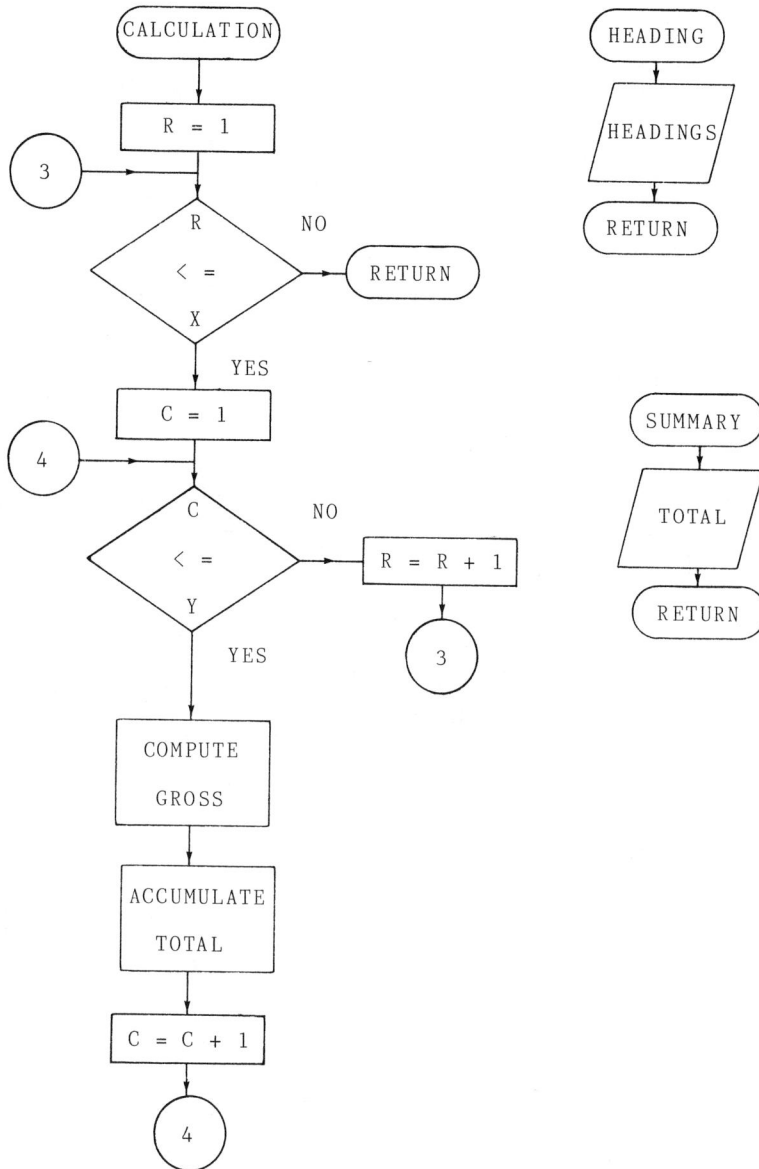

FIGURE 17-2
(Continued)

The following immediate mode statement causes the memory available to be printed. The key word may or may not be used in program mode depending upon the system.

PRINT FRE(1)
7271

The system displays the memory available on the next line. In this case, 7271 bytes are available.

The key word used to determine available memory varies with the system. APPLESOFT BASIC systems also use the FRE key word. TRS-80 BASIC systems use the MEM key word for the equivalent function. LOCATE or the equivalent key word can be used to locate the number of bytes that are free in any available screen position.

The format for the output edit lines used to print the headings and detail lines is established in statements 370 and 380. The output format statements are assigned to 01$ and 02$.

The mainline control module is shown in lines 400 to 490. The INPUT statements in lines 410 and 420 are used to enter the number of rows and columns to be used in the array processing. In this program, the arrays are 4 by 4. Therefore, the arrays contain

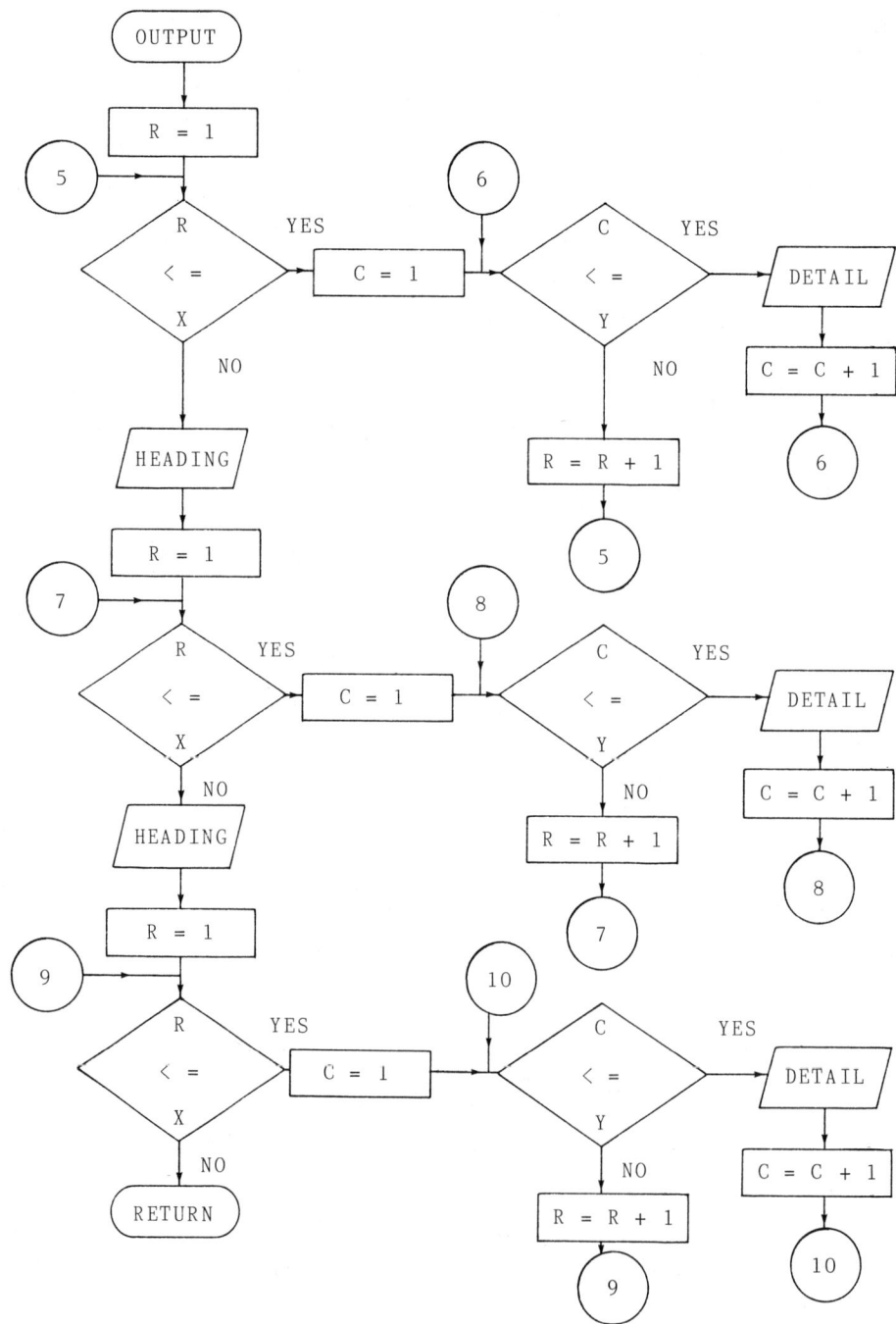

FIGURE 17–2
(Continued)

16 elements. The number of rows is entered as variable X, and the number of columns as Y.

The read module is called in line 430. Following is the nested FOR/NEXT loop used to enter the data.

```
610 FOR R = 1 TO X
620     FOR C = 1 TO Y
630         READ P(R,C), H(R,C)
640     NEXT C
650 NEXT R
660 RETURN
```

The outer loop is used to control the row (R) variable, and the inner loop controls

```
100             REM      FIGURE  17-3     WRITTEN BY LARRY FRY    7/27/83
110             REM      This program uses two-dimensional arrays to obtain
120             REM      gross pay.   Two-dimensional arrays are used for
130             REM      the pay rate, hours worked, and gross pay.
140                                                                       REM
150             REM      *****      Variable Identification
160             REM           R        .....  Row Subscript
170             REM           C        .....  Column Subscript
180             REM           P(R,C)   .....  Pay Rate Array
190             REM           H(R,C)   .....  Hours Worked Array
200             REM           G(R,C)   .....  Gross Pay Array
210             REM           X        .....  Loop Limit  -  Rows
220             REM           Y        .....  Loop Limit  -  Columns
230             REM           G(O,O)   .....  Summary Total
240                                                                       REM
300             REM      *****      Initialize System
310  CLEAR
320                                                                       REM
330             REM      *****      Dimension Arrays
340  DIM  P(10,10),   H(10,10),   G(10,10)
350                                                                       REM
360             REM      *****      Output Format
370  LET O1$ = "          Pay Rate Array"
380  LET O2$ = "###.##        ###.##        ###.##        ###.##"
390                                                                       REM
400             REM      *****      Mainline Control
410  INPUT "ENTER number of rows   "; X
420  INPUT "ENTER number of columns "; Y
430  GOSUB 610
440  GOSUB 810
450  GOSUB 1010
460  GOSUB 1210
470  GOSUB 1510
480  END
490                                                                       REM
600             REM      *****      Read Module
610  FOR R = 1 TO X
620      FOR C = 1 TO Y
630           READ P(R,C), H(R,C)
640      NEXT C
650  NEXT R
660  RETURN
670                                                                       REM
800             REM      *****      Calculation Module
810  FOR R = 1 TO X
820      FOR C = 1 TO Y
830           LET G(R,C) = P(R,C)   *   H(R,C)
840           LET G(O,O) = G(O,O)   +   G(R,C)
850      NEXT C
860  NEXT R
870  RETURN
880                                                                       REM
```

the column (C). An analysis of the nested statements shows that the inner loop (C) varies the fastest. A trace of the loop parameters follows.

FIGURE 17–3
Array program

Loop Pass	R	C
1	1	1
2	1	2
3	1	3
4	1	4
5	2	1
6	2	2
7	2	3
8	2	4
9	3	1
10	3	2
11	3	3

```
1000              REM      *****      Heading Module
1010   LPRINT CHR$(12)
1020   LPRINT TAB(12); "PORT-EX COMPANY"
1030   LPRINT
1040   LPRINT TAB(12); "PAYROLL  REPORT"
1050   LPRINT
1060   LPRINT O1$
1070   LPRINT
1080   RETURN
1090                                                                        REM
1200              REM      *****      Output Module
1210   FOR R = 1 TO X
1220        FOR C = 1 TO Y
1230             LPRINT USING O2$; P(R,C);
1240        NEXT C
1250     LPRINT : LPRINT
1260   NEXT R
1270   LPRINT  :  LPRINT  :  LPRINT
1280   LPRINT  "          Hours Worked Array"
1290   LPRINT
1300   FOR R = 1 TO X
1310        FOR C = 1 TO Y
1320             LPRINT USING O2$; H(R,C);
1330        NEXT C
1340     LPRINT : LPRINT
1350   NEXT R
1360   LPRINT  :  LPRINT  :  LPRINT
1370   LPRINT  "          Gross Pay Array"
1380   LPRINT
1390   FOR R = 1 TO X
1400        FOR C = 1 TO Y
1410             LPRINT USING O2$; G(R,C);
1420        NEXT C
1430     LPRINT : LPRINT
1440   NEXT R
1450   RETURN
1460                                                                        REM
1500              REM      *****      Summary Module
1510   LPRINT : LPRINT
1520   LPRINT USING "TOTAL PAYROLL   $$##,###.##";  G(O,O)
1530   RETURN
1540                                                                        REM
1550                                                                        REM
1560   STOP
1600              REM      *****      Data to be Processed
1610   DATA  4.50, 35, 5.00, 39.5, 3.35, 40, 3.75, 20
1620   DATA  7.55, 40, 6.50, 32.5, 9.95, 30, 8.80, 40
1630   DATA  9.99, 40, 8.75, 37.5, 9.00, 40, 9.50, 40
1640   DATA  9.75, 35, 9.25, 38.5, 8.00, 30, 6.50, 20
1650                                                                        REM
1660   STOP
```

FIGURE 17–4
Array program

Loop Pass	R	C
12	3	4
13	4	1
14	4	2
15	4	3
16	4	4

The read loop is executed a total of 16 times. The inner loop, which controls the column (C) element, varies the fastest. Therefore, the arrays are loaded row by row. After execution of the initial pass through the outer loop, the arrays appear as follows.

ARRAY P

Row	Column			
	1	*2*	*3*	*4*
1	4.50	5.00	3.35	3.75

ARRAY H

Row	Column			
	1	*2*	*3*	*4*
1	35	39.5	40	20

The arrays would be loaded row by row. They contain 4 rows and 4 columns for a total of 16 elements. The arrays are exhibited in figure 17–5.

The element in array P, which is known as row 1, column 1, corresponds to the same element in array H. Therefore, the pay rate value in P(1,1) corresponds to the hours worked value contained in array H(1,1). These values represent the pay rate and hours worked for one person. In the same manner, all of the remaining elements in arrays P and H correspond. The corresponding elements in the various arrays can be accessed and manipulated as necessary by using the appropriate subscripts.

Statement 440 calls the calculation module. A nested loop, which follows, is used to compute the gross pay and to accumulate the summary total.

```
810 FOR R = 1 TO X
820    FOR C = 1 TO Y
830        LET G(R,C) = P(R,C) * H(R,C)
840        LET G(0,0) = G(0,0) + G(R,C)
850    NEXT C
860 NEXT R
870 RETURN
```

```
               PORT-EX COMPANY

               PAYROLL  REPORT

               Pay Rate Array

    4.50        5.00        3.35        3.75

    7.55        6.50        9.95        8.80

    9.99        8.75        9.00        9.50

    9.75        9.25        8.00        6.50



               Hours Worked Array

   35.00       39.50       40.00       20.00

   40.00       32.50       30.00       40.00

   40.00       37.50       40.00       40.00

   35.00       38.50       30.00       20.00



               Gross Pay Array

  157.50      197.50      134.00       75.00

  302.00      211.25      298.50      352.00

  399.60      328.13      360.00      380.00

  341.25      356.13      240.00      130.00



   TOTAL PAYROLL    $4,262.85
```

FIGURE 17–5
Array processing output

The first four passes through the inner loop result in the computation of the first row in the gross pay array. Each corresponding element in the pay rate and hours worked arrays is multiplied to obtain the gross pay cells. This computes the gross pay for each individual worker. Following are the corresponding elements from the pay rate, hours worked, and gross pay arrays.

ARRAY P

Row	Column			
	1	*2*	*3*	*4*
1	4.50	5.00	3.35	3.75

ARRAY H

Row	Column			
	1	*2*	*3*	*4*
1	35	39.5	40	20

ARRAY G

Row	Column			
	1	*2*	*3*	*4*
1	157.50	197.50	134.00	75.00

During the first pass through the inner loop, variables R and C both contain the value 1. The value in element P(1,1) is multiplied by the corresponding element in H(1,1) to obtain G(1,1). The value 4.50 is multiplied by 35 to obtain 157.50. In the same manner, on the fourth pass through the inner loop, element P(1,4) is multiplied by H(1,4) to obtain G(1,4). The value 3.75 is multiplied by 20 to obtain 75.00. The nested loop is executed in this manner until all 16 elements in array G are computed. (See figure 17–5 for the completed arrays.)

Variable G(0,0) (zero subscript elements) is used to accumulate the summary total for gross pay. This computation is shown in line 840. The nested loop controls the accumulation of variable G(0,0). Each of the 16 elements in the gross pay are in turn added to G(0,0).

The headings module is called in line 450. Report and array headings are printed as a result of this routine. Line 1010 results in the printer advancing to a new page.

Statement 460 calls the output module. Nested loops are used to print the pay rate, hours worked, and gross pay arrays in sequence. The printed report shown in Figure 17–5 is the result of this module.

The nested loop in lines 1210 through 1260 prints the pay rate array. The 4 by 4 matrix is printed in array format. Each element is shown in its relative position. All 16 elements are printed. The LPRINT USING statement in line 1230, which follows, prints the array.

1230   LPRINT USING 02$; P(R,C);

The output format assigned to 02$ in statement 380 is used to edit the print line. The respective elements in array P(R,C) are printed according to loop parameters. Notice the semicolon at the end of the statement. This semicolon freezes the print head so that each element can be printed on the appropriate row. The first four elements are thus printed on row 1. This feature may not be available in the LPRINT USING format of some systems. The first four passes through the inner loop produce the following output.

4.50   5.00   3.35   3.75

Execution of the inner loop is terminated after the fourth pass. Parameter C exceeds the loop limit at that point. Control is then shifted to statement 1250 which advances printing to a new line. The second LPRINT statement in line 1250 produces double spacing between array rows as shown in figure 17–5.

Record the results of the following program segment.

```
1000 DIM P(5,5), Q(5,5), T(5,5)
1100 FOR I = 1 TO 3
1110      FOR J = 1 TO 4
1120           READ P(I,J), Q(I,J)
1130      NEXT J
1140 NEXT I
1200 FOR I = 1 TO 3
1210      FOR J = 1 TO 4
1220           LET T(I,J) = P(I,J) * Q(I,J)
1230           LET T(0,0) = T(0,0) + T(I,J)
1240      NEXT J
1250 NEXT I
1300 FOR I = 1 TO 3
1310      FOR J = 1 TO 4
1320           PRINT T(I,J); "   ";
1330      NEXT J
1340   PRINT : PRINT
1350 NEXT I
1360 PRINT : PRINT
1370 PRINT T(0,0)
1380 END
1500 DATA 2,40,3,15,4,20,3,25
1510 DATA 6,15,3,20,4,10,10,6
1520 DATA 3,15,4,10,5,5,4,15
```

80	45	80	75
90	60	40	60
45	40	25	60
700			

Record the results of the following program segment.

```
1000 CLEAR
2000 DIM P(5,5), H(5,5), T(5,5)
2100 FOR Y = 1 TO 5
2110      FOR Z = 1 TO 2
2120           READ P(Y,Z), H(Y,Z)
2130      NEXT Z
2140 NEXT Y
2200 FOR Y = 1 TO 5
2210      FOR Z = 1 TO 2
2220           LET T(Y,Z) = P(Y,Z) * H(Y,Z)
2230           LET T(0,0) = T(0,0) + T(Y,Z)
2240      NEXT Z
2250 NEXT Y
2300 FOR Y = 1 TO 2
```

```
2310   S = 0
2320      FOR Z = 1 TO 5
2330          LET S = S + T(Z,Y)
2340      NEXT Z
2350   PRINT S / 5
2360 NEXT Y
2400 PRINT : PRINT
2410 PRINT T(0,0) / (5 * 2)
2420 END
2500 DATA 20,3,40,4,30,3,25,3,40,4
2510 DATA 40,3,30,4,40,3,25,3,40,3
```

Answers for
Self-Test
17-2

101
119
110

Line 1260, which is NEXT R, increments the outer loop. The system then prints the second row. The loop is executed in this manner until each of the 16 elements are printed. In the completed array there are 4 rows of data values with 4 columns each.

Following execution of the loop in lines 1210 through 1260, the system prints the heading for the next array. The print statement in line 1280 causes the heading "Hours Worked Array" to be printed.

The nested loop in statements 1300 through 1350 prints the 16 elements in the hours worked array. Nested loop procedures are used to print the array.

This is followed by another heading line. Statement 1370 causes the heading "Gross Pay Array" to be printed.

The gross pay array is printed as a result of the nested loop in statements 1390 through 1440. The 16 array elements are printed in relative order.

After the output module is completed, the summary module is executed. This routine prints the summary total assigned to G(0,0) (zero subscript elements). The LPRINT USING format shown in statement 1520 prints the summary total. This module terminates program execution.

The data to be processed is shown in lines 1600 to 1650. The element values for the pay rate and hours worked arrays are alternated in the DATA statements. Four data records are shown on each line.

The program output is shown in figure 17–5. Each of the three arrays is printed. This is followed by the summary total. The amount printed for the summary total is $4,262.85. If the individual elements were added, the total would be $4,262.86. The one cent difference is caused by internal rounding.

PROGRAM DEVELOPMENT CHECKLIST

Use the following checklist to ensure that all components are included in the program.

_____   Flowcharts and documentation

_____   System initialization

_____   Housekeeping tasks

_____   DIMENSION statement

_____   Double subscripts

_____ Program loop control

_____ Data entry

_____ Computations

_____ Array output

_____ Summary totals

SUMMARY

The BASIC language contains procedures for processing data arranged in two-dimensional arrays. The term array, or matrix, is used to describe two-dimensional data arrangements. Two-dimensional arrays are arranged in rows and columns. Rows are in the horizontal plane, while columns are vertical. Arrays require the use of double subscripts which are written in the form A(R,C). The first character within the parentheses refers to the row, and the second refers to the column.

DIMENSION statements are used to reserve system memory for arrays. All arrays should be dimensioned.

Array elements are addressed and accessed by double subscripts. The total number of array elements is computed by multiplying the number of rows by the columns.

Caution should be exercised when declaring arrays. System memory can be exceeded when processing large arrays.

BASIC Key Words Learned

FRE — Determines the amount of system memory available.

MEM — Determines the amount of system memory available (TRS-80).

Instructions

Prepare the flowcharts and a structured BASIC program to print an inventory report. Use two-dimensional arrays to process the data. Create a 5 by 3 array for each of the following variables: product name, price, quantity on hand, and total. Load the data into the product name, price and quantity arrays, and compute the total array cells by multiplying the corresponding elements in the price and quantity arrays. Compute summary totals for the number of items and the total price. Print the arrays followed by the summary totals.

Following is the data to be processed. Use READ and DATA statements to enter the data into the 5 by 3 arrays.

PROGRAM ASSIGNMENT 17–1

Data

	Name Array	Price Array	Quantity Array
Row 1			
	Board, Circuit	625	20
	Board, Graphic	475	15
	Board, Memory	750	30

Row 2

	Board, Mother	975	100
	Circuit, Logic	56	78
	Circuit, Memory	35	400

Row 3

	Circuit, Processor	125	92
	Control, Expansion	93	31
	Control, Network	197	25

Row 4

	Display, Color	345	60
	Display, Monochrome	299	49
	Oscilloscope	325	5

Row 5

	Printer, Daisy	1100	20
	Printer, Matrix	475	15
	Tablet, Graphics	413	10

Output Format

Print the headings and the data arrays followed by the summary totals. Use output editing if available.

PORT-EX COMPANY

Inventory Report

Name Array

XXXXXXXXX   XXXXXXXXXXX   XXXXXXX

Price Array

XXX.XX   XXX.XX   XXX.XX

Quantity Array

XXX   XXX   XXX

Total Array

X,XXX.XX   X,XXX.XX   X,XXX.XX

SUMMARY TOTALS

PROGRAM ASSIGNMENT 17–2

Instructions

Prepare the flowcharts and a structured BASIC program to search an array for specified data. Use two-dimensional arrays to process the data. Create a 5 by 3 array for each of the following variables: product name, price, and quantity on hand. Load the data into the 5 by 3 arrays and print them. Use the product name array as the search key. The product storage location is determined by the element subscripts. Enter the search key in the transaction mode. If the specified value is present in the product name array, print the storage location (row and column). Include an error routine. Print the corresponding price and quantity.

The data to be processed is shown in Program Assignment 17–1. Use READ and DATA statements to enter the data into the 5 by 3 arrays.

Data

See Program Assignment 17–1.

Output Format

Print the headings and the arrays followed by the search transactions. Include an error handling routine. Use output editing if available. Execute at least six search transactions.

PORT-EX COMPANY

Storage Locations

Name Array

XXXXXXXX   XXXXXXXX   XXXXXXXXXXX

Price Array

XXX.XX   XXX.XX   XXX.XX

Quantity Array

XXX   XXX   XXX

Transaction Processing

PRODUCT NAME FROM INPUT = Circuit, Processor
STORAGE LOCATION = 3,1   PRICE = 125.00   QUANTITY = 92

Instructions

Prepare the flowcharts and a structured BASIC program to print an income distribution report. Use a 7 by 4 array to process the data. The Surfside Motel receives income from three major sources: rooms, meals, and drinks. Record room income in column one of the array. List income from meals in column two, and from drinks in column three. Place daily totals in column four. Use the rows for the days of the week. Print the complete array.

Compute the total daily income by adding the three income sources. This total becomes the fourth column. Accumulate and print the weekly summary of income from rooms, meals, and drinks, and the total income. Compute and print the average daily income for rooms, meals, and drinks, and the total income. Finally, identify and print the day of the week with the greatest income from rooms, meals, and drinks, and the total income.

Following is the data to be processed. Use INPUT statements to enter the data into the array.

Data

	Rooms	Meals	Drinks
Row 1			
	2,222.00	970.50	292.50
Row 2			
	2,333.33	1,002.85	243.75
Row 3			
	2,277.55	938.15	282.75
Row 4			
	2,166.45	969.81	214.94
Row 5			
	2,388.65	1,139.70	295.37
Row 6			
	1,667.67	1,435.46	309.81
Row 7			
	1,388.75	1,289.75	499.89

Output Format

Print the headings and the array followed by the summary and average values. Use output editing if available.

SURFSIDE MOTEL

Income Distribution

Income Array

Day	*Rooms*	*Meals*	*Drinks*	*Totals*
1	x,xxx.xx	x,xxx.xx	xxx.xx	x,xxx.xx
2	x,xxx.xx	x,xxx.xx	xxx.xx	x,xxx.xx
TOTAL	x,xxx.xx	x,xxx.xx	x,xxx.xx	xx,xxx.xx
AVERAGE	x,xxx.xx	x,xxx.xx	x,xxx.xx	x,xxx.xx
GREATEST DAY	x	x	x	x

TOTAL INCOME FOR WEEK $XX,XXX.XX

SEQUENTIAL DISK DATA FILES

OBJECTIVES

At the end of this chapter you should be able to perform the following operations:

- Create sequential disk data files.
- Load data into sequential disk data files.
- Read and display data from sequential disk data files.

STORING DATA ON MAGNETIC DISK

The textbook thus far has concentrated upon using data that has been entered through the use of INPUT statements (transaction processing) or READ-DATA statements (serial processing). These methods are used in business data processing operations. Routinely, however, businesses build data files on magnetic disks or diskettes. The advantages of this type of storage are: they enable faster access to and manipulation of data; they are easier to update; and, they enable faster execution of programs. In contrast, INPUT and READ-DATA statements require a longer period of time to enter data and they increase program execution time. Some disk data files commonly maintained by business organizations are files for personnel, customers, inventory, accounting, and budgeting.

A magnetic disk file is a collection of related data records. Files can consist of many records in any sequence. Records, in turn, are made up of related data fields, or variables. A data field is one unit of data, such as the employee name or the department name. Data fields must appear in the same relative sequence within a record. For example, the employee name is always entered first and the department name is always entered second within the record. Records usually can be placed in any sequence within the file; however, they are usually placed in some predetermined order.

The key concept in the use of magnetic disks is that data stored on magnetic disks can be used by different programs. It is not necessary to enter the data each time the program is executed as is required with INPUT statements. READ-DATA statements can only be used by the program in which the statements are contained. It is possible to link or chain programs together and pass the values when using READ-DATA statements, but this is a cumbersome process.

Disk files need only be constructed one time. They are then available for use by any program capable of reading disk files. The files are permanent and provide increased speed and flexibility. They can easily be updated by changing the appropriate data record values.

Many of today's business organizations use data base techniques for storing and/or retrieving data. A *data base* is one central file that contains all of the organization's data and information resources. The data base is stored on magnetic media.

There are three steps involved in creating a disk file. First, the file must be opened. Opening a file creates a buffer area, or a channel, to link the computer memory with the disk drive, or device. A *buffer* is a portion of main memory that is allocated to the creation of disk files. The buffer passes data to the disk from the system. Second, the data must be entered in the transaction mode. When the buffer is full of data values, the contents are transferred to the device. Finally, the file must be closed. The close statement transfers any data remaining in the buffer and secures the file.

The programs in this chapter use *sequential disk files*. This means that the data records are stored in a specific sequence. On most systems it is not possible to directly access a specific data record when using sequential files. In order to locate a particular data record, it is necessary to start at the beginning of the file and search the file record by record.

The data records are usually stored in a predetermined sequence. The relative arrangement of the data records within the file is accomplished at data entry. The data records can be entered in alphabetic or numeric order. Once the file is established, it is possible to search through it for specific records. The data records can be sorted into a different sequence and new records can be added at any time.

Another procedure used to access data on magnetic disks is referred to as random, or direct, access. When this procedure is used, it is possible to directly access a specific data record in the file. The disk file is not checked in sequence. Rather, the computer system accesses the specified data record directly. The disk is used in a dynamic, or random access, mode.

The creation of sequential disk data files is presented in Chapter 18. The process for updating sequential files is described in Chapter 19. Random access files are presented in Chapter 20.

FLOWCHARTS—CREATING AND READING SEQUENTIAL DISK FILES

The objective of this chapter is to illustrate the BASIC language procedures for creating and reading a sequential disk file. Two programs are used to do this: one program creates the file; and one reads the file and prints the data. The top-level flowchart shown in figure 18–1 is used to create the file. Figure 18–2 is the detailed logic flowchart for file creation.

The top-level flowchart in figure 18–1 contains the mainline routine which controls program execution. The subroutines are the data entry and output to disk blocks.

In the detailed logic flowchart in figure 18–2, housekeeping tasks, which consist of clearing the system and the monitor screen, are executed first.

The disk files must be opened before the device can be accessed. The open statement must be listed before there is any reference to the disk file.

The number of data records to be placed into the disk file is entered by an INPUT statement. There are 11 records to be processed, so 11 is entered. This number serves as the program loop limit The number of records to be processed can be found on the source document or in organization records.

A FOR/NEXT structure is used to control execution of the program loop. The loop will be executed 11 times according to the parameters. The loop body consists of the data entry and output to disk routines.

Variable values are entered in the data entry subroutine. Values are entered for the employee name, the department name, seniority, and year-to-date earnings. INPUT statements are used to enter the 11 data records, each of which has four fields.

The data records are placed in the disk file by the output to disk subroutine in the sequence entered.

Upon completion of the loop, the disk files are closed. The files must be closed or an error can result. This is followed by program termination.

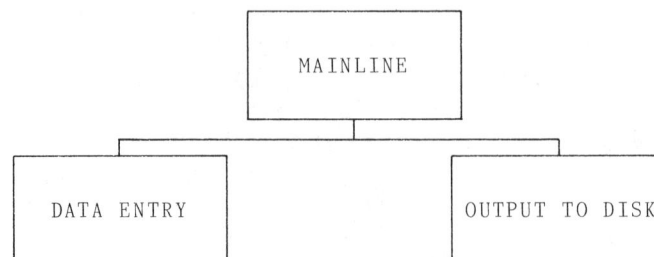

FIGURE 18–1
Top level flowchart

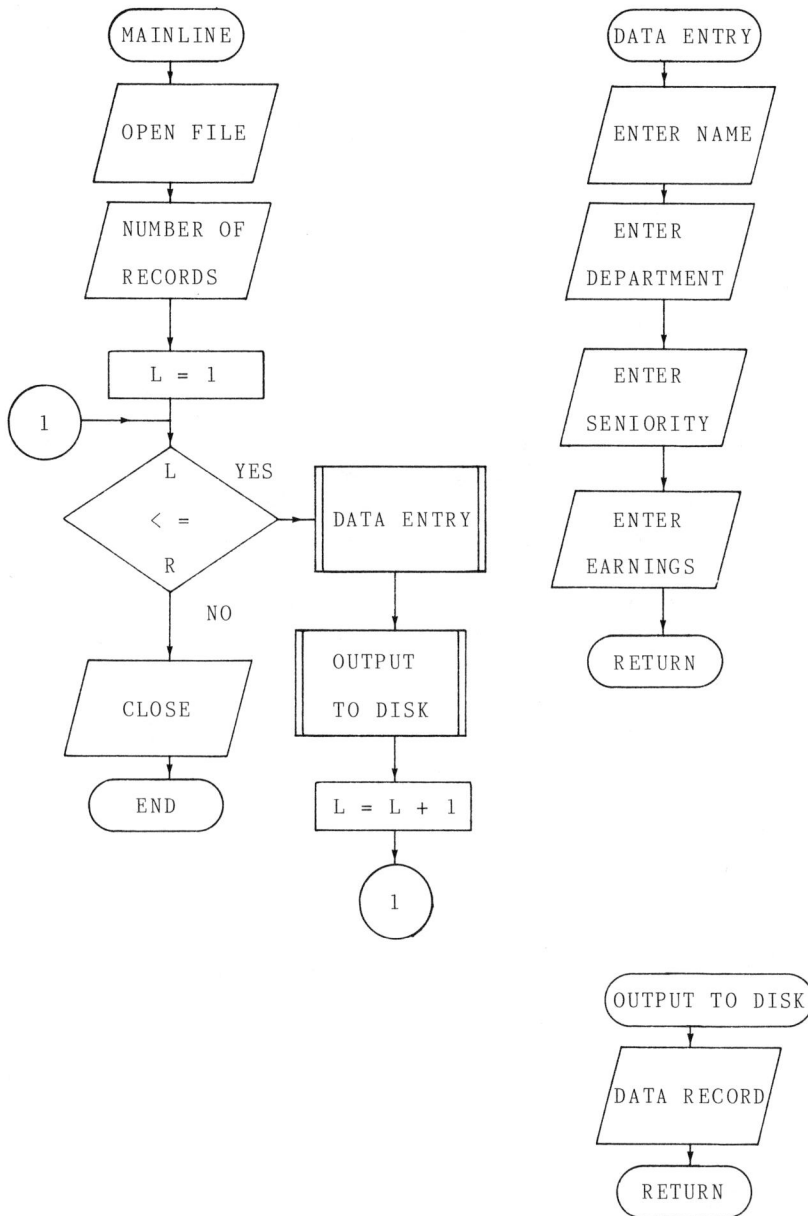

FIGURE 18–2
Detailed logic flowchart

This program creates a disk data file that contains 11 records.

The second program in this chapter, figure 18–8, reads the disk file created by the first program, figure 18–5. The data values are then printed. The top-level flowchart for the program that reads and prints the disk file is shown in figure 18–3. The mainline routine controls execution of the heading, read, output, and summary subroutines.

An independent error trap routine is also included in the flowchart. This routine is included to verify that the program has terminated correctly. When a data file is created, a pointer is placed at the end of the file to confirm that the entire file has been read. When the program terminates, the error trap routine determines if the program has terminated correctly (reached the pointer) or if it has terminated because of an error. This routine is not considered part of the mainline block. It is independent and is executed whenever the program terminates.

The detailed logic flowchart for reading and printing the file is shown in figure 18–4. Housekeeping tasks are performed before control of the program is passed to the mainline module. They include the statement used to clear the system and the monitor screen, the output format statements for heading and detail lines, and the error handling statement which detects errors and branches to the error routine.

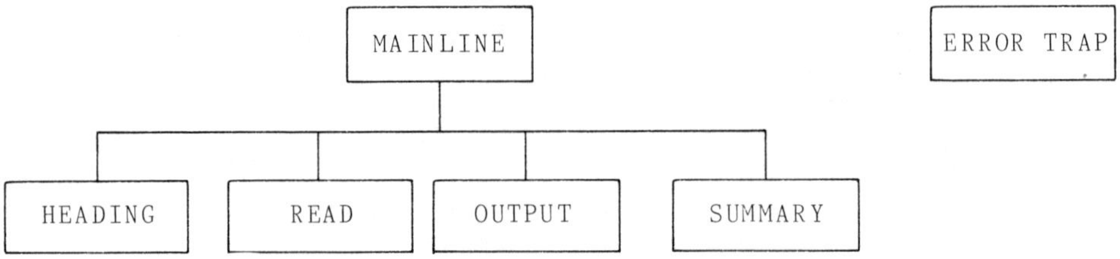

FIGURE 18–3
Top-level flowchart

The mainline routine is used as the driver module to control program execution. First, the disk file is opened to access the device.

A FOR/NEXT structure is used to control execution of the program loop. The limit is assigned a value of 100. The limit can be assigned any value as long as it exceeds the number of actual data records. There are 11 data records in the file, so 100 was selected for illustration purposes. Abnormal execution or an incorrect detail listing will result from entering a limit that is lower than the number of records. The program loop consists of a routine that reads data from the disk file, and an output block.

The read subroutine begins with a program branch statement that tests for the end of the disk file. When the end of the file is detected, the file is closed. This causes an error condition when the following statement, which reads data records from the file, is executed. Program control then shifts to the error routine. The error routine confirms that

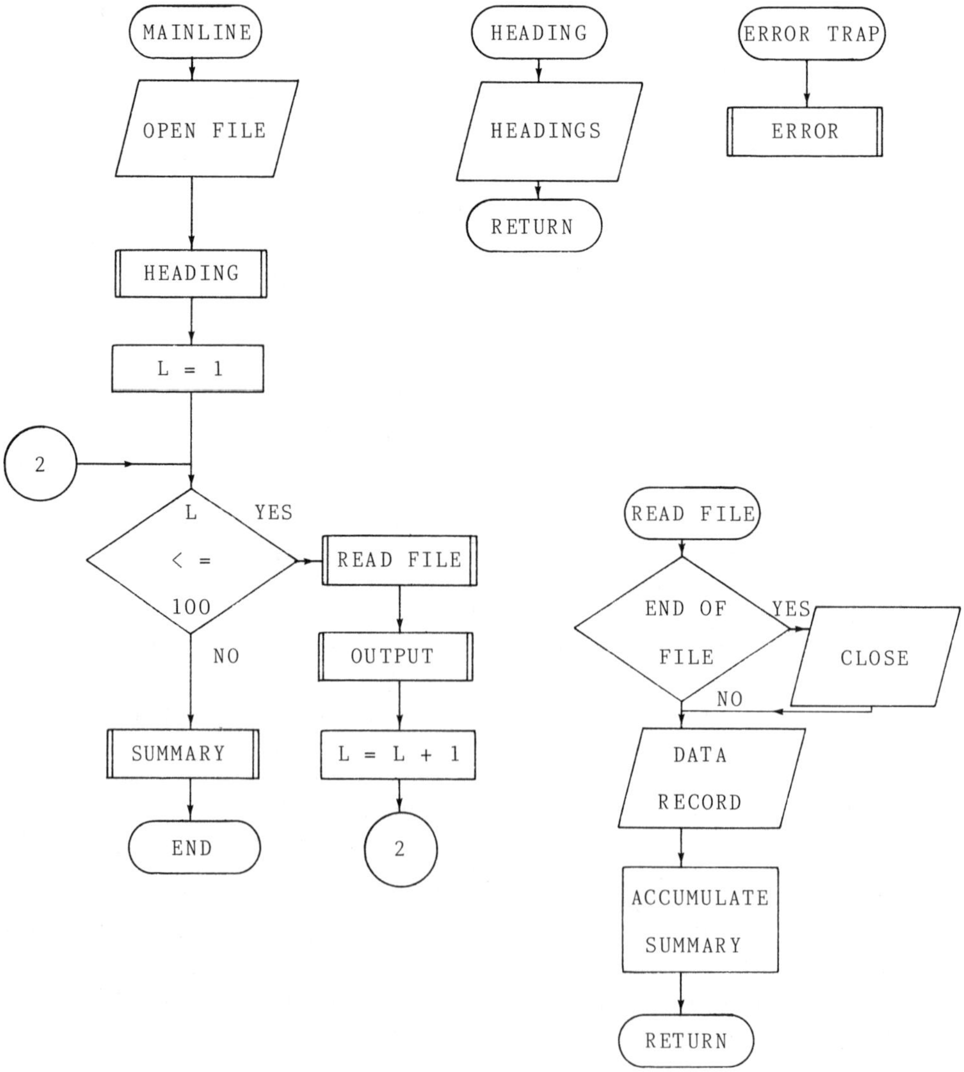

FIGURE 18–4
Detailed logic flowchart

the end of the file has been reached, or it produces an error message and a program break to alert the user that the program has terminated abnormally.

A variation of the BASIC INPUT statement is used to read data from the disk file. The summary total is accumulated in the read block. This total is used for footing and checking purposes. Footing totals are totals located at the bottom of a page. The invoice total or other totals available on the source form is compared with the total obtained at data entry to see if the two are equal.

The output subroutine prints the detail lines. In this program, 11 detail lines are printed.

The summary routine prints the accumulated total.

Errors, or abnormal program terminations, are provided for in the error routine. Program control branches to this routine when execution errors are detected. This routine checks the error code and the line number to confirm that the error is caused by attempting to read a file that is closed. If this is the case, program control shifts to the summary routine. If another error type is present, the program terminates abnormally.

EXAMPLE PROGRAMS—CREATING AND READING SEQUENTIAL FILES

The objective of this chapter is to demonstrate the BASIC language procedures for creating and reading sequential disk files. These usually are separate functions in business. One program is used to enter the variable values and create the disk file. A separate program is used to read the file and perform the necessary computations. The data entry operation is sometimes separate from the people who actually use the file.

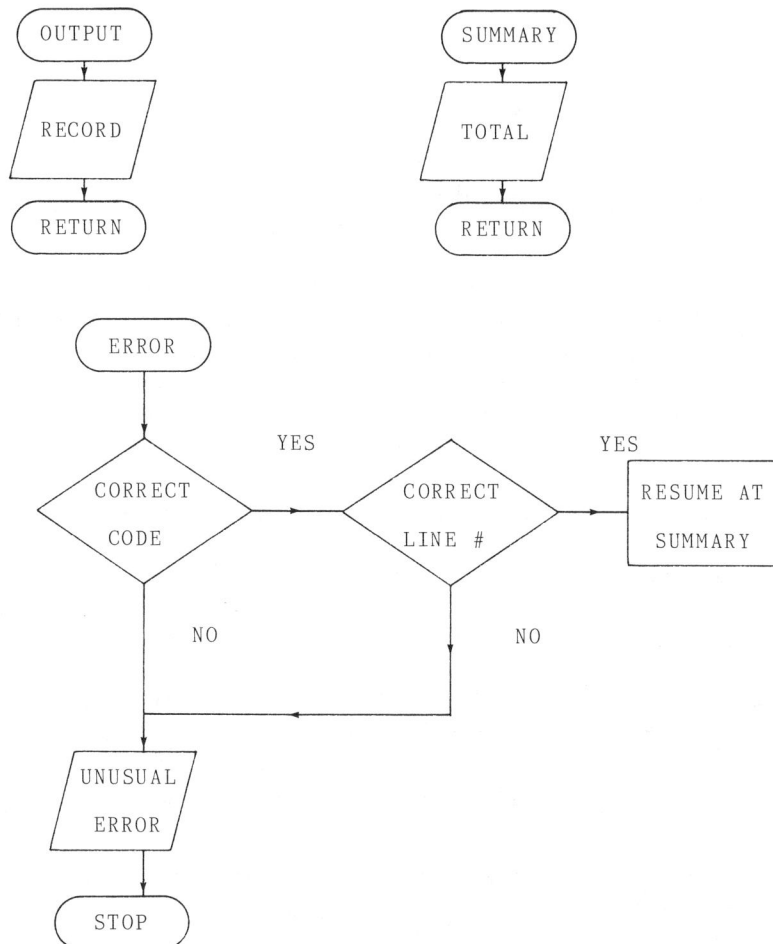

FIGURE 18–4
(Continued)

```
1000            REM    FIGURE 18-5    WRITTEN BY LARRY FRY    9/11/83
1010            REM    This program creates a sequential disk data
1020            REM    file.
1030                                                                    REM
1040                                                                    REM
1050            REM    ******    Variable  Identification
1060            REM    E$  .....  Employee Name
1070            REM    D$  .....  Department Name
1080            REM    S   .....  Seniority
1090            REM    YTD .....  Earnings Year-To-Date
1100            REM    L   .....  Loop Counter
1110            REM    R   .....  Loop Limit - Number of Records
1120                                                                    REM
1200            REM    ******    Housekeeping
1210            REM    ******    System Initialization
1220  CLEAR : CLS
1230                                                                    REM
1400            REM    ******    Mainline Module
1410  OPEN "O", #1, "B:PER.DAT"
1420  INPUT "ENTER Number of Records "; R
1430  FOR L = 1 TO R
1440        GOSUB 1610
1450        GOSUB 1810
1460  NEXT L
1470  CLOSE #1
1480  END
1490                                                                    REM
1600            REM    ******    Data Entry Module
1610  INPUT "ENTER Employee Name "; E$
1620  INPUT "ENTER Department Name "; D$
1630  INPUT "ENTER Seniority "; S
1640  INPUT "ENTER Y-T-D Earnings "; YTD
1650  PRINT
1660  RETURN
1670                                                                    REM
1800            REM    ******    Output to Disk File Module
1810  PRINT #1,  E$;   ",";  D$;   ",";  S;   ",";   YTD
1820  RETURN
1830                                                                    REM
1840  STOP
```

FIGURE 18-5
Sequential disk file
creation program

Disk data files are used because they can hold vast quantities of data, and because they provide fast access to the data. Magnetic disks can be accessed more rapidly than cassettes or magnetic tape.

Most of the data processing procedures and BASIC language key words used thus far are standard on all systems. The ANSI BASIC key words are used by the majority of systems. Applications programs to this point have used the standard BASIC key words with little variation. BASIC procedures for disk data files are different, however, because ANSI has not yet provided standards for them. Therefore, a wide divergence in procedures exists between the various systems making it imperative that system manuals be constantly and carefully checked for the proper procedures. Although it is not possible to include the procedures used by every manufacturer here, the key words and procedures used by the vast majority of systems are presented in the following text.

The program that illustrates creation of a sequential disk file is shown in figure 18–5. The top-level and detailed logic flowcharts for this program are shown in figures 18–1 and 18–2. Program documentation and variable identification are contained in lines 1000 to 1120. The system and monitor screen are cleared in statement 1220.

Disk data files must be opened before they can be used. All systems must use an open statement. The BASIC key word OPEN enables the use of a buffer for output to or input from a disk.

The OPEN statement on most systems includes the following parts.

1. The key word OPEN.
2. The file type, such as sequential output, sequential input, or random.
3. The channel, or buffer, reference number.
4. The file name.

5. The number of bytes per record (usually random files only).

Following is the OPEN statement format for this system.

1410 OPEN "⟨ File Type ⟩", # ⟨ Buffer No ⟩, "Drive:File Name"

The file type, or mode, must be specified as one of the following:

O—Output from computer to disk.
I—Input from disk to computer.
A—Append or add data records to the end of a sequential file. (E is used on some systems.)
R—Random access input/output file (presented in Chapter 20).

If the file type is a constant, it must be enclosed in quotation marks. It is possible to use a variable name for the mode.

The buffer number specifies the channel used in the program. There is a maximum number of files that can be accessed in any one program. This number varies according to the system. The # symbol preceding the buffer may be optional.

The file drive identifies the device or disk drive designation. Most systems have at least one drive which is identified as 1 or A. Some systems have two or more drives. In the system used for this textbook, drives A and B are used. The default drive is A. Therefore, if drive B is desired, it must be specified.

The file name is any name that is valid on the system being used. File names for this system may consist of two parts separated by a period. The format used for file name specification is File Name.Extension. Notice that the parts are separated by a period. The name may be from one to eight characters. The extension may not exceed three characters. Some systems do not use the extension. On others, the file name and extension separator may be a diagonal slash rather than a period. A colon separates the drive and file name specifications. If they are constants, they are both enclosed in one set of quotation marks. Record the file name procedures for the system being used in Exercise 18–1.

File Name Specifications

**EXERCISE
18–1**

Disk drive specification _____

File name specification _____

Extension specification _____

File extension separator _____

System file name format _____

The number of bytes per record may or may not be included in the OPEN statement. With this system the number of bytes is used only for random files.

Following is the OPEN statement for the example program.

1410 OPEN "O", #1, "B:PER.DAT"

The file buffer is opened as an output type with data being sent from the system to the disk. When any file is opened for output (mode O), existing files with the same name are destroyed. One buffer is to be used in this program.

The device used is identified as drive B. This is followed by the file name, which is PER.DAT.

The OPEN statement format used with MICROSOFT BASIC systems is the same as just described. (MICROSOFT provided the BASIC language interpreter and disk operating system for the INTERNATIONAL BUSINESS MACHINES PERSONAL COMPUTER.)

The OPEN statement format used with TRS-80 BASIC is the same as just described, except that mode E (for extend) is used rather than A.

The TRS-80 disk operating system uses a file designation step during the system boot procedure. The computer prompts the user with the question

HOW MANY FILES?

The user responds with the number of files to be used. This step assigns the number of buffers to be used in the program. A maximum of 15 may be specified.

Some BASIC systems allow the use of a number of files automatically. The system used for this textbook offers three files automatically.

In APPLESOFT BASIC, the BASIC control string CHR$(4) or Control-D (CRTL-D) is used to declare a file. All statements that reference disk files, such as OPEN, CLOSE, and WRITE, must be preceded by PRINT CHR$(4) or CTRL-D.

Following is the APPLESOFT BASIC procedure that is used to open a sequential file.

```
100 REM ** DECLARE FILE
110 LET F$ = CHR$(4)
120 PRINT F$; "OPEN PER"
```

Once a disk file is created in APPLESOFT, the catalog shows the file as type "T". Following is an example of a cataloged file.

```
CATALOG
T    003    PER
```

The file type is recorded as T or text. Text files in APPLESOFT refer to data files. Three disk sectors are used by the file. The file name is PER.

Mainframe computers or systems that use terminals use equivalent commands and key words to open data files. Instructor directions should be carefully followed.

Record the procedures to open a disk file on the system being used in Exercise 18–2.

EXERCISE 18–2

OPEN Statement

Mode specification _____

Buffer specification _____

Device specification _____

File name specification _____

Record size specification _____

Other _____

OPEN statement format _____

The INPUT statement in line 1420 is used to enter the number of records to be included in the file. This controls execution of the FOR/NEXT loop. The number of records is obtained from the source document or from organization records.

The loop in lines 1430 through 1460 controls execution of the data entry module and the output to disk file module. There are 11 data records to be entered, so loop parameters are set accordingly.

Department	Name	Seniority	Earnings
D$	E$	S	YTD
SHIPPING	ADAMS T	46	5431.85
RECEIVING	BAKER R	111	7875.31
TESTING	CHAN C	24	9499.88
COMPONENTS	DRIM L	37	8925.37
ASSEMBLY	ELFOR M	65	9897.75
DESIGN	FRY J	108	13421.00
OFFICE	FRY L	96	12941.99
ASSEMBLY	GEORGE B	21	8555.55
OFFICE	PULLING B	47	10000.00
TESTING	SKAR T	13	9779.00
DESIGN	SYLVIA L	72	11111.11

FIGURE 18–6
Data records

The data entry module in lines 1610 through 1660 consists of four INPUT statements that are used to enter variable values for the data records. One data record consists of four fields, or variable names. The data values entered are the employee name (E$), the department name (D$), seniority (S), and year-to-date earnings (YTD). The PRINT statement in line 1650 separates the records on the monitor screen at data entry. This is an aid provided for the program user. The data records entered are shown in figure 18–6.

The output to disk file module sends the data to the buffer. Line 1810, which follows, is the PRINT statement that sends the data record to the buffer.

1810 PRINT #1, E$; ","; D$; ","; S; ","; YTD

PRINT #1 is the buffer used to write the file. The PRINT # statement comprises one data record. There are four variable names in each record. These are E$, D$, S, and YTD. The variable names are followed by semicolons, which are used to separate the variables in the PRINT # statement. The semicolon is not part of the image recorded upon the disk. Commas or semicolons can be used to separate data names; however, semicolons are recommended. Semicolons cause the data to be compressed in the disk image, while commas cause the data to be recorded in system print zone format (14 spaces per zone). In effect, the use of commas or semicolons in a PRINT # statement produces the same results as a regular PRINT statement. The commas enclosed in quotation marks delimit and separate the variables on the disk. The "," is also followed by a semicolon.

String values which contain leading blank spaces, embedded commas, or embedded semicolons can be entered in a disk file, but they must be written to the file through the use of explicit quotation marks. The control string, CHR$(34) (ASCII code), is used to enter explicit quotation marks. For example, if the employee name field contains an embedded comma, as in ADAMS, T, the following PRINT # statement can be used.

1810 PRINT #1, CHR$(34); E$; CHR$(34); ","; D$; ","; S; ","; YTD

This control string for explicit quotation marks is used by most systems.

Some systems enable the use of PRINT # USING which provides editing of the disk file image.

The MICROSOFT BASIC and TRS-80 BASIC PRINT # statements use the same format to write the file.

Following is the APPLESOFT BASIC format for writing data to the disk. The statements used to open a file and print a record are also shown.

```
100 F$ = CHR$(4)
110 PRINT F$; "OPEN PER"
         .
         .
410 PRINT F$; "WRITE PER"
420 PRINT E$; ","; D$; ","; S; ","; YTD
430 PRINT F$
```

Statements 100 and 110 are used to open the disk file known as PER. This places the file name PER in the disk catalog. Line 410 is a disk file access command that causes output to be sent to the buffer. The statement PRINT F$; "WRITE PER" switches output to the buffer. The PRINT statement shown in line 420 actually writes the data record to the buffer. Line 430 terminates the disk access after the record is written to the buffer.

Following is an alternate method of writing to the file that is used by most systems.

```
1810 PRINT #1, E$
1811 PRINT #1, D$
1812 PRINT #1, S
1813 PRINT #1, YTD
```

When this format is used, a separate PRINT # statement is used for each data field. The INPUT # statements that read the file (discussed later in this chapter) must also be placed on separate lines if this format is used.

Record the statement for writing to disk files for the system being used in Exercise 18-3.

**EXERCISE
18-3**

Write to Disk Statement

PRINT # or WRITE statement _____

Variable names _____

Variable separation (field name) _____

Explicit quotation marks _____

Statement format _____

Following termination of the program loop, the disk file is closed. This statement transfers the data remaining in the buffer to the disk and secures the buffer and disk file. The buffer can then be used for other files or other purposes. Following is the CLOSE # statement format.

1470 CLOSE # ⟨ Buffer Number ⟩

The CLOSE statement in the example program follows.

1470 CLOSE #1

Buffer #1 was the only one opened in this program. Any file or buffer number previously opened should be closed. On most systems, the CLOSE statement listed by itself with no file number closes all files that have been opened. The END statement also closes files, but the use of this key word for that purpose is not recommended. The key word CLOSE should be used for the purpose of closing buffers and files.

MICROSOFT BASIC and TRS-80 BASIC use the same CLOSE statements as just described.

APPLESOFT BASIC uses the following form.

610 PRINT F$; "CLOSE PER"

Record the procedures used to close disk files on the system being used in Exercise 18–4.

Closing Disk Files

EXERCISE 18–4

CLOSE key word _____

Buffer number _____

File name _____

CLOSE statement format _____

The example program terminates after the CLOSE statement is executed.

The program segment shown in figure 18–7 is comprised of the APPLESOFT BASIC statements necessary for the creation of a sequential disk file. Documentation and variable identification statements are not included.

The second objective of this chapter is to demonstrate the BASIC language procedures for accessing, reading, and printing sequential disk data files. Figure 18–8 is the example program that reads and prints the sequential file created in figure 18–5. The top-level and detailed logic flowcharts for this program are contained in figures 18–3 and 18–4.

Program documentation and variable identification are shown in lines 2000 to 2130. Lines 2200 to 2260 contain the housekeeping statements. The system and monitor screen are cleared in line 2210. Statements 2240 and 2250 declare the output lines. Format statements are assigned to 01$ and 02$.

Statement 2280 is an error trap statement. This line, which follows, transfers control to statement 3310 when an error is detected.

2280 ON ERROR GOTO 3310

```
1000 REM    *****  FIGURE  18-7   APPLESOFT BASIC
1200 REM    *****   SYSTEM INITIALIZATION
1210 CLEAR : HOME
1220 LET F$ = CHR$(4)
1400 REM    *****  MAINLINE MODULE
1410 INPUT "ENTER NUMBER OF RECORDS ";R
1420 PRINT F$; "OPEN PER"
1430 FOR L = 1 TO R
1440 GOSUB 1610
1450 GOSUB 1810
1460 NEXT L
1470 PRINT F$; "CLOSE PER"
1480 END
1600 REM     *****  DATA ENTRY MODULE
1610 PR# 0
1620 INPUT "ENTER EMPLOYEE NAME "; E$
1630 INPUT "ENTER DEPARTMENT NAME "; D$
1640 INPUT "ENTER SENIORITY "; S
1650 INPUT "ENTER SALES "; YTD
1660 PRINT
1670 RETURN
1800 REM     *****  OUTPUT TO DISK FILE MODULE
1810 PRINT F$; "WRITE PER"
1820 PRINT E$; ","; D$; ","; S; ","; YTD
1830 PRINT F$
1840 RETURN
```

FIGURE 18–7
APPLESOFT BASIC sequential file creation program

```
2000            REM    FIGURE  18-8  WRITTEN BY LARRY FRY    9/11/83
2010            REM    This program  reads a  sequential disk data
2020            REM    file.  Selected variable values are then
2030            REM    printed.  A summary total is computed.
2040                                                                    REM
2050            REM    ******    Variable  Identification
2060            REM    E$  .....  Employee Name
2070            REM    D$  .....  Department Name
2080            REM    S   .....  Seniority
2090            REM    YTD .....  Earnings Year-To-Date
2100            REM    L   .....  Loop Counter
2110            REM    T   .....  Summary Total
2120                                                                    REM
2130                                                                    REM
2200            REM    ******    System Initialization
2210  CLEAR : CLS
2220                                                                    REM
2230            REM    ******    Format Output Lines
2240  LET O1$ = "Department          Name                Y-T-D Earnings"
2250  LET O2$ = "\              \    \          \         $$##,###.##"
2260                                                                    REM
2270            REM    ******    Error Trapping
2280  ON ERROR GOTO 3310
2290                                                                    REM
2300            REM    ******    Mainline Module
2310  OPEN "I", #1, "B:PER.DAT"
2320  GOSUB 2510
2330  FOR L = 1 TO 100
2340        GOSUB 2710
2350        GOSUB 2910
2360  NEXT L
2370  GOSUB 3110
2380  END
2390                                                                    REM
2500            REM    *****     Heading Module                         .
2510  LPRINT CHR$(12)
2520  LPRINT TAB(22);  "PORT-EX COMPANY"
2530  LPRINT
2540  LPRINT TAB(22);  "PERSONNEL  FILE"
2550  LPRINT
2560  LPRINT O1$
2570  LPRINT
2580  RETURN
2590                                                                    REM
2700            REM    ******    Read Data File Module
2710  IF EOF(1) THEN CLOSE
2720  INPUT #1, E$, D$, S, YTD
2730  LET T = T + YTD
2740  RETURN
2750                                                                    REM
2900            REM    ******    Output Module
2910  LPRINT
2920  LPRINT USING O2$; D$, E$, YTD
2930  RETURN
2940                                                                    REM
3100            REM    ******    Summary Module
3110  LPRINT : LPRINT
3120  LPRINT USING "TOTAL Y-T-D EARNINGS  $$##,###.##"; T
3130  RETURN
3140                                                                    REM
3300            REM    ******    Error Trapping Routine
3310  IF ERR <> 54 AND ERL <> 2720 THEN LPRINT "UNUSUAL ERROR CONDITION "; ERR
                                     ELSE RESUME 2370
3320  STOP
3330                                                                    REM
```

FIGURE 18–8
Sequential file access
program

The ON ERROR key word transfers control to the error trap routine when an error is detected. This procedure is used to confirm that the data file has been completely processed. The program should continue executing until the last data record has been entered. Following is the error trap routine in statement 3310. Statement segments are shown on separate lines for illustration purposes.

```
3310 IF ERR ⟨ ⟩ 54 and ERL ⟨ ⟩ 2720
       THEN LPRINT "UNUSUAL ERROR CONDITION"; ERR
       ELSE RESUME 2370
```

The ERR key word, which is used as a variable, returns the system error code for the detected error. BASIC error codes for the computer being used can be found in the system reference manual. Some systems may not support ERR and/or ERL.

Error code 54 for this system is defined as BAD FILE MODE. The program attempts to read a closed file, which causes an error. If the error code is not equal to 54 and the line number is not equal to 2720, an unusual error has occurred. The unusual error is not related to the end of the disk file. Therefore, the THEN portion of the IF statement, which prints the message UNUSUAL ERROR CONDITION, is executed. The error code is also printed. This message tells the user that there is an unusual error. The ERL key word, which is also used as a variable, returns the statement number in which the error was detected.

If the error code is equal to 54 and the line number is equal to 2720, the ELSE portion of the statement is executed. This causes the program to resume execution at statement 2370 which executes the summary module. The RESUME key word continues program execution at the referenced line number after an error handling procedure is executed. Execution resumes with statement 2370. The following options are available with the RESUME key word:

RESUME—execution resumes at the statement that caused the error.
RESUME NEXT—execution resumes at the statement following the one that caused the error.
RESUME 2370—execution resumes at the listed statement number.

The error in this program is actually caused in the read data file module. Following are lines 2710 and 2720.

```
2710 IF EOF(1) THEN CLOSE
2720 INPUT #1, E$, D$, S, YTD
```

The EOF(1) statement is used to check for the end of file condition. When a disk file is created, a pointer, or marker, is placed at the end of the file after the last data record is entered. The statement format follows.

```
EOF( ⟨ Buffer Number ⟩ )
```

The EOF(1) function is used with sequential files to determine if the last record has been processed. EOF means End of File. The buffer number is the one specified in the OPEN statement for that file. The program branch statement in line 2710, IF EOF(1) THEN CLOSE, closes the file when the end is reached. More specifically, it closes any open file. After the end of the file is reached, the THEN segment of line 2710 is executed. This closes any open file. Subsequent execution of line 2720 will cause an error. The error code returned by the ERR key word will be equal to 54. The ERL function will return line 2720 because the file is closed. The ON ERROR GOTO 3310 statement in line 2280 will transfer program control to line 3310.

Those systems that do not support the ERR and ERL functions can use the following procedure as part of the read module.

```
2710 IF EOF(1) THEN CLOSE: GOTO 2370
```

Obviously, the use of GOTO and the violation of the one entry point-one exit point rules are contrary to structured programming practices. Such program statements must be thoroughly documented with REMARK statements in the program.

MICROSOFT BASIC and TRS-80 BASIC systems use the same statements as the preceding example.

APPLESOFT BASIC uses the following procedures for end of file detection.

50 ONERR GOTO 710
710 LET E = PEEK(222)
720 IF E = 5 THEN PRINT F$; "CLOSE PER"
730 IF E ⟨ ⟩ 5 THEN PRINT "UNUSUAL ERROR CONDITION"; E

The ONERR statement is equivalent to the ON ERROR key word used in the example program. APPLESOFT BASIC examines the system memory location where error codes are stored. This is location 222. The BASIC key word PEEK is used for this purpose. PEEK is the BASIC function that examines system memory and returns the contents. Following is the PEEK statement format.

PEEK(⟨ Parameter ⟩)

The parameter is the storage location to be examined. It can range from 0 to 65535 (depending upon system memory capacity). The value returned can range from 0 to 255. In this example, location 222 is examined. Location 222 is the storage area in the APPLE computer that stores error codes. Statement 710 assigns the PEEK value to variable E.

Error code 5 is the one used for END OF DATA. If E is equal to 5, which is the END OF DATA code, statement 720 closes the file. If E is not equal to 5, the error message UNUSUAL ERROR CONDITION and the error code are printed. The user can then determine the reason for the error by checking the system reference manual.

Record the end of file detection procedure for the system being used in Exercise 18–5.

EXERCISE 18–5

End of File Detection

Error detection _____

Error code _____

Error location _____

Error trapping _____

Statement format _____

The mainline module is shown in lines 2300 to 2390. Statement 2310, which follows, opens the file for input from the disk to the system.

2310 OPEN "I", #1, "B:PER.DAT"

The file mode is I for input. Otherwise, the OPEN statement is the same as described in figure 18–5.

Line 2320 causes the heading module to be executed. The heading module is contained in lines 2510 to 2580. Report and column headings are printed as a result of this routine.

A FOR/NEXT structure is used to control execution of the program loop. The loop limit parameter is set at a number high enough to include all data records. There are 11 records in the file, but the limit is set at 100. If desired, an INPUT statement could be used to enter the limit parameter. Entering a loop limit higher than or equal to the actual number of data records in the file results in normal termination because of the error trap routine. Entering a limit smaller than the number of actual records in the file causes an error at execution. The user should be able to detect such an error. The user or programmer should ensure that the loop limit is high enough to include all records.

The loop body includes the read data file and output modules. The read data file module, which follows, causes the data records to be read from the file buffer.

    2710 IF EOF(1) THEN CLOSE
    2720 INPUT #1, E$, D$, S, YTD
    2730 LET T = T + YTD
    2740 RETURN

Line 2710 is the end of file detection statement. When the end of file marker is detected, the file is closed. Subsequent execution of statement 2720 after the file is closed results in an error. Control is then shifted to the error trap procedure previously described.

Data records are entered as a result of line 2720. The INPUT # statement is used to read from the file buffer. Following is the INPUT # statement format.

    2720 INPUT # (⟨ Buffer Number ⟩), Variable, Variable

The key word INPUT # causes data field values to be read from the sequential file and assigned to the referenced variables. The buffer number is the one referenced in the OPEN statement. Variables E$, D$, S, and YTD are assigned the respective data values. The variable names must be listed in the same sequence used in the PRINT # statement to write the file. If separate lines were used for each PRINT # statement as previously described, separate INPUT # statements must be used.

MICROSOFT BASIC and TRS-80 BASIC use the same statements as shown in the preceding example to read from a file.

APPLESOFT BASIC uses the following statements.

    100 LET F$ = CHR$(4)
    110 PRINT F$; "OPEN PER"
        .
        .
    710 PRINT F$; "READ PER"
    720 INPUT E$, D$, S, YTD
    730 PRINT F$

Statements 100 and 110 access and open the disk file. Line 710 programs the system to read from the referenced disk file, rather than from the keyboard. The INPUT statement in line 720 actually reads the data from the buffer. Line 730 disengages the file buffer access after the data record is entered.

Record the program statement to read data from the disk for the system being used in Exercise 18–6.

Reading Sequential Disk Files

**EXERCISE
18–6**

Disk access   _____

Key word   _____

Buffer number   _____

Statement format   _____

                    _____

```
                        PORT-EX COMPANY

                        PERSONNEL  FILE

       Department            Name            Y-T-D Earnings


       SHIPPING            ADAMS T                $5,431.85

       RECEIVING           BAKER R                $7,875.31

       TESTING             CHAN C                 $9,499.88

       COMPONENTS          DRIM L                 $8,925.37

       ASSEMBLY            ELFOR M                $9,897.75

       DESIGN              FRY J                 $13,421.00

       OFFICE              FRY L                 $12,941.99

       ASSEMBLY            GEORGE B               $8,555.55

       OFFICE              PULLING B             $10,000.00

       TESTING             SKAR T                 $9,779.00

       DESIGN              SYLVIA L              $11,111.11


       TOTAL Y-T-D EARNINGS   $107,438.80
```

FIGURE 18–9
Sequential personnel
data file

Line 2730 accumulates the summary total for year-to-date earnings. This value is printed in the summary module. The value is used for data validation purposes by comparing it with the source document.

Line 2350 calls the output module. This module prints the detail lines which are double-spaced. The LPRINT USING statement in line 2920 uses the format assigned to O2$ to print the detail lines.

After the program loop is terminated, the summary module is executed. The transfer

```
100 REM  ***  FIGURE    18-10    APPLESOFT PROGRAM
110 LET F$ = CHR$(4)
120 ONERR GOTO 910
200 REM  ***  MAINLINE MODULE
210 PRINT F$; "OPEN PER"
220 FOR L = 1 TO 100
230 GOSUB 410
240 GOSUB 610
250 NEXT L
260 PRINT F$; "CLOSE PER"
270 GOSUB 810
280 END
400 REM  ***  READ MODULE
410 PRINT F$; "READ PER"
420 INPUT D$, E$, S, YTD
430 PRINT F$
440 LET T = T + YTD
450 RETURN
600 REM  ***  OUTPUT MODULE
610 PR# 1
620 PRINT D$, E$, YTD
630 RETURN
800 REM  ***  SUMMARY MODULE
810 PR# 1
820 PRINT "TOTAL Y-T-D EARNINGS   "; T
830 RETURN
900 REM  ***  ERROR TRAP
910 LET E = PEEK(222)
920 IF E = 5 THEN 260
930 IF E <> 5 THEN PRINT "UNUSUAL ERROR "; E
940 STOP
```

FIGURE 18–10
APPLESOFT BASIC file
reading program

of control to the summary module is a result of the RESUME statement in the error trapping routine. This terminates program execution.

Output from the example program, which reads a sequential file, is shown in figure 18–9. The heading lines are printed first. They are followed by the 11 detail lines. Finally, the summary total is printed.

The APPLESOFT BASIC program shown in figure 18–10 could be used to read a sequential file. Program documentation and variable identification are the same as shown in figure 18–8.

PROGRAM DEVELOPMENT CHECKLIST

Use the following checklist to ensure that all components are included in the program.

_____ Flowcharts and documentation

_____ Program loop

Disk file creation

_____ Open for output

_____ Data entry

_____ Write to file

_____ Close file

Read disk files

_____ Open for input

_____ Read from file

_____ End of file detection

_____ Output

_____ Summary calculations

_____ Close

PROGRAM DEBUGGING

The following errors are commonly encountered when processing disk files.

1. BAD FILE MODE	Attempt to read from a closed file. Check for close before file read statement.	
2. BAD FILE NAME	Violation of file naming procedures.	
3. BAD FILE NUMBER	Incorrect buffer number. Check file buffer.	
4. DISK FULL or TOO MANY FILES	Disk/directory is full.	
5. DISK NOT READY	Disk is not in drive or the door is open.	
6. DISK WRITE PROTECTED	Attempt to write to disk that is write protected.	

7. END OF DATA	Attempt to read from file record that has not been stored. End of file has been passed.
8. FILE ALREADY OPEN	Attempt to open file that is already open.
9. FILE NOT FOUND	File name is not in directory. Check entry.
10. INPUT PAST END	End of file error. Attempt to read from file when already at end. Check for end of file detection.

SUMMARY

The BASIC language contains procedures for creating and reading sequential disk files. The process of creating and reading sequential files consists of three steps. First, the file buffer must be opened through the use of the OPEN statement. Next, the data must be printed to or read from the file. Finally, the file must be closed.

The different systems use a variety of key words and functions to create and read files. This variety is caused by the lack of standardized procedures. The ones commonly used are illustrated. System manuals must be carefully checked when using disk files.

The end of the file must be determined when executing a program that reads files. A variety of procedures is used by the different systems to determine if the end of the file has been reached.

BASIC Key Words Learned

CHR$(4)	APPLESOFT BASIC disk access control string.
CLOSE OR CLOSE #	Closes or secures file buffer and disk file.
EOF	Determines end of file.
ERL	Returns line number in which error is detected.
ERR	Returns system error code.
INPUT #	Reads record from file buffer.
ON ERROR (ON ERR)	Program control branches to referenced line upon detection of an error.
OPEN	Creates file buffer and accesses file for referenced mode.
PEEK	Examines system memory location.
PRINT #	Writes record to file buffer.
RESUME	Continues program execution after error trap or detection of error.

PROGRAM ASSIGNMENT 18–1

Instructions

Prepare the flowcharts and the structured BASIC programs to create, read, and print a sequential disk file. Use one program to create the file and another program to read and print the file. Use transaction processing to enter the data values. Compute and print a summary total in each program.

Following is the data to be processed. Use prompting INPUT statements to enter the data. Use the saleperson's name, sales region, and sales amount as the variables. (NOTE: Do not delete the file when completed.)

Data

Salesperson	Region	Sales
Smith	NE	3,455.70
Zenfor	SW	5,498.75
Smith	NE	2,677.33
Fores	SE	7,435.32
Hawes	NE	4,575.90
Zenfor	SW	3,666.67
Smith	NE	1,975.25
Fores	SE	3,276.75
Rastor	SW	8,999.99
Smith	NE	3,237.45
Zenfor	SW	4,475.55

Output Format

Print the headings. Include the summary total in the output for the file creation program. In the second program, print each data record and the summary total. Use output editing if available.

PORT-EX COMPANY

Sales Report

DATA ENTRY SALES SUMMARY TOTAL $XX,XXX.XX

Salesperson	Region	Sales
xxxxxxxx	xx	$xx,xxx.xx
xxxxx	xx	$xx,xxx.xx
xxxxxxx	xx	$xx,xxx.xx

DATA FILE SUMMARY TOTAL $XX,XXX.XX

Instructions

Prepare the flowcharts and the structured BASIC programs to create, read, and print a sequential disk data file. Use one program to create the file and another program to read and print the file. Use transaction processing to enter the data. Use the product name, cost, selling price, and quantity on hand as the variables. The total cost and total price fields are computed by multiplying the quantity by the cost and selling price respectively. The total markup is computed by subtracting the total cost from the total price. Compute summary totals for the total price, total cost, and markup in each program. The data fields to be written to the disk file are the name, price, cost, quantity, total price, total cost, and markup.

Following is the data to be processed. Use prompting INPUT statements to enter the data.

PROGRAM ASSIGNMENT 18–2

Data

Name	Cost	Price	Quantity
Board Circuit	355	625	20
Board Graphic	295	475	15
Board Memory	425	750	30
Board Mother	505	975	100
Circuit Logic	22	56	78
Circuit Memory	16	35	400
Circuit Processor	55	125	92
Control Expansion	66	93	31
Control Network	89	197	25
Display Color	215	345	60
Display Monochrome	99	299	49
Oscilloscope	175	325	5
Printer Daisy	675	1100	15
Tablet Graphics	200	413	10

Output Format

Print the headings. The output for the file creation program includes summary totals. The second program prints each data record and the summary totals. Use output editing if available.

PORT-EX COMPANY

Inventory Report

Data Entry Summary Totals

Cost	Price	Markup
$XXX,XXX	$XXX,XXX	$XXX,XXX

Name	Cost	Price	Quantity	Total Cost	Total Price	Total Markup
xxxxxxx	xxxxx	xxxxx	xxxx	xxxxxx	xxxxxx	xxxxxxxx
xxxxx	xxxxx	xxxxx	xxxx	xxxxxx	xxxxxx	xxxxxxxx

Data File Summary Totals

Cost	Price	Markup
$xxx,xxx	$xxx,xxx	$xxx,xxx

PROGRAM ASSIGNMENT 18-3

Instructions

Prepare the flowcharts and the structured BASIC programs to read and sort the contents of a sequential data file. After sorting, the data is entered in another file. Use two files: one is for the original data; the other is created after the data records are sorted. The contents of the sorted files are then read and printed.

The first program reads the data file created in Program Assignment 18–1 and loads the data into one-dimensional tables. The tables are sorted alphabetically by employee name. The sorted records create the second file. The second program then reads the sorted file and prints the data. Compute and print a summary total in each program.

The data file to be processed was created in Program Assignment 18–1. If it is not available, a new file must be created using the data from that assignment.

Data

See Program Assignment 18–1 for the data file.

Output Format

Print the headings. The output for the first program, which reads the file, sorts the data, and creates a new file, includes the summary total. The second program reads the sorted file and prints the data records and summary total. Use output editing if it is available.

PORT-EX COMPANY

Sales Report

DATA FILE SALES SUMMARY TOTAL $xxx,xxx.xx

Salesperson	Region	Sales
xxxxxxxx	xx	$xx,xxx.xx
xxxxxx	xx	$xx,xxx.xx

SORTED FILE SALES SUMMARY TOTAL $XX,XXX.XX

UPDATING SEQUENTIAL DISK FILES

OBJECTIVES

At the end of this chapter you should be able to perform the following operations:

- Update a sequential disk file by changing data values within a given record.
- Update a sequential disk file by adding new records to a previously existing file.

CHANGING DATA VALUES

The process of *updating disk files* at this programming level involves changing values in an existing sequential disk data file or appending additional data records to an existing file. The process of changing a value is described here.

Data entered into a file is sometimes incorrect. Certainly, data values change with each business day. Businesses are dynamic organizations, and change is a constant process. New clients are added. There are turnovers in personnel. Sales figures change (hopefully, by increasing). Therefore, disk files must be updated to reflect changes in the organization. Since the data values within records are changed on a daily or weekly basis, it is necessary to develop a programming procedure to do this.

The process of updating disk files also means that *archive*, or *backup*, copies of files and transactions must be kept. System failure or a computer room disaster can occur at any time. Archive copies of programs, data files, and daily transactions must be kept in a secure place.

The first program in this chapter demonstrates the creation of a sequential file. The second program demonstrates the procedure used to change a value within an existing data record.

ADDING DATA RECORDS

The other procedure to be considered in this chapter is the addition of new records to previously existing files. Customers, associates, and employees are constantly added or deleted. A programming procedure should exist to consider this fact.

Again, a procedure for creating archive copies of files and transactions for security reasons should be present. If there is a system failure or a computer room disaster, the organization must have a recovery procedure. Archive copies kept in a secure place are essential components of system recovery.

The third program in this chapter demonstrates appending data records to an existing file.

FLOWCHARTS—UPDATING DATA FILES

The objectives of this chapter are to demonstrate the BASIC language procedures used to change a data value in a sequential file or to add records to an existing file. Three programs are used to illustrate these features. The first program creates a sequential file

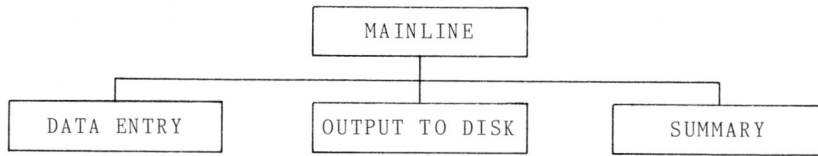

FIGURE 19–1
Top-level flowchart

for personnel sales records. The second program demonstrates updating an existing file by changing a variable value in a data record. The last program illustrates adding records to an existing file.

The top-level flowchart shown in figure 19–1 is for the file creation program. The mainline routine controls execution of the data entry, output to disk, and summary subroutines.

The detailed logic flowchart is exhibited in figure 19–2. The mainline routine is used

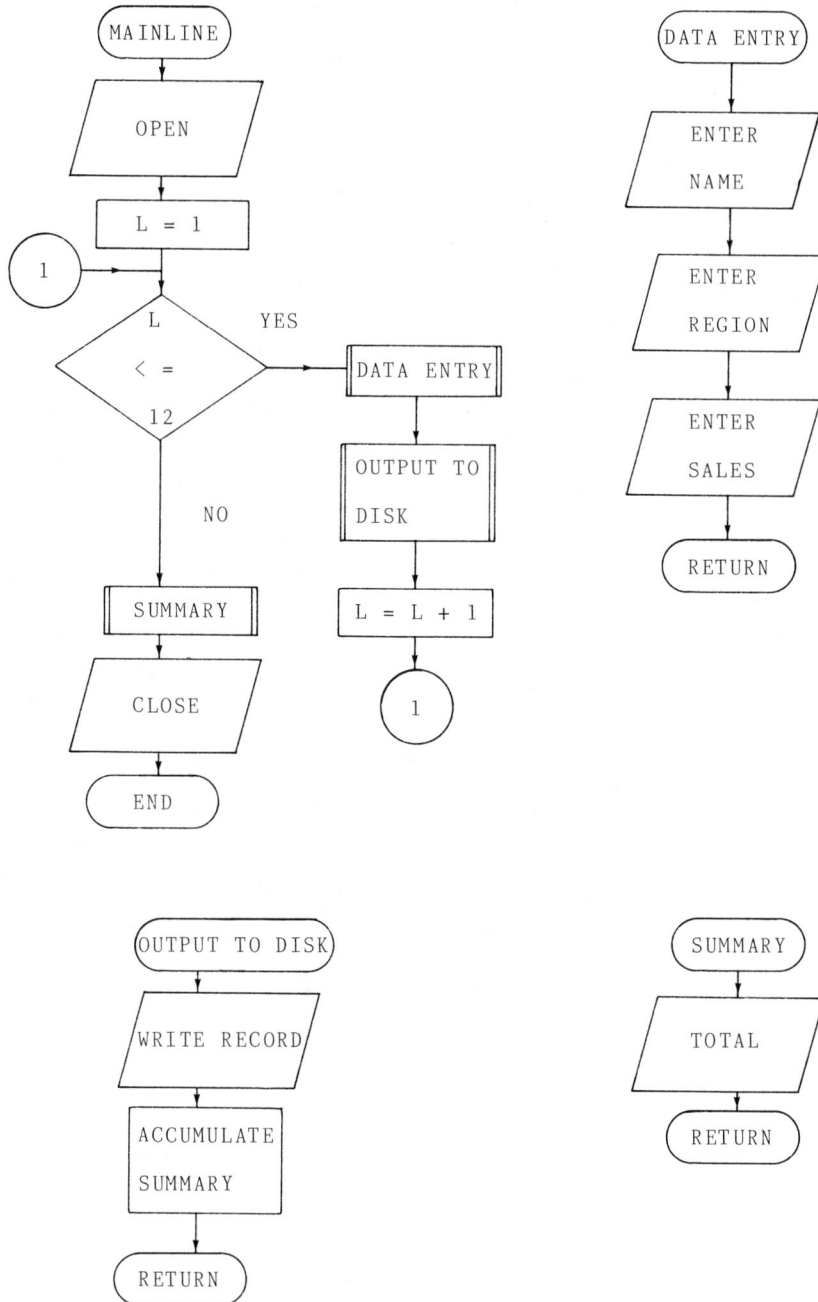

FIGURE 19–2
Detailed logic flowchart

as the driver module to control execution of the program. The file is opened to enable access to the disk buffer.

A FOR/NEXT structure is used to control execution of the program loop. There are 12 data records to be entered, so the loop parameters are set accordingly. The number of data records to be processed is obtained from the source document or the organization's records. The program loop consists of the data entry and output to disk subroutines.

The data records are entered in the data entry routine. There are three variable names to be entered. These are the employee's name, region, and sales amount. Data values are sent to the buffer as a result of the output to disk routine.

Following completion of the program loop, the summary routine prints the total sales amount. Program execution is then terminated.

The top-level flowchart for the file update program is shown in figure 19–3. Flowchart blocks include the mainline, read, update, rename, heading, output, and summary routines. The mainline routine controls execution of the program subroutines.

The detailed logic flowchart for the second program is exhibited in figure 19–4. The mainline routine controls execution of the program. INPUT statements are used to enter the file name, the record name, and the variable name to be updated. The appropriate disk file is then opened. An output file, which is referred to as the update file, is also opened.

A WHILE-WEND structure is used to control execution of the program loop. The sequential file created by the first program is read. The program loop is executed as long as there is data to read. When the end of the file is detected, the program loop is terminated.

The program loop consists of the read and update routines. The data records from the original file are entered in the read block. The update routine contains a program branch statement that checks for the proper record to be updated. When the correct record is entered, the sales amount is updated. The flag variable is assigned the value one. All records, including the one updated, are then written to the second disk file. This file is referred to as the *update file*. Twelve data records are entered. After the last record is processed, the program loop is terminated, and the files are closed.

A branch statement determines if the data record to be updated is located in the file. If the record to be updated is located, the flag variable contains the value one at the end of the update loop. If the flag contains a zero at the end of the update loop, the record was not located in the file. A warning message is printed if the record is not found.

A rename block is used to delete the original file. This is to avoid a duplicate file name error. The name of the updated file is then changed to the original file name.

Headings are printed next. Report and column headings are printed as a result of the heading routine.

The updated file is opened, so that it can be printed. A WHILE-WEND structure is used to read the file and print the records. The loop is executed as long as there is a record to read. There are 12 data records to process, so the loop is executed accordingly. The data records are entered from the disk in the read subroutine. The detail lines are printed in the output routine. A summary total is accumulated in the output block.

Following termination of the output loop, the summary total is printed. Program termination follows.

The third program updates the original and the updated files resulting from the first two programs by adding new data records. The top-level flowchart for this program is

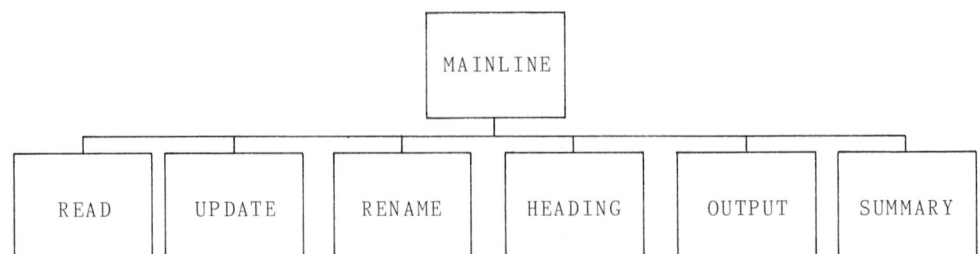

FIGURE 19–3
Top-level flowchart

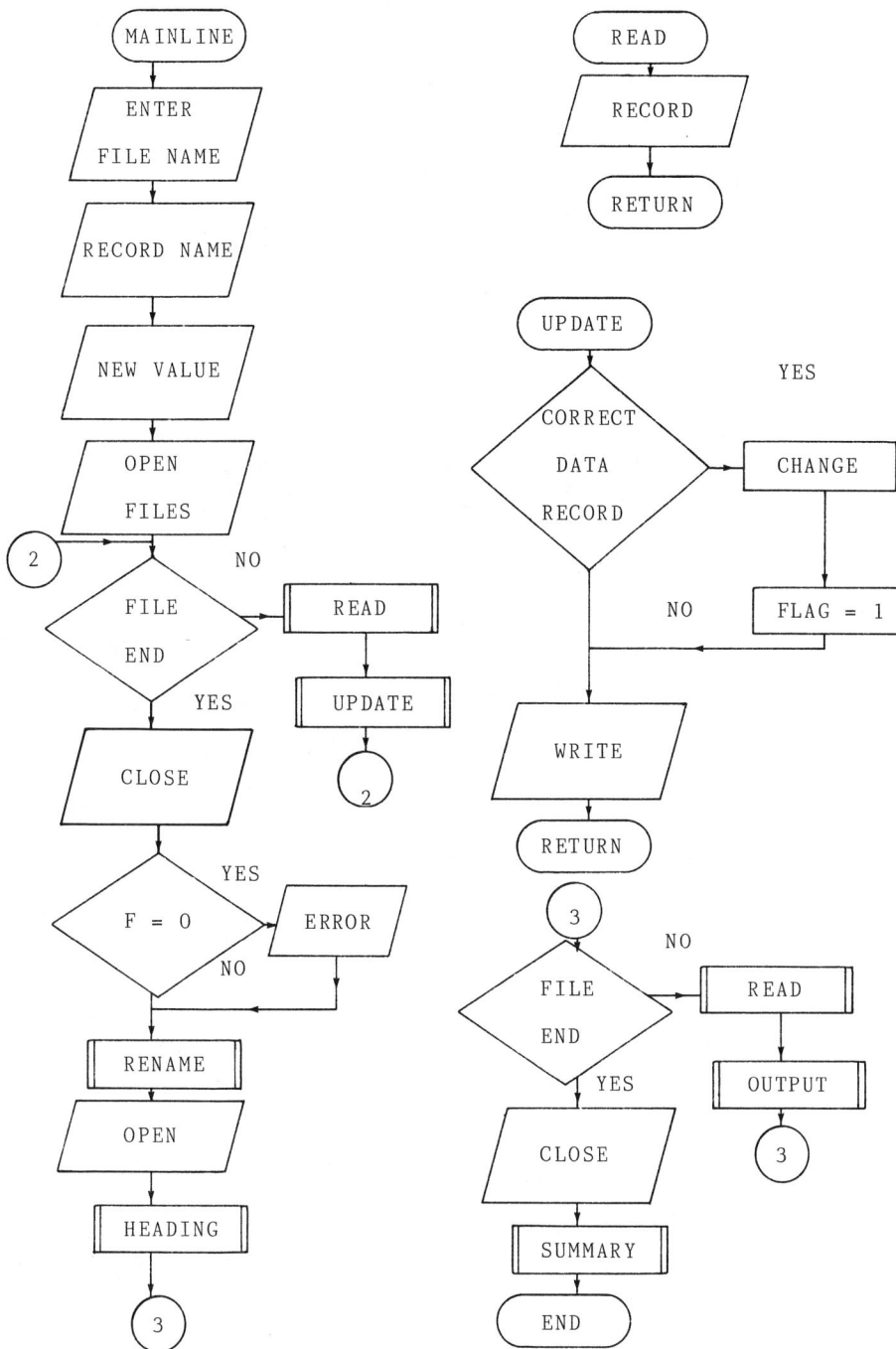

FIGURE 19–4
Detailed logic flowchart

shown in figure 19–5. The mainline routine controls execution of the program. The subroutines are the data entry, write to disk, heading, read file, output, and summary blocks.

The detailed logic flowchart is shown in figure 19–6. The data file created in the first program and updated in the second is used. Three new records are added to the file. The mainline routine acts as the driver module to control program execution.

An INPUT statement is used to enter the number of records to be added to the file. In this example, three records are appended. This number is used as the program loop limit. The number of records to be added is obtained from the source document. A FOR/NEXT structure is used to control execution of the append loop. The loop consists of the data entry and write to disk routines.

The file to be updated is opened as an *append* or *extend* file. Opening the file as an

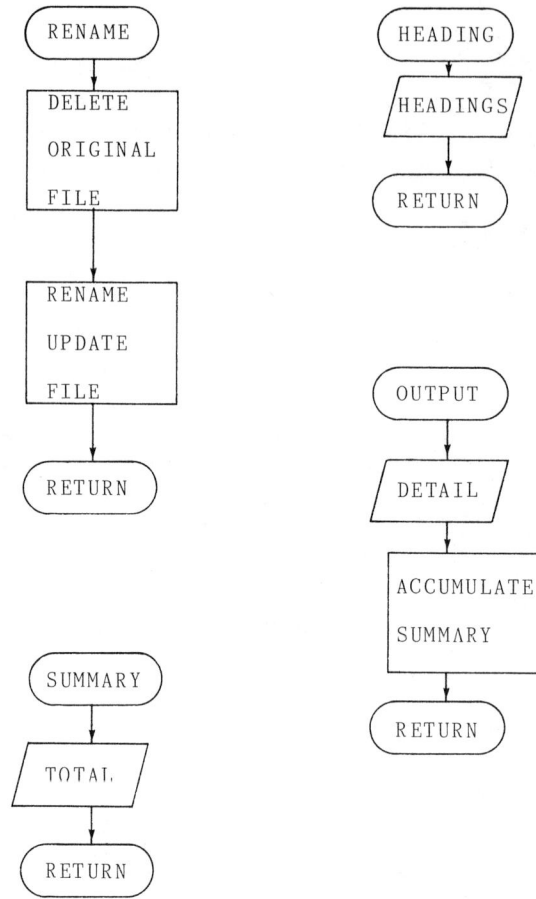

FIGURE 19–4
(Continued)

output file would destroy the existing file contents. Caution should be used when opening files because an incorrect entry could destroy a valuable data collection.

The data entry subroutine causes the new data records to be added. They must be entered and written according to the original file format. Three variable values are entered in each record.

The write to disk routine sends the data records to the file buffer. Following termination of the append loop, the file is closed.

The report and column headings are printed as a result of the heading routine.

The data file is opened for input purposes. The system can then access the file containing the 15 data records.

A WHILE-WEND structure is used to control execution of the output loop. The loop is executed until all records are processed. The loop consists of the read, file, and output subroutines.

Data records are entered as a result of the read subroutine. There are 15 data records to be processed. Summary totals for the sales amount and the number of records are accumulated in the read routine. The detail lines are printed in the output block.

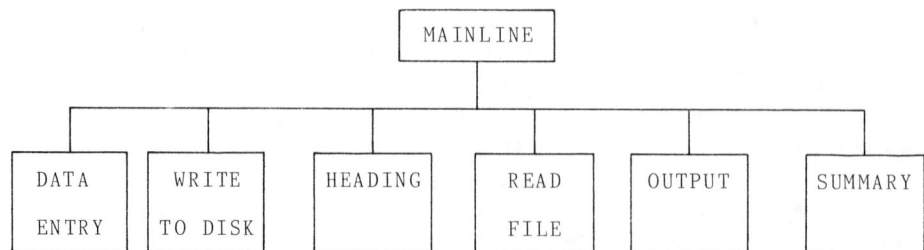

FIGURE 19–5
Top-level flowchart

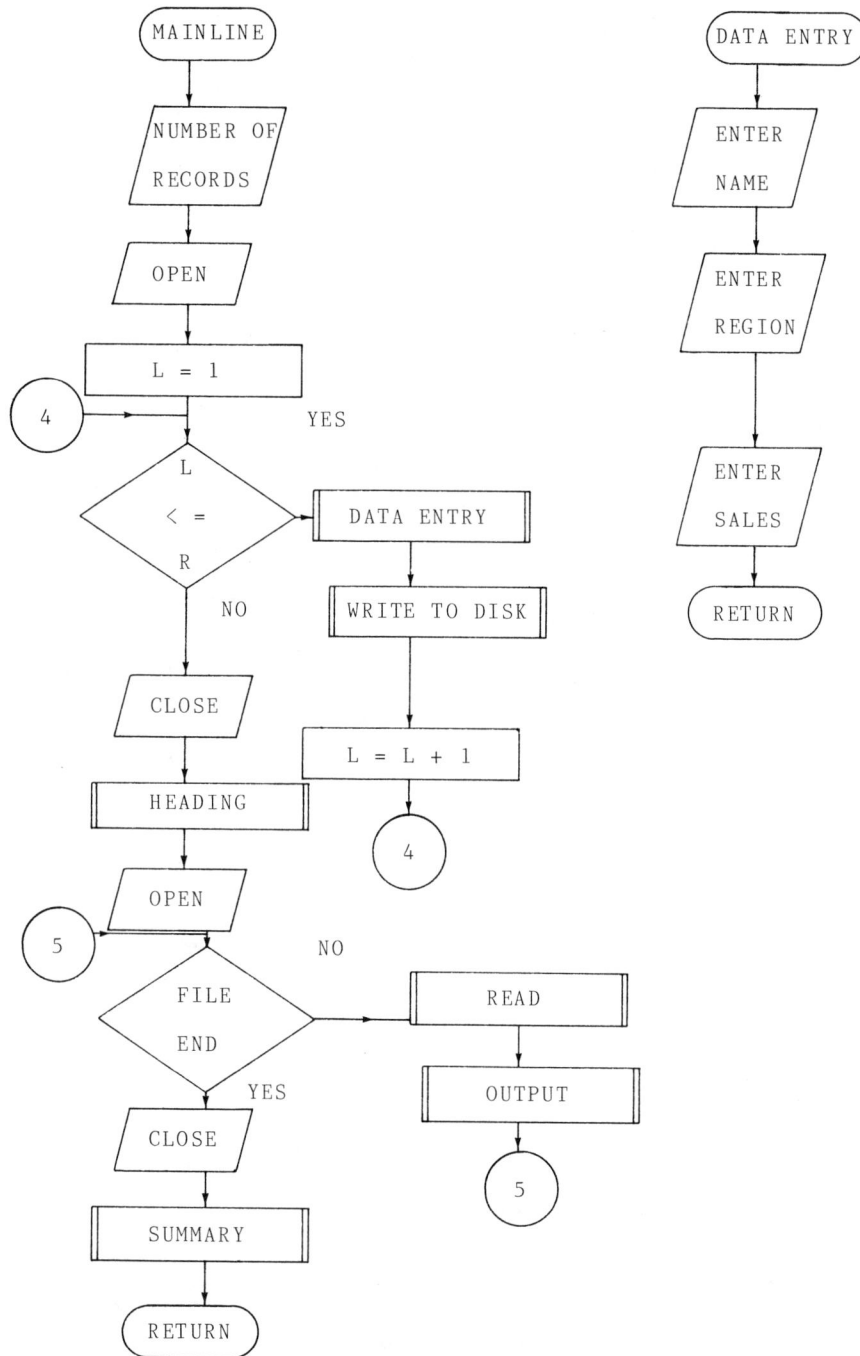

FIGURE 19–6
Detailed logic flowchart

Following execution of the output loop the file is closed, and the summary routine is executed. The summary totals for the sales amount and the number of records are printed. This terminates program execution.

EXAMPLE PROGRAMS—UPDATING SEQUENTIAL DISK FILES

The objective of this chapter is to demonstrate the BASIC language procedures for updating an existing sequential disk file by changing a value in a record and also by adding records to an existing file. Three programs are used to illustrate these procedures: the first program creates the file; the second program reads the file and changes a value

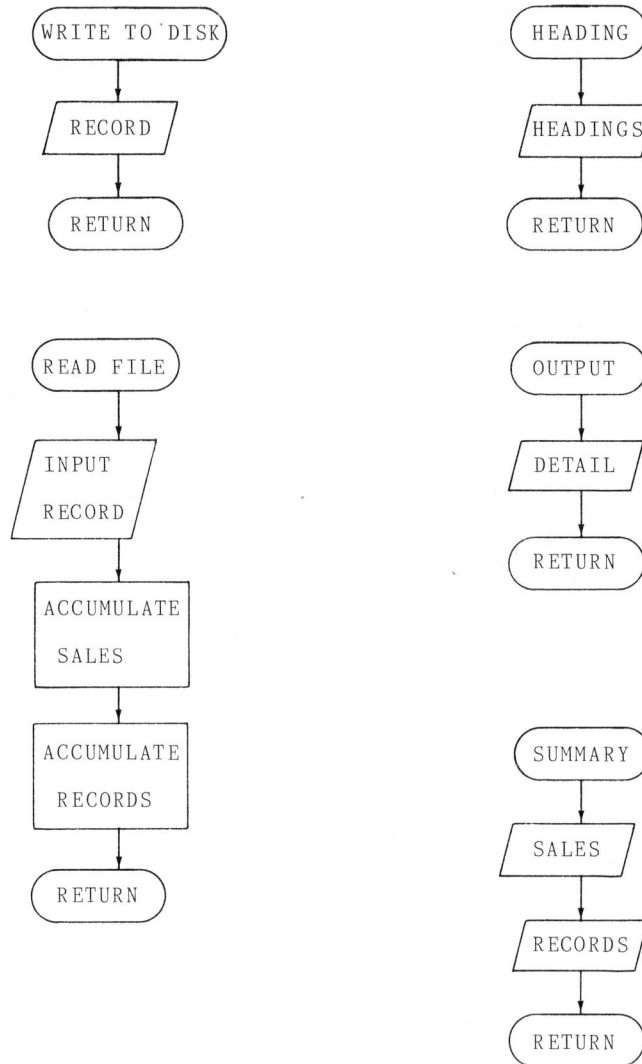

FIGURE 19–6
(Continued)

in a selected data record; and the third program adds data records to the previously updated file.

The program that creates the disk file is shown in figure 19–7. Twelve data records are entered. Each record contains three fields. The top-level and detailed logic flowcharts for this program are shown in figures 19–1 and 19–2.

Program documentation and variable identification appear in lines 3000 through 3090. The system and monitor screen are cleared in line 3220.

Statement 3410 opens the file for output mode. The file name used is EMPL.DAT. The file is assigned to disk drive B.

A FOR/NEXT structure is used to control execution of the program loop. There are 12 records to be processed, so loop parameters are set accordingly. The number of records is obtained from the source document or from the organization's records.

The program loop consists of the data entry and output to disk modules. The data entry module causes the three fields to be entered. The variables contained in each record are the employee name (E$), region (R$), and sales amount (S).

The output to disk module sends the data records to the file buffer. The records are written to the disk through the use of a WRITE # statement. Following is the WRITE # statement format.

3810 WRITE # ⟨Buffer Number ⟩, ⟨ Variable ⟩; ⟨ Variable ⟩

```
3000            REM     FIGURE  19-7   WRITTEN BY LARRY FRY    9/19/83
3010            REM     This program creates a sequential disk data
3020            REM     file for recording sales amounts.
3030                                                              REM
3040            REM     *****       Variable Identification
3050            REM     E$   .....       Employee Name
3060            REM     R$   .....       Region
3070            REM     S    .....       Sales Amount
3080            REM     T    .....       Summary Total
3090            REM     L    .....       Loop Counter
3100                                                              REM
3200            REM     *****       Housekeeping
3210            REM     *****       System Initialization
3220 CLEAR   :  CLS
3230                                                              REM
3400            REM     *****       Mainline Module
3410 OPEN "O", #2, "B:EMPL.DAT"
3420 FOR L = 1 TO 12
3430         GOSUB 3610
3440         GOSUB 3810
3450 NEXT L
3460 GOSUB 4010
3470 CLOSE #2
3480 END
3490                                                              REM
3600            REM     *****       Data Entry Module
3610 INPUT "ENTER Employee Name "; E$
3620 INPUT "ENTER Region "; R$
3630 INPUT "ENTER Sales "; S
3640 PRINT
3650 RETURN
3660                                                              REM
3670                                                              REM
3800            REM     *****       Output to Disk Module
3810 WRITE #2, E$; R$; S
3820 LET T = T + S
3830 RETURN
3840                                                              REM
4000            REM     *****       Summary Module
4010 LPRINT USING "Summary Total Sales $$##,###.##"; T
4020 RETURN
4030                                                              REM
4040 STOP
```

FIGURE 19–7
Sequential file creation
program

```
Summary Total Sales  $74,815.66
```

The WRITE # statement is more compact than the PRINT # statement because the "," delimiters are not needed. The "," delimit data fields and are required in the PRINT # statement. When WRITE # is used, the delimiting commas are inserted automatically by the system; they are not included in the program statement. The buffer number designated in the OPEN statement is used to identify the file. Semicolons or commas can be used to separate the variable names in the WRITE # statement. This affects the actual disk image as described in Chapter 18. Semicolons produce a compressed disk image. Commas spread the image because system print zones are used. The WRITE # statement from the example program follows.

3810 WRITE #2, E$; R$; S

MICROSOFT BASIC and TRS-80 BASIC use the same WRITE # statement. APPLESOFT BASIC does not support WRITE #. Those systems that do not support the WRITE # statement should use the PRINT # statement or its equivalent as described in Chapter 18.

Record the WRITE # statement format for the system being used in Exercise 19–1.

WRITE Statement Format

Key word _____

Buffer number _____

Variable names _____

WRITE statement format _____

_____

The summary total for sales is accumulated in the output to disk module. This value is compared with the footing numbers on the source document for data validation purposes. This total can be accumulated in the data entry module.

The program loop is executed 12 times. The data records entered are shown in figure 19–8.

Following execution of the program loop, the summary total is printed. This is shown in figure 19–7. The amount is $74,815.66.

The second program in this chapter reads the data file created in the first program and updates it by changing a value in a selected record. Figure 19–9 is the file update program. The top-level and detailed logic flowcharts for this program are shown in figures 19–3 and 19–4.

Program documentation and variable identification are contained in lines 5000 to 5130. Housekeeping tasks are shown in lines 5200 to 5270. The system and monitor screen are cleared in statement 5220. The output format for column headings and detail lines is declared in statements 5250 and 5260. The output formats are assigned to 01$ and 02$.

DATA RECORDS ENTERED

EMPLOYEE NAME	REGION	SALES
E$	R$	S
SMITH	NE	3,455.70
ZENFOR	SW	5,498.75
FORES	SE	7,435.32
HAWES	NE	4,575.90
RASTOR	SW	8,999.99
GRIMM	NE	6,578.78
DELP	SE	4,792.24
WINTERLIN	SW	8,767.77
HINDER	NW	6,790.00
LITTMAN	NE	5,455.55
MISTLE	NW	6,666.66
PRESTLE	NW	5,798.99
	TOTAL SALES	$74,815.66

FIGURE 19–8
Data records

```
5000              REM      FIGURE  19-9     WRITTEN BY LARRY FRY   9/19/83
5010              REM      This program reads a sequential disk file and
5020              REM      updates the sales amount in the selected record.
5030                                                                        REM
5040              REM      *****     Variable Identification
5050              REM      U$     .....   File Name to Update
5060              REM      UR$    .....   Record to Update
5070              REM      U      .....   Sales Update Amount
5080              REM      E$     .....   Employee Name
5090              REM      R$     .....   Region
5100              REM      S      .....   Sales Amount
5110              REM      T      .....   Summary Total
5120              REM      F      .....   Flag
5130                                                                        REM
5200              REM      *****     Housekeeping
5210              REM      *****     System Initialization
5220    CLEAR   :  CLS
5230                                                                        REM
5240              REM      *****     Format Output Lines
5250    LET O1$ = "Employee       Region         Sales"
5260    LET O2$ = "\           \         &         $$##,###.##"
5270                                                                        REM
5400              REM      *****     Mainline Module
5410    INPUT "ENTER File Name to Update "; U$
5420    INPUT "ENTER Record Name to Update "; UR$
5430    INPUT "ENTER Sales Update Amount "; U
5440    OPEN "I", #2, U$
5450    OPEN "O", #3, "B:EMPL.UPD"
5460    WHILE NOT EOF(2)
5470          GOSUB  5710
5480          GOSUB  5810
5490    WEND
5500    CLOSE
5510    IF F = 0 THEN LPRINT UR$, "RECORD NOT FOUND"
5520    GOSUB 6010
5530    OPEN "I", #2, "B:EMPL.DAT"
5540    GOSUB 6210
5550    WHILE NOT EOF(2)
5560          GOSUB  5710
5570          GOSUB  6410
5580    WEND
5590    CLOSE
5600    GOSUB 6610
5610    END
5700              REM      *****     Read Module
5710    INPUT #2, E$, R$, S
5720    RETURN
5730                                                                        REM
5800              REM      *****     Update Module
5810    IF E$ = UR$ THEN LET S = U : LET F = 1
5820    WRITE #3, E$; R$; S
5830    RETURN
5840                                                                        REM
6000              REM      *****     RENAME FILE MODULE
6010    KILL "B:EMPL.DAT"
6020    NAME "B:EMPL.UPD"   AS "B:EMPL.DAT"
6030    RETURN
6040                                                                        REM
6050                                                                        REM
6200              REM      *****     Heading Module
6210    LPRINT CHR$(12)
6220    LPRINT TAB(22); "PORT-EX COMPANY"
6230    LPRINT
6240    LPRINT TAB(22); "EMPLOYEE   SALES"
6250    LPRINT
6260    LPRINT O1$
6270    LPRINT
6280    RETURN
6290                                                                        REM
6400              REM      *****     Output Module
6410    LPRINT
6420    LPRINT USING O2$; E$, R$, S
6430    LET T = T + S
6440    RETURN
6450                                                                        REM
6600              REM      *****     Summary Module
6610    LPRINT : LPRINT
6620    LPRINT USING "Summary Total Sales   $$##,###.##"; T
6630    RETURN
6640                                                                        REM
6650    STOP
```

FIGURE 19–9
Sequential file update
program

The mainline module is contained in lines 5400 through 5610. The INPUT statements, which follow, are used to enter the file, record, and variable names to be updated.

5410 INPUT "ENTER File Name to Update"; U$
5420 INPUT "ENTER Record Name to Update"; UR$
5430 INPUT "ENTER Sales Update Amount"; U

The file name to be updated is entered as a result of statement 5410. Therefore, this program can be used to update more than one file name. It can only update files of the type specified, but more than one file of this type can be processed. This program can be used to update any sales file with the same record and field specifications. For example, it can be used to update sales files for different departments, stores, or regions.

Line 5420 is used to enter the specific record to be updated. The employee name field is used as the record identification key in this program. Other keys, such as the employee or customer number, could also be used. Finally, the updated sales amount is entered. This value replaces the previous sales amount in the file for the record specified.

The file is opened in statement 5440, which follows.

5440 OPEN "I", #2, U$

The OPEN statement, which was used previously, accessed files declared as a constant. The file name was enclosed in quotation marks. In this case, a variable (U$) is used in the OPEN statement. The file name that was entered in statement 5410, "B:EMPL.DAT", is opened as a result of statement 5440.

MICROSOFT BASIC and TRS-80 BASIC use the same procedures to open a variable file. APPLESOFT BASIC uses the following procedures to open a variable file.

100 LET F$ = CHR$(4)
5010 INPUT "ENTER FILE NAME TO BE UPDATED"; U$
5410 PRINT F$; "OPEN" U$

Program statement 5450 is used to open the update file. This file is created to receive the records from the original file. The original file is read and the records are written to the update file. Those records not being updated are written directly to the new file. The specified record receives the new data value and is then written to the update file. Following is the OPEN statement.

5450 OPEN "O", #3, "B:EMPL.UPD"

The update file is declared as an output file. This causes all records to be written to the file. Buffer #3 is used for the update file. The original file uses buffer #2. The update file name is "B:EMPL.UPD".

A WHILE-WEND structure, which follows, is used to control execution of the file update loop.

5460 WHILE NOT EOF(2)
5470   GOSUB 5710
5480   GOSUB 5810
5490 WEND
5500 CLOSE
5510 IF F = 0 THEN LPRINT UR$, "RECORD NOT FOUND"

The WHILE-WEND loop is executed as long as there is a record to process. The end of file marker, which is placed after the last record at file creation, is the key to the use of this control structure. The EOF(2) segment of the WHILE statement detects the end of file pointer. The EOF function returns a true response (-1 for the system being used) when the end of file pointer is detected. A false (0 for this system) is returned when there are additional records to process.

The WHILE NOT EOF(2) statement could be written as follows: WHILE NOT TRUE (or while there are records remaining), execute the loop. Upon detecting the end of file pointer, the WHILE statement would read, WHILE NOT FALSE (or WHILE TRUE) EOF(2), and terminate the loop.

Those systems that do not support the WHILE NOT EOF statement should use the end of file detection procedures described in Chapter 18 (see figure 18–8 or 18–10). APPLESOFT BASIC does not support the WHILE-WEND statements.

The update loop is executed as long as there are records to process. The loop consists of the read and update modules. The read module causes the data records to be entered. The three fields in each record are the employee name (E$), region (R$), and sales amount (S).

The record to be updated is determined in the update module, which follows.

```
5810 IF E$ = UR$ THEN LET S = U : LET F = 1
5820 WRITE #3, E$; R$; S
5830 RETURN
```

Line 5810 is the program branch statement that checks each record entered and selects the specified record for updating. The record identified as DELP is the one to be updated in this program. The value DELP is entered in the INPUT statement in line 5420 as variable UR$. If the employee name (E$) is equal to the specified update record (UR$), the update value (U) is assigned to the sales amount (S), and the flag variable is assigned the value one. The IF statement is evaluated as true only when the employee name entered from the disk and the update record name are equal.

When the IF statement is evaluated as false, program control drops to line 5820. Statement 5820 writes the records to the file buffer. It is executed for all records, including the one updated.

The WHILE-WEND loop is terminated after the last record in the original files has been processed. Statement 5500 then closes all files. The CLOSE key word closes all open files.

Line 5510, which follows, is the program branch statement used to determine if the update record was located in the file.

```
5510 IF F = 0 THEN LPRINT UR$, "RECORD NOT FOUND"
```

The flag variable is cleared at the beginning of the program. If the update record is located in the update process, the flag variable is assigned the value one in line 5810. If the specified update record is not located, the flag variable remains at zero causing the update record name and the warning message to be printed. Program control then drops to the next statement.

Statement 5520 calls the rename file module. This module is included in the program to retain the original file name. The file name EMPL.DAT is the personnel file name. The name is used as the personnel file reference name, so it should emerge from the program in a usable condition. The user should not be forced to keep track of many different file names. Therefore, the current file should emerge from the program with the original file name. Following is the rename module.

```
6010 KILL "B:EMPL.DAT"
6020 NAME "B:EMPL.UPD" AS "B:EMPL.DAT"
```

The KILL statement format follows.

```
6010 KILL ⟨ Device : File Name ⟩
```

The KILL key word in line 6010 deletes the original file, which is known as "B:EMPL.DAT". This file name is deleted to avoid a duplicate file name error condition. If an archive copy of the original file is desired, it is possible to rename the file as follows.

```
6010 NAME "B:EMPL.DAT" AS "B:EMPL.ARC"
```

The NAME key word transfers one file name to another. The NAME statement format follows.

```
6020 NAME " ⟨ Device:File Name ⟩ " AS " ⟨ Device:File Name ⟩ "
```

The update file is renamed with the original file name. In this case, file name "B:EMPL.UPD" is renamed as "B:EMPL.DAT". If the device is not specified, the default drive is used. As previously stated, this command can also be used to create archive copies.

MICROSOFT BASIC uses the same key words for file rename and deletion purposes.

TRS-80 BASIC uses the KILL key word to delete file names and the RENAME key word to change file names. The statement format follows.

6020 RENAME EMPL/UPD EMPL/DAT

APPLESOFT BASIC uses the following procedures to delete and rename file names.

910 PRINT F$; "DELETE EMPL"
920 PRINT F$; "RENAME EMPLUPD, EMPL"

Line 910 is the APPLESOFT statement used to delete the file known as EMPL. Statement 920 changes the EMPLUPD file to EMPL. The comma separating the two file names in line 920 is required.

Statement 5530 opens the update file, which is now known as "B:EMPL.DAT", as an input file.

The heading module is called in line 5540. Report and column headings are printed as a result of this module.

A WHILE-WEND structure is used to execute the output loop. The loop is executed as long as there are records to process. The output loop includes the read and output modules. The read module is contained in lines 5710 and 5720. This routine was used previously in the program. The output module prints the detail lines. The LPRINT US-ING statement in line 6420 prints the data. Output format statement 02$ is used to edit the printing. The summary total for sales is accumulated in the output module.

Twelve data records are present in the file. The WHILE-WEND loop is executed until all records have been processed. The files are closed after the loop is terminated.

The summary module is executed after the loop is terminated. Total sales are printed as a result of this module. Program execution ends after the summary total is printed.

```
                        PORT-EX COMPANY

                        EMPLOYEE  SALES

        Employee        Region        Sales


        SMITH           NE          $3,455.70

        ZENFOR          SW          $5,498.75

        FORES           SE          $7,435.32

        HAWES           NE          $4,575.90

        RASTOR          SW          $8,999.99

        GRIMM           NE          $6,578.78

        DELP            SE          $4,999.89

        WINTERLIN       SW          $8,767.77

        HINDER          NW          $6,790.00

        LITTMAN         NE          $5,455.55

        MISTLE          NW          $6,666.66

        PRESTLE         NW          $5,798.99

        Summary Total Sales    $75,023.31
```

FIGURE 19–10
File update program
results

```
8000            REM      FIGURE  19-11   WRITTEN BY LARRY FRY     9/20/83
8010            REM      This program updates a sequential disk file.
8020            REM      New records are added or appended to an existing
8030            REM      sequential disk file.
8040                                                                    REM
8050            REM      *****      Variable Identification
8060            REM      E$    .....      Employee Name
8070            REM      R$    .....      Region
8080            REM      S     .....      Sales
8090            REM      T     .....      Summary Sales
8100            REM      N     .....      Number of Records in File
8110            REM      L     .....      Loop Counter
8120            REM      R     .....      Loop Limit
8130                                                                    REM
8200            REM      *****      Housekeeping
8210            REM      *****      System Initialization
8220  CLEAR : CLS
8230                                                                    REM
8240            REM      *****      Format Output Lines
8250  LET O1$ = "Employee        Region        Sales"
8260  LET O2$ = "\          \        &         $$##,###.##"
8270                                                                    REM
8400            REM      *****      Mainline Module
8410  INPUT "ENTER Number of Records to Add to File "; R
8420  OPEN "A", #2, "B:EMPL.DAT"
8430  FOR L = 1 TO R
8440        GOSUB 8610
8450        GOSUB 8810
8460  NEXT L
8470  CLOSE #2
8480  GOSUB 8910
8490  OPEN "I", #2, "B:EMPL.DAT"
8500  WHILE NOT EOF(2)
8510        GOSUB 9010
8520        GOSUB 9210
8530  WEND
8540  CLOSE #2
8550  GOSUB 9410
8560  END
8570                                                                    REM
8600            REM      *****      Data Entry Module
8610  INPUT "ENTER Employee Name "; E$
8620  INPUT "ENTER Region "; R$
8630  INPUT "ENTER Sales "; S
8640  PRINT
8650  RETURN
8660                                                                    REM
8800            REM      *****      Write to Disk
8810  WRITE #2, E$; R$; S
8820  RETURN
8830                                                                    REM
8900            REM      *****      Heading Module
8910  LPRINT CHR$(12)
8920  LPRINT TAB(22); "PORT-EX COMPANY"
8930  LPRINT
8940  LPRINT TAB(16); "SALES  FILE "; DATE$
8950  LPRINT
8960  LPRINT O1$
8970  LPRINT
8980  RETURN
8990                                                                    REM
9000            REM      *****      Read File Module
9010  INPUT #2, E$, R$, S
9020  LET T = T + S
9030  LET N = N + 1
9040  RETURN
9050                                                                    REM
9200            REM      *****      Output Module
9210  LPRINT
9220  LPRINT USING O2$; E$, R$, S
9230  RETURN
9240                                                                    REM
9400            REM      *****      Summary Module
9410  LPRINT : LPRINT
9420  LPRINT USING "Total Sales       $$##,###.##"; T
9430  LPRINT
9440  LPRINT USING "Total Records in File   ###"; N
9450  RETURN
9460                                                                    REM
9470  STOP
```

FIGURE 19-11
Sequential file append
program

The results of the file update program are exhibited in figure 19–10. Twelve detail lines are printed. They are followed by the new summary total. The sales amount in the DELP record was changed from 4,792.24 to 4,999.89. The new summary total is 75,023.31.

The third program in this chapter demonstrates the BASIC language procedures for updating a sequential file by adding new records. Twelve records are present in the file at the conclusion of the program in figure 19–9. Three additional records are to be added in this program. The program to append records to an existing file is shown in figure 19–11. The top-level and detailed logic flowcharts for this program are shown in figures 19–5 and 19–6.

Program documentation and variable identification are shown in lines 8000 to 8130. Housekeeping tasks are contained in statements 8200 to 8270. The system and monitor screen are cleared in line 8220. Output format statements are declared in lines 8250 and 8260. Output formats are assigned to 01$ and 02$.

The mainline module is contained in lines 8410 to 8570. This module controls program execution. The number of records to be added to the file is entered through the INPUT statement in line 8410. This number is obtained from the source document or the organization's records.

The file to be updated is opened in line 8420. The file mode is "A". This means that the data records being entered will be added at the end of the file. The new records are added beginning at the end of file marker. Mode "A" must be used for this purpose. Opening a file as mode "O" for update purposes would destroy the file. Line 8420 follows.

8420 OPEN "A", #2, "B:EMPL.DAT"

MICROSOFT BASIC uses the same statement to append files.

The TRS-80 BASIC statement used to append files is equivalent to the preceding statement, except that mode "E" is used. Mode "E" means that the file is to be extended.

Following is the APPLESOFT BASIC statement used to append files.

410 PRINT F$; "APPEND EMPL"

Record the append statement for the system being used in Exercise 19–2.

EXERCISE 19–2

Append Statement Format

Key word _____

File mode _____

Buffer number _____

Device/file name _____

A FOR/NEXT structure controls execution of the append loop. Three additional records are to be added. The loop consists of the data entry and write to disk modules. The data records to be added are entered as a result of lines 8610 to 8640. The write to disk module sends the data records to the file buffer. Notice that the data fields are entered in the same sequence as in the original file.

The file is closed after the append loop is terminated.

Report and column headings are printed as a result of statement 8480.

The file is opened for input in line 8490. A WHILE-WEND structure is used to control execution of the output loop. There are now 15 records in the file, so the loop is executed accordingly.

```
                    PORT-EX COMPANY

                SALES  FILE 12-21-1984

      Employee        Region        Sales


        SMITH           NE          $3,455.70

        ZENFOR          SW          $5,498.75

        FORES           SE          $7,435.32

        HAWES           NE          $4,575.90

        RASTOR          SW          $8,999.99

        GRIMM           NE          $6,578.78

        DELP            SE          $4,999.89

        WINTERLIN       SW          $8,767.77

        HINDER          NW          $6,790.00

        LITTMAN         NE          $5,455.55

        MISTLE          NW          $6,666.66

        PRESTLE         NW          $5,798.99

        NORAN           SW          $7,442.14

        KANE            NE          $3,235.25

        CALFOR          SE          $5,115.55


      Total Sales     $90,816.24

      Total Records in File    15
```

FIGURE 19–12
Append program results

The output loop consists of the read and output modules. Statement 9010 reads the data records. The summary total for the amount of sales is accumulated in line 9020, and the number of records is tallied in statement 9030.

Detail lines are printed in the output module. The LPRINT USING statement in line 9220 uses the output format assigned to 02$ to edit the detail lines.

Following termination of the output loop, the summary totals are printed. The amount of sales and the number of records are printed. This terminates program execution.

The output from this program is shown in figure 19–12. Headings and detail lines are printed. There are 15 detail lines. The two summary totals are printed last.

PROGRAM DEVELOPMENT CHECKLIST

Use the following checklist to ensure that all components are included in the program.

_____ Flowcharts and documentation

_____ Program loop

Disk file update/append

_____ Open input file

_____ Open update/append file

_____ Update entries

_____ Write to file

Rename files

_____ Kill or delete files

_____ Name or rename files

Output

_____ Open for input

_____ Read file

_____ End of file detection

_____ Summary totals

_____ Output

_____ Close files

SUMMARY

The BASIC language contains procedures for updating sequential disk files. The update process includes changing data values in an existing record and/or adding records to a file. An existing file can be updated by changing a data value in a specified record. Two files must be opened for this process: one is the original file which is read; the other is the update file which is used for output. The identification key for the record and the data value to be updated are entered in transaction mode.

Records can also be added to an existing file. The new records are appended, or extended, to the existing file. The file must be opened in the append mode. Record addition procedures vary from system to system.

System reference manuals must be carefully checked when using disk files.

BASIC Key Words Learned

APPEND	APPLESOFT key word to append file.
DELETE	Deletes referenced file name.
KILL	Deletes referenced file name.
NAME	Renames file as specified.
RENAME	Renames file as specified.
WEND	Terminates WHILE loop.
WHILE	Loop control structure.
WRITE #	Sends record to file buffer.

Instructions

Prepare the flowcharts and structured BASIC programs to create, update, and print a sequential disk file. Use one program to create and print the file and another to update and print the file. Use transaction processing to enter the data to create and update the file. The variables are the account number, the account name, the transactions to date, and the current balance. Accumulate a summary total of account balances in each program. Use the account number as the key field. File updating consists of deleting an existing record from the file. Rename the original file and save it as an archive file.

Following is the data to be processed. Use prompting INPUT statements to enter the data. (NOTE: Do not delete the file when completed.)

Data

Account Number	Account Name	Transactions To Date	Current Balance
1570	Bro-Kemp	37	1,137.94
3900	Space Air	10	3,450.00
2480	Office Mod	20	750.00
1170	Phil Dirt Co	19	0.00
1660	Pete Moss Assoc	23	2,450.00
1220	Chuck Roast Ent	17	0.00
1490	X-Y Games	9	497.15

Transaction Data

ACCOUNT NUMBER—3900. Delete from file.

Output Format

Print the headings. Include detail lines and the summary total in the output for the file creation program. Print the data file and the summary total in the second program. Use output editing if available.

PORT-EX COMPANY

Account Status Report

Account Number	Account Name	Transactions to Date	Current Balance
XXXX	XXXXXX	XX	$X,XXX.XX
XXXX	XXXXXX	XX	$X,XXX.XX

SUMMARY TOTAL $XX,XXX.XX

Updated File

Account Number	Account Name	Transactions to Date	Current Balance
XXXX	XXXXXX	XX	$X,XXX.XX
XXXX	XXXXXX	XX	$X,XXX.XX

SUMMARY TOTAL $XX,XXX.XX

PROGRAM ASSIGNMENT 19–2

Instructions

Prepare the flowcharts and the structured BASIC program to update and print a sequential disk file. The program adds five records to the sequential file created in Program Assignment 19–1. The records append, or extend, the original file. Accumulate a summary total for the five records added. Print the detail lines and the summary total for the file.

The data records to be added follow. Use prompting INPUT statements to enter the data.

Data

Account Number	Account Name	Transactions to Date	Current Balance
1270	A–Z Assoc	29	1,157.40
1380	BYTO Computers	32	995.55
1870	Hi Tech Comp	8	632.47
1470	Able Mable Ent	18	575.25
1650	Compware	4	348.77

Output Format

Print the headings, the summary total for the added data records, and the data records and summary total for the updated file. Use output editing if available.

PORT-EX COMPANY

Account Status Report

UPDATE SUMMARY TOTAL $XX,XXX.XX

Account Number	Account Name	Transactions toDate	Current Balance
XXXX	XXXXXX	XX	X,XXX.XX
XXXX	XXXXXX	XX	X,XXX.XX

SUMMARY TOTAL $XX,XXX.XX

PROGRAM ASSIGNMENT 19–3

Instructions

Prepare the flowcharts and the structured BASIC program to update a sequential disk file. The program uses the file produced in Assignments 19–1 and 19–2. Develop a program menu to consider the following options:

1. Changing a data value within a specified record.
2. Adding additional records to the file.
3. Deleting a record.
4. Printing the file with summary total.

A file rename procedure must be included in the program after each processing step. Use prompting INPUT statements to enter the transactions.

The file to be processed was created as a result of Program Assignments 19–1 and 19–2. Following is the transaction data.

Transaction Data

1. Delete the following record: Account 1220.
2. Append the following records:

Account Number	Account Name	Transactions to Date	Current Balance
1580	Ramtech	2	445.75
1670	Image Tech	1	179.85
1680	Bits and Bytes	3	333.33

3. Change the following values in the specified record:

1490	X–Y Games	10	814.00

4. Print the updated file and the summary total.

Output Format

Print the headings, including the current date, the detail lines, and the summary total. Use output editing if available.

PORT-EX COMPANY

Account Status Report 10–20–84

Account Number	Account Name	Transactions to Date	Current Balance
XXXX	XXXXXXXXXX	XX	X,XXX.XX
XXXX	XXXXXXX	XX	X,XXX.XX

SUMMARY TOTAL $XX,XXX.XX

RANDOM ACCESS DISK FILES

20

OBJECTIVES

At the end of this chapter you should be able to perform the following operations:

- Create random, or direct, access disk data files.
- Access, retrieve, and display records from random access disk files.
- Update random access disk files.

DIRECT ACCESS FILES

The sequential disk files described in the previous chapters are adequate for serial or batch data processing tasks. They are used in situations where the entire file is accessed, such as in the preparation of customer account statements or payroll. Sequential access procedures are used when the response time is not critical.

When response time is critical, business data processing procedures require the use of *direct*, or *random*, access files. Commonly, the response time to a query is less than three to five seconds (at maximum). Some situations in which immediate disk access is required are making reservations for airlines or hotels, checking bank account balances, determining customer account status, and responding to such situations as fire or medical emergencies. Time is critical in these situations. The inquiry cannot hold while the computer cranks through an entire disk file to find the correct record. Direct, immediate access is necessary. In these time critical situations, random access processing must be used.

Inquiry, or transaction-oriented, processing utilizes a random access file. Any given record in the file can be accessed directly. Different records can be directly accessed with no time penalty, regardless of where the record is physically located in the disk file. Thus, the record for customer number 1234 can be accessed in the same time frame as the record for customer number 9876, even though they are physically located at different places on the disk. The only time difference involved is movement of the read-write head (or heads) on the disk drive. This is measured in thousandths of a second.

Business data base development and utilization require direct access files. Data base inquiries and transactions require an immediate response. Therefore, direct access files are used.

FLOWCHARTS—CREATING AND ACCESSING RANDOM ACCESS FILES

The objective of this chapter is to illustrate the BASIC language procedures for creating and accessing a random access file. Two programs are used to do this: one program creates the file; the other accesses the file and retrieves selected records. The process for updating a random file is simpler than that involved in updating sequential files because any given record can be directly accessed. The flowcharts shown in figures 20–1 and 20–2 are used to create the file.

The top-level flowchart in figure 20–1 contains the mainline routine which controls program execution. The subroutines are the data entry, write to random file, and summary blocks. Housekeeping tasks, which consist of clearing the system and the monitor screen, are executed before the mainline routine assumes control of the program.

The detailed logic flowchart is shown in figure 20–2. The mainline routine controls execution of the program subroutines.

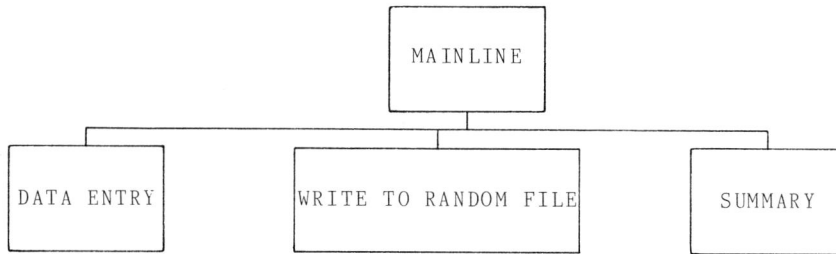

FIGURE 20–1
Top-level flowchart

The disk file must be opened before the device can be accessed. The OPEN statement must be listed before there is any reference to the disk file.

Random access files for the system being used are stored in binary form. It is necessary to describe the image that is to be recorded upon the disk for each record. Please note that all records in any given file must be described with the same length parameter. A FIELD statement is used to describe the record as it will appear in the buffer. The statement actually allocates the buffer area for the record as described. The data is recorded in the buffer in string form. It is converted to binary form as it is written on the disk.

The number of data records to be placed in the disk file is entered by an INPUT statement. There are 12 records to be processed, so this number is entered. It serves as the program loop limit. The number of records is available on the source document.

A FOR/NEXT structure is used to control execution of the program loop. The loop will execute 12 times according to the parameters. The loop body consists of the data entry and write to random disk routines.

Variable values are entered in the data entry routine. The values entered are the product number, product name, product cost, selling price, and quantity on hand. INPUT statements are used to enter the values. A data validation procedure is used to check the values entered to insure that they are correct. The user can verify that the data values entered are correct. Detection of an incorrect value causes the program to branch back to the INPUT statements.

The data values are sent to the buffer as a result of the LSET (or RSET) function. This command sends the data to the buffer and left-justifies (or right-justifies) it within the space allocated in the FIELD statement.

With this system it is necessary to convert numeric variables to string form when using random files. The MKx$ function is used to convert the numeric values into string form. It is included as part of the LSET function in this program. The proper numeric format (integer, single-precision, or double-precision) must be specified in the conversion process.

The PUT statement transfers the data record from the buffer to the disk. Each individual record is written on the disk by the PUT function.

Summary totals for the cost and price are accumulated in the write to random file routine.

The disk file is closed following termination of the program loop. Summary totals are printed at this point. This is followed by program termination.

The second program in this chapter accesses the random file and retrieves selected records. Once any given record is retrieved and is in current memory, it is available for any type of processing. The flowcharts shown in figures 20–3 and 20–4 are used for the file access program.

The top-level flowchart in figure 20–3 contains the mainline routine which controls program execution. The subroutines are the search disk and output blocks. Housekeeping tasks, which include clearing the system and monitor screen, and formatting the output lines, are performed before the mainline block takes control of the program.

The detailed logic flowchart is shown in figure 20–4. The mainline routine controls execution of the subroutines.

The disk file is opened before any processing tasks occur. The FIELD statement describes the buffer record format.

MAINLINE

```
        ( MAINLINE )
              │
              ▼
         ┌─────────┐
         │  OPEN   │
         └─────────┘
              │
              ▼
         ┌─────────┐
         │  FIELD  │
         └─────────┘
              │
              ▼
        ╱NUMBER OF╱
        ╱ RECORDS ╱
              │
              ▼
         ┌─────────┐
         │  L = 1  │
         └─────────┘
              │
    (1)───────┤
              ▼
            ╱  L  ╲         YES
           ╱  < =  ╲──────────────┐
           ╲   R   ╱              ▼
            ╲     ╱         ┌────────────┐
              │ NO          │ DATA ENTRY │
              ▼             └────────────┘
        ╱ CLOSE ╱                 │
              │                   ▼
              ▼             ┌──────────────┐
         ┌─────────┐        │ WRITE TO FILE│
         │ SUMMARY │        └──────────────┘
         └─────────┘                │
              │                     ▼
              ▼             ┌────────────┐
          (  END  )        │ L = L + 1  │
                           └────────────┘
                                  │
                                  ▼
                                 (1)
```

DATA ENTRY

```
        ( DATA ENTRY )
  (2)────────┤
              ▼
        ╱ ENTER  ╱
        ╱ NUMBER ╱
              │
              ▼
        ╱ ENTER ╱
        ╱ NAME  ╱
              │
              ▼
        ╱ ENTER ╱
        ╱ COST  ╱
              │
              ▼
        ╱ ENTER ╱
        ╱ PRICE ╱
              │
              ▼
        ╱  ENTER  ╱
        ╱QUANTITY╱
              │
              ▼
         ┌─────────┐
         │  PRINT  │
         └─────────┘
              │
              ▼
            ╱ DATA ╲        NO
           ╱CORRECT╲──────────────(2)
            ╲      ╱
              │ YES
              ▼
          ( RETURN )
```

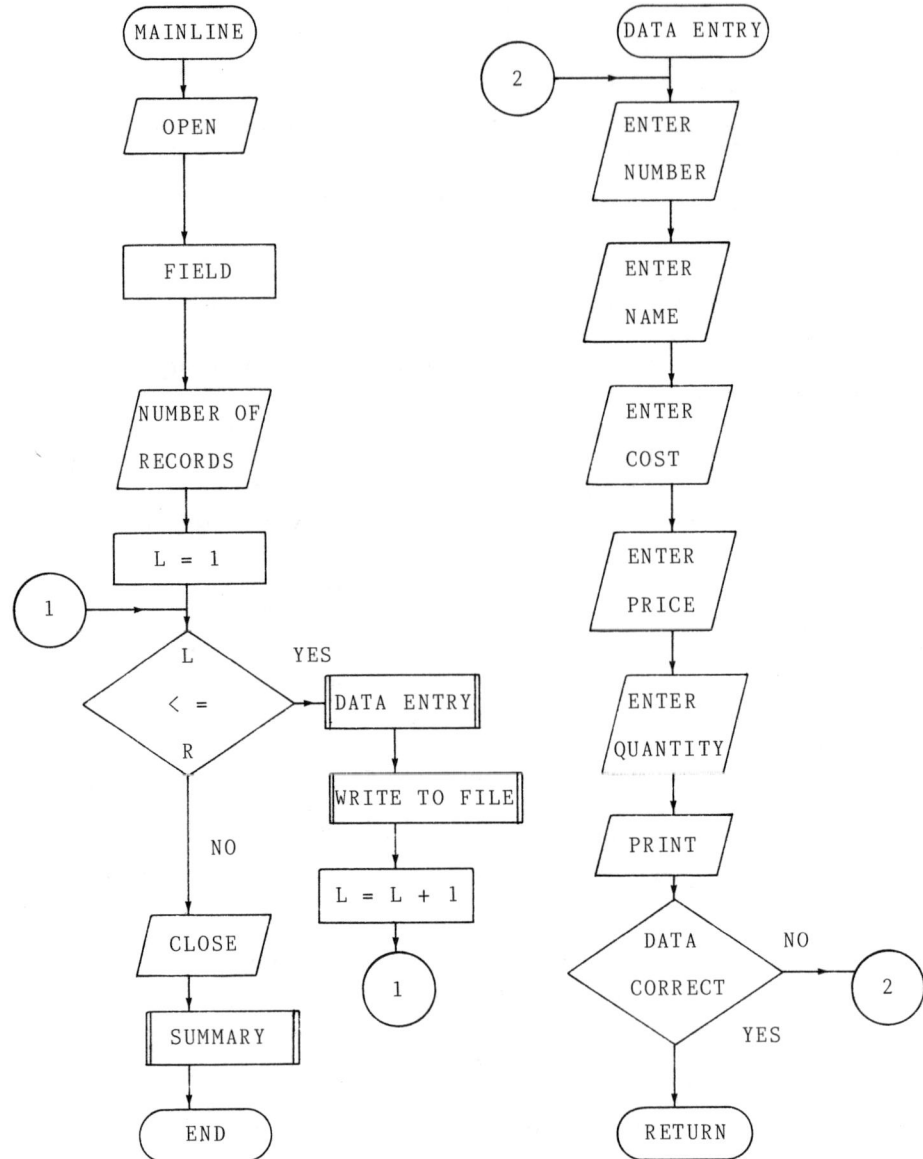

FIGURE 20–2
Detailed logic flowchart

The number of data records to be retrieved from the file is entered by an INPUT statement. Five records are to be recovered, so this number is entered. This number serves as the program loop limit.

A FOR/NEXT structure is used to control execution of the program loop. The loop will be executed five times according to the parameters. The loop body consists of the search disk and output subroutines.

The search disk file routine accesses the file and retrieves the selected data record. The search key is entered by an INPUT statement. In this program, it is the product number.

The GET statement is used to retrieve the selected record. When a record is retrieved by the GET statement, the numeric values must be converted from string format to numeric format. The product number, cost, price, and quantity fields are converted to the appropriate numeric format (integer, single-precision, or double-precision) as specified.

The output routine prints the selected data records. The FOR/NEXT loop results in five data records being printed. The program terminates after the records are retrieved and printed.

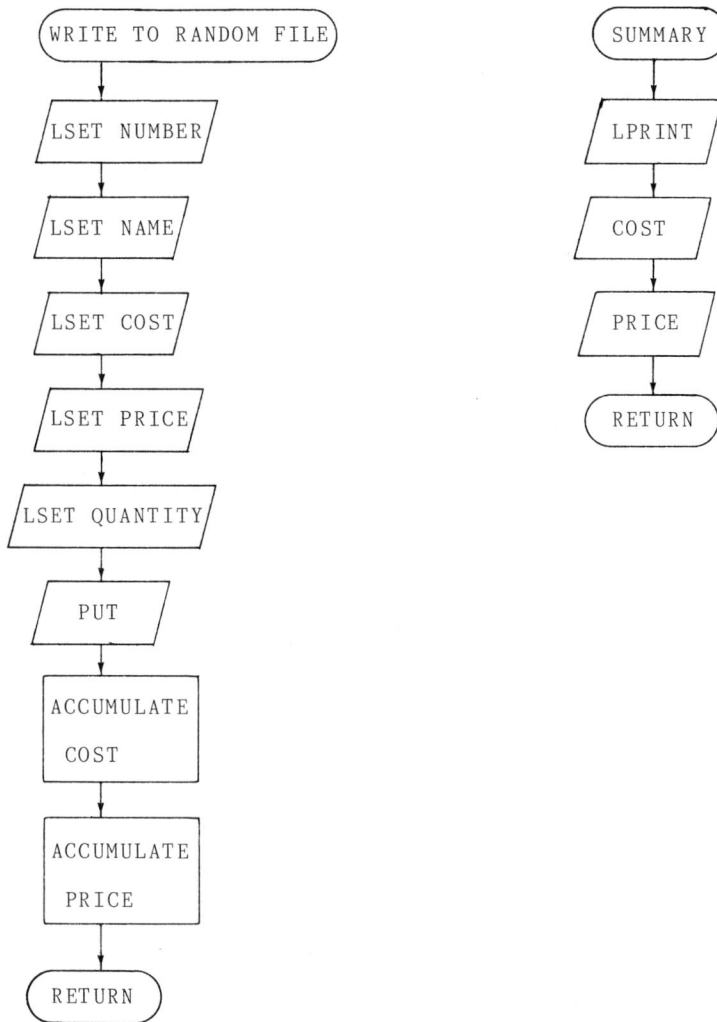

FIGURE 20–2
(Continued)

EXAMPLE PROGRAMS—CREATING AND ACCESSING RANDOM DISK FILES

The objective of this chapter is to demonstrate the BASIC language procedures for creating and accessing random disk files. Two programs are used to do this: one program creates the file; the other program accesses the file and retrieves selected data records. The process of updating a random access file is simpler than updating a sequential file because a specific record can be retrieved from the file, changed, and put back into the file. Thus, GET and PUT operations are involved in random file updating.

The program that illustrates creation of a random access file is shown in figure 20–5. The top-level and detailed logic flowcharts for this program are shown in figures 20–1 and 20–2.

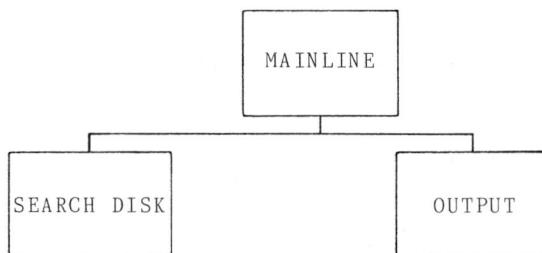

FIGURE 20–3
Top-level flowchart

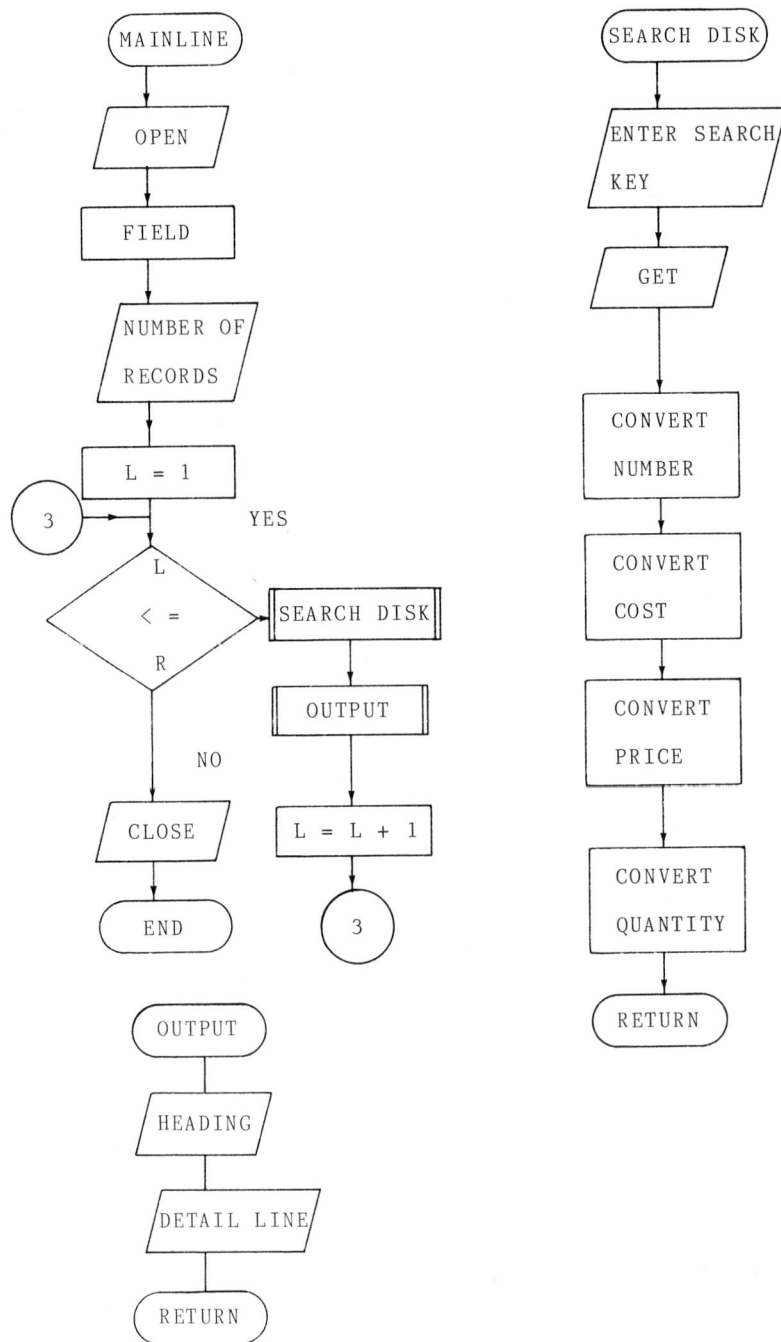

```
          ( MAINLINE )                              ( SEARCH DISK )
                |                                          |
          / OPEN /                                /ENTER SEARCH/
                |                                 /   KEY    /
          [ FIELD ]                                        |
                |                                    / GET /
        /NUMBER OF/                                        |
        / RECORDS /                               [ CONVERT  ]
                |                                 [ NUMBER   ]
          [ L = 1 ]                                        |
                |                                 [ CONVERT  ]
   ( 3 )----->  |            YES                  [ COST     ]
                |                                          |
              / L \                                [ CONVERT  ]
             <  =  >----->[ SEARCH DISK ]          [ PRICE    ]
              \ R /               |                         |
                |          [ OUTPUT ]             [ CONVERT  ]
              NO                  |               [ QUANTITY ]
                |          [ L = L + 1 ]                    |
          / CLOSE /              |                  ( RETURN )
                |              ( 3 )
            ( END )

          ( OUTPUT )
                |
          / HEADING /
                |
          /DETAIL LINE/
                |
          ( RETURN )
```

FIGURE 20–4
Detailed logic flowchart

Program documentation and variable identification are contained in lines 2000 to 2200. The system and monitor screen are cleared in line 2320.

Random access files are opened through the use of the OPEN statement. The OPEN statement format is much the same as that used with sequential files, except that the file mode is "R". Mode "R" means that the file can be used for random access <u>input</u> and/or <u>output</u>. The OPEN statement for random access files also must include a record length declaration. Following is the random access OPEN statement format.

2410 OPEN "R", # ⟨Buffer⟩, ⟨"Device:File Name"⟩, ⟨Record Length⟩

Following is the OPEN statement used in the program.

2410 OPEN "R", #3, "B:INV.DAT", 42

The file mode is declared as "R", which enables input and/or output operations with

```
2000            REM     FIGURE   20-5     WRITTEN BY LARRY FRY    10/20/83
2010            REM     This program creates a random access disk file.
2020            REM     Twelve data records are entered in a direct file.
2030                                                                        REM
2040            REM     *****         Variable Identification
2050            REM     N    .....   Product Number
2060            REM     P$   .....   Product Name
2070            REM     C    .....   Product Cost
2080            REM     P    .....   Selling Price
2090            REM     Q    .....   Quantity on Hand
2100            REM     L    .....   Loop Counter
2110            REM     R    .....   Loop Limit
2120            REM     I$   .....   Data Entry Verification
2130            REM     T1   .....   Summary Cost Total
2140            REM     T2   .....   Summary Price Total
2150            REM     F1$  .....   FIELD # 1 - Random Binary
2160            REM     F2$  .....   FIELD # 2 - Random Binary
2170            REM     F3$  .....   FIELD # 3 - Random Binary
2180            REM     F4$  .....   FIELD # 4 - Random Binary
2190            REM     F5$  .....   FIELD # 5 - Random Binary
2200                                                                        REM
2300            REM     *****         Housekeeping
2310            REM     *****         System Initialization
2320  CLEAR : CLS
2330                                                                        REM
2400            REM     *****         Mainline Module
2410  OPEN "R", #3, "B:INV.DAT", 42
2420  FIELD #3, 4 AS F1$, 20 AS F2$, 7 AS F3$, 7 AS F4$, 4 AS F5$
2430  INPUT "ENTER Number of Records to Load  ";  R
2440  FOR L = 1 TO R
2450        GOSUB  2610
2460        GOSUB  2810
2470  NEXT L
2480  CLOSE # 3
2490  GOSUB 3010
2500  END
2510                                                                        REM
2600            REM     *****         Data Entry
2610  CLS
2620  INPUT "ENTER  Product Number  ";  N
2630  INPUT "ENTER  Product Name  ";  P$
2640  INPUT "ENTER  Product Cost  ";  C
2650  INPUT "ENTER  Selling Price  ";  P
2660  INPUT "ENTER  Quantity on Hand  ";  Q
2670  PRINT
2680  INPUT "Are the above entries correct  (Y/N)  ";  I$
2690  IF LEFT$(I$,1) <> "Y" THEN GOSUB 2620
2700  RETURN
2710                                                                        REM
2800            REM     *****         Write to Random File
2810  LSET F1$ = MKI$(N)
2820  LSET F2$ = P$
2830  LSET F3$ = MKS$(C)
2840  LSET F4$ = MKS$(P)
2850  LSET F5$ = MKI$(Q)
2860  PUT # 3, N
2870  LET T1 = T1 + C * Q
2880  LET T2 = T2 + P * Q
2890  RETURN
2900                                                                        REM
3000            REM     *****         Summary Module
3010  LPRINT : LPRINT
3020  LPRINT USING "Summary Total Cost  $###,###.## "; T1
3030  LPRINT
3040  LPRINT USING "Summary Total Price  $###,###.## ";  T2
3050  RETURN
3060                                                                        REM
3070  STOP
```

Summary Total Cost $110,705.10

Summary Total Price $209,803.40

FIGURE 20–5
Random file creation
program

the named file. Buffer number three is used in the program. The file name is INV.DAT, and it is recorded upon disk drive B. The record length is declared as being 42 bytes. One *byte* is one character. For example, the letter A and the number 6 would require one byte each to store. A maximum of 42 bytes can be contained in each record. The inclusion of more characters in the record will cause an error, or the excess characters will be truncated.

The record consists of five data fields. The format and length for each of the five fields follows.

Field	Field Name	Format	Type	Length
Number	N	XXX	Integer	4
Name	P$	Alphabetic—19 Characters	String	20
Cost	C	XXX.XX	Real	7
Price	P	XXX.XX	Real	7
Quantity	Q	XXX	Integer	4
				TOTAL 42

The field length should be declared with one more character than the actual format to allow for system overhead or accounting procedures. For example, an integer field that contains three characters should be counted as four bytes. Blank spaces or other symbols used in string data fields should be counted in the record length. Numeric data includes only digits or decimals, which are counted as one character each. The sum of the field lengths must equal the record length.

If a record length is not included when referencing random access files, the default length is used. A default length of 128 or 256 bytes is used with most systems.

MICROSOFT BASIC and TRS-80 BASIC systems use the same OPEN statement as shown here for random access files.

APPLESOFT BASIC uses the following OPEN statement format for random access files.

```
100 LET F$ = CHR$(4)
200 PRINT F$; "OPEN INV, L42"
```

Line 100 is the control string used to reference disk files. The APPLESOFT BASIC OPEN statement for random access files is much the same as the one used for sequential files, except that the record length is included. The L parameter must be included when referencing random access files. The parameter L42 sets the record length at 42 bytes. The comma separator between the file name and the L parameter must also be included. Record the random access OPEN statement for the system being used in Exercise 20–1.

EXERCISE 20–1

Random Access OPEN Statement Format

Key word   _____

Buffer number   _____

File name/device   _____

Record length   _____

OPEN statement format   _____

The FIELD statement in line 2420 is used to allocate and assign the buffer record space for the various fields. Following is the FIELD statement format.

2420 FIELD # ⟨Buffer⟩, ⟨Integer⟩ AS ⟨String Field Name⟩

Following is the FIELD statement used in the program.

2420 FIELD #3, 4 AS F1$, 20 AS F2$, 7 AS F3$, 7 AS F4$, 4 AS F5$

All variable values must be in string form when sent to the buffer. Numeric values must be converted to string values through the make function. This conversion process is described in the write to random disk file segment of the chapter. Therefore, string names must be used in the assignment portion of the FIELD statement. Buffer number three is used for the file. The first assignment segment allocates four bytes to string F1$ as follows.

4 AS F1$

The AS portion assigns four bytes to F1$. Twenty bytes are allocated to F2$, seven to F3$, seven to F4$, and four to F5$. There are five variables in each record, and each variable is listed in the FIELD statement. There is a mixture of string, integer, and real numbers in this program, so a separate buffer area is declared for each. The variable names declared in the FIELD statement, such as F1$, should not be used for any other purpose in the program.

When a program is used for random access input and output, only one OPEN and one FIELD statement are necessary. The buffer space can be reallocated within the program. In such cases, another FIELD statement is required.

MICROSOFT BASIC and TRS-80 BASIC systems use the same statement format to assign buffer space.

APPLESOFT BASIC does not require a function that corresponds to the FIELD statement.

Record the FIELD statement format for the system being used in Exercise 20–2.

Buffer Allocation Statement

EXERCISE 20–2

Key word _____

Buffer number _____

FIELD allocation/assignment _____

_____

FIELD statement format _____

_____

The number of records to be contained in the file is entered by the INPUT statement in line 2430. This sets the program loop limit. The number of records is obtained from the source document or the organization's records.

A FOR/NEXT structure is used to control execution of the program loop. The loop consists of the data entry and write to random file modules. There are 12 data records to be entered, so loop parameters are set accordingly.

The data entry module consists of INPUT statements which are used to enter the variable values and a data verification step. The variables are the product number (N), the product name (P$), the product cost (C), the selling price (P), and the quantity on hand (Q). The data records entered are shown in figure 20–6.

PRODUCT NUMBER	PRODUCT NAME	PRODUCT COST	SELLING PRICE	QUANTITY
N	P$	C	P	Q
111	BOARD CIRCUIT	335.33	625.50	20
121	BOARD GRAPHIC	295.15	475.75	15
131	BOARD MEMORY	425.25	750.50	30
141	BOARD MOTHER	505.05	975.75	100
211	CIRCUIT LOGIC	22.22	56.50	78
221	CIRCUIT MEMORY	16.16	35.35	400
231	CIRCUIT PROCESSOR	55.55	125.25	92
311	CONTROL EXPANSION	66.66	93.39	31
321	CONTROL NETWORK	89.89	197.97	25
411	DISPLAY COLOR	215.15	345.45	60
421	DISPLAY MONOCHROME	99.99	199.99	49
511	OSCILLOSCOPE	175.75	325.25	5

FIGURE 20–6
Data records

Statements 2680 and 2690, which follow, are used to verify data entry.

2680 INPUT "Are the above entries correct (Y/N) "; I$
2690 IF LEFT$(I$,1) ⟨ ⟩ "Y" THEN GOSUB 2620

Statement 2680 displays the referenced message upon the monitor screen. The user can then check the data values and enter the appropriate response. A Y or YES response means that the values are correct and execution can continue. Any other response causes control to be shifted back to the INPUT statements for reentry. Notice that the values entered originally are still displayed on the screen. This occurs because control is shifted to line 2620 and not to the CLS statement.

The write to random file module causes the data values to be sent to the buffer. The records are then written to the disk. The statements used to send the data values to the buffer are contained in lines 2810 through 2850, which follow.

2810 LSET F1$ = MKI$(N)
2820 LSET F2$ = P$
2830 LSET F3$ = MKS$(C)
2840 LSET F4$ = MKS$(P)
2850 LSET F5$ = MKI$(Q)

The LSET key word sends the referenced string value to the proper buffer location. Numeric values must be converted to string values through the make function, an explanation of which follows, before being sent to the buffer. LSET is used to left-justify data values, and RSET is used to right-justify values. Left-justification means that the data values are aligned on the extreme left side of the assigned area. Right-justification means that data values are aligned on the extreme right side of the assigned area. LSET is used with both string and numeric data. The numeric values have already been converted to string format before being LSET. Following is the LSET (or RSET) statement format.

LSET = ⟨ Variable ⟩

When string values are declared in the LSET function, the assignment is performed directly because string data values do not have to be converted. Line 2820 assigns the product name (P$) to F2$ directly. When the value is numeric, it must be converted to string format through the use of the MKx$ function. MKx$ converts a numeric value into string format. Following is the MKx$ format.

MKx$ (⟨ Variable Name ⟩)

The x parameter is determined by the type of numeric value. Following is the MKx$ format for different numeric values.

MKx$ Format	Data Type
MKI$	Integer
MKS$	Real—single-precision
MKD$	Real—double-precision

Statement 2810 converts the integer value for the product number (N) variable into the string F1$. Line 2830 converts the single-precision real value for the cost (C) variable into the string F3$.

The LSET (or RSET) function sends the data values to the buffer area where the values are assigned to the storage location allocated in the FIELD statement. Notice that the string fields assigned in the FIELD statement, such as F1$ and F2$, are referenced in the corresponding LSET statements. There must be correspondence between the FIELD and LSET statements as in the following example.

FIELD Parameter	Variable Name	Length
F1$	N	4
F2$	P$	20
F3$	C	7
F4$	P	7
F5$	Q	4

The field lengths in the preceding example include system overhead. The numeric values are converted to strings by the MKx$ function. This string value is then assigned to a string variable name. It is sent to the buffer by the LSET statement. Notice that the string names and the field lengths as described in the FIELD statement correspond with the LSET functions.

MICROSOFT and TRS-80 BASIC systems use the same statement to convert numeric values and send them to the buffer.

APPLESOFT BASIC systems do not use a function that corresponds to the LSET or MKx$ operations.

Record the conversion and send statements utilized by the system being used in Exercise 20–3.

Conversion and Buffer Transmission Statement

EXERCISE 20–3

Conversion key word _____

Integer value _____

Real—single-precision _____

Real—double-precision _____

Send key word _____

Statement format _____

The records in the buffer are written to the disk through the use of the PUT statement. Following is the PUT statement format.

2860 PUT # ⟨ Buffer Number ⟩, ⟨ Record Number ⟩

The buffer number is the number used in the OPEN and FIELD statements. The record number can be an integer or variable name. In this program, the product number (N) is used as the record number. The system may have an upper limit for the record number; on this system, the limit is 32767. If the record number is omitted, the default record number is used. Following is the PUT statement used in the program.

2860 PUT # 3, N

MICROSOFT BASIC and TRS-80 BASIC systems use the same statement to transfer data from the buffer to the disk.

APPLESOFT BASIC systems use the following procedures to write to the random file.

```
100 LET F$ = CHR$(4)
200 PRINT F$; "OPEN INV, L42"
610 PRINT F$; "WRITE INV, R" L
620 PRINT N
630 PRINT P$
640 PRINT C
650 PRINT P
660 PRINT Q
670 PRINT F$
680 RETURN
```

The R in the WRITE statement shown in line 610 refers to the record number in the random file. The loop counter (L) is the record number. The WRITE INV procedure accesses the buffer. The separate PRINT statements transfer the referenced data values to the disk.

Figure 20–7 is an APPLESOFT BASIC program segment that creates a random access file. Program documentation is omitted.

```
100   LET F$ = CHR$(4)
200   PRINT F$; "OPEN INV, L42"
300   REM   ****   MAINLINE MODULE
310   INPUT "ENTER NUMBER OF RECORDS "; R
320   FOR L = 1 TO R
330   GOSUB 510
340   GOSUB 610
350   NEXT L
360   PRINT F$; "CLOSE INV"
370   END
380   REM
500   REM   ****   DATA ENTRY
510   HOME
520   INPUT "ENTER PRODUCT NUMBER "; N
530   INPUT "ENTER PRODUCT NAME "; P$
540   INPUT "ENTER COST   "; C
550   INPUT "ENTER PRICE   ";  P
560   INPUT "ENTER QUANTITY  ";  Q
570   RETURN
580   REM
600   REM   ****   WRITE TO DISK
610   PRINT F$; "WRITE INV, R" L
620   PRINT N
630   PRINT P$
640   PRINT C
650   PRINT P
660   PRINT Q
670   PRINT F$
680   RETURN
690   REM
```

FIGURE 20–7
APPLESOFT BASIC
random file creation
program

Record the program statement used to write records to the random file for the system being used in Exercise 20–4.

Write to Disk Statement		**EXERCISE 20–4**
Key word		
Buffer		
File name		
Record length		
Record number		
Write to disk format		

Summary totals for the product cost and selling price are accumulated in lines 2870 and 2880. T1 is the summary cost and T2 is the summary price. This concludes the write to random disk module.

Following termination of the FOR/NEXT loop, the random file is closed. The CLOSE statement is shown in line 2480. It is similar to the CLOSE statement used in sequential files. The APPLESOFT BASIC CLOSE statement for random files is shown in line 360 in figure 20–7.

The summary module is executed next. Summary totals for cost and price are printed. The summary totals are shown in figure 20–5. This terminates program execution.

The second objective of this chapter is to demonstrate the BASIC language procedures used to access a random file and retrieve selected data records. Figure 20–8 is the example program that accesses and retrieves selected records from the random file created by the program in figure 20–5. The top-level and detailed logic flowcharts for this program are shown in figures 20–3 and 20–4.

Program documentation and variable identification are shown in lines 4000 to 4340. Lines 4400 to 4460 contain the housekeeping statements. The system and monitor screen are cleared in line 4420. Statements 4440 and 4450 declare the output lines. Format statements are assigned to 01$ and 02$.

The mainline module is shown in lines 4600 to 4700. Statement 4610 opens the random access file known as INV.DAT. The OPEN statement is the same as the one used to create the file. Line 4610 follows.

4610 OPEN "R", #3, "B:INV.DAT", 42

Statement 4620 allocates the fields in the buffer. The FIELD statement is the same as in the file creation program. Line 4620 follows.

4620 FIELD #3, 4 AS F1$, 20 AS F2$, 7 AS F3$, 7 AS F4$, 4 AS F5$

When random access input and output operations are executed in the same program, only one OPEN and one FIELD statement are required. If necessary, buffer space can be reassigned during a program by including additional FIELD statements.

The number of records to be retrieved from the random file is entered through the INPUT statement in line 4630. This sets the loop limit parameter. The number of records to be retrieved varies depending upon the task to performed. Five records are retrieved in this program.

```
4000            REM      FIGURE  20-8    WRITTEN BY LARRY FRY   10/23/83
4010            REM      This program retrieves a specified record from
4020            REM      a random access disk file.
4030                                                                        REM
4200            REM      *****      Variable Identification
4210            REM      N   .....  Product Number
4220            REM      P$  .....  Product Name
4230            REM      C   .....  Product Cost
4240            REM      P   .....  Selling Price
4250            REM      Q   .....  Quantity on Hand
4260            REM      L   .....  Loop Counter
4270            REM      R   .....  Loop Limit
4280            REM      S   .....  Transaction Search Key
4290            REM      F1$ .....  FIELD # 1 - Random Binary
4300            REM      F2$ .....  FIELD # 2 - Random Binary
4310            REM      F3$ .....  FIELD # 3 - Random Binary
4320            REM      F4$ .....  FIELD # 4 - Random Binary
4330            REM      F5$ .....  FIELD # 5 - Random Binary
4340                                                                        REM
4400            REM      *****      Housekeeping
4410            REM      *****      System Initialization
4420 CLEAR : CLS
4430            REM      *****      Format Output Lines
4440 LET O1$ = "Number        Name              Cost      Price      Quantity"
4450 LET O2$ = " ####      \                 \   ###.##    ###.##      ###"
4460                                                                        REM
4600            REM      *****      Mainline Module
4610 OPEN "R", #3, "B:INV.DAT", 42
4620 FIELD #3, 4 AS F1$, 20 AS F2$, 7 AS F3$, 7 AS F4$, 4 AS F5$
4630 INPUT "ENTER  Number of Records to Seek from File  ";  R
4640 FOR L = 1 TO R
4650      GOSUB  4810
4660      GOSUB  5010
4670 NEXT L
4680 CLOSE #3
4690 END
4700                                                                        REM
4800            REM      *****      Search Disk File
4810 CLS
4820 INPUT "ENTER Product Number  ";  S
4830 GET #3,  S
4840 LET N% = CVI(F1$)
4850 LET C! = CVS(F3$)
4860 LET P! = CVS(F4$)
4870 LET Q% = CVI(F5$)
4880 RETURN
4890                                                                        REM
5000            REM      *****      Output Module
5010 LPRINT : LPRINT
5020 LPRINT O1$
5030 LPRINT USING O2$;  N%, F2$, C!, P!, Q%
5040 RETURN
5050                                                                        REM
5060 STOP
```

FIGURE 20–8
Random disk file access program

A FOR/NEXT structure controls execution of the program loop. The loop consists of the search disk file and output modules.

The search disk file module is contained in lines 4800 to 4890. The monitor screen is cleared in line 4810. An INPUT statement in line 4820 causes the search key to be entered. The search key for this program is the record (product) number.

Statement 4830 retrieves the selected record from the disk. A GET statement is used for this purpose. Following is the GET statement format.

4830 GET ⟨ Buffer Number ⟩, ⟨ Record Number ⟩

The buffer number is the one used in the OPEN and FIELD statements. The record number is the search key entered through the INPUT statement in line 4820 which follows.

4830 GET #3, S

Buffer number 3 is used in this program. The record number being sought is identified as variable S.

MICROSOFT BASIC and TRS-80 BASIC systems use the same statement to retrieve a given record from a random file.

APPLESOFT BASIC uses the following procedure.

```
100 LET F$ = CHR$(4)
200 PRINT F$; "OPEN INV, L42"
810 PRINT F$; "READ INV, R"; S
820 INPUT N
830 INPUT P$
840 INPUT C
850 INPUT P
860 INPUT Q
870 PRINT F$
```

The "READ INV, R" procedure in line 810 identifies the record to be retrieved. Separate PRINT statements are used in the file creation program; therefore, separate INPUT statements are required in the access program.

Record the statement used to retrieve a record from a random file for the system being used in Exercise 20–5.

Random File Access Statement

Key word _____

Buffer _____

File name/device _____

Record number _____

Access statement format _____

_____

Since data is stored in the buffer in string form, it is necessary to convert numeric data from string back to numeric values after retrieving them from the disk. The CVx function is used to convert from string to numeric form. Following is the CVx statement used to convert the product number.

```
4840 LET N% = CVI(F1$)
```

The variable name N% identifies the product number as an integer variable. The CVx function used is determined by whether the variable is an integer, a single-precision variable, or a double-precision variable. These functions are shown in the following table.

Variable Name	CVx	Format
N%	CVI	Integer
C!	CVS	Real—single-precision
(#)	CVD	Real—double-precision

Double-precision variables are not used in this program. The suffix for double-precision is the # symbol.

The following statements convert the product number, cost, price, and quantity values into the appropriate numeric format.

```
4840 LET N% = CVI(F1$)
4850 LET C! = CVS(F3$)
4860 LET P! = CVS(F4$)
4870 LET Q% = CVI(F5$)
```

Notice the correspondence between the variable names and the string assignments as declared in the FIELD and conversion statements.

The product name field (P$, which is declared as F2$ in the buffer) does not have to be converted because it is string data. Variable name F2$ as declared in the field statement can be used to print the value.

MICROSOFT BASIC and TRS-80 BASIC systems use the same statement format to convert from string to numeric values.

APPLESOFT BASIC does not utilize an equivalent statement. Record the conversion statement for the system being used in Exercise 20–6.

**EXERCISE
20–6**

String Conversion Statement

Key word

_____

Integer

_____

Single-precision

_____

Double-precision

_____

Conversion statement format

_____

_____

The output module prints the data records that have been retrieved. The heading 01$ is printed for each record. Following is the detail line that prints the record.

5030 LPRINT USING 02$; N%, F2$, C!, P!, Q%

Five data records are printed as a result of the output module. If garbage is printed as a detail line, an invalid product number was entered as the search key. The five records retrieved are shown in figure 20–9.

The file is closed following termination of the FOR/NEXT loop. This ends program execution.

The update procedure for random files is a three step process. First, the appropriate record is retrieved from an existing file. Numeric variable values are converted from string to numeric form. Second, the appropriate changes are made by altering the vari-

Number	Name	Cost	Price	Quantity
211	CIRCUIT LOGIC	22.22	56.50	78
Number	Name	Cost	Price	Quantity
511	OSCILLOSCOPE	175.75	325.25	5
Number	Name	Cost	Price	Quantity
321	CONTROL NETWORK	89.89	197.97	25
Number	Name	Cost	Price	Quantity
111	BOARD CIRCUIT	335.33	625.50	20
Number	Name	Cost	Price	Quantity
231	CIRCUIT PROCESSOR	55.55	125.25	92

FIGURE 20–9
**Random disk file access
program execution**

```
100   LET F$ = CHR$(4)
200   PRINT F$; "OPEN INV, L42"
300   REM   ****  MAINLINE CONTROL
310   INPUT "ENTER NUMBER OF RECORDS TO SEEK "; R
320   FOR L = 1 TO R
330   GOSUB 810
340   GOSUB 910
350   NEXT L
360   PRINT F$; "CLOSE INV"
370   END
380   REM
800   REM   ****  ACCESS DISK
810   INPUT "ENTER RECORD ID NUMBER   "; S
820   PRINT F$; "READ INV, R"; S
830   INPUT N
840   INPUT P$
850   INPUT C
860   INPUT P
870   INPUT Q
880   PRINT F$
890   RETURN
900   REM   ****   OUTPUT
910   PRINT N, P$, C, P, Q
920   RETURN
930   REM
940   STOP
```

FIGURE 20–10
APPLESOFT BASIC
random file access
program

able value. Finally, the numeric values are converted back to string form, and the record is sent back to the disk.

New records can be added at any time because the random access OPEN statement enables input or output operations. The new record number may not duplicate an existing record identification.

An APPLESOFT BASIC program that accesses a random file and retrieves a selected record is shown in figure 20–10. Documentation statements are omitted.

The APPLESOFT BASIC program to update a random file requires reading from and writing to the file. Three steps are involved in the procedure. First, a read module accesses the file and retrieves the desired record. Next, the selected field values are changed. Finally, the record is sent back to the disk file. New records are added using a write to disk routine. Existing record numbers may not be duplicated.

PROGRAM DEVELOPMENT CHECKLIST

Use the following checklist to ensure that all components are included in the program.

Random access files

_____ Flowcharts and documentation

_____ Program loop

Disk file creation

_____ Open for input/output

_____ Data entry

_____ Write to file

_____ Close file

Access disk files

_____ Open for input/output

_____ Search for record

_____ Output

_____ Close file

Update random files

_____ Open for input/output

_____ Retrieve selected record

_____ Update value

_____ Write to file

_____ Close file

SUMMARY

The BASIC language contains procedures for creating and accessing random disk files. The process of creating a random file consists of four steps. First, the file is opened. Second, on some systems, the buffer space is assigned, or allocated, by using the FIELD statement. Next, the values are entered in transaction mode and they are written to the disk. Numeric values may have to be converted to string form on some systems. Finally, the file is closed.

The different systems use a variety of key words and functions to create files because there are no standardized procedures. The processes commonly used are illustrated. System manuals must be carefully checked when using disk files.

The process of accessing a random disk file to retrieve data records consists of four steps. First, the file is opened. Second, on some systems, a FIELD statement is used to allocate buffer space. Next, the selected record is retrieved from the file. If necessary, numeric values are converted to string form. Processing tasks are then executed. Finally, the file is closed.

File update procedures are simplified when random files are used because the selected record can be directly accessed, updated, and then written back to the disk.

BASIC Key Words/Operations Learned

CHR$(4)	APPLESOFT BASIC disk access.
CVD	Double-precision conversion.
CVI	Integer conversion.
CVS	Single-precision conversion.
FIELD	Buffer allocation.
GET	Transfers data from disk to buffer.
LSET	Transfers data to disk and aligns at left side.

MKD$	Converts real numeric data to string form (double-precision).
MKI$	Converts integer numeric data to string form.
MKS$	Converts real numeric data to string form (single-precision).
OPEN	Opens files for random access. Must include record length.
PUT	Transfers record from buffer to disk.
READ	APPLESOFT BASIC disk access.
RSET	Transfers data values to buffer and aligns at right side.
WRITE	APPLESOFT BASIC transfer statement to buffer.

Instructions

PROGRAM ASSIGNMENT 20–1

Prepare the flowcharts and the structured BASIC programs to create, access, and print a random file. Use one program to create the file and another program to access the file and print each of the records. Use transaction processing to enter the data values and the records to be retrieved and printed. Compute a summary total in each program. Process all records in the file.

Following is the data to be processed. Use prompting INPUT statements to enter the data. The variables are the employee number, employee name, sales region, and sales amount.

Data

Employee Number	Employee Name	Region	Amount
101	Smith	NE	3,455.70
102	Zenfor	SW	5,489.75
103	Fores	SE	7,435.32
104	Hawes	NE	4,575.90
105	Rastor	SW	8,999.99
106	Grimm	NE	6,578.78
107	Delp	SE	4,792.24
108	Winterlin	SW	8,767.77
109	Hinder	NW	6,790.00
110	Littman	NE	5,455.55
111	Mistle	NW	6,666.66
112	Prestle	NW	5,798.99

Output Format

Print the headings. Include the summary total in the output for the file creation program. Print each data record and the summary total in the second program. Use output editing if available.

PORT-EX COMPANY

Sales Report

DATA ENTRY SALES SUMMARY TOTAL			$XX,XXX.XX
Employee Number	*Name*	*Region*	*Sales*
XXX	XXXXXXX	XX	X,XXX.XX
XXX	XXXXXXX	XX	X,XXX.XX
DATA FILE SUMMARY TOTAL			$XX,XXX.XX

PROGRAM ASSIGNMENT 20–2

Instructions

Prepare the flowcharts and the structured BASIC programs to create, access, and print a random file. One program creates the file and another program accesses the file and retrieves the records. Use transaction processing to enter the data values. Compute and accumulate a summary total for the product cost in the file creation program. Use transaction processing to retrieve the data records. If the quantity on hand is less than the reorder point, print a product order message. Compute and accumulate the summary total for reorder cost. Retrieve and process all records.

Following is the data to be processed. Use prompting INPUT statements to enter the data. The variables to be entered are the product number, the description, the reorder point, the quantity on hand, the reorder quantity, and the cost.

Data

Product Number	Description	Reorder Point	Quantity on Hand	Reorder Quantity	Cost
3541	Munchkins	500	790	250	20.99
4034	Number-0	500	450	150	19.97
5222	Sweet Peas	900	800	200	14.70
5333	Corn Nib	900	750	250	13.00
1011	Excess Towel	300	400	150	22.22
7555	Frozen Corn	75	50	50	10.00
3056	Flake Chip	300	400	100	21.75
4323	Flaky Frost	250	300	75	28.75
5335	Beets	200	150	125	19.97
5447	Green Beans	350	275	150	23.35
7131	Orange Sherbert	75	65	50	12.45

Output Format

Print the headings, including the current date. Include the summary total cost in the output for the file creation program. Print headings and reorder messages as necessary in the second program. Compute the summary total cost for the reorder quantities specified. Use output editing if available.

FOOD CIRCUS GROCERIES

Reorder Summary Report 11–11–84

DATA ENTRY COST SUMMARY TOTAL $XXX,XXX.XX

Number	Description	Reorder Quantity	Item Cost
XXXX	XXXXXXXXX	XXX	XX.XX
XXXX	XXXXXXXXXXX	XXX	XX.XX

SUMMARY REORDER COST $XX,XXX.XX

Instructions

Prepare the flowcharts and the structured BASIC program to create and update a random access file. Use one program to create the file. Accumulate a summary total in this program. Use another program to update the file created as a result of the first program. Develop a program menu to consider the following options.

1. Changing a data value within a specified record.
2. Adding additional records to the file.
3. Printing the entire file with a summary total.

Following is the data to be processed. Use prompting INPUT statements to enter the data to create the file. The variables are the account number, the account name, the transactions to date, and the current balance.

Data

Account Number	Account Name	Transactions to Date	Current Balance
1170	Phil Dirt Co	19	0.00
1270	A–Z Assoc	29	1,157.40
1380	BYTO Computers	32	995.00
1470	Able Mable Ent	18	575.25
1490	X-Y Games	10	814.00
1570	Bro Kemp	37	1,137.94
1580	Ramtech	2	445.75
1650	Compware	4	348.77
1660	Pete Moss Assoc	23	2,450.00
1670	Image Tech	1	179.85
1680	Bits and Bytes	3	333.33
1870	Hi Tech Comp	8	632.47
2480	Office Mod	20	750.00
3900	Space Air	10	3,450.00

Use prompting INPUT statements to enter the transactions. Following is the transaction data.

Transaction Data

1. Add the following records to the file.

Account Number	Account Name	Transactions to Date	Current Balance
1580	Star Quest	3	416.47
1640	Half Wit Comp	2	132.23

2. Change the following values in the selected record.

1870	Hi Tech Comp	10	487.91

3. Print all data records and the summary balance.

Output Format

Print the headings, including the current date. Include the summary total in the file creation program. The update program should result in the printing of all data records in the file after updating has occurred. Include the summary total balance. Use output editing if available.

PORT-EX COMPANY

Account Status Report 11–28–84

DATA ENTRY ACCOUNT BALANCE SUMMARY TOTAL $XXX,XXX.XX

Account Number	Account Name	Transactions to Date	Current Balance
XXXX	XXXXXXXXX	XX	X,XXX.XX
XXXX	XXXXXXXXX	XX	X,XXX.XX

SUMMARY TOTAL BALANCE $XXX,XXX.XX

APPENDIX A
ANSI MINIMAL
BASIC KEY WORDS

Following are the 26 key words established in the *American National Standard for Minimal BASIC*.

Key word	Function
BASE	Declares table/array element less than one. FORMAT: 100 OPTION BASE 0
DATA	Serial data entry statement that is paired with READ. FORMAT: 300 DATA 14, "PAST DUE"
DEF	Declares user-defined function. FORMAT: 100 DEF FX(A) = INT(A*100 + .5)/100
DIM	Declares number of elements in table/array. FORMAT: 100 DIM X(25)
END	Program termination. FORMAT: 1000 END
FOR	Program loop control structure. FORMAT: 500 FOR L = 1 TO R
GO	Program control jump. FORMAT: 500 GOTO 250
GOSUB	Program branch to subroutine. FORMAT: 600 GOSUB 1110
GOTO	Program control jump. FORMAT: 500 GOTO 250
IF	Program decision or branch. FORMAT: 300 IF A = 40 LET P = H * R
INPUT	Transaction mode data entry. FORMAT: 250 INPUT "ENTER HOURS"; H
LET	Assignment statement. FORMAT: 350 LET A = 40
NEXT	Terminates body of FOR loop and increments loop counter. FORMAT: 750 NEXT L
ON	Program branch structure, commonly referred to as CASE OF, that is used with program menu operations. FORMAT: 250 ON A GOSUB 1010, 2010, 3010
OPTION	Declares table/array element less than one. FORMAT: 100 OPTION BASE 0
PRINT	Displays or prints output. FORMAT: 600 PRINT A, A$
RANDOMIZE	Random number generator that declares new random seed value. FORMAT: 200 RANDOMIZE(X)
READ	Serial data entry statement that is paired with DATA. FORMAT: 300 READ A, B$
REM	Documentation within program. FORMAT: 150 REM THIS WILL NOT COMPUTE
RESTORE	Enables reuse of DATA statement values. FORMAT: 400 RESTORE
RETURN	Terminates subroutine and returns control to statement following GOSUB. FORMAT: 700 RETURN

Key word	Function
STEP	FOR/NEXT loop parameter other than +1. FORMAT: 250 FOR L = 1 to R STEP 10
STOP	Program halt with program BREAK message. FORMAT: 1000 STOP
SUB	Calls subroutine. FORMAT: 400 GOSUB
THEN	IF statement qualification parameter. FORMAT: 300 IF H = 40 THEN LET P = H * R
TO	Program jump. FORMAT: 400 GOTO 250

APPENDIX B
NON-ANSI KEY WORDS

More than 100 additional non-ANSI commands/statements/key words are supported by most computer systems. There are differences between individual manufacturers in the implementation of the BASIC language. Individual implementations result in differences in key words, statements, and functions. Therefore, system reference manuals must be carefully checked. Following are the BASIC key words commonly found on most systems. (NOTE: The statement numbers are omitted from the format.)

Key word	Function
ABS	Returns absolute value. FORMAT: PRINT ABS(A)
AND	Logical operator. Both stated conditions must be TRUE for a TRUE result. FORMAT: IF A = B AND A > 100 THEN GOSUB 400
ASC	Returns ASCII code for first character in string value. FORMAT: PRINT ASC(A$)
ATN	Returns arctangent. FORMAT: PRINT ATN(A)
APPEND	Sequential disk file operation (APPLESOFT BASIC) that enables the user to add records to an existing file. FORMAT: PRINT F$; "APPEND INV"
AUTO	Generates program line numbers according to parameters. FORMAT: AUTO
BEEP	Returns sound or beep. PRINT CHR$(7) or CONTROL-G can also be used. FORMAT : IF A > 20 THEN BEEP
BREAK	Message printed after program interrupt. FORMAT: BREAK in 1430
BYE	Used on time-sharing systems to disconnect the terminal from the system. (Some systems use GOODBYE.) FORMAT: BYE
CATALOG	Displays an inventory of program/data files stored upon disk/diskette. (APPLESOFT BASIC and some time-sharing systems.) FORMAT: CATALOG
CDBL	Converts to double-precision. FORMAT: LET A = CDBL(B)
CHR$	Converts ASCII code to character code. FORMAT: LET X$ = CHR$(Y)
CINT	Rounds to nearest integer. FORMAT: LET A = CINT(B)
CLEAR	Assigns all numeric variables the value of zero and all string variables the value of blank. FORMAT: CLEAR
CLOAD	Load BASIC program stored on cassette. FORMAT: CLOAD"A"
CLOSE	Disengages input/output disk file. FORMAT: CLOSE #3
CLS	Clears monitor screen. FORMAT: CLS

Key word	Function
CONT	Resumes execution after program BREAK. FORMAT: CONT
COS	Returns cosine. FORMAT: LET A = COS(B)
CSAVE	Saves program on cassette. FORMAT: CSAVE"A"
CSNG	Converts to single-precision. FORMAT: LET A = CSNG(B)
CSRLIN	Returns vertical cursor position. (See POS for horizontal.) FORMAT: LET A = CSRLIN
CVD	Random disk file operation that converts a string variable to a double-precision value. FORMAT: LET A# = CVD(B$)
CVI	Random disk file operation that converts a string variable to an integer value. FORMAT: LET A% = CVI(B$)
CVS	Random disk file operation that converts a string variable to a single-precision value. FORMAT: LET A! = CVS(B$)
DATE$	Returns the current date from system. FORMAT: PRINT DATE$
DELETE	Deletes a group of program statements. FORMAT: DELETE 10–200
EDIT	Displays the referenced line upon the monitor, and enables editing. FORMAT: EDIT 2000
ELSE	IF-THEN-ELSE program branch parameter. FORMAT: IF A > B THEN GOSUB 1000 ELSE GOSUB 2000
EOF	Sequential disk file function that determines end of file condition. FORMAT: WHILE NOT EOF(2)
ERASE	Cancels the referenced table/array. FORMAT: ERASE A, X$
ERL	Returns the line number that caused an error condition. FORMAT: PRINT ERL
ERR	Returns current error code. FORMAT: PRINT ERR
ERROR	Generates error condition. FORMAT: ERROR = 240
EXP	Computes exponential function. FORMAT: PRINT EXP (A − 1)
FIELD	Random disk file operation that allocates buffer space. FORMAT: FIELD 7 AS A$
FILES	Displays an inventory of program/data files stored upon disk/diskette. FORMAT: FILES
FIX	Truncates value to integer form. FORMAT: FIX(A)
FLASH	Monitor screen blinks or flashes output. FORMAT: FLASH
FRE	Returns the number of free bytes in memory. FORMAT: PRINT FRE
GET	Keyboard operation that enables the entry of a single character from the keyboard. FORMAT: GET A$
GET	Random disk file operation that reads the referenced record and transfers it to the buffer. FORMAT: GET N
GR	Initializes low-resolution graphics mode, which is used for computer low-resolution graphics. FORMAT: GR

Key word	Function
HEX	Returns a hexadecimal value. FORMAT: PRINT HEX(A)
HOME	Clears the monitor screen and places the cursor at the top left position. FORMAT: HOME
HTAB	Sets the horizontal cursor position. FORMAT: HTAB 10
INKEY$	Enables entry of one character from the keyboard. FORMAT: LET A$ = INKEY$
INPUT#	Sequential disk file operation that reads the record from file. FORMAT: INPUT #3, A$, B
INT	Returns the largest integer value that is less than or equal to the argument. FORMAT: LET B = INT(A)
INVERSE	Changes or reverses screen background and foreground. FORMAT: INVERSE
KILL	Deletes referenced file name. FORMAT: KILL PROG1.BAS
LEFT$	String processing function that returns the left-most referenced character(s). FORMAT: LET A$ = LEFT$(B$,1)
LEN	String processing function that returns the number of characters in the referenced string value. FORMAT: PRINT LEN(A$)
LINE INPUT	Enters entire line from keyboard ignoring delimiters, such as commas, in the data value. LINE INPUT can also be used in disk file operations. FORMAT: LINE INPUT "CITY ADDRESS"; A$
LIST	Displays program or referenced lines. FORMAT: LIST 1000–2000
LLIST	Displays program or referenced lines on the printer. FORMAT: LLIST 1000–2000
LOAD	Loads program file name from the device specified into main memory. FORMAT: LOAD PROG1
LOC	Disk file operation that returns record number processed (random) or number of records accessed (sequential). FORMAT: PRINT LOC INV.DAT
LOCATE	Positions the cursor on the monitor screen. FORMAT: LOCATE(10, 16)
LOF	Disk file operation that returns the number of bytes in the file. FORMAT: PRINT LOF(#3)
LOG	Returns the natural logarithm (log to base e). FORMAT: PRINT LOG(A)
LOGOFF	Time-sharing system disconnect operation that terminates access to computer system. FORMAT: /LOGOFF or @LOGOFF
LOGON	Time-sharing system access command that obtains terminal access to system. FORMAT: /LOGON or @LOGIN LOGON is usually followed by the system access command for the BASIC language. FORMAT: /BASIC or @BASIC
LPRINT	Sends output to the printer. FORMAT: LPRINT A, B, C$
LPRINT USING	Sends the edited output to the printer. FORMAT: LPRINT USING 01$; A, B, C$
LSET	Random file operation that left-justifies the data in the buffer according to the FIELD statement parameters. MKD$, MKI$, or MKS$ may be used with LSET (or RSET). FORMAT: LSET A$ = MKI$(B)
MID$	String processing function that returns the referenced characters from the string. FORMAT: LET B$ = MID$(A$,5,2)

Key word	Function
MKD$	Random file operation that converts double-precision values to string form. FORMAT: LSET A$ = MKD$(B)
MKI$	Random file operation that converts integer values to string form. FORMAT: LSET A$ = MKI$(B)
MKS$	Random file operation that converts single-precision values to string form. FORMAT: LSET A$ = MKS$(B)
NAME	Alters existing file name. FORMAT: NAME "PROG1.BAS" AS "X1.BAS"
NEW	Microcomputer system command that clears system main memory (RAM). FORMAT: NEW
NEW	Time-sharing system command that creates a new file name. The system prompt is OLD OR NEW? FORMAT: OLD OR NEW?
NORMAL	Sets the monitor screen at normal background/foreground color. FORMAT: NORMAL
NOT	Logical operator known as the logical complement. FORMAT: IF NOT A = B THEN GOSUB 1000
NOTRACE	Cancels TRACE (APPLESOFT). FORMAT: NOTRACE
OLD	Time-sharing system operation that accesses a program file previously saved. The system prompt is OLD OR NEW? FORMAT: OLD OR NEW?
ONERR	Program branch to referenced line when an error is detected (APPLESOFT). FORMAT: ONERR GOTO 4100
ON ERROR	Program branch to referenced line when an error is detected. FORMAT: ON ERROR GOTO 4100
OPEN	Disk file operation that enables disk file access for input/output. FORMAT: OPEN #3
OR	Logical operator. One stated condition must be TRUE for a TRUE response. FORMAT: IF A = B OR A > 1000 GOSUB 1000
PEEK	Examines system storage location and returns the value stored there. FORMAT: LET P = PEEK (222)
POKE	Inserts a value into the referenced system storage location. FORMAT: POKE 222, 5
POP	Replaces a RETURN in a subroutine operation to cancel the last referenced GOSUB statement. FORMAT: POP
POS	Returns the current horizontal cursor location (see also CRSLIN). FORMAT: LET A = POS(B)
PRINT USING	Edits output sent to the monitor screen (see also ANSI PRINT in Appendix A). FORMAT: PRINT USING 01$; A, B, C$
PRINT #	Sequential file operation that writes the sequential record to the file (PRINT # USING can also be used). FORMAT: PRINT # 2, A, B
PUT	Random file operation that transfers a record from the buffer to the disk file. FORMAT: PUT #3, N
RENAME	Alters the file name (TRS-80 BASIC). FORMAT: RENAME INV/DAT INV/ARC
RENUM	Renumbers program line numbers in a predetermined fashion (RENUMBER on some systems may be a utility program). FORMAT: RENUM 1100, 1000, 100
RESET	Disk file operation that closes all files and clears the buffer. FORMAT: RESET
RESUME	Continues program execution after an error routine. FORMAT: RESUME

Key word	Function
RIGHT$	String processing function that returns the right-most referenced characters from a string value (see also LEFT$, MID$, and LEN). FORMAT: LET A$ = RIGHT$(B$, 5)
RND	Returns the random number generated by the computer with a value between 0 and 1. ANSI RANDOMIZE is used to alter the random seed value which is the beginning number that the computer uses to generate a random number. FORMAT: LET A = RND(B)
RSET	Random file operation that right-justifies a string value in the buffer. FORMAT: RSET A$ = MKI$(B)
RUN	Executes the program in current memory. FORMAT: RUN
SAVE	Transfers the program file from current memory to permanent memory and saves it. FORMAT: SAVE "P1"
SCRATCH	Time-sharing system command that cancels or clears current work space. FORMAT: SCRATCH or SCR
SGN	Returns the sign of the variable. FORMAT: PRINT SGN(A)
SIN	Returns the trigonometric sine. FORMAT: PRINT SIN(A)
SPACE$	Returns a string of blank spaces. FORMAT: LET A$ = SPACE$(10)
SPC	Inserts blank spaces in printed output. FORMAT: PRINT A; SPC (10); B
SPEED	Controls the display rate of screen output. FORMAT: SPEED = 100
SQR	Returns the square root. FORMAT: LET A = SQR(B)
STOP	Terminates program execution with a program BREAK message. FORMAT: STOP
STR$	String processing function that returns a string representation of a numeric value. FORMAT: LET A$ = STR$(B)
SWAP	Switches, or swaps, two variable values. FORMAT: SWAP A$, B$ or SWAP A$(I), A$(J)
SYSTEM	Quits BASIC and returns control to the operating system. FORMAT: SYSTEM
TAB	Tabulates output to the referenced print column. FORMAT: PRINT TAB(20); A
TAN	Returns the tangent. FORMAT: LET A = TAN(B)
TIME$	Returns the current time from the operating system. FORMAT: PRINT TIME$
TRACE	Debugging tool that traces statement numbers and variable values as the program is executed. FORMAT: TRACE
TROFF	Terminates trace (TRON). FORMAT: TROFF
TRON	Debugging tool that traces statement numbers and variable values as the program is executed (some systems). FORMAT: TRON
UNSAVE	Time-sharing system command that deletes the referenced file name. FORMAT: UNSAVE FRY1
VAL	String processing function that returns the numeric value of a string. FORMAT: LET A = VAL(B$)
VTAB	Sets cursor or output at the referenced line (row). FORMAT: VTAB 10

Key word	Function
WAIT	Suspends execution pending entry of the correct value by the user at the referenced device/address. FORMAT: WAIT
WEND	Marks the end of a WHILE loop. FORMAT: WEND
WHILE	Program loop structure that tests conditions before entering a loop. FORMAT: WHILE A < B
WIDTH	Sets output width. Alters print line width. FORMAT: WIDTH LPT1, 132
WRITE	Displays output including delimiters on the screen. FORMAT: WRITE A, B$
WRITE#	Sequential file operation that writes a record from the buffer to the file. FORMAT: WRITE #1, A, B$, C

APPENDIX C
COMPUTER
SYSTEM ACCESS

PART I. TIME-SHARING SYSTEMS (Mainframes and/or Minicomputers)

Those computer systems that support terminals are commonly referred to as time-sharing systems. Access to the computer system is provided to different terminals. The system is operating at such high speed that each user is seemingly conducting an individual dialog with the computer. Most time-sharing systems can also support a variety of programming languages concurrently. This is called multiprogramming. Thus, one user may be programming in BASIC while other users are working in PASCAL, COBOL, or FORTRAN.

The utilization of terminals or video display units (VDTs) with a time-sharing system can be divided into five phases. First, the user must gain access to the system. This procedure is usually referred to as logging on the system. Second, the user must access the BASIC language (or another language) and the files stored on auxiliary devices. Third, the program statements are entered or revised as necessary. Fourth, the program is executed in current memory. Finally, the user must disconnect or logoff from the system. Following are detailed explanations of these phases. Individual computer systems may require different commands. Record the commands (key words) for the system being used in Exercise C–1.

Time-Sharing System Operation Procedures

  I. The operations/commands commonly used to logon the system are:
     A. Physically connect the acoustic coupler or connect the modem to the system (if necessary).
     B. //LOGON or @LOGON
     C. Provide personal identification or password.
 II. The operations/commands commonly used to access the BASIC language are:
     A. BASIC language—//BASIC or @BASIC or/SYSTEM/BASIC.
     B. Program file access—the system prompt OLD OR NEW?
        1. OLD—the system responds by asking for the existing file name.
        2. NEW—the system responds by asking for the file name to be created.
        3. CATALOG—the system lists the program file names assigned to that user/password.
        4. SAVE—transfers the program from current memory to permanent memory (disk).
        5. UNSAVE— deletes the referenced file name from permanent memory.
        6. SCRATCH—clears the assigned user work space, or current memory.
III. The operations/commands commonly used with BASIC program statements are:
     A. Display existing program statements—LIST command.
     B. Program statement entry mode—follow the standard BASIC language procedures for the system being used.
     C. Program statement edit mode
        1. Replace referenced statement—rekey statement. New statement replaces the old.

    2. Statement editing commands

        a.) Erase the last character—RUBOUT key, ERASE key, or CONTROL-Z.

        b.) Erase current statement—CONTROL-Y or CONTROL-X.

    3. Move pointer or current statement marker—follow system procedures.

IV. The command commonly used for program execution is RUN which executes the program in the assigned user work space, or current memory.

  V. The operations/commands commonly used to logoff the system are:

    A. Quit BASIC—BYE or GOODBYE quits the BASIC language and returns to system command level.

    B. Disconnect terminal from system—@FIN or @TERMINATE or/LOGOFF.

    C. Physically disconnect the acoustic coupler or modem (if necessary).

Record the time-sharing access or quit procedures for the system being used in Exercise C–1.

EXERCISE C–1

Time-sharing Procedures

Logon procedures _____

_____

_____

_____

Password procedures _____

_____

_____

BASIC language access _____

_____

_____

Program file access _____

_____

_____

_____

Program statement entry _____

_____

_____

_____

Program statement edit mode   _____

_____

_____

_____

Delete last character   _____

_____

Delete current statement   _____

_____

Quit BASIC language   _____

_____

_____

_____

Logoff   _____

_____

_____

PART II. MICROCOMPUTER SYSTEMS

The introduction of the microcomputer has resulted in widespread access to computers and computing. The most popular microcomputer configuration includes diskette drives, but cassette recorders are also available. Program storage procedures will be presented later in this appendix.

The development of the microprocessor circuit, or chip, led directly to the microcomputer. The microprocessor is often referred to as the "computer on a chip." The microprocessor performs logic and computation functions. Early microcomputers consisted of an 8-bit microprocessor chip. The microprocessor size in bits determines the largest size of data that the computer can transfer at one time. Thus, an 8-bit microprocessor is limited to 8 bits per pass. The microprocessor size also determines the maximum amount of random memory that can be addressed at any one time. Microcomputers now provide 8-bit or 16-bit microprocessors. The 16-bit microprocessor can pass larger pieces of data at one time and can address more random memory.

The microcomputer main memory is commonly referred to as the random access memory (RAM). The RAM area is equivalent to the current, or temporary, work space assigned in time-sharing systems. RAM memory is volatile and is erased each time the computer is turned off. BASIC key words, such as NEW, can also be used to clear current memory.

Microcomputer RAM memory is expressed in terms of 1024 bytes, commonly referred to as one K. One byte is one character, such as the letter A. The most popular microcomputers contain 48K to 128K of RAM. Thus, a microcomputer with 64K of memory can store 65,536 bytes.

Microcomputers usually also contain read-only memory (ROM) circuits. These circuits contain the BASIC language interpreter, the control programs, and/or the system start-up routines. The ROM area of storage is not volatile, which means that it is not erased. The BASIC interpreter or control program remains stored there at all times.

Input and/or output devices, such as cassette recorders, diskette drives, printers, hard disk drives, and modems for telecommunications are usually attached to the computer through slots, or plug-in boards or modules. Most systems can support any or all of these devices.

Microcomputer Auxiliary Storage

Microcomputer main memory is volatile and must be supplemented by auxiliary storage devices, such as cassette recorders or diskette drives. The vast majority of business and educational microcomputer systems are equipped with diskette drives. Some systems may be equipped with cassette recorders for permanent storage of programs or data. Following is a summary of the procedures for using cassette recorders and diskette drives. Record the procedures for the system being used in Exercises C–2 through C–5.

Cassette Recorders

Cassette recorders are usually connected to the computer system through a plug-in. System reference manuals should be checked carefully because of the differences between systems. Recording or volume settings must be precisely set when saving or loading files. Most recorders must use specified cassette tapes. Two commands that are universally used for saving and loading programs are: CSAVE, which is used to save program files on tape; and CLOAD, which is used to load files. Record the procedures used with cassette recorders for the system being used in Exercise C–2.

EXERCISE C–2

Cassette Recorder

File name rules _____

_____

_____

Saving program files (CSAVE) _____

_____

_____

_____

Loading program files (CLOAD) _____

_____

_____

_____

Volume or record settings _____

_____

_____

_____

Diskette Drives

Most microcomputer systems in business and educational organizations are equipped with one or more diskette drives. The cost difference between cassette and diskette systems is more than offset by the benefit of increased operational and set-up speed. Diskettes are more convenient to use.

New diskettes must be initialized, or formatted, before they can be used. *Initialization* means that the disk operating system is copied from a disk that is already formatted, which is called the master, to a new one, called the slave. The system reference manual should be checked for proper initialization procedures. Diskettes must be initialized, or formatted, before they can be used to store programs or data. Record the initialization procedures for the system being used in Exercise C–3.

Diskette Initialization

**EXERCISE
C–3**

Diskette technical characteristics _____

_____

_____

_____

Initialization procedures (format) _____

_____

_____

_____

Disk operating system copy procedures _____

_____

_____

_____

Microcomputer System Startup

At system startup, the disk operating system must be transferred from auxiliary storage into the computer's memory. This procedure is referred to as *booting the system*. Booting the system means that the input/output functions of the diskette drive can be accessed. Most systems automatically boot when the computer is turned on. A diskette must be in the booting, or controlling, drive position. This procedure is known as a *cold boot*. The other method used to boot the system when the computer system is already on is known as a *warm boot*. A warm boot is accomplished by referencing the slot in which the drive is connected or by the use of CONTROL and other keys. Record cold and warm boot procedures for the system being used in Exercise C–4.

EXERCISE
C–4

System Boot Procedures

Cold boot procedures _____

_____

_____

_____

Warm boot procedures _____

_____

_____

_____

Microcomputer Diskette Access

Procedures for saving, loading, creating inventories, and deleting file names from diskettes vary from system to system. Summarize the key words and commands used to create, save, and load file names in Exercise C–5.

EXERCISE
C–5

Disk Operating System Procedures

File name rules _____

_____

_____

_____

Inventory of _____

file names _____

_____

_____

Save file name _____

_____

_____

_____

Load file name _____

_____

_____

_____

Delete file name _____

_____

_____

_____

Change file name _____

_____

_____

_____

PART III. PRINTED OUTPUT FROM SYSTEM

Time-sharing systems and microcomputers must access a printer to obtain a printed, or hard-copy, version of the program or execution results. The different systems use a variety of procedures, such as LPT1, LPRINT, SYS-xxxxx-x, and PR# 1, to access the printer. Various procedures are used to set print line width. Record the procedures used to obtain printed output from the system being used in Exercise C–6.

Obtaining Printed Output

EXERCISE C–6

Printer access command _____

_____

_____

_____

Print line width command _____

_____

_____

_____

APPENDIX D COMPARISON OF BASIC KEY WORDS FOR SELECTED COMPUTER SYSTEMS

ENTER THE APPROPRIATE COMMANDS/KEY WORDS FOR THE SYSTEM BEING USED IN THE SPACE PROVIDED.

Function	APPLESOFT	TRS-80	IBM PC	Time-sharing	System Being Used
BASIC Input/Output Operations					
Serial data entry	READ	READ	READ	READ	_____
Serial data entry	DATA	DATA	DATA	DATA	_____
Interactive data entry	INPUT	INPUT	INPUT	INPUT	_____
Printed output—zone format	PRINT(,)	PRINT(,)	PRINT(,)	PRINT(,)	_____
Printed output—non-zone format	PRINT(;)	PRINT(;)	PRINT(;)	PRINT(;)	_____
Edited output		PRINT USING	PRINT USING	PRINT USING	_____
BASIC Computation Operations					
Calculations	+ − * /	+ − * /	+ − * /	+ − * /	_____
Exponentiation	^	[or ^	^	^ or **	_____
Precedence	( )	( )	( )	( )	_____
BASIC Comparison Operations					
Simple conditional	IF-THEN	IF-THEN	IF-THEN	IF-THEN	_____
Complex conditional		IF-THEN-ELSE	IF-THEN-ELSE	IF-THEN-ELSE	_____
BASIC Program Loop Control Operations					
Unrestricted jump	GO TO	GO TO	GO TO	GO TO	_____
Loop control	FOR/NEXT	FOR/NEXT	FOR/NEXT	FOR/NEXT	_____
Loop control			WHILE-WEND		_____

Function	APPLESOFT	TRS-80	IBM PC	Time-sharing	System Being Used

BASIC Subroutine Operations

Subroutine call	GOSUB	GOSUB	GOSUB	GOSUB	_____
Subroutine termination	RETURN	RETURN	RETURN	RETURN	_____
CASE OF subroutine call	ON-GOSUB	ON-GOSUB	ON-GOSUB	ON-GOSUB	_____

BASIC Monitor Screen Commands

Vertical placement (column)	VTAB	PRINT @	LOCATE		_____
Horizontal placement (row)	HTAB	PRINT @	LOCATE		_____

BASIC Table/Array Operations

Declare table/array	DIM	DIM	DIM	DIM	_____
Element option	OPTION BASE	OPTION BASE	OPTION BASE	OPTION BASE	_____

BASIC Sequential Data File Operations

Engage data file	OPEN	OPEN	OPEN	OPEN	_____
Write record to file	WRITE and PRINT	PRINT #	PRINT # or WRITE #		_____
Read record from file	READ and INPUT	INPUT #	INPUT #		_____
Disengage Data File	CLOSE	CLOSE	CLOSE		_____

(APPLESOFT data file commands are preceded by PRINT CHR$ (4) or CONTROL-D)

BASIC Random Access Data File Operations

Engage data file	OPEN - L	OPEN	OPEN	OPEN	_____
Assign buffer space		FIELD	FIELD		_____
Move data to buffer		LSET or RSET	LSET or RSET		_____
Write record to file	WRITE and PRINT	PUT	PUT		_____
Read record from file	READ and INPUT	GET	GET		_____
Disengage file	CLOSE	CLOSE	CLOSE	CLOSE	_____

BASIC String Processing Functions

Returns left-most portion of string	LEFT$	LEFT$	LEFT$	LEFT$	_____
Returns right-most portion of string	RIGHT$	RIGHT$	RIGHT$	RIGHT$	_____
Returns middle segment of string	MID$	MID$	MID$	MID$	_____
Returns length of string	LEN	LEN	LEN	LEN	_____

Function	APPLESOFT	TRS-80	IBM PC	Time-sharing	System Being Used

BASIC Error Isolation Operations

Program branch to error handling routine	ONERR	ON ERROR	ON ERROR	ON ERROR	_____

BASIC Debugging Operations

Enable system trace of program	TRACE	TRON	TRON	TRACE	_____
Terminate trace	NOTRACE	TROFF	TROFF	NOTRACE	_____

BASIC Miscellaneous Commands/Operations

User-defined function	DEF FN	DEF FN	DEF FN	DEF FN	_____
Return integer part of value	INT	INT	INT	INT	_____
Return random number	RND	RND	RND	RND	_____

GLOSSARY

Accumulate—Increment a variable, such as a summary total.

Acoustic coupler—Telecommunications interface between computer system and phone.

ADA—The programming language that has been selected as the standard high-level language by the U.S. Department of Defense.

Alphabetic data—A data value with alphabetic characters. BASIC uses the term string data to describe alphabetic/alphanumeric values.

Alphanumeric data—A data value that has a mixture of alphabetic, numeric, and other special characters. BASIC uses the term string data to describe alphanumeric values.

American National Standards Institute (ANSI)—An organization made up of representatives from business, commerce, educational institutions, and government that is concerned with standardization. A data processing subcommittee is concerned with equipment, software, and languages.

American Standard Code for Information Interchange (ASCII)—The ANSI approved standard character code.

Applications program—A computer program used to accomplish a specific task. Applications programs are usually written in high-level languages, such as BASIC or COBOL.

Arithmetic Operators—Symbols, such as +, −, *, and /, used in BASIC for computation operations.

Array—An arrangement of data values that uses two dimensions. The data is arranged in rows and columns.

Assembly language—A mid-level programming language that is used to prepare software, interpreters, and compilers.

Assignment operation—An operation in which a specific value, formula, or function is assigned to a variable.

Auxiliary storage—A magnetic storage device that is connected to the computer system. Disk, diskette, cassette, or tape devices may be used.

Backup—Separate copies of software, programs, or data that are kept in case of disk failure.

Batch processing—Data is processed in a group, usually in a predetermined sequence.

Baud—Telecommunications data transmission rate that is equivalent to bytes per second. Three hundred baud is roughly equivalent to three hundred characters per second.

BASIC (Beginners All-Purpose Symbolic Instruction Code)—A high-level programming language developed by John Kameny and Thomas Kurtz at Dartmouth College in 1963–1964.

Binary—The computer internal numbering system that uses binary code (0 and 1).

Bit—The binary digit (0 or 1) used in the internal language of the computer system, which is commonly called machine language.

BOOLEAN—A logical decision with a TRUE or FALSE response.

Boot—Microcomputer system access to the disk drive.

Branch—A shift in program control usually resulting from a program decision.

Break point—A key test value used in comparison operations.

Buffer—The area of main memory reserved for input/output operations.

Bugs—Creepy little creatures known as errors.

Byte—One character in storage. The byte is the smallest unit of storage that the system can address.

CASE OF structure—A program branch structure commonly used in menu operations.

CRT (Cathode Ray Tube)—The monitor screen, now commonly referred to as VDT (Video Display Terminal).

Central Processing Unit (CPU)—The system's central processing unit which consists of main memory, logic, and control circuits.

Command level—The computer system is in control of operations. The system is usually in command level, except when a program is running.

CODASYL (Committee On Data Systems And Languages)—A joint committee that developed the COBOL language in 1960.

COBOL (Common Business Oriented Language)—A high-level programming language used primarily for business applications programming.

Coding—Writing program instructions.

Core—A term that was formerly used to describe obsolete main memory components, and is now used to describe main computer memory.

Compiler—A control program that converts high-level language to object code before execution.

Concatenation—A string processing function that combines string values.

Control break—Data processing methodology that produces subtotals.

Control Program—A program that monitors/supervises the computer system or other programs.

Cursor—A system-supplied prompt used to enter or edit program statements or data.

Data base—One central data file that supports the organization's data processing requirements.

Data field—One item or unit of data. BASIC uses the term variable to describe a data field.

Data item—One unit of data, which is referred to as a variable in BASIC.

Data list—A system supplied table(s) in which data values are arranged at execution. Data values are arranged in the table and processed according to program parameters.

Data pointer—A system supplied pointer that tracks data items to be processed in the data list.

Debugging—The process of removing errors, or bugs.

Detail printing—Output of one print line for each data record entered.

Diagnostics—Error messages provided by the system.

Digital computer—A computer system that uses a numbering system, such as binary, to process data.

Dimension—The number of data items or elements in a table/array.

Disk Operating System (DOS)—The control program that supervises and controls the system access to the disk/diskette.

Do loop structure—A program loop control structure. The BASIC language uses the FOR/NEXT loop for this structure. This structure is used to execute loops at least one time.

Documentation—The paper trail of documents that supports and records the development of a program.

Double-precision—The accuracy, or precision, of real data values. Double precision values go to 16 or more decimal places.

DIP switch (Dual In-line Parallel)—A physical switch that is used to control printer or memory functions.

Dummy data—The data record used for program termination. The dummy DATA statement is listed after the significant DATA statements.

Emulation—A computer system or portion of a computer simulates another computer or device.

Error trap—A routine that checks for error types/codes when the system detects an error.

Exception printing—Output of print line for conditions that are not within normal or acceptable ranges.

Execution—Program statements are performed or executed. The program is run.

Fatal error—A program error that results in termination.

Field—A data item or variable.

File—A collection of related data records.

Flowchart—A logical step-by-step graphic solution to a given problem. Standard symbols are used.

FOR/NEXT loop structure—The primary BASIC language loop control structure. This structure is used when the loop is to execute at least one time.

FORTRAN (Formula Translation)—A high-level programming language used primarily for scientific/mathematic applications.

Function—A numeric or string processing operation. Functions may be system or user supplied.

GIGO—Garbage In = Garbage Out. Errors in data values do not correct themselves.

Hardware—Computer equipment.

Hexadecimal—Numbering system with a base of 16 that is used in assembly language programming.

Hierarchy—A formal programming structure in which selected modules control other modules that execute procedures or computations.

High-Level Language—A programming language that is "close to English." High-level languages must be translated into a language that the machine can process internally.

Icon—Portion of a window display on monitor screen used in selecting options.

International Standards Organization (ISO)—An international group that establishes standards for computers and languages.

Increment—Add to a counter or variable.

Information Resource Management (IRM)—Control or management of the organization's computer, programming, data, and information resources.

Initialization of diskettes—Formatting new diskettes for use on microcomputer systems.

Initialize variables—Assignment of an initial value to a variable.

Instruction—One program step.

Integer data—Whole number value.

Integrated circuit (IC)—Electronic device with circuitry integrated on a silicon chip.

Integrated software—Software that combines data processing, word processing, and computer-generated graphics. Data can be passed from one type of integrated software to another.

Interactive—Computer system with time-sharing ability. The system prompts the user to perform tasks that control execution of the program.

Interface—A device used to connect devices or systems.

Interpreter—A control program that converts high-level language to machine language, and also detects syntax errors. The interpreter translates the high-level program one line at a time.

I/O—Input/Output.

Job Control Language (JCL)—The commands entered to link the operating system to the program being executed. The term is usually associated with mainframe systems.

Jump—A program branch to another statement.

K—1024 bytes or characters. 64K of memory is 65,536 bytes.

KISS—The first law of programming. KISS = Keep It Simple, Stupid!!

Key word—System reserved word set aside for a specific function or purpose.

Left-justified—Data value aligned at extreme left side of space.

Logic error—An error in implementation, programming logic, or follow through.

Logical operator—AND, OR, and NOT are logical operators used to test for specified conditions.

Log on—The user gains access to a time-sharing system.

Loop—A program control procedure that causes certain statements to be executed repeatedly until parameters are satisfied. FOR/NEXT loops are commonly used.

Low-level program—The internal language of the computer that is referred to as machine language.

Management Information System (MIS)—Management of the organization's computer, programming, data, and information resources.

Machine language—The language (binary code) used internally by the machine to process data.

Mainframe—A large central computer capable of storing mass quantities of data, supporting many terminals, and also multiprogramming.

Menu—A display that enables the program user to select between options, functions, or procedures.

Microprocessor—An electronic circuit that is capable of performing logic, control, or computation functions.

Microprocessor size—The largest number of bits that the computer can transfer in one pass. Microcomputers are commonly 8-bit, 16-bit, or 32-bit machines.

Mid-level language—The language that is used to prepare software, interpreters, and compilers. An intermediate numbering system is used to prepare mid-level, or assembly, language programs.

Minicomputer—A computer system that is smaller than a mainframe, but is capable of supporting terminals and multiprogramming.

Modem (Modulator/Demodulator)—Telecommunications interface between the computer and telephone system.

Module—A portion of a program that considers one processing task, such as input, calculations, or output.

Mouse—A user-friendly device that accesses the computer system/software.

Multifunctional system—A general purpose computer system capable of supporting different program applications, terminals, and multiprogramming.

Multiprogramming—The computer system supports a number of different programming languages concurrently.

Murphy's law—A postulate to remember: If anything can go wrong, it will.

Nested loop—One loop structure is nested within another loop. FOR/NEXT or WHILE loops may be nested inside another loop.

Nesting—Placing a program loop or decision within a similar operation.

Network—Computer systems linked together by telecommunications.

Non-zone printing—Output is displayed in a packed or non-zone format. The semicolon (;) is used in PRINT statements for this purpose.

Null string—An "empty" string that is composed of blank spaces.

Numeric variable—One item of data that consists of digits and decimals. No other characters are permitted. Computations must use numeric variables.

Object program—The machine language program that results from compilation of the source program.

Operating system (OS)—The control program that supervises computer system operations.

Output editing—The insertion of editing symbols such as dollar signs, percent symbols, and commas. The procedure places string or numeric output into a specified format. PRINT USING is used for editing output.

Output format—The arrangement of the output display or printing into a specified format.

Packing—Output is in non-zone format.

Parameter—A condition or procedure that is used to complete BASIC program statements or operations.

PASCAL—A high-level programming language compatible with structured methodology.

Permanent memory—An auxiliary storage device, such as a disk, used for permanent storage of programs/data.

Password—A personal (sometimes confidential) identification that must be presented to the system before access is obtained.

Port—A slot or plug-in that is used to connect disks or modems to the computer.

Print zone—A system-supplied format that separates output into columns of data. Standard zone width varies from 5 to 16 columns. The comma (,) is used in PRINT statements for this purpose.

Program—A series of individual instructions that solves a given problem.

Program control structures—Three main structures are used to control execution of programs. The program control structures used with BASIC are the simple sequential, the branch, and the loop.

Prompt—The system-supplied character, cursor, or word that informs the user that the system is waiting for a command/statement. Some systems use a cursor, while others use OK, READY, or DONE.

Random access memory (RAM)—Microcomputer current, or temporary, work space which is volatile.

Random number—A number that is generated by the computer system. Any number within the system provided parameter has an equal chance of being generated.

Read only memory (ROM)—The read only memory area stores the control program, system start-up routine, or BASIC interpreter. ROM is not volatile.

Real data—A decimal or fraction value.

Record—A collection of related data items or variables that is used in input/output operations.

Relational operator—Tests for relational conditions, such as <, >, =, or <>, between specified values.

Right-justified—The data value is aligned at the extreme right side.

Scientific notation (E format)—This format is automatically invoked when the size of a data value exceeds system limits. It converts very large or small numbers to exponential (E format) form.

Scrolling—Moving the area displayed on the monitor screen up, down, left, or right.

Search—A routine designed to search data tables or arrays for a specified key value.

Sector—A segment of one track on the disk.

Serial processing—The processing of data in a series or batch. READ and DATA statements can be used in BASIC for this purpose. Sequential disk files are also used for serial processing.

Single-precision—The precision of real data valves. Single-precision values go to 6 or 7 decimal places.

Software—Programming languages or system programs.

Sort—A procedure or utility that arranges string or numeric data values into a predetermined sequence.

Source document—The business form, such as an invoice or purchase order, that is the origin of data values.

Source program—The high-level language program that is entered into the computer before compilation. The result following compilation is called the object program.

Statement—One instruction or program line.

String data—BASIC language terminology for alphabetic or alphanumeric data values. String variable names must include a $ suffix.

Structured programming—Programming methodology that uses a modular format. Each processing task is considered in a module.

Subroutine—The module, or portion, of a program that accomplishes one task such as input or calculations. The subroutine is the BASIC language format for structured programming.

Summary printing—Output of totals that summarize a report or data set.

Syntax—The word structure of a programming language. The word usage, or grammar, of a programming language.

Syntax error—An error wherein the rules of syntax, usage, or grammar are violated.

System—The overall view of a process. A series of interrelated steps that, when combined, cause an organization or a group to perform tasks.

System-defined function—A procedure, such as a random number generator or a trigonometric function, that is provided by the computer system.

Table—The arrangement of data in a single dimension. A list of data values in column form.

Tally—Addition in increments of one.

Temporary memory—The current user work space in main memory. Temporary memory is volatile.

Telecommunications—The connection of computer systems through telecommunications devices.

Test data—Data values used to test program validity.

Time-sharing—A system of terminals that share access to the computer system's central processing unit.

Top-down programming—The structured programming methodology that uses a step-by-step process to break a problem into small programmable units.

Track—One concentric circle around a disk which is divided into sectors.

Transaction mode—The data processing procedure wherein data values are entered directly from a terminal as the transaction occurs.

Translator—The control program that translates high-level programming languages into a language the machine understands.

Truncation—The computer system drops that portion of a data value which is not considered significant or which cannot fit in the assigned area.

User—The person in the organization who requests and uses data processing resources.

User-defined function—A procedure or arithmetic function defined by the programmer.

Utility software—System-supplied programs or functions provided to assist the user in performing tasks such as sorting data values or renumbering program statements.

Variable—The BASIC language terminology used to describe a data item. One unit of data.

VLSI (Very Large Scale Integration)—Current integrated circuit technology that results in very high circuit capacity/density.

VDT (Video Display Terminal)—Computer input/output unit with keyboard and video display.

Volatile storage—The contents in memory are erased when the system is turned off.

WHILE loop structure—A BASIC language loop control structure in which the loop parameters are tested before the loop is executed.

Window—A video display procedure in which more than one program or utility can be shown on the screen at the same time.

Zone printing—Output is formatted in system-defined columns.

MANUALS CITED

American National Standards Institute. *American National Standard for Minimal BASIC.* New York, NY: American National Standards Institute, 1978.

Apple Computer Inc. *Applesoft.* Cupertino, CA: Apple Computer Inc., 1981.

_____. *The DOS Manual.* Cupertino, CA: Apple Computer Inc., 1981.

International Business Machines Corporation. *IBM BASIC.* Second edition. Boca Raton, FL: IBM, 1982.

Microsoft Corporation. "Microsoft BASIC Interpreter." In *Microsoft Softcard.* Bellevue, WA: Microsoft Corporation, 1982.

National Cash Register Company. *Expenses in Retail Business.* Dayton, OH: National Cash Register Company, 1973.

Tandy Corporation. *TRS-80 Disk System Owner's Manual.* Fort Worth, TX: Tandy Corporation, 1980.

_____. *TRS-80 Model III Operation and BASIC Language Reference.* Fort Worth, TX: Tandy Corporation, 1980.

INDEX